Federated Deep Learning for Healthcare

This book provides a practical guide to federated deep learning for healthcare including fundamental concepts, framework, and the applications comprising domain adaptation, model distillation, and transfer learning. It covers concerns in model fairness, data bias, regulatory compliance, and ethical dilemmas. It investigates several privacy-preserving methods such as homomorphic encryption, secure multi-party computation, and differential privacy. It will enable readers to build and implement federated learning systems that safeguard private medical information.

Features:

- Offers a thorough introduction of federated deep learning methods designed exclusively for medical applications.
- Investigates privacy-preserving methods with emphasis on data security and privacy.
- Discusses healthcare scaling and resource efficiency considerations.
- Examines methods for sharing information among various healthcare organizations while retaining model performance.

This book is aimed at graduate students and researchers in federated learning, data science, AI/machine learning, and healthcare.

Advances in Smart Healthcare Technologies
Editors: Chinmay Chakraborty and Joel J. P. C. Rodrigues

This book series focus on recent advances and different research areas in smart healthcare technologies including Internet of Medical Things (IoMedT), e-Health, personalized medicine, sensing, Big Data, telemedicine, etc. under the healthcare informatics umbrella. Overall focus is on bringing together the latest industrial and academic progress, research, and development efforts within the rapidly maturing health informatics ecosystem. It aims to offer valuable perceptions to researchers and engineers on how to design and develop novel healthcare systems and how to improve patient's information delivery care remotely. The potential for making faster advances in many scientific disciplines and improving the profitability and success of different enterprises is to be investigated.

Blockchain Technology in Healthcare Applications: Social, Economic and Technological Implications
Bharat Bhushan, Nitin Rakesh, Yousef Farhaoui, Parma Nand Astya, and Bhuvan Unhelkar

Digital Health Transformation with Blockchain and Artificial Intelligence
Chinmay Chakraborty

Smart and Secure Internet of Healthcare Things
Nitin Gupta, Jagdeep Singh, Chinmay Chakraborty, Mamoun Alazab, and Dinh-Thuan Do

Practical Artificial Intelligence for Internet of Medical Things: Emerging Trends, Issues, and Challenges
Edited by Ben Othman Soufiene, Chinmay Chakraborty, and Faris A. Almalki

Intelligent Internet of Things for Smart Healthcare Systems
Edited by Durgesh Srivastava, Neha Sharma, Deepak Sinwar, Jabar H. Yousif, and Hari Prabhat Gupta

Future Health Scenarios: AI and Digital Technologies in Global Healthcare Systems
Edited by Maria Jose Sousa, Francisco Guilherme Nunes, Generosa do Nascimento, and Chinmay Chakraborty

Machine Learning and Deep Learning Techniques for Medical Image Recognition
Edited by Ben Othman Soufiene and Chinmay Chakraborty

Artificial Intelligence Technology in Healthcare: Security and Privacy Issues
Edited by Neha Sharma, Durgesh Srivastava, and Deepak Sinwar

Federated Deep Learning for Healthcare: A Practical Guide with Challenges and Opportunities
Edited by Amandeep Kaur, Chetna Kaushal, Md. Mehedi Hassan, and Si Thu Aung

For more information about this series, please visit: www.routledge.com/Advances-in-Smart-Healthcare-Technologies/book-series/CRCASHT

Federated Deep Learning for Healthcare
A Practical Guide with Challenges and Opportunities

Edited by
Amandeep Kaur, Chetna Kaushal,
Md. Mehedi Hassan, and Si Thu Aung

CRC Press is an imprint of the
Taylor & Francis Group, an **informa** business

Designed cover image: © Shutterstock Images

First edition published 2025
by CRC Press
2385 NW Executive Center Drive, Suite 320, Boca Raton FL 33431

and by CRC Press
4 Park Square, Milton Park, Abingdon, Oxon, OX14 4RN

CRC Press is an imprint of Taylor & Francis Group, LLC

© 2025 selection and editorial matter, Amandeep Kaur, Chetna Kaushal, Md. Mehedi Hassan, and Si Thu Aung; individual chapters, the contributors

Reasonable efforts have been made to publish reliable data and information, but the author and publisher cannot assume responsibility for the validity of all materials or the consequences of their use. The authors and publishers have attempted to trace the copyright holders of all material reproduced in this publication and apologize to copyright holders if permission to publish in this form has not been obtained. If any copyright material has not been acknowledged please write and let us know so we may rectify in any future reprint.

Except as permitted under U.S. Copyright Law, no part of this book may be reprinted, reproduced, transmitted, or utilized in any form by any electronic, mechanical, or other means, now known or hereafter invented, including photocopying, microfilming, and recording, or in any information storage or retrieval system, without written permission from the publishers.

For permission to photocopy or use material electronically from this work, access www.copyright. com or contact the Copyright Clearance Center, Inc. (CCC), 222 Rosewood Drive, Danvers, MA 01923, 978-750-8400. For works that are not available on CCC please contact mpkbookspermissions@ tandf.co.uk

Trademark notice: Product or corporate names may be trademarks or registered trademarks and are used only for identification and explanation without intent to infringe.

ISBN: 978-1-032-68955-5 (hbk)
ISBN: 978-1-032-69486-3 (pbk)
ISBN: 978-1-032-69487-0 (ebk)

DOI: 10.1201/9781032694870

Typeset in Times
by codeMantra

Contents

About the Editors.. viii

List of Contributors.. x

Chapter 1 Revolutionizing Healthcare through Federated Learning:
A Secure and Collaborative Approach.. 1

Amrina Rahman, Md. Mushfiqur Rahman, and Farhana Yasmin

Chapter 2 Revolutionizing Healthcare: Unleashing the Power of
Digital Health 17

Renu Vij

Chapter 3 Federated Deep Learning Systems in Healthcare............................ 31

*Ashraful Reza Tanjil, Fahim Mohammad Adud Bhuiyan,
Mohammad Abu Tareq Rony, and Kamanashis Biswas*

Chapter 4 Applications of Federated Deep Learning Models in
Healthcare Era 50

Monika Sethi, Jyoti Snehi, Manish Snehi, and Aadrit Aggarwal

Chapter 5 Machine Learning for Healthcare: Review and Future Aspects........ 59

*Aadrita Nandy, Jyoti Choudhary, Joanne Fredrick,
T. S. Zacharia, Tom K. Joseph, and Veerpal Kaur*

Chapter 6 Federated Multi-Task Learning to Solve Various
Healthcare Challenges... 78

Seema Pahwa and Amandeep Kaur

Chapter 7 Smart System for Development of Cognitive Skills Using
Machine Learning 89

*Rashmi Aggarwal, Uday Devgan, Sandhir Sharma,
Tanvi Verma, and Aadrit Aggarwal*

Chapter 8 Patient-Driven Federated Learning (PD-FL): An Overview 101

A. Menaka Devi and V. Megala

v

Chapter 9 An Explainable and Comprehensive Federated Deep Learning in Practical Applications: Real World Benefits and Systematic Analysis Across Diverse Domains 109

Khalid Aziz, Sakshi Dua, and Prabal Gupta

Chapter 10 Federated Deep Learning System for Application of Healthcare in Pandemic Situation 131

Vandana and Chetna Kaushal

Chapter 11 The Integration of Federated Deep Learning with Internet of Things in Healthcare 143

Hirak Mondal, Md. Mehedi Hassan, Anindya Nag, and Anupam Kumar Bairagi

Chapter 12 FireEye: An IoT-Based Fire Alarm and Detection System for Enhanced Safety 160

Md. Moynul Islam, Nahida Fatme, Md AL Mahbub Hossain, and Muhammad Fiazul Haque

Chapter 13 Safeguarding Data Privacy and Security in Federated Learning Systems 170

Wasswa Shafik, Kassim Kalinaki, Khairul Eahsun Fahim, and Mumin Adam

Chapter 14 Diseases Detection System Using Federated Learning 191

P. Dhiman, S. Wadhwa, and Amandeep Kaur

Chapter 15 Tailoring Medicine through Personalized Healthcare Solutions 199

Tejinder Kaur, Madhav Aggarwal, Krish Wason, and Pragati Duggal

Chapter 16 FedHealth in Wearable Healthcare, Orchestrated Federated Deep Learning for Smart Healthcare: Health Monitoring and Healthcare Informatics Lensing Challenges and Future Directions.... 207

Bhupinder Singh and Christian Kaunert

Contents vii

Chapter 17 From Scarce to Abundant: Enhancing Learning with Federated
Transfer Techniques 224

*Rezuana Haque, Md. Mehedi Hassan, and Sheikh Mohammed
Shariful Islam*

Chapter 18 Federated Learning-Based AI Approaches for
Predicting Stroke 233

*Satyajit Roy, Fariha Ferdous Mim, Md. Mehedi Hassan, and
Sheikh Mohammed Shariful Islam*

Index...251

About the Editors

Dr. Amandeep Kaur currently holds the position of a professor at the Chitkara University Institute of Engineering and Technology, Chitkara University, Punjab. She earned her doctorate degree from I. K. Gujral Punjab Technical University, Jalandhar. Dr. Kaur's academic achievements include receiving both her M.Tech (Computer Science and Engineering) and B.Tech (Computer Science and Engineering) degrees with distinction. Additionally, she has successfully qualified UGC-NET in Computer Science. Dr. Kaur boasts an extensive research portfolio, with approximately 100 publications in renowned international journals and fully refereed international conferences. She has accumulated 24 years of valuable experience in her field and has filed and published more than 107 patents. Dr. Kaur has played a significant role in mentoring the academic growth of over 30 Ph.D. and PG students. Her primary research areas encompass medical informatics, machine learning, IoT (Internet of Things), artificial intelligence, and cloud computing. Notably, Dr. Kaur has been recognized for her exceptional contributions, winning the Excellence Award in the "Filing Patent" category for three consecutive years (2021, 2022, and 2023) and the Best Ph.D. Supervision Award in 2023. Furthermore, she has achieved recognition on a global scale, as she is included in Stanford University's prestigious list of the top 2% most influential scientists among Indian researchers. This underscores her significance in the field of computer science and research.

Dr. Chetna Kaushal works as an assistant professor in Chitkara University, Punjab. She has done a Ph.D. in Computer Science and Engineering from Chitkara University, Punjab, M.Tech in Computer Science and Engineering from DAV University, Punjab, and B.Tech in Information Technology from Punjab Technical University. Her areas of expertise are machine learning, soft computing, pattern recognition, image processing, and artificial intelligence. She has around ten years of experience in research, training, and academics. She has published numerous research papers in various international/national journals, books, and conferences. She has filed and published more than 50 patents to her name. She is a reviewer of many prestigious journals. Dr. Chetna Kaushal is an exceptionally motivated and talented researcher deeply dedicated to advancing human health and well-being through pioneering scientific investigations. Her remarkable achievements thus far are a testament to her capabilities, and her potential for making significant future contributions to her field is undeniably bright.

Md. Mehedi Hassan is a dedicated young researcher, holding a B.Sc. Engineering degree in computer science and engineering from 2022 and currently pursuing his M.Sc. Engineering degree at Khulna University, Bangladesh. His remarkable aptitude for research has propelled him to excel in biomedical engineering, data science, and expert systems, earning him recognition as a respected leader in these fields. He is the founder and CEO of the Virtual BD IT Firm and the lab head of the VRD

About the Editors

Research Laboratory in Bangladesh. With over three filed patents, three of which have been granted, Mehedi is not only an innovative thinker but also a practical problem solver. He also serves as a reviewer for prestigious journals, further underscoring his influence in the scientific community. Mehedi's research interests encompass a broad spectrum, ranging from human brain imaging, neuroscience, machine learning, and artificial intelligence to software engineering. Driven by his notable accomplishments and promising potential, Mehedi remains dedicated to leveraging cutting-edge scientific research to enhance human health and well-being.

Dr. Si Thu Aung received his B.E. from Technological University, Myanmar, in 2014, the Master of Engineering in Electronics from Mandalay Technological University, Myanmar, in 2017, and a Ph.D. in Biomedical Engineering from the Faculty of Engineering, Mahidol University, Thailand, in 2021. Previously, he worked as a post-doctoral researcher at the Rail and Modern Transports Research Center under the National Science and Technology Development Agency, Thailand Science Park, Pathum Thani, Thailand. Now, he is working as a post-doctoral research associate at the Department of Mathematics at the State University of New York, Buffalo. His current research interests include biomedical signal processing, digital image processing, machine learning, and deep learning.

Contributors

Mumin Adam
Department of Computer Engineering
King Fahd University of Petroleum and
    Minerals (KFUPM)
Dhahran, Saudi Arabia

Aadrit Aggarwal
JP Morgan Chase & Co.
Bangalore, India

Madhav Aggarwal
Chitkara University Institute of
    Engineering and Technology,
    Chitkara University,
    Rajpura, India

Rashmi Aggarwal
Chitkara Business School
Chitkara University
Rajpura, India

Khalid Aziz
SCA
Lovely Professional University
Phagwara, India

Anupam Kumar Bairagi
Computer Science and Engineering
    Discipline
Khulna University
Khulna, Bangladesh

Kamanashis Biswas
Department of Computer Science and
    Engineering
North Western University
Khulna, Bangladesh

Fahim Mohammad Adud Bhuiyan
Department of Computer Science and
    Engineering
East West University
Dhaka, Bangladesh

Jyoti Choudhary
Computer Science and Engineering
Lovely Professional University
Phagwara, India

Uday Devgan
Chitkara Business School
Chitkara University
Rajpura, India

P. Dhiman
Department of Computer Science
Government PG College
Ambala Cantt, India

Sakshi Dua
SCA
Lovely Professional University
Phagwara, India

Pragati Duggal
Chitkara University Institute of
    Engineering and Technology
Chitkara University
Rajpura, India

Khairul Eahsun Fahim
Information Technology Management
ZNRF University of Management
    Sciences
Dhaka, Bangladesh

Contributors

Nahida Fatme
Department of CSE
Bangladesh University of Business and
Technology
Dhaka, Bangladesh

Joanne Fredrick
Computer Science and Engineering
Lovely Professional University
Phagwara, India

Prabal Gupta
Department of ECE, SCSE
Lovely Professional University
Phagwara, India

Muhammad Fiazul Haque
Department of CSE
Bangladesh University of Business and
Technology
Dhaka, Bangladesh

Rezuana Haque
Computer Science and Engineering
Chittagong University of Engineering &
Technology
Chittagong, Bangladesh

Md. Mehedi Hassan
Computer Science and Engineering
Discipline
Khulna University
Khulna, Bangladesh

Md AL Mahbub Hossain
Department of CSE
Bangladesh University of Business and
Technology
Dhaka, Bangladesh

Md. Moynul Islam
Department of CSE
Bangladesh University of Business and
Technology
Dhaka, Bangladesh

Sheikh Mohammed Shariful Islam
Institute for Physical Activity and
Nutrition
Deakin University
Melbourne, VIC, Australia

Tom K. Joseph
Computer Science and Engineering
Lovely Professional University
Phagwara, India

Kassim Kalinaki
Department of Computer Science
Islamic University in Uganda
Mbale, Uganda
and
Borderline Research Laboratory
Kampala, Uganda

Christian Kaunert
School of Law and Government
Dublin City University
Ireland

Amandeep Kaur
Chitkara University Institute of
Engineering and Technology
Chitkara University
Rajpura, India

Tejinder Kaur
Chitkara University Institute of
Engineering and Technology
Chitkara University
Rajpura, India

Veerpal Kaur
Computer Science and Engineering
Lovely Professional University
Phagwara, India

Chetna Kaushal
Chitkara University Institute of
Engineering and Technology
Chitkara University
Rajpura, India

V. Megala
Data Centre, Vellalar College for
  Women
Erode, India

A. Menaka Devi
Cooperation, Vellalar College for
  Women
Erode, India

Fariha Ferdous Mim
Computer Science and Engineering
North Western University
Khulna, Bangladesh

Hirak Mondal
Department of Computer Science and
  Engineering
North Western University
Khulna, Bangladesh

Anindya Nag
Computer Science and Engineering
  Discipline
Khulna University
Khulna, Bangladesh

Aadrita Nandy
Computer Science and Engineering
Lovely Professional University
Phagwara, India

Seema Pahwa
Chitkara University Institute of
  Engineering and Technology
Chitkara University
Rajpura, India

Amrina Rahman
Department of Management
  Information Systems (MIS)
University of Dhaka
Dhaka, Bangladesh

Md. Mushfiqur Rahman
Department of Statistics
University of Dhaka
Dhaka, Bangladesh

Mohammad Abu Tareq Rony
Department of Statistics
Noakhali Science and Technology
  University
Noakhali, Bangladesh

Satyajit Roy
Computer Science and Engineering
  Discipline
Khulna University
Khulna, Bangladesh

Monika Sethi
Chitkara University Institute of
  Engineering and Technology
Chitkara University
Rajpura, India

Wasswa Shafik
Dig Connectivity Research Laboratory
  (DCRLab)
Kampala, Uganda

Sandhir Sharma
Chitkara Business School
Chitkara University
Rajpura, India

Bhupinder Singh
School of Law
Sharda University
Greater Noida, India

Jyoti Snehi
Computer Science and Engineering
Punjabi University Patiala
Patiala, India

Manish Snehi
Computer Science and Engineering
Punjabi University Patiala
Patiala, India

Contributors

Ashraful Reza Tanjil
Department of Computer Science and
Engineering
East West University
Dhaka, Bangladesh

Vandana
Chitkara University Institute of
Engineering and Technology
Chitkara University
Rajpura, India

Tanvi Verma
Chitkara Business School
Chitkara University
Rajpura, India

Renu Vij
Debarment of AIT-Management,
University School of Business
Chandigarh University
Mohali, India

S. Wadhwa
Chitkara University Institute of
Engineering and Technology
Chitkara University
Rajpura, India

Krish Wason
Chitkara University Institute of
Engineering and Technology
Chitkara University
Rajpura, India

Farhana Yasmin
School of Computer and Software
Nanjing University of Information
Science and Technology
Nanjing, China

T. S. Zacharia
Computer Science and Engineering
Lovely Professional University
Phagwara, India

1 Revolutionizing Healthcare through Federated Learning
A Secure and Collaborative Approach

Amrina Rahman, Md. Mushfiqur Rahman, and Farhana Yasmin

1.1 INTRODUCTION

The advancement of technology and its computational power has enabled the healthcare sector to exploit vast records of medical information stored in the form of big data [1]. For example, Electronic Health Record (EHR), which is an electronic documentation of patients' clinical recordings, opens doors for analyzing data and extracting valuable insights to better disease diagnosis and patient treatment. Considering the volume of data in the healthcare industry, machine learning (ML) models are often used for analysis and pattern recognition [2]. However, ML techniques come with their own limitations. To maintain the accuracy of a model, a huge and inclusive dataset is required. This can pose a problem in the medical sector as clinical data are often sensitive and private. Not only that, employing a ton of infrastructures to manage this large pool of data is not always the most effective idea. Moreover, laws like General Data Protection Regulation (GDPR) of the European Union, the California Consumer Privacy Act (CCPA), and Health Insurance Portability and Accountability Act (HIPAA) can put restrictions on data sharing, which can ultimately hinder the development of an effective ML model [2]. Again, computational resource limitations, infrastructural costs, network connectivity, ethical considerations, inaccurate calculations of model parameters, and so on can create catastrophe here as the discussed field is pretty much sensitive.

Being a collaborative and incremental approach, federated learning (FL) can be a solution here. Instead of depending on data centrally stored on the cloud, FL enables remote devices to collaborate on a shared model and fine-tune it based on their data. This approach brings copies of models to remote devices, unlike the other way around, from central servers. The edge devices train local models using their own data and the updated model parameters are sent to the central servers. Secure aggregation techniques are used by the main model to average these newly found inputs [3]. Each time edge devices are used to evaluate updated parameters until convergence is achieved. This technique brings an ocean of opportunities for confidential

DOI: 10.1201/9781032694870-1

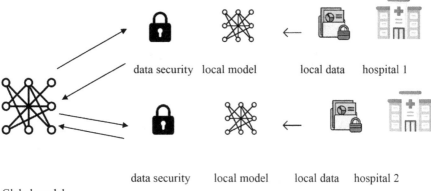

FIGURE 1.1 Federated learning applying local updates to the central model with proper data security.

data like medical images and recordings. As the data never leaves the device in FL, it maintains the privacy and secrecy of individuals. Figure 1.1 illustrates FL, wherein local updates are applied to the central model while ensuring proper data security.

Our study mainly focuses on the applications and contributions of FL in the healthcare sector while discussing the already applied FL models and their working procedures. There is also an attempt to find answers to the following questions:

- What studies have been conducted in different years with a focus on healthcare application using FL?
- What models or architectures were used in specific medical purposes, for example, disease prediction, patient monitoring, drug discovery, and personalized medicine?
- How can FL ensure a more secure model training approach than traditional ML for medical data?

1.2 RELATED WORKS

ML has become a substantial practice in healthcare in recent years. Increased computational power and data availability have made it possible for machines to diagnose and predict diseases early, design personalized treatment for patients, conduct predictive analytics, and what not. Several studies have also been conducted over the years utilizing ML models that are relevant and appropriate for the problems. Hassan et al. brought an unsupervised cluster-based model that groups features to detect diabetes early. Algorithms like Random Forest (RF), Multi-layer Perceptron (MLP), and K-nearest Neighbors (KNN) were employed in this study that brought 99.57%, 98.70%, and 96.10% accuracy, respectively [4]. In another study, Hassan et al. applied K-means clustering and XGBoost feature selection algorithm in a study conducted for chronic kidney disease (CKD) prediction. Among Neural Network (NN), Support Vector Machine (SVM), Random Tree (RT), RF, and Bagging Tree

Model (BTM) used in this article, NN yielded the highest 100% accuracy on full dataset (25 attributes) while SVM showed so in the XGBoost dataset (7 attributes) [5]. For discovering patterns and retrieving significant rules from human intoxication data, Hassan et al. utilized apriori algorithm in a research article. The result showed 95% confidence and 45% support level with a finding of eight important rules [6]. Furthermore, a comparative discussion was made on different algorithms like SVM, MLP, RF, Gradient Boost, eXtreme GBoost, KNN, and Logistic Regression (LR), which were used to detect and predict breast cancer by Hassan et al. Least Absolute Shrinkage and Selection Operator (LASSO) approach was followed to select features and, among others, the RF algorithm demonstrated the highest accuracy using the LASSO technique [7]. However, traditional ML techniques require a vast amount of data and computational power to achieve a satisfactory level of accuracy. But in the healthcare industry, the data-sharing approach can pose a threat to clinical record privacy and security. FL can be a solution to this problem as local data is never required to leave devices to train the ML model. As today's world is flooded with data, utilizing proper tools and techniques to extract information from this data can give any company a competitive edge over others. On top of that, patients' data require high-level security and privacy, which can be ensured by FL. As a result, studies have been conducted on FL regarding medical applications in recent times.

At the budding stage, Google introduced federated stochastic gradient descent (FedSGD) and federated averaging (FedAvg) algorithms which work in such a fashion. Implemented in a federated setting, these algorithms do not require local data sharing and the central server only works with the model parameter updates to refine the global model. However, there remains a chance of an individual device's information being decrypted from the updates sent to the server. The secure aggregation technique helps to prevent this as it allows the server to decrypt only the average update upon participation of a large number of devices [8]. FL has already made significant contributions in the healthcare sector. For example, a significant source of modern medical data that is used in clinical research is EHR. Boughorbel et al. designed a novel FL model named Federated uncertainty-aware learning algorithm (FUALA) using EHR that refines FedAvg. The algorithm handled uncertainty in information by reducing highly uncertain models' contribution and bringing in model ensembling techniques [9]. On a different note, Lim et al. utilized IoT data in healthcare and worked on the dynamic contract design to assure intertemporal incentive compatibility (IIC). The design increased profitability and reduced the negative effects of information asymmetry [10]. Again, Qayyum et al. employed clustered federated learning (CFL) to diagnose COVID-19 automatically. The trained model achieved a 16% improvement in F-1 score in terms of X-ray datasets while the percentage was 11% in the case of ultrasound datasets [11]. To apply FL in artificial intelligence (AIoT) applications, Zhang et al. demonstrated Big.Little branch architecture in which the big branch was used for forecasting purposes and little branches were used for AIoT applications. This model achieved better results in terms of precision of prediction and inference period [12]. In another study conducted by Nilsson et al., FedAvg algorithm showed the best performance among other algorithms like Federated Stochastic Variance Reduced Gradient, and CO-OP, depending little on IID and Non-IID partitionings of the datasets. However, FedAvg and conventional ML demonstrated the same performance in terms of IID data when the latter did better on Non-IID data [13].

A few already conducted review works discussed the advancement made by FL in the healthcare arena. Antunes et al. made a review on the contemporary FL applications related to EHR data, and the study also discussed ML procedures, research challenges and possible solutions, and relevant case studies [14]. Another review work conducted by Nguyen et al. showed current FL advancements in the medical sector and FL designs for smart healthcare, for example, secure and privacy-aware FL, resource-aware FL, personalized FL, and incentive FL [15]. Some of the studies focused on the specific aspects of FL applications in this sector. Kaissis et al. showed how FL can be used in medical imaging to protect data privacy and security. The article mentioned techniques like differential privacy, homomorphic encryption (HE), secure multi-party computation, and secure hardware implementations [16]. A federated transfer learning framework named FedHealth was proposed by Chen et al. to address issues like fragmented clinical data and lack of personalization. The technique was particularly designed for wearable healthcare and was able to attain result accuracy during the investigation of wearable activities [17]. Hao et al. proposed the PRCL (Privacy-aware and Resource saving Collaborative Learning) protocol to address problems related to privacy and energy requirement by local devices during FL training. The article proposed a splitting method to lessen local computing cost and the large computational part was executed by cloud servers [18]. Yang et al. conducted a study on a collaborative model for COVID area division using 3D chest Computed Tomography (CT). Computer-assisted characterization and detection using chest CT performed quite well in terms of COVID tests. However, challenges came with distributed data and variation of annotations in local data, which can ultimately affect COVID diagnosis. The mentioned article solved these issues by employing semi-supervised learning and FL. FL diminished data-sharing requirement while semi-supervised learning lessened the annotation hassle in a decentralized system [19]. Some recent works on ML and Fl are shown in Table 1.1.

1.3 APPLICATIONS OF FEDERATED LEARNING IN HEALTHCARE

Applications of FL in healthcare cover a wide range of areas – disease prediction, patient monitoring, drug discovery, personalized medicine, understanding of medicines, and diagnosis, especially cancer and tumor detection. As the term FL was coined by Google, several research works had been conducted since then, particularly from 2018 to 2021. A number of algorithms were deployed in different studies for different medical research purposes:

1.3.1 DISEASE PREDICTION

FL can be used to leverage EHR to design a more effective central model using distributed and private data [20]. Using patients' history documented in EHRs, Brisimi et al. designed an iterative cluster Primal Dual Splitting (cPDS) algorithm in order to work on a sparse (soft-margin l1-regularized) Support Vector Machine (sSVM) problem. The approach is a decentralized one and does not require exchange of patients' data. cPDS algorithm is used in this study to predict hospitalization of cardiovascular

TABLE 1.1
Some Recent Works on ML and FL in the Healthcare Sector

Author's Name with Published Year	Database	Applied Models and Algorithms/Techniques	Contribution
Hassan et al. [4]	Early stage diabetes risk prediction dataset (520 instances, 17 features)	Unsupervised cluster-based model, Random Forest (RF), Multi-layer Perceptron (MLP), and K-nearest Neighbors (KNN)	Early diabetes detection, accuracy: Random Forest (RF) – 99.57%, Multi-layer Perceptron (MLP) – 98.70%, and K-nearest Neighbors (KNN) – 96.10%
Hassan et al. [5]	Chronic kidney disease (400 instances, 25 features)	K-means clustering, XGBoost feature selection algorithm, Neural Network (NN), Support Vector Machine (SVM), Random Tree (RT), Random Forest (RF), and Bagging Tree Model (BTM)	Chronic kidney disease (CKD) prediction
Hassan et al. [6]		Apriori algorithm	Discovered patterns and retrieved significant rules from human intoxication data, 95% confidence and 45% support level with a finding of eight important rules
Hassan et al. [7]	Seer breast cancer data	SVM, MLP, RF, GB, XGB, KNN, LR Least Absolute Shrinkage and Selection Operator (LASSO) approach to select features	Breast cancer detection and prediction
McMahan and Ramage [8]	N/A	Federated stochastic gradient descent (FedSGD) and federated averaging (FedAvg) algorithms	Introduced the concept and working procedure of FL, secure aggregation technique
Boughorbel et al. [9]	CERNER Health Facts (HF) database	Federated Uncertainty-Aware Learning Algorithm (FUALA)	Handled uncertainty by reducing highly uncertain models' contribution and bringing in model ensembling techniques
Lim et al. [10]			Dynamic contract design to assure intertemporal incentive compatibility (IIC)

(Continued)

TABLE 1.1 (*Continued*)

Some Recent Works on ML and FL in the Healthcare Sector

Author's Name with Published Year	Database	Applied Models and Algorithms/Techniques	Contribution
Qayyum et al. [11]	COVID-chestxray-dataset, POCOVID-Net: Automatic detection of COVID-19 from a new lung ultrasound imaging dataset (POCUS) (1,103 images sampled from 64 videos)	Clustered federated learning (CFL)	COVID-19 diagnosis, 16% improvement in F-1 score in X-ray datasets, 11% improvement in ultrasound datasets
Zhang et al. [12]	N/A	Big.Little branch architecture	Used for forecasting and IoT applications, achieved better results in precision of prediction and inference
Nilsson et al. [13]	MNIST dataset (Modified National Institute of Standards and Technology dataset)	Federated Averaging (FedAvg) algorithm, Federated Stochastic Variance Reduced Gradient, CO-OP	FedAvg and conventional ML demonstrated the same performance for IID data, traditional ML did better on Non-IID data
Antunes et al. [14]	N/A	N/A	Reviewed contemporary FL applications related to EHR data
Nguyen et al. [15]	N/A	N/A	Showed current FL advancements in the medical sector, secure and privacy-aware FL, resource-aware FL, personalized FL, incentive FL
Kaissis et al. [16]	N/A	N/A	FL in medical imaging to protect privacy, mentioned techniques like differential privacy, homomorphic encryption, secure multi-party computation
Chen et al. [17]		A federated transfer learning framework named FedHealth	Addressed issues like fragmented clinical data and lack of personalization and was designed for wearable healthcare

(*Continued*)

TABLE 1.1 (*Continued*)
Some Recent Works on ML and FL in the Healthcare Sector

Author's Name with Published Year	Database	Applied Models and Algorithms/Techniques	Contribution
Hao et al. [18]		PRCL (Privacy-aware and Resource saving Collaborative Learning) protocol	Addressed privacy and energy requirement issues during FL training, proposed a splitting method to lessen local computing cost
Yang et al. [19]	The LIDC/IDRI Database and data from National Institutes of Health	Semi-supervised and federated learning	COVID area division using 3D chest Computed Tomography (CT), computer-assisted characterization and detection performed well in COVID tests

patients proposing a decentralized framework [21]. In another study, Yaqoob et al. proposed an FL-based framework for HSP systems to tackle data privacy related problems. A federated matched averaging (FedMA) algorithm was used to maintain medical data privacy here. On top of that, a hybrid approach of a modified artificial bee colony and support vector machine (MABC-SVM) ultimately improved prediction accuracy [22].

However, studies showed there are possibilities that samples used in FL can be also learnt by reverse engineering the trained model. Khana et al. integrated differential privacy in their proposed model to address this issue. To keep the samples unrevealed, this method applied controlled noise to weight parameters to prevent significant changes in the summary statistics. The research made an effort to predict breast cancer conditions using gene expression data [23].

1.3.2 PATIENT MONITORING

Remote patient monitoring (RPM) application is used nowadays in patient monitoring without hampering patients' daily activities. Classifying vital signs and body movements is challenging in this field of monitoring where artificial intelligence can help. Shaik et al. utilized FL to design a personalized monitoring system. Through this study, the researchers designed a heterogeneous stacked FL architecture, FedStack, and merged tri-axial data to monitor a patient's spontaneous body movements with the help of FL. They also used sensor data for effective positioning of sensors for patient monitoring, which ultimately led to categorizing label activities [24].

Wu et al. worked on an FL model, which is a cloud-based approach named FedHome, to monitor in-home health-related activities. Here, a proposed generative convolutional autoencoder (GCAE) fine tuned the model for an error-free health monitoring. Moreover, GCAE also cut down costs of FL in the application of FedHome [25]. In another study, Khoa et al. brought Fed xData framework to work on issues like parameter complexity, huge costs, lack of personalization, and accuracy. It established an incessant data balancing-supplemented framework that utilizes RandomOverSample technique. It also solved the issue related to not independent and identically (Non-IID) distribution by modifying the model in a better way and thus achieved higher accuracy [26].

1.3.3 Drug Discovery

Increasing the training data incurs higher time and financial costs of traditional machine learning models in the pharmaceutical industry [27]. Moreover, protecting intellectual properties and company interests can often limit the sharing of data and collaborative initiatives in drug discovery [28]. A secure multi-party computation (MPC) encryption method helps to tackle this issue in data sharing while making a way to work on private datasets without disclosing them [29]. However, some companies are not interested in sharing even their encrypted data, and regulations like GDPR and CCPA are making the necessity of an alternative approach more obvious [30].

FL can bring a solution to this problem. Among different categories of FL, HFL (horizontal federated learning) is more appropriate for drug discovery than others with an additional advantage of sharing encrypted parameters instead of raw data. Again, QSAR (Quantitative structure-activity relationship) is a widely used technique in drug discovery for predicting and analyzing the characteristics of compounds [31]. Chen et al. established FL-QSAR (Federated learning-Quantitative structure-activity relationship), which was integrated into the HFL framework. However, it was found in this study that HFL showed the same accuracy as cleartext learning algorithms which generally use shared information [30].

In another study related to drug discovery, Xiong et al. showed that FL has a better regularization effect than conventional ML models when it comes to biased datasets. According to this study, FL can also contribute to drug discovery by solving the issue of small and biased data dilemma [32].

1.3.4 Personalized Medicine

Precision or Personalized Medicine (PM) can be defined as "prevention and treatment strategies that take individual variability into account" [33]. The leaders of the National Institutes of Health (NIH) and the Food and Drug Administration (FDA) shared the concept of personalized medicine [34]. It was found that patients' individual genetic, biochemical, physiological, structural, environmental, behavioral, and other factors should be tailored to personalize the treatment or even the prevention of a disease. Although the terms "personalized" and "precision" are used here interchangeably, there are some differences between them [35].

Personalized medicines become effective by targeting the right patients based on diagnostic tests that identify patients, which helps to design targeted therapies [34].

Often these therapies are tailored using diverse data stored on local devices. As the patient data does not need to be shared, FL thus protects the privacy and sensitivity of clinical data.

1.4 ALGORITHMS USED IN FEDERATED LEARNING IN THE HEALTHCARE ARENA

FL leverages the FL algorithms to implement the technique to ensure data security, privacy, and utilization of local data. FL includes implementation of steps like local training, model aggregation, and global model update [36]. On top of that, FedSGD, FedAvg, and FedDyn models contribute to the usage of FL. A description of each can be helpful for a proper understanding of the model architecture of FL.

1.4.1 FEDERATED STOCHASTIC GRADIENT DESCENT (FEDSGD)

FedSGD is an optimized ML algorithm that is based on the conventional SGD algorithm and is implemented in a federated setting. The algorithm includes the FL steps mentioned before:

- **Initialization**: To solve a particular problem, a global model is sent to participating edge devices.
- **Local Training**: Next comes the step of local training of the sent model by the participating devices based on their local data. The SGD algorithm is used in this phase to update the model.
- **Model Updates**: The devices share gradients or model updates after local training is done, rather than sharing data. This approach strengthens the privacy of the personal data used in training.
- **Aggregation**: Using the aggregation technique, the server utilizes the model updates proposed by the local devices. Thus, the server leverages the collaborative effort put in by the devices to improve the model quality.
- **Global Model Update**: The aggregation technique is iterated multiple times by the central server on sending and receiving the model back and forth. The updates are adjusted to the model until convergence is reached.

According to McMahan et al., optimization based on SGD has accelerated the successful implementation of deep learning. In federated optimization, SGD involves calculating single batch gradients per round. Although the algorithm shows efficiency, good models only come with numerous rounds of training in this case [37]. Another study by Chen et al. mentioned that stochastic optimization comes with synchronous and asynchronous approaches and each of the two has its own cons. Asynchronous approach creates the additional burden of noise when the synchronous one has idle time issues. As a solution, the same study proposed synchronous optimization with backup workers, which addressed the noise issue and proposed to lessen stragglers in the synchronous technique [38].

1.4.2 Federated Averaging (FedAvg)

The FedAvg algorithm can be said as the extension of the previously mentioned algorithm, FedSGD. In FedAvg, according to McMahan et al., client devices take one step of gradient descent at a time and the server considers the weighted average of the resulting model. Going forward, the devices can be utilized for multiple times repeating the procedure for more local updates and then averaging takes place. This technique is known as FederatedAveraging or FedAvg. Three main parameters generally influence the amount of computation: the portion of clients participating in each round for computation or C, number of training passes on each round performed by each client or E, and the size of local minibatch clients use for updates or B [37]. The working procedure of the FedAvg algorithm includes some steps similar to those of the FedSGD algorithm:

- **Initialization**: To initiate the procedure of model training, a global model is determined first.
- **Data Sources**: As local devices participate in making updates of the initial model without sharing their data, training data is sourced from numerous devices in place of a central one.
- **Local Training**: Each device uses its own local data to update the model parameters of the initial global model. The process is generally iterative.
- **Model Updates**: Model updates by participating devices come from local training, relying on local data. Without the need for data sharing, the global model thus gains insights from distributed data.
- **Communication**: This step involves transferring local updates derived from distributed devices to the central server. Sharing only the updates protects data privacy.
- **Aggregation**: The local updates received from the devices are utilized by the central server as it averages the updates. An averaging technique is used in this step to make a change in the initial global model.
- **Global Model Update**: Aggregation does not stop after one shot, and the process repeats until convergence. Each time the global mode is updated on the central server, it is sent back to the devices to make further parameter changes if necessary.
- **Repetition**: As mentioned earlier, the FedAvg algorithm follows an iterative approach to achieve convergence. Here, steps from 3 to 7 are repeated to leverage the knowledge learnt from devices to attain improved accuracy and generalization.

The distinctive key features of the FedAvg algorithm include:

Data Privacy: FedAvg protects the privacy and security of local data because training data never leaves the device in this approach, unlike traditional ML models.

Communication Efficiency: Instead of sending local data, updates for model parameters are communicated only to ensure security. These updates are then aggregated in the central server.

Decentralization: The idea of decentralization brings a breakthrough because the conventional, centralized approach involves greater computational capacity and is

Revolutionizing Healthcare through Federated Learning 11

not suitable for scaling often. Again, local data is not needed to be shared, so information remains private in this method.

Robustness: Single point failure in case of participating devices does not affect the FedAvg algorithm. This makes it more stable than other models used in traditional approaches.

1.4.3 FEDDYN (FEDERATED LEARNING WITH DYNAMIC REGULARIZATION)

Complex models can lead to huge communication overhead of mobile devices in conventional FL. Federated Distillation (FD), which is a federated form of knowledge distillation, can bring a solution to this problem. However, FD does not show a good performance in terms of non-IID cases, for example, Federated Recommendation (FR). As an initiative to solve this, FedDyn method was proposed by Jin et al. that relies on focus distillation instead of averaging technique in order to address the non-IID issue. The results derived from this technique demonstrated better convergence speed and less communication overhead [39]. Acar et al. also proposed FedDyn in a study where the central server sends the global model to the active devices. The sum of each active device's local empirical loss and penalized risk function, known as the local empirical risk objective, is optimized. Penalized risk is dynamically updated generally [40].

Apart from the mentioned algorithms, there are other ones like FedProx, FedOpt, FedBN, SiloBN, FedDAR, and Scaffold, which are also used in FL to advance the healthcare industry [41].

1.5 HOW FL IS MORE SECURE THAN TRADITIONAL APPROACHES

FL can be distinguished from traditional ML by the additional privacy and security it offers. And this also remains true for clinical data. The additional security integration can be considered in this way. FL does not require local data sharing like traditional ML models, therefore data never leaves the owner's device. In place of data, updated parameters are sent to the central server by the participating devices. However, without proper encryption and secure aggregation, there remains the possibility of data leak, endangering personal security. Additionally, this technique includes inadvertent remembrance which can result in revealing training data from suggested updates. The following techniques can be helpful for improving privacy and security of the data involved.

1.5.1 DIFFERENTIAL PRIVACY

Differential privacy involves retrieving global statistical distribution and lessening individual identifiable information at the same time [42]. A dataset is considered to be differentially private when an outsider cannot specifically judge whether a particular individual was utilized to extract a particular outcome. This method reorganizes data, includes additional noise, or even applies differentially private stochastic gradient descent in NNs [43]. FL in healthcare applications, particularly medical imaging, can greatly benefit from this method while ensuring security.

1.5.2 Homomorphic Encryption

HE performs computation on encrypted data considering it as unencrypted. This particular technique needs proper definition of operations to be performed within the algorithm, and standard encryption algorithms cannot be used in this case. HE has notable implementations in areas like convolutional neural network (CNN), ML as a service [44], and also in FL. It contributes to the secure aggregation of suggested updates [45].

1.5.3 Secure Multi-Party Computation

Secure multi-party computation (SMPC) is applied on data parts that are divided in such a way that prevents disclosure of the data to any individual party. Due to the feature of "secret sharing" in certain environments, SMPC has been explored in recent days [16]. Without the need to disclose the patient's genome, this technique has contributed to the field of genome sequencing [46]. SMPC can also be applied to the analysis of medical imaging. It helps to prevent the leakage of personal information and thus ensures a secure FL approach.

1.5.4 Secure Hardware Implementations

Along with the above-mentioned techniques, hardware-level security, which can include processors or edge devices like mobile devices, is also important [47]. Despite the occurrence of operating system kernel breaches, this technique can be implemented in FL to ensure algorithm and data security [16].

1.6 CONCLUSION

In this article, we have tried to shed light on different healthcare applications of FL with examples of recent algorithms, architectures, and techniques used in the related studies. FL helps healthcare institutions to collaboratively work on building models without compromising patients' data privacy and sensitivity. Our paper has highlighted the beneficiary approach of FL that can create a breakthrough in fields like personalized medicine, drug discovery, disease detection, and patient monitoring – all these have the potential to save millions of lives. The specialty of FL lies in ensuring enhanced privacy and security in comparison with traditional ML methods. The paper has delved into the several techniques that are employed to make sure local data remains secure and private in FL. An overview of recent studies and findings related to FL in the healthcare sector has also been presented in this study, pointing to the state-of-the-art in this prospect. Limitations of FL in this sector include statistical heterogeneity, communication issues in FL, and necessity of strengthening security to design a more sustained FL network – these can guide researchers to conduct further studies in this arena. Finally, FL can revolutionize the healthcare sector in many ways and it holds enormous potential to serve the greater humanity.

REFERENCES

1. Hong, L., Luo, M., Wang, R., Lu, P., Lu, W., & Lu, L. (2018). Big data in health care: Applications and challenges. *Data and Information Management*, 2(3), 175–197. https://doi.org/10.2478/dim-2018-0014
2. Bates, D. W. W., Saria, S., Ohno-Machado, L., Shah, A., & Escobar, G. (2014). Big data in health care: Using analytics to identify and manage high-risk and high-cost patients. *Using Big Data to Transform Care*, 33(7). https://doi.org/10.1377/hlthaff.2014.0041
3. Shastri, Y. (2023). Retrieved from https://www.v7labs.com/blog/federated-learning-guide#:~:text=Federated%20learning%20(often%20referred%20to,model%20locally%2C%20increasing%20data%20privacy
4. Hassan, Md. M., Mollick, S., & Yasmin, F. (2022). An unsupervised cluster-based feature grouping model for early diabetes detection. *Healthcare Analytics*, 100112. https://doi.org/10.1016/j.health.2022.100112
5. Hassan, Md. M., Hassan, Md. M., Mollick, S., Asif, M., Yasmin, F., Bairagi, A. K., Raihan, M., Arif, S. A., & Rahman, A. (2023). A comparative study, prediction and development of chronic kidney disease using machine learning on patients clinical records. *Human-Centric Intelligent Systems*. https://doi.org/10.1007/s44230-023-00017-3
6. Hassan, Md. M., Zaman, S., Mollick, S., Hassan, Md. M., Raihan, M., Kaushal, C., & Bhardwaj, R. (2023). An efficient Apriori algorithm for frequent pattern in human intoxication data. *Innovations in Systems and Software Engineering*. https://doi.org/10.1007/s11334-022-00523-w
7. Hassan, Md. M., Hassan, Md. M., Yasmin, F., Khan, Md. A. R., Zaman, S., Galibuzzaman, Islam, K. K., & Bairagi, A. K. (2023). A comparative assessment of machine learning algorithms with the Least Absolute Shrinkage and Selection Operator for breast cancer detection and prediction. *Decision Analytics Journal*, 7, 100245. https://doi.org/10.1016/j.dajour.2023.100245
8. McMahan, B., & Ramage, D. (2017). Retrieved from https://blog.research.google/2017/04/federated-learning-collaborative.html
9. Boughorbel, S., Jarray, F., Venugopal, N., Moosa, S., Elhadi, H., & Makhlouf, M. (2019). Federated uncertainty-aware learning for distributed hospital EHR data. *Semantic Scholar*. https://doi.org/10.48550/arXiv.1910.12191
10. Lim, W. Y., Garg, S., Xiong, Z., Niyato, D., Leung, C., Miao, C., & Guizani, M. (2021). Dynamic contract design for federated learning in smart healthcare applications. *IEEE Internet of Things Journal*, 8(23), 16853–16862. https://doi.org/10.1109/jiot.2020.3033806
11. Qayyum, A., Ahmad, K., Ahsan, M. A., Al-Fuqaha, A., & Qadir, J. (2022). Collaborative federated learning for healthcare: Multi-modal COVID-19 diagnosis at the edge. *IEEE Open Journal of the Computer Society*, 3, 172–184. https://doi.org/10.1109/ojcs.2022.3206407
12. Zhang, X., Hu, M., Xia, J., Wei, T., Chen, M., & Hu, S. (2021). Efficient federated learning for cloud-based AIOT applications. *IEEE Transactions on Computer-Aided Design of Integrated Circuits and Systems*, 40(11), 2211–2223. https://doi.org/10.1109/tcad.2020.3046665
13. Nilsson, A., Smith, S., Ulm, G., Gustavsson, E., & Jirstrand, M. (2018). A performance evaluation of Federated Learning Algorithms. *Proceedings of the Second Workshop on Distributed Infrastructures for Deep Learning*. https://doi.org/10.1145/3286490.3286559
14. Antunes, R. S., André da Costa, C., Küderle, A., Yari, I. A., & Eskofier, B. (2022). Federated learning for healthcare: Systematic review and architecture proposal. *ACM Transactions on Intelligent Systems and Technology*, 13(4), 1–23. https://doi.org/10.1145/3501813

15. Nguyen, D. C., Pham, Q.-V., Pathirana, P. N., Ding, M., Seneviratne, A., Lin, Z., Dobre, O., & Hwang, W.-J. (2023). Federated learning for smart healthcare: A survey. *ACM Computing Surveys, 55*(3), 1–37. https://doi.org/10.1145/3501296

16. Kaissis, G. A., Makowski, M. R., Rückert, D., & Braren, R. F. (2020). Secure, privacy-preserving and federated machine learning in medical imaging. *Nature Machine Intelligence, 2*(6), 305–311. https://doi.org/10.1038/s42256-020-0186-1

17. Chen, Y., Qin, X., Wang, J., Yu, C., & Gao, W. (2020). FedHealth: A federated transfer learning framework for wearable healthcare. *IEEE Intelligent Systems, 35*(4), 83–93. https://doi.org/10.1109/mis.2020.2988604

18. Hao, M., Li, H., Xu, G., Liu, Z., & Chen, Z. (2020). Privacy-aware and resource-saving collaborative learning for healthcare in cloud computing. *ICC 2020-2020 IEEE International Conference on Communications (ICC).* https://doi.org/10.1109/icc40277.2020.9148979

19. Yang, D., Xu, Z., Li, W., Myronenko, A., Roth, H. R., Harmon, S., Xu, S., Turkbey, B., Turkbey, E., Wang, X., Zhu, W., Carrafiello, G., Patella, F., Cariati, M., Obinata, H., Mori, H., Tamura, K., An, P., Wood, B. J., & Xu, D. (2021). Federated semi-supervised learning for COVID region segmentation in chest CT using multi-national data from China, Italy, Japan. *Medical Image Analysis, 70,* 101992. https://doi.org/10.1016/j.media.2021.101992

20. Kavitha Bharathi, S., Dhavamani, M., & Niranjan, K. (2022). A federated learning based approach for heart disease prediction. *2022 6th International Conference on Computing Methodologies and Communication (ICCMC).* https://doi.org/10.1109/iccmc53470.2022.9754119

21. Brisimi, T. S., Chen, R., Mela, T., Olshevsky, A., Paschalidis, I. Ch., & Shi, W. (2018). Federated learning of Predictive models from Federated Electronic Health Records. *International Journal of Medical Informatics, 112,* 59–67. https://doi.org/10.1016/j.ijmedinf.2018.01.007

22. Yaqoob, M. M., Nazir, M., Khan, M. A., Qureshi, S., & Al-Rasheed, A. (2023). Hybrid classifier-based federated learning in health service providers for cardiovascular disease prediction. *Applied Sciences, 13*(3), 1911. https://doi.org/10.3390/app13031911

23. Khanna, A., Schaffer, V., Gürsoy, G., & Gerstein, M. (2022). Privacy-preserving model training for disease prediction using federated learning with differential privacy. *2022 44th Annual International Conference of the IEEE Engineering in Medicine & Biology Society (EMBC).* https://doi.org/10.1109/embc48229.2022.9871742

24. Shaik, T., Tao, X., Higgins, N., Gururajan, R., Li, Y., Zhou, X., & Acharya, U. R. (2022). FedStack: Personalized activity monitoring using stacked federated learning. *Knowledge-Based Systems, 257,* 109929. https://doi.org/10.1016/j.knosys.2022.109929

25. Wu, Q., Chen, X., Zhou, Z., & Zhang, J. (2020). FedHome: Cloud-edge based personalized federated learning for in-home health monitoring. *IEEE Transactions on Mobile Computing,* 1–1. https://doi.org/10.1109/tmc.2020.3045266

26. Khoa, T. A., Nguyen, D.-V., Dao, M.-S., & Zettsu, K. (2021). Fed xData: A federated learning framework for enabling contextual health monitoring in a cloud-edge network. *2021 IEEE International Conference on Big Data (Big Data).* https://doi.org/10.1109/bigdata52589.2021.9671536

27. Ma, R., Li, Y., Li, C., Wan, F., Hu, H., Xu, W., & Zeng, J. (2020). Secure multiparty computation for privacy-preserving drug discovery. *Bioinformatics, 36*(9), 2872–2880. https://doi.org/10.1093/bioinformatics/btaa038

28. Hie, B., Cho, H., & Berger, B. (2018). Realizing private and practical pharmacological collaboration. *Science, 362*(6412), 347–350. https://doi.org/10.1126/science.aat4807

29. Yao, A. C. (1982, November 1). Protocols for secure computations. https://doi.org/10.1109/SFCS.1982.38

Revolutionizing Healthcare through Federated Learning   15

30. Chen, S., Xue, D., Chuai, G., Yang, Q., & Liu, Q. (2020). FL-QSAR: A federated learning-based QSAR prototype for collaborative drug discovery. *Bioinformatics, 36*(22–23), 5492–5498. https://doi.org/10.1093/bioinformatics/btaa1006

31. Ma, J., Sheridan, R. P., Liaw, A., Dahl, G. E., & Svetnik, V. (2015). Deep neural nets as a method for quantitative structure-activity relationships. *Journal of Chemical Information and Modeling, 55*(2), 263–274. https://doi.org/10.1021/ci500747n

32. Xiong, Z., Cheng, Z., Lin, X., Xu, C., Liu, X., Wang, D., Luo, X., Zhang, Y., Jiang, H., Qiao, N., & Zheng, M. (2021). Facing small and biased data dilemma in drug discovery with enhanced federated learning approaches [Review of Facing small and biased data dilemma in drug discovery with enhanced federated learning approaches]. *Science China Life Sciences, 65*, 529–539. https://link.springer.com/article/10.1007/s11427-021-1946-0

33. Collins, F. S., & Varmus, H. (2015). A new initiative on precision medicine. *New England Journal of Medicine, 372*(9), 793–795. https://doi.org/10.1056/nejmp1500523

34. Hamburg, M. A., & Collins, F. S. (2010). The path to personalized medicine. *New England Journal of Medicine, 363*(4), 301–304. https://doi.org/10.1056/nejmp1006304

35. Goetz, L. H., & Schork, N. J. (2018). Personalized medicine: Motivation, challenges, and progress. *Fertility and Sterility, 109*(6), 952–963. https://doi.org/10.1016/j.fertnstert.2018.05.006

36. Shastri, Y. (2023, February 3). A step-by-step guide to federated learning in computer vision. Www.v7labs.com. https://www.v7labs.com/blog/federated-learning-guide#:~:text=Federated%20Learning%3A%20Key%20takeaways

37. McMahan, B., Moore, E., Ramage, D., Hampson, S. & Arcas, B.A.Y. (2017). Communication-efficient learning of deep networks from decentralized data. *Proceedings of the 20th International Conference on Artificial Intelligence and Statistics, in Proceedings of Machine Learning Research, 54*, 1273–1282. https://proceedings.mlr.press/v54/mcmahan17a.html

38. Chen, J., Monga, R., Bengio, S., & Jozefowicz, R. (2016). Revisiting distributed synchronous SGD. Google Research. https://research.google/pubs/pub45187/

39. Jin, C., Chen, X., Gu, Y., & Li, Q. (2023, March 27). FedDyn: A dynamic and efficient federated distillation approach on recommender system. *IEEE Xplore. 2022 IEEE 28th International Conference on Parallel and Distributed Systems (ICPADS)*, Nanjing, China. https://ieeexplore.ieee.org/abstract/document/10077950

40. Acar, D. A. E., Zhao, Y., Navarro, R. M., Mattina, M., Whatmough, P. N., & Saligrama, V. (n.d.). Federated learning based on dynamic regularization. ICLR. https://arxiv.org/pdf/2111.04263.pdf

41. Hwang, H., Yang, S., Kim, D., Dua, R., Kim, J., Yang, E. & Choi, E. (2023). Towards the practical utility of federated learning in the medical domain. *Proceedings of the Conference on Health, Inference, and Learning, in Proceedings of Machine Learning Research, 209*, 163–181. https://proceedings.mlr.press/v209/hwang23a.html

42. Dwork, C., & Roth, A. (2013). The algorithmic foundations of differential privacy. *Foundations and Trends(r) in Theoretical Computer Science, 9*(3–4), 211–407. https://doi.org/10.1561/0400000042

43. Rajkumar, A. & Agarwal, S. (2012). A differentially private stochastic gradient descent algorithm for multiparty classification. *Proceedings of the Fifteenth International Conference on Artificial Intelligence and Statistics, in Proceedings of Machine Learning Research, 22*, 933–941. https://proceedings.mlr.press/v22/rajkumar12.html

44. Gilad-Bachrach, R., Dowlin, N., Laine, K., Lauter, K., Naehrig, M. & Wernsing, J. (2016). CryptoNets: Applying neural networks to encrypted data with high throughput and accuracy. *Proceedings of the 33rd International Conference on Machine Learning, in Proceedings of Machine Learning Research, 48*, 201–210. https://proceedings.mlr.press/v48/gilad-bachrach16.html

45. Li, X., Chen, D., Li, C., & Wang, L. (2015). Secure data aggregation with fully homomorphic encryption in large-scale wireless sensor networks. *Sensors*, *15*(7), 15952–15973. https://doi.org/10.3390/s150715952
46. Jagadeesh, K. A., Wu, D. J., Birgmeier, J. A., Boneh, D., & Bejerano, G. (2017). Deriving genomic diagnoses without revealing patient genomes. *Science*, *357*(6352), 692–695. https://doi.org/10.1126/science.aam9710
47. Secure Enclave. (2021, May 17). Apple support. https://support.apple.com/guide/security/secure-enclave-sec59b0b31ff/web

2 Revolutionizing Healthcare

Unleashing the Power of Digital Health

Renu Vij

2.1 INTRODUCTION: BACKGROUND AND DRIVING FORCES

As digital health continues to gain momentum, a plethora of innovative technologies are transforming the healthcare landscape. This chapter explores the various digital health technologies that are revolutionizing healthcare delivery, empowering patients, and enabling healthcare professionals to make data-driven decisions. By understanding these technologies and their potential applications, we can unlock the power of digital health and pave the way for a future where healthcare is more accessible, efficient, and patient-centric.

2.2 RESEARCH AIM AND OBJECTIVES

The primary aim of this chapter is to set the stage for understanding the significance and potential impact of digital health in revolutionizing healthcare. The specific objectives of this chapter include:

Providing an overview of the healthcare landscape and its challenges
Defining digital health and its scope
Highlighting the need for transformation in healthcare

This chapter begins by highlighting the enhanced access to healthcare services facilitated by digital health solutions. Telemedicine and virtual care platforms are examined as tools that break down geographical barriers, allowing patients in remote or underserved areas to consult with healthcare professionals remotely. The potential of mobile health applications in providing on-demand healthcare information and resources is also explored.

This chapter further examines how digital health technologies enhance care coordination and collaboration among healthcare providers. Electronic health records (EHRs), health information exchange (HIE) systems, and tele-consultation platforms streamline communication, enabling seamless information sharing and multidisciplinary care. The challenges of interoperability and data privacy are addressed, emphasizing the need for standardized systems and robust security measures.

DOI: 10.1201/9781032694870-2

Improved patient safety and quality of care are significant outcomes of the digital health revolution. This chapter explores the impact of technologies such as medication management systems, clinical decision support tools, and remote patient monitoring in reducing errors, preventing adverse events, and enabling early intervention. User-centered design and usability testing are highlighted as essential factors for ensuring the effectiveness and acceptance of these solutions.

Cost efficiency and healthcare resource optimization are key considerations in this chapter. The potential of telemedicine, remote patient monitoring, and predictive analytics in reducing healthcare costs, minimizing hospital readmissions, and optimizing resource allocation are discussed. This chapter also addresses barriers to adoption, including infrastructure requirements, reimbursement models, and regulatory frameworks.

Ethical considerations and patient privacy are given due importance throughout this chapter. Informed consent, data security, and confidentiality are emphasized to maintain trust between patients and healthcare providers. The role of regulatory bodies in ensuring compliance with privacy regulations and ethical guidelines is also acknowledged.

2.3 REVIEW OF LITERATURE

The integration of digital technologies in healthcare has brought about a paradigm shift in how medical services are delivered. Digital health encompasses a wide range of tools and platforms, including telemedicine, health apps, wearable devices, EHRs, remote monitoring, artificial intelligence (AI), and genomics. This chapter explores how these technologies have revolutionized healthcare, benefiting both patients and healthcare providers. The literature review, drawing from esteemed authors, delves into the transformative impact of digital health on healthcare practices.

Telemedicine, as championed by Bashshur et al. (2016), has emerged as a transformative force in patient care. With the ability to conduct remote consultations and provide virtual care, telemedicine has significantly improved access to healthcare services, especially in underserved and remote areas. Patients can now receive timely medical advice, leading to early diagnosis and better management of chronic conditions.

The work of Rajkomar et al. (2019) highlights the potential of AI in revolutionizing diagnostics and treatments. AI-powered algorithms can analyze vast amounts of medical data, assisting clinicians in making more accurate diagnoses and treatment decisions. Moreover, AI-driven predictive analytics enable early detection of diseases and personalized treatment plans, thereby enhancing patient outcomes.

Steinhubl et al. (2015) underscore the empowering nature of health apps and wearable devices for patients. These tools allow individuals to monitor their health, track fitness levels, and access personalized health insights. By encouraging self-management and preventive healthcare, health apps and wearables can lead to healthier lifestyles and reduced burden on healthcare facilities.

The adoption of digital health technologies raises concerns about data security and privacy. Rothstein et al. (2016) emphasized the need for robust data protection measures to safeguard sensitive patient information. This chapter discusses the challenges of maintaining data privacy in the digital health era and the importance of implementing secure information-sharing practices.

Revolutionizing Healthcare

Wang et al. (2018) shed light on the regulatory challenges faced by digital health innovations. Striking a balance between promoting innovation and ensuring patient safety requires flexible and adaptive regulatory frameworks. This chapter explores the role of regulatory bodies in fostering responsible digital health practices.

The potential of digital health extends into the realm of personalized medicine and genomics. Collins and Varmus (2015) explained how advancements in genomics can lead to tailored treatment plans based on an individual's genetic makeup. Integrating genomic data with digital health technologies holds the promise of improved treatment efficacy and patient outcomes.

The transformative potential of blockchain technology in healthcare, as explored by Zhang et al. (2018), lies in ensuring data interoperability, security, and integrity. Blockchain's decentralized nature and encrypted data sharing can enhance data management, patient consent, and medical record security.

Rajkomar et al. (2019) highlighted how AI has transformed diagnostics in healthcare. Machine learning algorithms can analyze complex medical data, including imaging, pathology, and genetic information, to aid in disease detection and diagnosis. AI-powered diagnostic tools have shown promising results in various fields, such as radiology, pathology, and cardiology, improving accuracy and reducing interpretation time.

Advancements in genomics, as discussed by Collins and Varmus (2015), are playing a pivotal role in personalized medicine. By integrating genomic data with digital health platforms, clinicians can develop tailored treatment plans based on an individual's genetic makeup. This approach allows for more targeted therapies, minimizing adverse reactions and optimizing treatment efficacy.

Telemedicine and remote monitoring, as championed by Bashshur et al. (2016), have transformed chronic disease management. Patients with chronic conditions, such as diabetes, hypertension, and heart disease, can now be remotely monitored through wearable devices and home health monitoring systems. Healthcare providers can track patients' vital signs and health indicators in real time, enabling timely interventions and reducing hospital readmissions.

AI's impact on drug discovery and development, as studied by Topol (2019), is revolutionizing the pharmaceutical industry. Machine learning algorithms can analyze vast datasets to identify potential drug candidates and predict their efficacy and safety profiles. This has the potential to accelerate the drug development process, reducing costs and improving the chances of finding effective treatments for various diseases.

Virtual reality (VR) and augmented reality (AR) technologies are transforming surgical training, as explored by Steinhubl et al. (2015). Surgeons can now practice complex procedures in a simulated environment, enhancing their skills and confidence before performing surgeries on real patients. VR and AR also offer a platform for collaborative surgeries, enabling experts to guide less-experienced surgeons remotely.

Big data analytics and clinical decision support systems (CDSSs) are empowering healthcare providers to make informed decisions. By integrating patient data from EHRs, medical literature, and clinical guidelines, CDSS can suggest personalized treatment plans and alert clinicians to potential drug interactions and adverse events.

2.4 HEALTHCARE IN INDIA

India, as one of the world's most populous countries, faces significant challenges in providing adequate healthcare to its citizens. The healthcare system in India has undergone considerable improvements over the years, but it also grapples with various barriers that hinder its ability to deliver comprehensive and accessible healthcare services. This essay will examine the current state of healthcare in India, highlighting its achievements, identifying persistent challenges, and proposing potential solutions for a healthier future.

India has made notable progress in improving healthcare indicators over the years. The government has implemented various initiatives to enhance healthcare accessibility and affordability, resulting in improved life expectancy and decreased infant mortality rates. The expansion of the National Health Mission (NHM) has strengthened the primary healthcare infrastructure, including the establishment of community health centers and rural hospitals. Additionally, successful vaccination drives have significantly reduced the prevalence of diseases such as polio and measles.

India's pharmaceutical industry has also played a crucial role in providing cost-effective generic drugs to both its citizens and the world. With its prowess in manufacturing medicines, India has become a global supplier of essential medications, helping combat diseases and making treatments more affordable for millions of people worldwide.

A traditional health system refers to the conventional model of healthcare delivery, which relies heavily on face-to-face interactions between patients and healthcare providers, such as doctors, nurses, and pharmacists. The system focuses on in-person consultations and patients visit healthcare facilities, clinics, or hospitals to consult with healthcare providers. The diagnosis and treatment are primarily based on physical examinations, medical history, and direct interactions.

Patient records, including medical histories, test results, and treatment plans, are often maintained in physical paper files. This can lead to challenges in data accessibility, storage, and retrieval. Healthcare services are geographically constrained. Patients may face barriers to accessing care due to distance, mobility issues, or the availability of healthcare professionals in their area.

Scheduling Challenges as Appointments are typically scheduled through phone calls or in-person, and waiting times for appointments can be lengthy, leading to potential delays in diagnosis and treatment.

Sharing patient information between different healthcare providers can be cumbersome and time-consuming, often relying on fax machines or physical document transfer.

Traditional health systems and digital health systems represent two distinct paradigms of healthcare delivery. Traditional systems rely on in-person consultations and paper-based records, while digital health systems leverage technology to enhance patient care, data management, and accessibility. The shift toward digital health systems is driven by the need for greater efficiency, improved patient engagement, and enhanced diagnostic and treatment capabilities. While traditional health systems continue to play a vital role in healthcare, the integration of digital technologies is reshaping the landscape and offering new opportunities to improve healthcare

Revolutionizing Healthcare

quality and outcomes. The future of healthcare likely lies in a harmonious coexistence of these two approaches, with digital health systems augmenting and enhancing the strengths of traditional care delivery.

2.5 CHALLENGES IN HEALTHCARE IN INDIAN SCENARIO

Despite the progress, India's healthcare system faces several challenges. One of the most significant obstacles is the unequal distribution of healthcare resources between urban and rural areas. Urban centers typically enjoy better healthcare facilities, while rural regions suffer from inadequate infrastructure, shortage of healthcare professionals, and limited access to essential services.

Another pressing concern is the high out-of-pocket expenditure on healthcare by individuals and families. The lack of comprehensive health insurance coverage leaves many vulnerable to financial hardships when facing medical emergencies. Additionally, the public healthcare system often grapples with overcrowded hospitals and long waiting times, leading some individuals to seek private healthcare, which can be financially burdensome for many.

Malnutrition remains a significant health issue in India, especially among children and pregnant women, leading to stunted growth and increased susceptibility to infections. Non-communicable diseases (NCDs) like diabetes, cardiovascular diseases, and cancer are on the rise due to changing lifestyles, contributing to the burden on the healthcare system.

2.6 THE FUTURE DIRECTION

To address these challenges and improve the healthcare status in India, a multi-pronged approach is necessary. The government must increase its healthcare expenditure to enhance infrastructure and improve the quality of healthcare services across rural areas. This includes recruiting and retaining skilled healthcare professionals in underserved regions and providing them with adequate facilities and resources.

Investments in preventive healthcare should be prioritized to reduce the burden of NCDs. Health education and awareness campaigns can promote healthier lifestyles and disease prevention, while vaccination drives must continue to curb infectious diseases effectively.

Universal health coverage, through a comprehensive health insurance scheme, can protect individuals from catastrophic health expenses and ensure equitable access to healthcare services. By integrating public and private healthcare sectors, the government can leverage the strengths of both systems to create a more robust and responsive healthcare framework.

India's healthcare system has come a long way, but significant challenges still persist. By focusing on addressing disparities in access, increasing investments, and promoting preventive healthcare, India can work toward a more inclusive and efficient healthcare system. Collaborative efforts from the government, healthcare professionals, and society as a whole are essential to achieve the vision of a healthier India, where quality healthcare is accessible to all citizens, regardless of their economic status or geographical location.

2.7 DEFINING DIGITAL HEALTH

Digital health, also known as eHealth or health informatics, refers to the integration of technology and information into healthcare practices to enhance patient care, improve outcomes, and streamline healthcare processes. It encompasses a wide range of digital tools, applications, and systems that leverage data, communication technologies, and AI to revolutionize the healthcare industry. From EHRs to telemedicine, digital health is reshaping how healthcare is delivered, making it more accessible, efficient, and patient-centric.

Digital health encompasses a wide range of technologies, systems, and applications that leverage digital tools to improve healthcare delivery, enhance patient engagement, and enable data-driven decision-making. It encompasses areas such as EHRs, telemedicine, mobile health (mHealth), wearable devices, HIE, AI, and data analytics. Digital health solutions have the potential to empower individuals to take control of their health, enable remote care delivery, facilitate seamless communication between healthcare providers, and unlock valuable insights from health data.

Digital health solutions also hold the promise of expanding access to healthcare services, especially in underserved areas, and improving overall health outcomes. However, as digital health continues to evolve, it is essential to address concerns related to data privacy, security, and ensuring equitable access to these technologies for all individuals. Through continuous innovation, collaboration between stakeholders, and a commitment to patient-centered care, digital health will play an instrumental role in shaping the future of healthcare.

2.8 THE NEED FOR TRANSFORMATION IN HEALTHCARE

The traditional healthcare model faces limitations in terms of accessibility, affordability, and patient-centricity. The need for transformation in healthcare is evident to overcome these limitations and create a healthcare system that is more proactive, preventive, and personalized. Digital health serves as a catalyst for this transformation, offering innovative approaches to healthcare delivery, data management, and patient engagement.

EHRs have emerged as a fundamental component of digital health. This section explores the benefits of EHRs in terms of improving healthcare coordination, enhancing patient safety, and facilitating seamless data sharing among healthcare providers. The challenges associated with EHR implementation, interoperability, and data privacy are also discussed, along with potential solutions to overcome these obstacles.

2.9 TELEMEDICINE AND REMOTE PATIENT MONITORING

Telemedicine and remote patient monitoring technologies have revolutionized the way healthcare services are delivered. This section delves into the advantages of telemedicine, including improved access to care, reduced healthcare costs, and enhanced patient convenience. Additionally, this chapter explores remote patient monitoring devices and their impact on chronic disease management, preventive care, and post-operative monitoring.

Revolutionizing Healthcare

2.10 MOBILE HEALTH (mHEALTH) APPLICATIONS

The proliferation of smartphones has paved the way for mobile health (mHealth) applications, empowering individuals to take control of their health and well-being. This section highlights the diverse range of mHealth applications, including fitness trackers, medication reminders, symptom trackers, and telehealth platforms. The potential benefits, challenges, and ethical considerations associated with mHealth applications are also discussed.

2.10.1 WEARABLE DEVICES AND SENSOR TECHNOLOGIES

Wearable devices and sensor technologies are transforming healthcare by providing real-time health monitoring and personalized insights. This section explores the applications of wearable devices in areas such as fitness tracking, remote patient monitoring, and early disease detection.

2.10.2 AI AND MACHINE LEARNING AI

Machine learning holds immense potential in revolutionizing healthcare through advanced analytics, predictive modeling, and decision support systems. This section explores the applications of AI in radiology, pathology, drug discovery, and personalized medicine.

2.10.3 DATA ANALYTICS AND HEALTH INFORMATION EXCHANGE

Data analytics and HIE are integral to leveraging the power of digital health. This section examines the role of data analytics in improving clinical outcomes, population health management, and healthcare operations. The importance of interoperability and secure health data exchange is emphasized, along with the potential benefits and challenges associated with HIE implementation.

2.10.4 EMERGING TECHNOLOGIES

This section explores the potential of emerging technologies such as blockchain and the Internet of Medical Things (IoMT) in revolutionizing healthcare. The benefits of blockchain in data security, interoperability, and supply chain management are discussed, while IoMT's impact on connected healthcare devices, remote monitoring, and patient engagement is explored.

Blockchain is a distributed ledger technology that ensures secure, transparent, and tamper-proof record-keeping. In the context of healthcare, blockchain can help in securely storing and sharing patient data, medical records, and other sensitive information. The decentralized nature of blockchain ensures that patient data is not controlled by a single entity, reducing the risk of data breaches and unauthorized access. Additionally, blockchain's smart contracts enable automated and secure execution of agreements, streamlining processes like insurance claims and supply chain management. By enhancing data security and interoperability, blockchain can improve the efficiency and accuracy of healthcare systems, leading to better patient outcomes.

IoMT refers to the interconnected network of medical devices, wearables, and sensors that collect and transmit health data. IoMT devices monitor patients in real time, providing continuous health insights and enabling remote patient monitoring. These devices can track vital signs, medication adherence, and disease progression, empowering healthcare providers to make data-driven decisions and deliver personalized care. IoMT also facilitates telemedicine and telehealth services, expanding access to healthcare, particularly in remote or underserved areas.

Combining blockchain with IoMT holds immense potential for healthcare transformation. Blockchain's data security and privacy features complement IoMT's data generation capabilities. By utilizing blockchain, IoMT data can be securely stored, shared, and accessed by authorized parties, ensuring data integrity and patient privacy. This integration can enhance the accuracy of patient data, facilitate real-time data exchange between healthcare providers, and streamline healthcare processes. Additionally, blockchain can assist in tracking the provenance and authenticity of medical devices, reducing the risk of counterfeit products entering the market.

Overall, the combination of blockchain and IoMT promises to create a more efficient, secure, and patient-centric healthcare ecosystem, leading to improved healthcare outcomes and better patient experiences. However, challenges related to regulatory compliance, interoperability, and scalability need to be addressed for successful and widespread implementation in the healthcare industry.

2.10.5 Enhanced Access to Healthcare Services

Digital health solutions have paved the way for enhanced access to healthcare services. This explores how telemedicine and virtual care platforms enable patients to consult with healthcare professionals remotely, breaking down geographical barriers and improving healthcare accessibility for individuals in rural or underserved areas. These platforms have become increasingly popular, especially in recent years, due to their convenience, accessibility, and ability to bridge the gap between patients and healthcare providers, regardless of geographical distances.

1. **Scheduling and Booking:** Patients can schedule appointments through these platforms at their convenience, without the need for physical visits to the healthcare facility. Some platforms may also allow patients to book urgent or on-demand consultations, providing timely medical advice.
2. **Real-Time Consultations:** Telemedicine platforms facilitate real-time consultations with healthcare professionals. Patients can discuss their symptoms, medical history, and concerns with the doctor, similar to an in-person visit. Doctors can assess the patient's condition remotely and provide appropriate medical advice or treatment plans.
3. **Remote Monitoring:** Some telemedicine platforms integrate with wearable devices or remote monitoring tools. This enables healthcare providers to track patients' vital signs, chronic conditions, or post-surgical recovery remotely, ensuring continuous monitoring and timely interventions.
4. **E-Prescriptions and Test Orders:** Through telemedicine platforms, doctors can electronically send prescriptions to the patient's preferred

Revolutionizing Healthcare

pharmacy, eliminating the need for physical prescriptions. They can also order diagnostic tests or lab work, which the patient can conduct locally.

5. **Patient Education and Follow-ups:** Telemedicine platforms can facilitate patient education by sharing relevant resources and information. After the consultation, healthcare professionals can conduct follow-up sessions virtually to track the patient's progress and adjust treatment plans if necessary.

6. **Secure and Private:** Telemedicine platforms prioritize patient privacy and security. They use encrypted communication and secure data storage to protect patient information, complying with healthcare regulations and guidelines.

7. **Access to Specialists:** Telemedicine and virtual care platforms can connect patients with specialized healthcare professionals who may not be available locally. This expands access to expert opinions and specialized care for patients, particularly those in remote areas.

Telemedicine and virtual care platforms empower patients to consult with healthcare professionals remotely, providing timely and accessible healthcare services while maintaining the privacy and security of patient information. These platforms play a vital role in enhancing patient experiences, reducing healthcare costs, and improving overall healthcare accessibility.

2.10.6 Successful Digital Health Initiatives and Their Potential to Revolutionize India's Healthcare System

2.10.6.1 Improved Healthcare Accessibility

One of the primary benefits of digital health in India is the improved accessibility of healthcare services, especially in rural and remote areas. India's vast geography and diverse population pose challenges to traditional healthcare delivery, making it difficult for everyone to access quality care. Digital health technologies, such as telemedicine and mobile health applications, have bridged the gap between patients and healthcare providers.

The eSanjeevani telemedicine platform, launched by the Ministry of Health and Family Welfare in 2019, is a prime example of how digital health is transforming healthcare accessibility in India. It allows patients to consult with doctors remotely through video calls and receive medical advice and prescriptions without the need to travel long distances to healthcare facilities. This initiative has brought specialized medical services to underserved areas, benefiting millions of patients across the country.

2.10.6.2 Enhancing Patient Care and Management

Digital health technologies have revolutionized patient care and management, enabling better monitoring, diagnosis, and personalized treatment plans. By leveraging EHRs and wearable health devices, healthcare professionals can access real-time patient data, leading to more informed decisions and improved outcomes.

Niramai, an Indian health tech startup, has developed an AI-based breast cancer screening solution that uses thermal imaging and machine learning algorithms. The non-invasive, radiation-free technique detects early-stage breast cancer with high accuracy, aiding early intervention and improving survival rates. This innovative approach has the potential to transform breast cancer screening and diagnosis in India, especially for women in rural areas with limited access to specialized healthcare facilities.

2.10.6.3 Government Initiatives and Support

The Indian government has recognized the transformative potential of digital health and has taken various initiatives to promote its adoption across the healthcare ecosystem. These efforts focus on creating a conducive regulatory environment, promoting innovation, and ensuring data security and privacy.

The National Digital Health Mission (NDHM), launched in 2020, aims to create a comprehensive digital health ecosystem in India. Under this mission, every citizen is provided with a unique health ID, which serves as a single point of access for their health records and enables seamless healthcare service delivery across the country. The NDHM also facilitates interoperability among healthcare providers, ensuring efficient exchange of patient data while maintaining data privacy and security.

Digital health in India has emerged as a powerful force, revolutionizing the country's healthcare landscape. Through improved accessibility, enhanced patient care, and government support, digital health technologies have the potential to transform India's healthcare system for the better. As these initiatives gain momentum and more innovations come to the forefront, India is poised to witness a significant improvement in healthcare outcomes and a more inclusive and efficient healthcare ecosystem for all its citizens.

Institutions are actively utilizing digital health technologies to enhance patient care, improve medical education, and streamline administrative processes. However, it's essential to note that the specific applications and implementations of digital health may have evolved since then.

1. **EHRs:** Both PGI and GMCH have likely implemented EHR systems to digitize and centralize patients' medical records. EHRs enable healthcare providers to access patient information securely and in real time, promoting coordinated and efficient care. EHRs also facilitate data sharing and communication among different departments within the institutions.
2. **Telemedicine and Virtual Consultations:** In response to the COVID-19 pandemic and the need to maintain social distancing, PGI and GMCH have likely integrated telemedicine solutions. Telemedicine platforms allow doctors to provide remote consultations to patients, reducing the need for physical visits and minimizing the risk of infection transmission. Telemedicine has been particularly beneficial in reaching patients in rural and remote areas.
3. **Mobile Health Applications:** Mobile health applications or apps can play a significant role in healthcare delivery. These apps may be used by both institutions to provide health information, appointment booking, medication reminders, and self-management tools to patients. Additionally, they may facilitate communication between patients and healthcare providers, leading to better engagement and adherence to treatment plans.
4. **Medical Education and Training:** PGI and GMCH likely leverage digital technologies for medical education and training purposes. These nstitutions

Revolutionizing Healthcare

might use virtual learning platforms, online courses, and webinars to enhance the knowledge and skills of medical students, residents, and healthcare professionals. Digital tools can also support simulation-based training for medical procedures.

5. **Data Analytics and Research:** Both institutions are likely utilizing data analytics to gain insights from the vast amount of medical data they generate daily. Data-driven approaches can help in improving patient outcomes, identifying trends, and conducting research to address specific healthcare challenges prevalent in India.

6. **NHM Initiatives:** As premier medical institutions, PGI and GMCH are likely actively participating in national health initiatives such as the NDHM and Ayushman Bharat. These initiatives aim to create a more integrated and efficient healthcare ecosystem across the country.

It's important to remember that technology adoption and implementation can vary across different departments and units within these institutions. While they may have integrated digital health solutions in various aspects of their operations, the specific applications and technologies employed may differ based on individual requirements and resources.

2.10.7 Digital Health Initiatives Have Significantly Benefited Rural Areas and Tribal Areas in India

By addressing some of the unique healthcare challenges they face, here are some ways in which digital health has made a positive impact in these underserved regions:

1. **Improved Access to Healthcare:** Rural and tribal areas often lack adequate healthcare infrastructure, with limited or no access to healthcare facilities and specialists. Digital health technologies, such as telemedicine, have brought healthcare services closer to these communities. Patients can now consult with doctors remotely, reducing the need for long and costly journeys to urban centers for medical attention.

2. **Timely Diagnosis and Treatment:** Through digital health tools like mobile health applications and remote diagnostics, rural and tribal residents can access early diagnosis and timely treatment. This helps in managing chronic diseases, identifying health risks, and initiating appropriate interventions, leading to better health outcomes and reduced healthcare costs.

3. **Health Awareness and Education:** Digital health platforms offer valuable health information and education materials in local languages, making it easier for people in rural and tribal areas to understand and adopt healthy practices. These platforms play a crucial role in promoting health literacy and disease prevention in underserved communities.

4. **Maternal and Child Health:** Maternal and child health is a significant concern in rural and tribal areas. Digital health initiatives, including mobile apps for maternal and child care, can provide essential guidance to expectant mothers, new mothers, and caregivers. They can access information

about antenatal care, vaccinations, nutrition, and postnatal care, leading to better health outcomes for mothers and children.

5. **Disease Surveillance and Outbreak Management:** Digital health technologies are instrumental in disease surveillance and early outbreak detection. In remote areas, where access to healthcare reporting may be limited, digital tools enable faster reporting and tracking of disease trends, allowing health authorities to respond promptly and contain potential outbreaks.

6. **Data Collection and Research:** Digital health platforms facilitate the collection of healthcare data from rural and tribal areas. This data can be used for research purposes, helping policymakers and healthcare professionals gain insights into regional health needs, disease prevalence, and the effectiveness of interventions.

7. **Empowerment of Community Health Workers:** Community health workers (CHWs) play a crucial role in delivering healthcare services in rural and tribal areas. Digital health tools equip these CHWs with mobile applications that support remote consultations, record-keeping, and health education, making their work more efficient and impactful.

8. **E-Pharmacy and Supply Chain Management:** Digital health initiatives may include e-pharmacy services that ensure timely delivery of medicines and healthcare products to remote areas. Additionally, digital supply chain management systems help in reducing stockouts and wastage of essential drugs and medical supplies.

Overall, digital health has proven to be a game-changer in reaching underserved populations in rural and tribal areas of India. By overcoming geographical barriers and improving healthcare access, these initiatives contribute to reducing health disparities and enhancing the overall health and well-being of these communities. However, continued efforts are required to ensure that digital health solutions are accessible, affordable, and culturally relevant for the diverse populations in these regions.

Digital health systems are instrumental in supporting medical practitioners in the diagnosis of diseases and the creation of effective treatment plans, and research identifies as follows:

1. **Access to Patient Data:** Digital health systems maintain EHRs, containing a patient's complete medical history, including past illnesses, medications, lab results, and imaging data. This comprehensive information provides doctors with a holistic view of the patient's health, assisting in accurate diagnoses and informed treatment choices.

2. **CDSSs:** These systems include clinical decision support tools offering evidence-based guidelines, best practices, and alerts for potential drug interactions or contraindications. They help practitioners make informed decisions in disease diagnosis and treatment selection.

3. **Data Analytics and AI:** Digital health systems use data analytics and AI to analyze extensive datasets, identifying patterns and trends. Machine learning algorithms can aid in early disease detection, risk assessment, and prognosis prediction, improving diagnostic accuracy.

Revolutionizing Healthcare

4. **Telemedicine and Remote Consultations:** Integrated telemedicine platforms facilitate remote consultations, enabling doctors to assess patients' symptoms and progress. This technology supports timely diagnoses and treatment initiation, even when physical presence is impractical.
5. **Access to Medical Literature and Research:** Digital health systems provide access to vast repositories of medical literature and research papers, keeping healthcare professionals updated on the latest advancements and treatments.
6. **Streamlined Workflow:** These systems streamline administrative tasks, reducing paperwork and allowing clinicians to spend more time with patients and on diagnostic processes.
7. **Interoperability:** Digital health systems are designed for interoperability, ensuring seamless data exchange among healthcare providers and institutions. This facilitates collaborative diagnosis and treatment planning.
8. **Patient Engagement:** Patient portals encourage active patient engagement by providing access to records, progress tracking, and communication with healthcare providers. This engagement can lead to more accurate symptom reporting and faster diagnoses.
9. **Remote Monitoring and Wearables:** Connected devices and wearables transmit real-time patient data to digital health systems, allowing for continuous monitoring and early intervention for chronic conditions.
10. **Data Security:** Robust data encryption and protection measures safeguard patient information, ensuring privacy and compliance with healthcare regulations.

2.11 CONCLUSION

Digital health technologies have indeed revolutionized healthcare, transforming patient care, diagnostics, and treatment. While the benefits are immense, challenges related to data security, regulation, and ethical considerations must be addressed. As we look to the future, personalized medicine and genomics, as well as blockchain technology, hold great promise in shaping a patient-centered and efficient healthcare ecosystem.

The digital health revolution has significantly transformed diagnostics and treatments in healthcare. AI-powered diagnostic tools, genomics, remote monitoring, AI-driven drug discovery, VR/AR in surgical training, and data-driven CDSS have all contributed to improved patient care and outcomes. As the field of digital health continues to advance, the integration of these technologies will revolutionize healthcare further, providing a patient-centered, efficient, and personalized approach to diagnosis and treatment.

REFERENCES

Bashshur, R. L., Shannon, G. W., Bashshur, N., & Yellowlees, P. M. (2016). The Empirical Evidence for Telemedicine Interventions in Mental Disorders. *Telemedicine Journal and e-Health*, 22(2), 87–113.

Collins, F. S., & Varmus, H. (2015). A New Initiative on Precision Medicine. *The New England Journal of Medicine*, 372(9), 793–795.

Rajkomar, A., Dean, J., & Kohane, I. (2019). Machine Learning in Medicine. *The New England Journal of Medicine*, 380(14), 1347–1358.

Rothstein, M. A., Wilbanks, J. T., Brothers, K. B., & Magnus, D. C. (2016). Ethical and Legal Implications of Preemptive Pharmacogenetic Testing. *JAMA*, 316(15), 1543–1544.

Steinhubl, S. R., Muse, E. D., & Topol, E. J. (2015). Can Mobile Health Technologies Transform Health Care? *JAMA*, 314(12), 1235–1236.

Topol, E. J. (2019). High-Performance Medicine: The Convergence of Human and Artificial Intelligence. *Nature Medicine*, 25(1), 44–56.

Wang, T. D., Wongsuphasawat, K., & Plaisant, C. (2018). Visual Exploration of Big Spatio-Temporal Urban Data: A Study of New York City Taxi Trips. *IEEE Transactions on Visualization and Computer Graphics*, 24(12), 3437–3450.

Zhang, P., White, J., Schmidt, D. C., Lenz, G., & Rosenbloom, S. T. (2018). FHIRChain: Applying Blockchain to Securely and Scalably Share Clinical Data. *Computational and Structural Biotechnology Journal*, 16, 267–278.

3 Federated Deep Learning Systems in Healthcare

*Ashraful Reza Tanjil, Fahim Mohammad
Adud Bhuiyan, Mohammad Abu Tareq
Rony, and Kamanashis Biswas*

3.1 INTRODUCTION

When it comes to extracting medical data from Electronic Medical Records (EMRs), discovering new knowledge from medical data, ensuring data privacy and security, managing data heterogeneity, and maintaining scalability and efficiency, federated deep learning (FDL) systems have emerged as a game-changing solution.

To begin with, FDL helps hospitals and clinics gain valuable insights from EMRs without centralizing private patient information. Using a decentralized approach, medical facilities may work together on studies and diagnoses while protecting patients' personal information under laws like Health Insurance Portability and Accountability Act (HIPAA) and General Data Protection Regulation (GDPR).

Further, FDL draws on the expertise of several hospitals to make breakthrough discoveries in the healthcare field. Patterns, connections, and unusual illnesses may be uncovered by algorithms trained on several datasets from different sources. This method of working together hastens medical research and encourages the use of evidence-based practice. FL ensures the security and privacy of sensitive medical data through its local storage and encryption at rest. Instead of disclosing the original data, each organization distributes model updates while retaining its data rights. This measure mitigates the likelihood of theft or unauthorized entry, which is advantageous for all parties concerned. A significant obstacle is the wide variety of EMR formats, imaging modalities, and clinical procedures in healthcare today. FL accounts for this variety by letting models learn from the specific data available at each institution while harmonizing the findings, which improves the models' overall quality and applicability. For deep learning models to be used in extensive healthcare networks, they must be efficient and scalable. FL systems may increase, adding additional users without requiring extensive system modifications. This flexibility means that a wide variety of healthcare professionals may reap the advantages of joint research and diagnostic tools. FDL systems have changed healthcare by making it easier to extract information from EMRs, encouraging discovery, protecting data privacy and security, managing data heterogeneity, and guaranteeing scalability and efficiency. Better patient care, ground-breaking research, and a promising future for the healthcare business may all be attributed to the interoperability made possible by these technologies.

DOI: 10.1201/9781032694870-3

3.2 INFORMATION EXTRACTION AND KNOWLEDGE DISCOVERY WITH FEDERATED DEEP LEARNING

3.2.1 EXTRACTING MEDICAL INFORMATION FROM ELECTRONIC MEDICAL RECORDS

EMRs are a patient's medical history converted into digital format. Particularly in collecting crucial medical information from EMRs, information extraction and knowledge discovery by FDL is a cutting-edge methodology that can transform healthcare. EMRs have become a highly significant repository of patient information since they contain a plethora of data that can be used for clinical research, improving patient care, disease management, and decision-making in healthcare, as well as developing novel medicines. However, the difficulty lies in swiftly and accurately retrieving relevant information from these massive and frequently unstructured records. This presents a significant hurdle. Numerous healthcare institutions, national legislations, and regulatory entities such as the GDPR and the HIPAA have implemented recent regulations aimed at governing the exchange of data in a manner that upholds user security and privacy (Li et al., 2020). Furthermore, managing and regulating medical data storage, transmission, and utilization play a pivotal role in safeguarding patient rights. The requirement for an effective system to retrieve information from healthcare organizations and hospitals while preserving data privacy is prompted by the dispersed and delicate characteristics of EMRs in practical environments. This motivates us to inquire into the significance and potential of FDL within the healthcare industry. FDL is an advanced approach to distributed learning that leverages datasets from multiple institutions, thereby circumventing the need for explicit centralization or data sharing during training (T. Li et al., 2019; Yang et al., 2019; Joshi et al., 2022). The data contained in EMR systems are frequently unstructured, making it challenging to extract them. It is usually delicate. Thus, care must be taken to protect it. The machine learning (ML) method of FDL can securely retrieve sensitive medical data from EMRs without compromising patient confidentiality. By fusing the benefits of deep learning with those of FL, FDL offers a novel approach to overcoming this difficulty. There are many benefits to using FDL to glean medical data from EMRs. First, it can extract information from unstructured data, such as clinical notes. Second, it is possible to train models on big datasets of EMRs, which is challenging to perform using conventional ML methods. Third, it protects users' privacy, which is essential when dealing with sensitive medical information. Due to the rigorous regulations and apprehensions regarding data privacy, this assumes paramount significance within the healthcare industry. Regarding EMRs, keeping patient information private and following data security laws like HIPAA in the USA or GDPR in Europe are very important. This is because patient data can be hacked.

FDL encompasses both centralized and decentralized methodologies. Centralized FL involves data collection by a central server, whereas the decentralized variant maintains data distribution across client devices. Both approaches facilitate collaborative model training while upholding data privacy within specific contexts. Extracting medical information from EMRs through FDL encompasses complex and detailed stages.

3.2.1.1 Data Collection and Preparation

The initial stage involves the acquisition of a diverse dataset of EMRs obtained from various healthcare facilities, such as hospitals or clinics. Before transmission to a central server, the data undergoes encryption. Subsequently, the server does data preprocessing procedures to render the data amenable for training the deep learning model.

3.2.1.2 Model Selection

The model selection process entails carefully considering deep learning models, such as recurrent neural networks (RNNs) or transformer-based models, which may effectively serve as the foundation for extracting information in the given job. The architectural design of this model is specifically tailored to handle the sequential and unstructured characteristics of medical information efficiently.

3.2.1.3 Local Model Training

Each institution conducts individual training in a deep learning model using its respective EMR data. This stage is crucial in enabling the model to acquire knowledge from institution-specific patterns and nuances, leading to a substantial enhancement in the accuracy of information extraction.

3.2.1.4 Model Distribution

Model distribution determines a statistical model's probability distribution. After completing the training, the model is disseminated to the many devices that own the EMR data. The model undergoes local training on individual devices utilizing the EMR data specific to each device.

3.2.1.5 Updates to the Model

At regular intervals, regional models transmit changes to a central server in the form of model weights or gradients while ensuring the privacy of patient data remains undisclosed. This server serves as a platform for consolidating these updates, aiding the enhancement of global models.

3.2.1.6 Global Model Training/Aggregation

The central server aggregates the updates from participating universities to produce a single global model during global training. The aforementioned global model benefits from including many data sources while upholding privacy principles.

3.2.1.7 Evaluation of the Model

The performance of the newly generated global model is tested by assessing it on a dataset that has been held out.

3.2.1.8 Knowledge Extraction

Following training on the global model, it applies to various medical information extraction activities. For instance, the artificial intelligence (AI) system can recognize and classify multiple diseases, extract pertinent prescription information, analyze trends within patient medical records, and potentially forecast disease outcomes.

3.2.1.9 Privacy Preservation

Privacy preservation is a crucial aspect of this process, wherein stringent measures are implemented to safeguard the confidentiality of individual patient data. These measures include using privacy-preserving techniques such as differential privacy or FL with secure aggregation.

3.2.1.10 Iterative Refinement

The iterative refinement method involves periodic updates and retraining of the global model to enhance its accuracy and accommodate evolving healthcare trends.

3.2.1.11 Model Deployment

After a comprehensive evaluation, the model is implemented into a production environment and if the model is deemed satisfactory, it is deployed for production use.

One typical architecture is "centralized FL," in which a central server collects data from various client devices, refines a global model, and then delivers the refined model back to the clients. Google uses this layout in Android keyboards to gather user feedback for future model iterations. A single point of failure could result in a catastrophic collapse even if it functions. The Federated Averaging (FedAvg) method is a well-known case in point. Another architecture, decentralized FL, eliminates the need for a centralized server by enabling direct communication and model updates among client devices. The SimFL system is wholly distributed. The model is refined iteratively by updating, exchanging, and incorporating new local gradients—algorithms like Online Push Sum attempt to mitigate its trust-dependent shortcomings in single-sided trust situations. Hospitals use blockchain and other decentralized healthcare technologies to diagnose cancer.

3.3 FEDERATED LEARNING'S SCALABILITY

Cross-silo refers to the integration and collaboration between different organizational units or departments. In Cross-silo FL, a small number of data centers, such as those in the medical industry, train a global model with a large amount of data and computational resources. Cross-silo FL is a feasible alternative when organizations cannot share information due to privacy and security considerations. The cross-silo setting has a high computing and storage capacity on a very tiny scale, but its stability is comparatively low compared to the cross-device configuration (Joshi et al., 2022). Cross-device refers to the ability of devices to communicate and interact with one another seamlessly. Cross-device FL presents a scenario wherein many clients possess substantial data quantities unlike a cross-silo scenario where only a few are endowed with such data. As a result, models are generated by the cross-device system for vast and dispersed data within a unified application. The clients, often mobile and IoT devices, may be activated or deactivated based on specific needs. The system should possess the computational capabilities to effectively manage a large number of devices and effectively address frequent operational challenges, such as unreliable network connections and power outages (Joshi et al., 2022).

Federated Deep Learning Systems in Healthcare

3.3.1 Federated Learning Aggregation

The server acquires the revised global models from all participating devices and consolidates them through the selected aggregation methodology. This concludes the solitary iteration of the FL procedure.

3.3.1.1 The FedAvg Algorithm

FedAvg is an algorithmic decentralized ML framework wherein many devices or clients engage in collaborative training to develop a shared global model. During each iteration, participants calculate model updates based on their local datasets. These changes are then aggregated to a central server, and the average is computed. The procedure above involves an iterative approach to train a collaborative model while ensuring the confidentiality of the data, which is the most popular FL algorithm.

3.3.1.2 The FedGKT Algorithm

The primary objective of the FedGKT framework is to maintain privacy while addressing the computational limitations inherent in the peripheral nodes within the framework of FL. Convolutional neural networks (CNNs) improve the efficacy of the model. This strategy reduces communication expenses by effectively reducing the burden on peripheral devices. FedGKT asserts that it requires a substantially diminished quantity of computational resources, varying between 9 and 17 times less, compared to FedAvg. Notwithstanding this diminution, FedGKT is purported to attain accuracy levels that are comparable to or marginally superior.

3.3.1.3 The FedMA Algorithm

FedMA refers to an FL methodology well-suited for contemporary neural network structures, such as CNNs and long short-term memory (LSTM) networks. The global model is constructed sequentially, where each layer is built by aligning and averaging hidden components with comparable feature extraction properties. These components include channels for convolution layers, hidden states for LSTM, and neurons for fully connected layers. This approach facilitates collaborative training, leading to improved model performance.

3.3.1.4 Secured Weighted Aggregation

The Secured Weighted Aggregation technique employs homomorphic encryption to calculate client weights confidentially. The system employs a Zero-Knowledge Proof (ZKP) verification methodology to mitigate fraudulent interactions between central servers and clients. The aforementioned innovative aggregation method effectively tackles discrepancies in data and protects misleading communications, guaranteeing the data's confidentiality and accuracy.

3.3.1.5 The FedNAS Algorithm

Federated Neural Architecture Search (FedNAS) is a framework designed to address the challenge posed by identically distributed (Non-IID) and non-independent (Non-IID) data in FL. This technology streamlines the labor-intensive procedure for creating and choosing architectures and hyperparameters. FedNAS improves model accuracy and reduces computing overhead and communication cycles in cases where data is dispersed by allowing distant workers to seek superior model designs collectively.

3.3.1.6 Inprivate Digging

The methods shown in Inprivate Digging may be used for Differential Privacy in Regression and Binary Classification, and the focus is on privacy-protecting tree-based data mining. It presents a safe Gradient Boosting Decision Tree (GBDT) approach, allowing private tree training on local machines for each data owner. Data privacy is maintained while combining these trees into an ensemble.

3.3.1.7 Federated Matrix Factorization

Using homomorphic encryption and distributed ML, the Federated Matrix Factorization (FedMF) architecture is introduced in Secure FedMF. Uploading gradient information rather than raw preferences to the server enables user-level collaborative matrix factorization. Homomorphic encryption is more secure because it prevents data leakage caused by gradients.

3.3.1.8 Federated Forest

Training random forests in a vertical FL setting is made possible by the Federated Forest method. To protect users' anonymity, nodes communicate their split decisions to one another in an encrypted fashion. The methodology is secure, enables classification and regression tasks, and maintains accuracy on par with non-federated approaches.

Herein lie several concrete illustrations of how Federated Learning (FDL) might be employed to extract medical data from EMRs:

The objective is to identify and isolate diagnoses from clinical notes. The utilization of Federated Learning (FDL) has the potential to facilitate the training of a model that can effectively extract diagnoses from clinical notes. These notes typically lack structure and pose challenges in terms of parsing. This data can potentially enhance patient care by facilitating more precise identification of diseases and disorders by medical practitioners.

Federated Learning (FDL) can be employed to train a model capable of extracting drug-related data from EMRs. This includes extracting information such as the medication name, dosage, and frequency of administration. This data can be utilized to enhance patient safety through the identification of potential drug interactions and allergies.

The process information is obtained from EMRs. FDL can be employed to train a computational model to extract pertinent procedure-related information from EMRs. This includes details such as the nature or category of the procedure, the specific day on which the treatment was conducted, and the resulting outcome. Utilizing this data can enhance patient care by helping physicians monitor the efficacy of various therapies and detect any potential problems.

The objective is to ascertain the individuals who are susceptible to being readmitted. Federated Learning (FDL) can be employed to train a predictive model that can effectively discern patients susceptible to readmission. This information can be utilized for early intervention to mitigate readmission, resulting in cost savings and enhanced patient outcomes.

Federated Deep Learning Systems in Healthcare 37

The objective is to forecast the potential results for patients. Federated learning (FDL) can be utilized for training a predictive model that may estimate patient outcomes, including survival rates or the likelihood of experiencing specific complications. This data can enhance the customization of patient care and facilitate more informed treatment decisions.

By applying FDL to the evaluation of medical data extracted from EMRs, researchers and healthcare providers can maximize the value of this invaluable resource while maintaining patient confidentiality and compliance with data protection regulations. This methodology enhances the precision of clinical decision-making and expedites the exploration of novel medical knowledge and perspectives that can ultimately result in improved patient care and outcomes.

The FL system collects the models sent by all participating clients, modifies the global model, and then transmits it back to everyone. Nonetheless, this raises some severe difficulties. Integrating blockchain into FL frameworks could improve the robustness, scalability, and efficiency of the underlying FL model. In its most basic form, blockchain is a distributed public ledger or database that facilitates collaborative learning among devices without requiring a trusted third party to act as an intermediary or aggregator (Bao et al., 2019).The FL and blockchain approaches are decentralized.

Intelligent devices comprise the Internet of Medical Things (IoMT), a revolutionary technology in the healthcare and medical industries .. The rapid expansion of these technologies has led to the generation of substantial volumes of data daily by integrated devices. By using FL methodologies in a decentralized manner, data scientists can evaluate the produced data on edge devices at a local level, eliminating the necessity of uploading and storing the unprocessed data on a central server. This approach guarantees the privacy of the data from IoT devices. Retaining personal data, particularly within the healthcare industry, offers significant security and privacy advantages. This section emphasizes a fundamental differentiation between the FL approaches and conventional centralized ML methodologies. FL can be an enabling tool for Mobile Edge Computing (MEC) system-wide collaborative model training. Since edge computing is not meant to involve transferring data between edge devices and a centralized cloud, it is best suited for usage in edge computing applications. This enables FL to leverage the computational capacity of the edge server and the data collected by dispersed edge devices with relative ease. This article focuses on the practical applications of FL in the medical area. Hakak et al. (2020) describe a custom-tailored FL framework with edge support to allow healthcare analytics utilizing user-generated data. The authors delineate a methodology that leverages pre-trained models to extract user-specific insights for assessing ailments via monitoring mobility levels and behaviors with data gathered from wearable devices—all while safeguarding privacy and cloud resources. As was previously said, the integrity and security of the dispersed IoT devices may be maintained and improved by combining the edge computing setup with other new technologies. One example of an in-depth discussion on the challenges of integrating FL and blockchain in edge computing is in Nguyen et al. (2021). These challenges encompass communication costs, resource allocation, incentive mechanisms, security, and privacy protection.

3.4 DISCOVERING NEW KNOWLEDGE FROM MEDICAL DATA

The "Information extraction and knowledge discovery with FDL" methodology is considered at the forefront of data analysis and medical research. It provides a robust method for discovering new insights and essential information from large and varied collections of medical data. To acquire an explicit knowledge of the significance of this technique, it is necessary to analyze the intricacies of each component properly. Federated Learning (FDL) is particularly advantageous within the medical field, as patient data is frequently susceptible, and preserving privacy is paramount. "Information extraction" refers to recognizing and extracting pertinent data or insights from sources that lack a defined framework or have only a partial structure. Within the realm of medical data, the scope of this concept extends to various sources such as EMRs, medical imaging, clinical notes, and even health-related data supplied by patients through wearable devices. The task involves the intricate process of interpreting and systematically arranging this abundant pool of information, converting it into a well-organized framework that can be subjected to efficient analysis. One of the primary benefits of Federated Learning (FDL) lies in its capacity to facilitate the training of models using extensive and heterogeneous datasets that would otherwise provide challenges or be unfeasible to consolidate in a centralized manner. For instance, Federated Learning (FDL) can be employed to train a predictive model that assesses the likelihood of having a specific ailment by utilizing data sourced from numerous hospitals across the globe. By adopting a decentralized strategy, the model would be able to acquire knowledge from a more extensive array of patients and data categories compared to what might be achieved using a centralized approach. One additional benefit of FDL is its enhanced privacy preservation compared to conventional centralized ML methods. The non-disclosure of individual datasets effectively mitigates the potential for patient data breaches. The significance of this matter is particularly pronounced in the context of medical data, as it often encompasses confidential information such as genetic data, medical history, and treatment strategies. The "knowledge discovery" process involves utilizing sophisticated computer methods to uncover concealed patterns, correlations, and trends within the retrieved data. The process might be likened to discovering hidden treasures within an expansive mine, wherein these treasures symbolize significant knowledge or insights previously buried from view. Within medicine, these insights may encompass novel diagnostic indicators, treatment methods, or even previously unidentified disease risk factors. The medical area encompasses several applications of FDL, primarily focused on pursuing novel insights and knowledge. It may be employed in a multitude of manners, as mentioned below.

3.4.1 IDENTIFY NOVEL ILLNESS BIOMARKERS

Presently, novel biomarkers associated with conditions including cancer, Alzheimer's disease, and Parkinson's disease are being identified using FDL. By analyzing extensive and varied datasets, FDL can discern patterns that would be challenging to find utilizing conventional methodologies.

Federated Deep Learning Systems in Healthcare

3.4.2 Create More Precise Risk Prediction Models

FDL is currently being used to enhance the precision of risk prediction models for many diseases, including heart disease, stroke, and diabetes. By integrating data derived from several sources, FDL can encompass a broader spectrum of influential aspects of risk, including genetics, lifestyle choices, and medical background.

3.4.3 Discover Novel Drug Targets

FDL is now employed in exploring novel therapeutic targets for cancer and HIV/ AIDS. By examining extensive datasets comprising genomic and clinical information, FDL can discern the specific genes and proteins that play a role in advancing diseases. Subsequently, this data can be utilized to develop novel pharmaceuticals that specifically interact with the genes above and proteins.

3.4.4 Improve the Personalization of Treatment Regimens

The enhancement of treatment plan personalization is currently being pursued through the utilization of FDL, which aims to create tailored treatment plans for individuals diagnosed with cancer and several other medical conditions. By examining and evaluating the unique data about each patient, FDL can discern the treatments that yield the highest efficacy for the individual in question. This phenomenon has the potential to result in improved results and a reduction in adverse effects.

FL has been employed in the development of diverse illness-detection models. These are the outcomes of new knowledge from medical data using FL. During severe pandemic, significant progress has been made in addressing the challenges related to COVID-19 detection, DNA sequencing, and other pertinent issues. These advancements have demonstrated commendable efficacy in detecting capabilities. Ouyang et al. presented a collaborative early warning framework for COVID-19 that employed intelligent contracts and blockchain technology. The system aims to anticipate the outcomes of new case detections. Establishing a framework enabled the assignment of responsibilities to medical institutions, social institutions, and individuals to promote early warning collaboration. Dayan et al. [2] presented an FL model to predict the impending oxygen requirement of patients who manifest symptoms of COVID-19. By incorporating vital signs, laboratory data, and chest X-rays as input variables, this model demonstrates enhanced precision in forecasting the clinical outcome of individuals afflicted with COVID-19. This research thus establishes a foundational framework for implementing FL in the healthcare sector. Ma et al. (2022) have additionally proposed an FL-based auxiliary diagnosis model for cancer patients (Wen et al., 2023).

Large datasets from multiple centers and countries are being employed to train deep learning (DL) models in medical image analysis via FL (Roth et al., 2020; Sheller et al., 2020; Remedios et al., 2020). This technology facilitates the collaborative training of a global model by individual medical centers within an FL framework. There are several benefits associated with cross-domain collaborative and decentralized learning. Data annotation is a vital and arduous undertaking within medical imaging. Through the utilization of FL, diverse institutions have the potential to get advantages from one another's annotations without the need for direct exchange of these annotations. Training deep learning algorithms necessitates significant CPU resources and memory capacity. The use of FL can enhance the efficacy of training and reduce memory usage in algorithms designed for AI-assisted medical image analysis (Rauniyar et al., 2022). Among all cancers, breast cancer has the highest fatality rate and is the third leading cause of death overall. It accounts for 6.9% of deaths and 11.7% of new cases, per data from the Global Cancer Observatory (GLOBOCAN). According to research findings from (Sung et al., 2021). Breast density was categorized using a DL model trained with the help of transfer learning (FL) in the work by Roth et al. [16]. To refine the performance of pre-trained deep learning models, we modified the uppermost layers to aid in the classification operation while leaving the initial layers in a fixed state (Ahsan et al., 2023). Seven clinical institutions from around the world worked together to come up with this classification. Compared to a model trained outside of an FL framework, which requires data sharing and violates privacy standards, the experimental results showed that the trained model performed better. Prostate cancer is the second leading cause of cancer death in American men [20], behind only lung cancer (Aldoj et al., 2020). Early cancer identification, patient monitoring, treatment planning, and surgery planning are only some diagnostic and therapeutic applications that can benefit significantly from precise and automated prostate segmentation (Wang et al., 2016). Segmenting the prostate and prostatic regions manually is a common practice despite being a laborious and sometimes inaccurate process. In this context, a multicenter investigation was conducted by Sarma et al. (2021) to examine entire prostate segmentation on axial T2-weighted MRI (magnetic resonance imaging) images. Each institution's data was utilized to train a 3D Hybrid Anisotropic Hybrid Network (Liu et al., 2017) model. In addition, all three organizations used FL to train a unified model with 15 nodes. The FL-based model performed better and was more generalizable than a model trained on data from a single institution. The federated domain generalization issue was offered as a solution by Xia et al. (2021). The authors proposed a generalizable framework known as federated domain generalization (FedG) to construct a federated model from a collection of distant source generalizations whose performance deteriorated when applied to unknown data outside the federation. FrequentG was trained with information from six prostates. The experimental results demonstrate that FedG is more effective than the current gold standard methods (Rauniyar et al., 2022).

The implementation of an automated segmentation method for brain tumors possesses the capacity to impact the procedures of brain tumor diagnosis and treatment substantially. In their study, W. Li et al. (2019) investigated the feasibility of implementing differential privacy to protect patient data within the FL framework. The researchers employed the BraTS 2018 dataset (Bakas et al., 2017; Menze et al., 2015) as a case study to analyze the practical learning systems' segmentation capabilities for brain tumors. In the evaluation, a comparison was made between federated and centralized data training methods. The decentralized model reached convergence after 300 training epochs, whereas the FL approach achieved convergence after around 600. The training process focused on data centralization required an average of 205.70 seconds for each epoch, while an additional 65.45 seconds were needed for modest overhead tasks.

The most widely used method of diagnosis and subsequent therapy is liver segmentation. Recent interest in FL-based solutions can be attributed to the fact that remote

Federated Deep Learning Systems in Healthcare 41

users can train a centralized collection of models using a wide variety of image datasets. In their paper, Bernecker et al. (2022) presented two FL algorithms: FedNorm and FedNorm+, both of which used modality-based normalization strategies. They used data from several sources to verify their approach (6 medical facilities, 428 patients). Dice coefficients of up to 0.9610 were achieved, and overall performance was superior to locally trained models developed at each location. Additionally, federated models have sometimes outperformed their centralized counterparts. These examples demonstrate the utilization of Federated Learning (FDL) to extract novel insights from medical data while ensuring privacy preservation. By integrating data from many sources, FDL can potentially advance novel and enhanced methodologies for diagnosing, treating, and preventing illnesses.

In summary, combining information extraction and knowledge discovery using FDL in medicine has significant promise for advancing healthcare research and application. Utilizing medical data enables stakeholders to effectively leverage its complete capabilities, leading to the exploration of novel insights and eventually improving the standard of healthcare and the overall welfare of patients. This is achieved while simultaneously safeguarding data privacy and adhering to regulatory requirements.

3.5 CHALLENGES AND OPPORTUNITIES OF FEDERATED DEEP LEARNING SYSTEMS IN HEALTHCARE

The effectiveness of FDL systems in healthcare scenarios involving remote datasets and hesitant data proprietors to share their raw data is demonstrated through their implementation. Medical data is more sensitive and patients do not share their data. The traditional deep learning algorithms are hungry for data trained on the centralized publicly accessible data repository that may have data leakage, which could not provide data security to the user. The FDL approach can overcome these problems and be built to ensure the privacy of users' data. FDL is a collaborative and decentralized learning system that, without sharing the user's raw data, trains their model in the local system such as mobile phones, tablets, smartwatches, cameras, vehicles, thermostats, telescopes, and so on, and then aggregates model parameters for sending gradient updates to the server and retaining private user information on a device. The use of FDL comes with many privacy and security challenges and opportunities.

3.6 DATA PRIVACY

FDL in healthcare has provided opportunities for its low cost, data robustness, strict data privacy and security, etc. Several fundamental challenges are inherently linked to the field of FDL. Although it has strict privacy and security, ensuring a full guarantee of patient data is more challenging. This chapter will describe the challenges and opportunities of data privacy and security, heterogeneity of data, and scalability of data approaches in healthcare, which is striving to allow more deep learning models. Privacy is the most important factor nowadays. People are very concerned about their data privacy. They do not want to share their data with open-source or centralized systems, but traditional ML approaches only focus on user data analysis. They are unconcerned with privacy and security (Hassan et al., 2023; Yasmin et al., 2023).

The FDL approach ensures the privacy of its user's data. The central concept of FDL builds on its privacy. The privacy of FDL is keeping the secure user's raw data in the system. Although local device data are not sure with the global model, there are possibilities that data can be leaked during the training process. Under privacy, we will discuss data privacy in FDL systems in healthcare. The FDL structure can be divided into three categories: privacy on the local system side, server side, and FDL side.

3.6.1 PRIVACY ON THE LOCAL SYSTEM SIDE

In the FDL system, the local system needs to upload its parameters and weights to the global system, but it cannot wholly rely on the server because it might not trust the server because a shady server could look at the information sent and figure out private information from it. Some privacy on the local system is discussed below.

3.6.1.1 Differential Privacy (DP)

DP is the most used privacy method on the local network. This privacy technique is mainly used in industry and education domains. The main idea behind DP is to protect privacy by adding noise to sensitive information. The utilization of DP offers a structured approach for the creation of intelligent algorithms that possess the capability to assess the privacy implications associated with data analysis while simultaneously ensuring a level of accuracy that is deemed acceptable. It injects a slight statical noise with the gradient update to reduce the attack risk. However, it has another problem: the injected noise can contaminate the learning model. The DPFedAvgGAN framework employs DP techniques to hinder the effectiveness of Generative Adversarial Network (GAN)-based attacks on FL settings that infer training data from other users.

3.6.1.2 VerifyNet

It provides privacy by a double masking technique, making it challenging for attackers to deduce training data, and it can handle multiple dropouts. It offers clients a method to verify the findings obtained from the central server, which ensures the primary server's reliability.

3.6.2 PRIVACY ON THE SERVER SIDE

Privacy on the server side controls access to unauthorized local systems. Once the server has gathered the modified parameters from clients, it will calculate a weighted average of these values, considering the data size. It reduces the probability of attack on and synchronous gradient aggregation to the local system. This privacy in FDL is the following.

3.6.2.1 Aggregation

The server can restrict the local system using aggregation. It can control the global model's accumulation of local system training parameters. As the server cannot validate local system data, the FDL policy aggregation can select the trustable model for receiving the model parameters.

3.6.2.2 Secure Multi-Party Computation

The Secure Multi-Party Computation (SMC) is well known for its robust security protocol in FDL. It ensures its protocol by using the encryption methodology.

Federated Deep Learning Systems in Healthcare

The fundamental methodology utilized in this research entailed the integration of DP and homomorphic encryption. Within the FL framework, SMC has been utilized to ensure the security of client updates. Compared to the conventional iteration of SMC, FL demonstrates a substantial improvement in computational efficiency through the encryption of parameters only, as opposed to the substantial quantity of data inputs. SMC is a four-round interactive mechanism that may be optionally employed within the context of the reporting process during the contact round. During each protocol iteration, the server gathers messages from all devices. Then, it employs the collected user messages to evaluate an individual response sent to each respective device. In the third round, participants engage in a commit round when devices upload encrypted data-masked model modifications to the server. In the final round, the local system discloses the encrypting secret to the server. Due to its encrypting technique, the final model's accuracy decreased.

3.6.3 PRIVACY ON THE FL FRAMEWORK SIDE

This section is most important for FDL to ensure the security of the entire system participating in the training and learning process. Most of the time, attackers steal the information from the finalized version. They try to guess the security and individual information of a particular participant. The following privacy can be employed in this section.

3.6.3.1 Homomorphic Encryption (HE)

HE is commonly utilized for securing clients' data during the communication of model updates among clients and the server. Before being uploaded, the parameters undergo encryption, and it is often necessary to transmit public-private decoding keys. Consequently, the server can compute encrypted model changes without having first to decode them. HE is widely recognized for its significant computational overhead, requiring extensive computer resources to perform computations on encrypted data. For performing this encrypting technology, performers must consider the computational requirement for FDL. Along with this, we have to consider homomorphic algorithms so that they can optimize the computational requirement to perform the FDL.

3.7 DATA AND SECURITY

Included in FDL, data privacy and security are solvable primary challenges in healthcare that will be discussed in this chapter. Data sharing is challenging and, if possible, constrained by ethical and legal considerations since medical data is more sensitive and private than others. Security and privacy in the healthcare sector, particularly in FDL systems, are of the utmost importance due to the sensitive characteristics of medical information. The task of balancing data privacy and promoting collaborative model training is a multifaceted undertaking. Ensuring the security of healthcare data is challenging due to the necessity of sharing model parameters, weights, or gradients. Due to these factors, specific security concerns emerge. Part of this chapter will discuss security challenges and opportunities. The security in FDL can be summarized as follows.

44 Federated Deep Learning for Healthcare

3.7.1 POISONING ATTACKS

A poisoning attack is one of the most common ways to inject malicious data into the global model. The main idea of poisoning attacks differs in many ways, but the fundamental idea remains. The attacker transmits the manipulated data to influence the global model. The occurrence of poisoning is possible during the training phase, which might impact either the training dataset or the local model. Consequently, this can indirectly compromise the integrity of the global model. In this chapter, two primary poisoning attacks are described.

3.7.1.1 Data Poisoning

As discussed in this chapter, it is a decentralized training system with participants from different places that only shares its parameters with the global system. There is some risk of data poisoning as there is no authority to validate the parameters before the international system is received. Data poisoning in FDL in healthcare is one kind of attack. It would happen in two ways. The first one is labeling flipping; label flipping does not necessitate the adversary to know the global distribution. The second is an attack by adversaries during local system training and parameter transfer to the global model at this time. Attackers may also introduce malicious data into the global model, causing it to become biassed and erroneous in terms of classification, accuracy, recall, precision, and generating inaccurate health condition predictions for the patient.

3.7.1.2 Model Poisoning

This is one kind of attacking technique in FDL where an adversary deliberately introduces malicious data into the training process to impair the performance of the global model. In this type of poisoning, malicious data is applied more directly, manipulating the model updates. Typically, these types of assaults endeavor to get further information through various means.

3.7.1.2.1 Model Inversion

In FDL, it is another type of security threat where the attackers analyze the training output of the globally trained model, such as mathematical analysis (gradient), and they find out the user information from it.

3.7.1.2.2 Membership Inference

By examining model outputs, adversaries can ascertain whether a specific data point was utilized in the training process. This kind of attack can be divided into active inference and passive inference. In passive inference attacks, the user can only observe the model output. In active inference attacks, the adversary actively participates within the global model by the shadow and local training models, crafting the input and observing the model output.

3.7.1.3 System Vulnerabilities

The processes of FDL encompass multiple local devices that possess diverse adversarial capabilities. A vulnerability refers to a specific flaw an attacker may exploit to breach privilege boundaries (Aldoj et al., 2020). In the FDL in healthcare, millions of local devices can participate in training multiple rounds or phases. It is impossible to

Federated Deep Learning Systems in Healthcare **45**

confirm that all devices are secure without their parameters, so that the global model can know nothing about the details of local devices. To build an FL-based healthcare system that protects the data's security and safety, it is necessary to look for all possible points of weakness and tighten security. Managing and defending against potential threats are easier when we know where a system or framework is weak. The following are the most common system vulnerabilities in FDL.

3.7.1.3.1 Communication

The FDL method incorporates exchanges of information among the decentralized devices after many repeats of communication rounds. As there can be millions of local machines in the training process, insecure devices are considered a significant vulnerability. When many local devices join during the training process, the Byzantine nodes will likely send models to the general mode, which is nothing but data poisoning. Eavesdropping in communication channels creates interruption, injects malicious data between participating devices and the global model, and steals information from them.

3.7.1.3.2 Gradient Leakage

Although data is not shared during training, it could be leaked by gradient update. The attacker can reconstruct the raw data. It could discover the sensitive data from the gradient updates. In Aldoj et al. (2020), they categorized gradient updates by type-0, type-1, and type-2. The term "type-0" pertains to executing gradient leaking attacks on the server, wherein per-client shared gradient updates are intercepted. Type-1 pertains to gradient leakage attacks conducted by a client on its gradient updates, which occur after the conclusion of local training. The third category of gradient leaking attacks refers to type-2 leakage, which involves executing such attacks on individual training instances during the local training process at a client.

3.7.1.3.3 Compromised Clients and Server

In the traditional deep learning system, clients do not play any roles without sharing their training data. However, in FDL, clients (local devices) play a crucial role in the developing process. They can observe intermediate global model states and provide updates as part of the decentralized training procedure. This makes the system insecure and opens the door for malicious attacks. A server can be centralized or decentralized. In centralized FDL, the primary responsibilities reside with the server. The duties above encompass the dissemination of preliminary model parameters, the consolidation of model updates, and the correspondence of the global model to the selected clientele. When considering decentralized server compromise, the compromised server can manipulate the aggregation procedure and examine all gradient updates transmitted throughout the training iterations.

3.7.2 GENERATIVE ADVERSARIAL NETWORK-BASED ATTACKS

They can execute poisoning and inference attacks. Based on the experiments of this kind of attack, it may be active or passive. When user inputs are analyzed at the server level, it is referred to as a passive attack; and when global updates are sent to the targeted isolated model, that is referred to as the active GAN attack.

3.7.3 Free-Riding Attack

This particular form of assault does not actively engage in the training process but receives updates made to the global model. The responsibility of providing gradient updates or parameters for contributing to the global model lies with the client. However, the client will get the updated final global model. In this form of assault, clients can introduce spurious data; nevertheless, the likelihood of such an attack is relatively low, and the resulting impact is considered moderate severity.

3.7.4 Backdoor Attacks

This enhanced version of the poisoning attack is similar to the data poisoning attacks. In this attacking way, attackers inject malicious data within the existing FDL. The attacker's main target is to reduce the task performance. The data poisoning attacks would be classified by image backdoor image classification and backdoor word prediction. The backdoor image classification model exhibits misclassification behavior when pictures possessing specific attributes are erroneously classified into an attacker's chosen class. The backdoor word-prediction model predicts the words from the mode the attacker chooses.

3.7.5 Man-in-the-Middle (MITM) Attacks

This attack intercepts when transmitting the gradient update between the local devices and the global server. MITM can launch attacks by getting involved in assuming the role of a legitimate participant or eavesdropping. MVD proposed a new attacking technique that can lead to model misclassification against the black-box classifier Rauniyar, A., et al. (2022) [3].

3.7.6 Adversarial Attacks

In this attack, old data is used for updating global model parameters. After completing the updates, it gathers information from the other participants, and so this kind of act is called an adversarial attack. The study by Bernecker et al. (2022) proposed two attacking models: PoisonGAN and DataGen. They can reconstruct the client's sample from the global parameters.

3.8 HETEROGENEITY OF DATA

Healthcare data exhibits significant heterogeneity, encompassing format, organization, and content variations. This heterogeneity of data exists because FDL models are trained in different data types in different locations. Healthcare data can be obtained from diverse sources, including medical equipment, EMRs, and patient surveys. Each of the sources above may employ distinct methodologies for data gathering, leading to the acquisition of data that exhibits varying formats and structures. The data that is transferred between nodes is almost always non-IID. In addition, the quantity of data stored on each node is rarely evenly distributed. This chapter will focus on the following type of heterogeneity of data.

3.9 NON-INDEPENDENT AND IDENTICALLY DISTRIBUTED DATA

The existence of non-IID data across nodes tends to result in a biased global model in the FDL systems. Models trained on non-IID data may exhibit inferior performance compared to models trained on IID data. This limitation arises because of the models' potential inability to exhibit generalization capabilities when confronted with novel input that deviates from the training data. Training models using non-IID data may require longer than training on IID data. This is due to the potential requirement of additional training iterations for the models to achieve convergence. FDL provides the capability to collect data from numerous participants, enabling the training of models on more extensive and diversified datasets compared to what can be achieved by conventional ML methods. This phenomenon can result in models that exhibit higher accuracy and generalizability, even in cases where the data is non-IID.

3.10 SCALABILITY AND EFFICIENCY

The scalability issue holds significant importance within FL, given that these systems can involve many participants on massive bank customer data. The intrinsic challenges associated with these systems and concerns over data heterogeneity and privacy make solving FL exceedingly complex. Scalability pertains to the capacity of a system to effectively manage a substantial volume of participants and data. Scalability is a crucial requirement for FDL as it enables training models on extensive and heterogeneous datasets, a critical aspect of healthcare applications. In the FDL system, the global model would be trained using billions of data where the participants attend training sessions from different locations and data are heterogeneous. The scalability of FDL provided is high and effective. For this scalability, some security issues are described in this chapter. Some challenges are considerable in reducing the scalability of FDL, such as data heterogeneity and communication overhead.

Efficiency refers to the capacity of a system to expediently and resource-efficiently train models. It is an essential prerequisite for the effective deployment of FDL systems in healthcare applications, considering the critical nature of timely and accurate results in this field. FDL lacks security in healthcare data and can still not prove data security with a guarantee, which made this technique unreliable to the users.

3.11 CONCLUSION

The FDL system in healthcare is a relatively new field; not much work has been done yet. The study found that FLD can work well on medical EMRs data stored in different places. It can ensure that the patient's data is confidential, which obeys the European GDPR and American HIPAA. FDL in healthcare could provide data privacy and security to ensure medical data safety. FDL can provide the security protocol so that users can share model parameters or weights with the global model discussed in this chapter. Along with security, it also can take the step for central privacy before data leakage.

REFERENCES

Ahsan, M. M., Ali, M. S., Hassan, M. M., Abdullah, T. A., Gupta, K. D., Bagci, U., Kaushal, C., & Soliman, N. F. (2023). Monkeypox diagnosis with interpretable deep learning. *IEEE Access, 11*, 81965–81980. https://doi.org/10.1109/ACCESS.2023.3300793

Aldoj, N., Lukas, S., Dewey, M., & Penzkofer, T. (2020). Semi-automatic classification of prostate cancer on multi-parametric MR imaging using a multi-channel 3D convolutional neural network. *European Radiology, 30*(2), 1243–1253. https://doi.org/10.1007/s00330-019-06417-z

Bakas, S., Akbari, H., Sotiras, A., Bilello, M., Rozycki, M., Kirby, J. S., Freymann, J. B., Farahani, K., & Davatzikos, C. (2017). Advancing the cancer genome atlas glioma MRI collections with expert segmentation labels and radiomic features. *Scientific Data, 4*. https://doi.org/10.1038/sdata.2017.117

Bao, X., Su, C., Xiong, Y., Huang, W., & Hu, Y. (2019). FLChain: A blockchain for auditable federated learning with trust and incentive. *Proceedings -5th International Conference on Big Data Computing and Communications, BIGCOM 2019*, 151–159. https://doi.org/10.1109/BIGCOM.2019.00030

Bernecker, T., Peters, A., Schlett, C. L., Bamberg, F., Theis, F., Rueckert, D., Weiß, J., & Albarqouni, S. (2022). *FedNorm: Modality-Based Normalization in Federated Learning for Multi-Modal Liver Segmentation*. https://arxiv.org/abs/2205.11096

Hakak, S., Ray, S., Zada Khan, W., & Scheme, E. (2020). *A Framework for Edge-Assisted Healthcare Data Analytics Using Federated Learning*. https://www.ieee.org/publications

Hassan, M. M., Hassan, M. M., Yasmin, F., Khan, M. A. R., Zaman, S., Galibuzzaman, Islam, K. K., & Bairagi, A. K. (2023). A comparative assessment of machine learning algorithms with the Least Absolute Shrinkage and Selection Operator for breast cancer detection and prediction. *Decision Analytics Journal, 7*. https://doi.org/10.1016/j.dajour.2023.100245

Joshi, M., Pal, A., & Sankarasubbu, M. (2022). Federated learning for healthcare domain - pipeline, applications and challenges. *ACM Transactions on Computing for Healthcare, 3*(4). https://doi.org/10.1145/3533708

Li, T., Sahu, A. K., Talwalkar, A., & Smith, V. (2019). *Federated Learning: Challenges, Methods, and Future Directions*. https://doi.org/10.1109/MSP.2020.2975749

Li, W., Milletarì, F., Xu, D., Rieke, N., Hancox, J., Zhu, W., Baust, M., Cheng, Y., Ourselin, S., Cardoso, M. J., & Feng, A. (2019). *Privacy-Preserving Federated Brain Tumour Segmentation*. https://arxiv.org/abs/1910.00962

Li, X., Gu, Y., Dvornek, N., Staib, L., Ventola, P., & Duncan, J. S. (2020). *Multi-Site fMRI Analysis Using Privacy-Preserving Federated Learning and Domain Adaptation: ABIDE Results*. https://arxiv.org/abs/2001.05647

Liu, S., Xu, D., Zhou, S. K., Mertelmeier, T., Wicklein, J., Jerebko, A., Grbic, S., Pauly, O., Cai, W., & Comaniciu, D. (2017). *3D Anisotropic Hybrid Network: Transferring Convolutional Features from 2D Images to 3D Anisotropic Volumes*. https://arxiv.org/abs/1711.08580

Ma, Z., Zhang, M., Liu, J., Yang, A., Li, H., Wang, J., Hua, D., & Li, M. (2022). An assisted diagnosis model for cancer patients based on federated learning. *Frontiers in Oncology, 12*. https://doi.org/10.3389/fonc.2022.860532

Menze, B. H., Jakab, A., Bauer, S., Kalpathy-Cramer, J., Farahani, K., Kirby, J., Burren, Y., Porz, N., Slotboom, J., Wiest, R., Lanczi, L., Gerstner, E., Weber, M. A., Arbel, T., Avants, B. B., Ayache, N., Buendia, P., Collins, D. L., Cordier, N., ... Van Leemput, K. (2015). The multimodal brain tumor image segmentation benchmark (BRATS). *IEEE Transactions on Medical Imaging, 34*(10), 1993–2024. https://doi.org/10.1109/TMI.2014.2377694

Nguyen, D. C., Ding, M., Pham, Q.-V., Pathirana, P. N., Le, L. B., Seneviratne, A., Li, J., Niyato, D., & Poor, H. V. (2021). *Federated Learning Meets Blockchain in Edge Computing: Opportunities and Challenges.* https://arxiv.org/abs/2104.01776

Yang, S., Ren, B., Zhou, X., & Liu, L. (2019). Parallel Distributed Logistic Regression for Vertical Federated Learning without Third-Party Coordinator. CoRR. https://dblp.uni-trier.de/db/journals/corr/corr1911.html#abs-1911-09824

Rauniyar, A., Hagos, D. H., Jha, D., Håkegård, J. E., Bagci, U., Rawat, D. B., & Vlassov, V. (2022). *Federated Learning for Medical Applications: A Taxonomy, Current Trends, Challenges, and Future Research Directions.* https://arxiv.org/abs/2208.03392

Remedios, S. W., Butman, J. A., Landman, B. A., & Pham, D. L. (2020). Federated gradient averaging for multi-site training with momentum-based optimizers. *Lecture Notes in Computer Science (Including Subseries Lecture Notes in Artificial Intelligence and Lecture Notes in Bioinformatics), 12444 LNCS,* 170–180. https://doi.org/10.1007/978-3-030-60548-3_17

Roth, H. R., Chang, K., Singh, P., Neumark, N., Li, W., Gupta, V., Gupta, S., Qu, L., Ihsani, A., Bizzo, B. C., Wen, Y., Buch, V., Shah, M., Kitamura, F., Mendonça, M., Lavor, V., Harouni, A., Compas, C., Tetreault, J., ... Kalpathy-Cramer, J. (2020). *Federated Learning for Breast Density Classification: A Real-World Implementation.* https://doi.org/10.1007/978-3-030-60548-3_18

Sarma, K. V., Harmon, S., Sanford, T., Roth, H. R., Xu, Z., Tetreault, J., Xu, D., Flores, M. G., Raman, A. G., Kulkarni, R., Wood, B. J., Choyke, P. L., Priester, A. M., Marks, L. S., Raman, S. S., Enzmann, D., Turkbey, B., Speier, W., & Arnold, C. W. (2021). Federated learning improves site performance in multicenter deep learning without data sharing. *Journal of the American Medical Informatics Association, 28*(6), 1259–1264. https://doi.org/10.1093/jamia/ocaa341

Sheller, M. J., Edwards, B., Reina, G. A., Martin, J., Pati, S., Kotrotsou, A., Milchenko, M., Xu, W., Marcus, D., Colen, R. R., & Bakas, S. (2020). Federated learning in medicine: facilitating multi-institutional collaborations without sharing patient data. *Scientific Reports, 10*(1). https://doi.org/10.1038/s41598-020-69250-1

Sung, H., Ferlay, J., Siegel, R. L., Laversanne, M., Soerjomataram, I., Jemal, A., & Bray, F. (2021). Global cancer statistics 2020: GLOBOCAN estimates of incidence and mortality worldwide for 36 cancers in 185 countries. *CA: A Cancer Journal for Clinicians, 71*(3), 209–249. https://doi.org/10.3322/caac.21660

Wang, Y., Cheng, J. Z., Ni, D., Lin, M., Qin, J., Luo, X., Xu, M., Xie, X., & Heng, P. A. (2016). Towards personalized statistical deformable model and hybrid point matching for robust MR-TRUS registration. *IEEE Transactions on Medical Imaging, 35*(2), 589–604. https://doi.org/10.1109/TMI.2015.2485299

Wen, J., Zhang, Z., Lan, Y., Cui, Z., Cai, J., & Zhang, W. (2023). A survey on federated learning: challenges and applications. *International Journal of Machine Learning and Cybernetics, 14*(2), 513–535. https://doi.org/10.1007/s13042-022-01647-y

Xia, Y., Yang, D., Li, W., Myronenko, A., Xu, D., Obinata, H., Mori, H., An, P., Harmon, S., Turkbey, E., Turkbey, B., Wood, B., Patella, F., Stellato, E., Carrafiello, G., Ierardi, A., Yuille, A., & Roth, H. (2021). *Auto-FedAvg: Learnable Federated Averaging for Multi-Institutional Medical Image Segmentation.* https://arxiv.org/abs/2104.10195

Yang, Q., Liu, Y., Chen, T., & Tong, Y. (2019). *Federated Machine Learning: Concept and Applications.* https://arxiv.org/abs/1902.04885

Yasmin, F., Hassan, M. M., Hasan, M., Zaman, S., Kaushal, C., El-Shafai, W., & Soliman, N. F. (2023). PoxNet22: A fine-tuned model for the classification of monkeypox disease using transfer learning. *IEEE Access, 11,* 24053–24076. https://doi.org/10.1109/ACCESS.2023.3253868

4 Applications of Federated Deep Learning Models in Healthcare Era

Monika Sethi, Jyoti Snehi, Manish Snehi, and Aadrit Aggarwal

4.1 INTRODUCTION

In intelligent medical applications, deep learning (DL) research has demonstrated encouraging outcomes in supporting clinical data-driven medical diagnosis and therapy. As an example, DL helps with brain tumor segmentation and classification from magnetic resonance imaging (MRI) [1,2], textual identification of healthcare lab records [3], and cancer evaluation as well as forecasting [4]. A large and diversified set of training data is essential for the DL framework to perform effectively well on innovative medical applications [5]. Such training datasets are gathered from a variety of laboratory reports, comprising biological gauges, distinct individuals, medical centers, clinical environments, and drug firms, as well as healthcare insurance organizations. Nevertheless, limited individuals and illnesses that have modest rates of incidence can be obtained from just one healthcare center; obtaining the medical data necessary for building an algorithm using DL may prove difficult. Moreover, as demonstrated in Figure 4.1 DL architectures built on a single institutional dataset are susceptible to organizational data biases. Studies employing data from an identical healthcare organization have proven the tremendous accuracy of

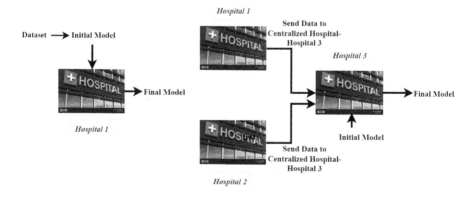

FIGURE 4.1 Single institution learning vs. collaborative institution learning.

this institution-specific bias. But, when the dataset is used from an entirely distinct organization and even within departments inside the same organization, then is proven to be less efficient. Concurrently, individual confidentiality and regulatory constraints pertaining to healthcare data make it impractical to train DL algorithms in a centralized data warehouse. Therefore, in order to construct a single DL framework while preserving individual confidentiality and secrecy, numerous healthcare providers have to work together in order to improve both the range and availability of data for training.

As the healthcare industry and its protocols are extremely complicated, health-related records are often dispersed. As an example, patient medical records might be provided only to certain healthcare organizations exclusively. Such medical details may only be approved by law to be disclosed and published to third parties under strict guidelines as protected health information (PHI). Regulations bodies and procedures, such as the Health Insurance Portability and Accountability Act (HIPAA), firmly restrict who has access to and examination of health-related information [6]. Furthermore, there's a universal consensus concerning the necessity of privacy and data protection due to a rising rate of data thefts at hospitals. As an illustration, in the most recent healthcare information breach at the American Medical Collection Agency (AMCA), around 12 million individuals' economic, health, and billing information were compromised by cybercriminals [7]. As a consequence, more robust laws are being passed in several nations to ensure the privacy of information. In particular, the European Union implemented the General Data Protection Regulation (GDPR) in 2018 to guarantee the confidentiality of users while securing their information [8]. Companies need to give individuals an opportunity to cancel or remove their information and supply a clear explanation of why companies want accessibility to their personal information according to the GDPR. Companies that break the rule would be subject to harsh punishments.

Federated learning (FL) is one new strategy that has been established to address the issue of designing a viable DL architecture using federated health datasets when maintaining individual anonymity [9]. Such technique facilitates decentralized development of machine learning (ML) architectures without demanding the transmission of health data via a centralized aggregated server. As client node locations, healthcare organizations train their DL algorithms independently prior to delivering them to the aggregated server at regular intervals. The individual models from every single node are coordinated and aggregated through the main server to form a centralized framework, which is then shared with every other node. This is important to mention that, throughout the training procedure, the data used for training never gets communicated and remains secret within every node in the network. Health-related information is treated as confidential since simply the model's weight and settings are supplied. Considering these factors, FL reduces a great deal of security issues by shielding private and confidential information yet enabling collaboration across different healthcare centers. FL has great potential to enhance medical facilities for individuals and institutions in the healthcare industry. This chapter discusses the use of FL in addressing a variety of diseases, including Parkinson's, cancer, and Alzheimer's.

4.2 FEDERATED LEARNING FRAMEWORKS FOR ALZHEIMER'S DISEASE CLASSIFICATION

Alzheimer's disease (AD) has become a hazardous disorder, which is frequent in human civilizations and is tragically getting more prevalent each year [10,11]. The number of people in need continues to rise, however there are currently fewer healthcare professionals accessible and the ones who are accessible have hectic schedules. As a result, the incorporation of electronic medical care platforms for AD has grown, with the goal of reducing the workload for professionals and individuals with AD. Nevertheless, the substantial computational cost for AD diagnosis activities has presented difficulties for the deployment of techniques such as fog, cloud, and DL approaches. A variety of factors, comprising data locally, outsourcing, extraction and selection of feature, and implementation, are incorporated in the Evolutionary Deep Convolutional Neural Network Scheme (EDCNNS) by the researcher's group in Ref. [12]. An FL framework provided the foundation for the AD design, facilitating reliable training as well as validation of data across multiple locations. To optimally manage transferred data while taking into consideration its limitations, a consolidation approach with FL is offered. Numerous labs provided real-time AD data, which included neuro-scans (such as MRIs, EEGs) and other clinical reports like blood tests. Each lab served as a node where pus, MRI brain images, and EEG data were given by AD sufferers. The specimens that were retrieved were then used for generating data which was reliably transmitted to a server in the vicinity for further examination and assessment. With blood biosamples, the researchers in Ref. [13] offered a diagnosis framework for AD classification that employed hardware acceleration (HA) and FL. The authors compared and analyzed the efficiency of the classifiers employing blood biosample data that were made available on the Alzheimer's Disease Neuroimaging Initiative (ADNI) portal. With the goal to ensure privacy, FL has been used to train a shared model without forwarding the raw data from individual devices to a centralized server. Their FL framework was built using the HA approach, enabling to expedite the testing and training operations. The HA technique was implemented via an Altera 10 GX FPGA (Field-Programmable Gate Array) and the VHDL hardware description languages. The simulation's findings demonstrated that the recommended methods outperformed prior state-of-the-art techniques in terms of training time while obtaining accuracy and sensitivity for early detection of 89% and 87%, respectively. The proposed techniques could be applied to systems with reduced energy demand since their usage falls between 35 and 39 mW. Another research team in Ref. [14] presented a federated conditional mutual learning (FedCM) to enhance efficiency by taking into account similarities across users and the regional efficiency of users. The presented study was the initial instance of FL on multi-dataset 3DCNN (3 Dimensional Convolutional Neural Network) to classify AD with neuro-scans namely T1w (T1 weighted) MRI. In comparison to FedMD (Federated Learning via Model Distillation) along with additional structures, the technique offered the highest degree of recognition. Further research and significance rating on the human brain's region of interest (ROI) indicated that the left hemisphere might be more relevant in comparison to the right side. The authors in Ref. [15] employed AD dataset and applied Internet of Things (IoT) devices and security methods to develop a

Applications of Federated Deep Learning Models in Healthcare Era 53

user-friendly and preserving confidentiality solution known as ADDetector. More specifically, ADDetector leveraged novel topic-based language elements to boost detection efficiency and solely obtained users audio via IoT gadgets which are often employed in intelligent home environments for the purpose to achieve robust AD diagnosis. ADDetector implemented a specialized three-layered (i.e., user, client, cloud, etc.) framework to provide confidentiality-preserving across breaches of privacy occurring at data, feature, and model tiers. Furthermore, ADDetector employed a FL-based approach that guarantees that the user maintains the confidentiality of the classified framework; maintains the authenticity of the raw data, and implements a differential privacy (DP) methodology that raises the feature's degree of confidentiality. Also, a unique asynchronous privacy-preserving aggregation approach is established to protect the model aggregating operation involving users with the cloud in FL-based approaches. Considering 1010 AD detection trials from 99 health and AD people, researchers analyzed ADDetector. The experimental findings demonstrated that, while all confidentiality strategies (i.e., FL, DP, and cryptography-based aggregation) are implemented, ADDetector achieved high accuracy of 82% and a relatively small overhead of 0.7 seconds.

The researchers in Ref. [16] and Ref. [17] offered a novel end-to-end approach to multidimensional AD digital biomarker assessment in real-world scenarios incorporating multi-modal sensing with FL strategies. The authors acknowledged that there remained a number of significant barriers to overcome while developing a real-world FL structure, which includes a scarcity of computational resources, diverged data, and limitations on data annotations. Researchers developed a small-sized hardware system with multiple modes of operation and implemented it in a 4-week clinical study with 61 aged subjects. The findings illustrated that, on average, the technique can detect a wide range of digital biomarkers with up to 95% accuracy and identify AD with an accuracy of 87.5%.

4.3 FEDERATED LEARNING FRAMEWORKS FOR CANCER CLASSIFICATION

The tremendous progress of AI has led to the broad adoption of ML techniques in intelligent healthcare assessment [18–20]. A substantial volume of well-labeled, high-quality data is needed for intelligent healthcare assessment, which is how algorithms develop. But in order to protect individual privacy and data secrecy, access to medical data is severely limited [21]. Nonetheless, due to individual confidentiality and data security concerns, access to medical data is severely limited. Applying AI to intelligent healthcare assessment involves two key obstacles: eradicating data outliers and improving both integrity and confidentiality. FL, a type of shielded data integration methods, lets data owners develop their algorithms independently followed by aggregate model parameters instead of simply integrating data. In a variety of medical imaging analysis applications, both the volume and variation in datasets play a crucial role for training models. Real-world scenarios, yet, present a couple of challenges: the quantity and kind of disease of individuals could stop just one organization from having the data it needs, and healthcare confidentiality policies frequently make patient information interchange problematic. Therefore, protecting personal information is necessary and has made it more difficult to use input gathered from multiple sources to train a healthcare algorithm. The authors in Ref. [22] provided an FL architecture to address the shortcomings. Alternative to exchanging data, their strategy enabled knowledge integration by transferring each client's model specifications by FL. The FL experiments validated the viability and effectiveness of the presented paradigm by attaining the intended outcomes, which are comparable to the performances of the centralized learning, with the breast cancer histopathology dataset (BreakHis). The research team in Ref. [23] provided a system that ensures the privacy of individuals during training by using FL. The authors combined two modalities: medical information and images of skin lesions. The outcomes of a centralized learning (CL) paradigm were contrasted against the efficacy of the globally federated architecture. With only 0.39% and 0.73% higher F1-score and accuracy results, respectively, attained through the CL approach, the FL strategy performed on par compared to the CL paradigm. Extended fine-tuning may help to further reduce the performance disparity. Additionally, the FL model accurately identified more positives than the CL model due to its 3.27% greater sensitivity. The findings show that FL is capable of efficiently developing highly predictive architectures while enforcing no training data is sent across the involved users. A CNN-based adaptive FL method was suggested by the authors in Ref. [24] to identify skin diseases utilizing dermo-scopy images. The authors took advantage of an adaptive ensemble CNN pooling approach for the global model. They used a gradient-based technique to set up the ensemble CNN at the user's side. with steady settings, their suggested strategy produced 95% accuracy, and with complicated data 89% accuracy. Using the International Skin Imaging Collaboration (ISIC) 2019 dataset, they evaluated their approach.

To produce precise pseudo-labels, the contributors in Ref. [25] presented a semi-supervised FL methodology which established networks and motivated participants to impart learning. Peer learning and ensembled averaging from committee machines are implemented in this methodology. Furthermore, they recommended the peer anonymization (PA) methodology as a key component. PA protected confidentiality, reduced communication costs, and retained effectiveness without introducing complication. To reduce the transmission expenses an asynchronous weighted aggregation technique for skin cancer diagnosis using CNN is presented in Ref. [26]. This method accumulated the received weights asynchronously. By splitting the CNN layers between shallower and deeper layers, with the shallower levels being revised more often, their proposed strategy maximizes transmission cycles. In the FL contexts for skin cancer, the effectiveness of CNN is evaluated in Ref. [27].

4.4 FEDERATED LEARNING FRAMEWORKS FOR PARKINSON'S DISEASE CLASSIFICATION

Parkinson's disease (PD) is a progressive disorder spurred by a breakdown of nerve cells in the substantia nigra, the area of the cerebral cortex responsible for movements. Such neurons degenerate or die, which prevents them from producing dopamine, a vital neurotransmitter. Whenever substantia nigra synapses get damaged in significant quantities, their normal activity is prevented by the loss of dopamine in the basal ganglia. PD motor signs, such as shaking, stiffness, impaired balancing, and

Applications of Federated Deep Learning Models in Healthcare Era 55

reduced impulsive motion, are brought on by disease. Several studies have employed common ML strategies for PD detection. However, there always exists a possibility that patients' sensitive details will be exposed by conventional ML techniques. The research presented in Ref. [28] suggested an innovative methodology for PD detection using blockchain-based FL, which maintained confidentiality and anonymity. As an enhanced version of the ML technique, FL might train a single technique over numerous decentralized local servers rather than exchanging gradient statistics. Blockchain technology is a useful tool for securing gradient transactions—transactions between local and central servers—and maintaining anonymity. Several CNN transfer learning-based approaches (VGG16, VGG19, and InceptionV3) were used to test and assess a proposed method; of these designs, VGG19 provided the best performance (97%). The outcome demonstrated that this model, which used blockchain-based FL to protect users' confidentiality and security, is extremely effective for identifying PD. PD patients experience Freezing of Gait (FoG), a motor sign that impairs a patient's everyday tasks by causing an intermittent impairment of movement. To assist such people, it is therefore essential to track and notify the FoG development. Gathering sufficient accurate data and confidentiality of participants are the two main challenges to creating medical applications for FoG, which have been taken into account in Ref. [29]. For this purpose, the authors recommended an FL healthcare application that uses mobile sensors to identify FoG signs. Researchers analyzed the proposed methodology and contrasted it with a centralized ML strategy. For both model training and testing, the team utilized a dataset consisting of ten PD patients divided into uneven subgroups. The findings indicate that, after employing the balanced technique of SMOTETomek, the model's precision alters by only 1% from that of the CL and by 5% while utilizing the imbalanced training subgroups. The researchers in Ref. [30] described how a cutting-edge PD detection classifier was trained and inferred using individual voice data utilizing various FL techniques. While the aim was to solve issues related to the strategy's viability, several FL techniques produced outcomes that were on par with a CL-trained framework, showing the promise of collaborative and privacy-preserving model training for the identification of PD. It is evident that the FL techniques offer a decentralized and safe environment for training ML designs, guaranteeing patient data privacy, even though they somewhat impair performance. These findings unequivocally demonstrate FL's potential for additional use in the healthcare industry. Some FL techniques have been shown to be effective in utilizing distributed speech data while resolving data privacy concerns, as evidenced by their capacity to achieve performance levels that are comparable to centralized models.

4.5 CONCLUSION AND FUTURE SCOPE

Developments in diagnostic technology have led to the continuous collection of vast amounts of health-related imaging data. As the amount of information available to professionals increases, they can develop data-driven strategies to enhance patient care. However, large amounts of data are required for well-trained data-driven algorithms. There is a limited amount of data that is available in any data center. As a result, DL algorithms that are created on nearby data centers might not function as intended. One potential approach could be to combine all of the data from many sites into a single center. However, confidentiality regulations prevent healthcare institutions from easily merging their data, and the process becomes even more difficult when businesses from various countries are involved. Another option is to use privacy-preserving techniques, which might make use of all the data available across several centers while protecting the privacy of sensitive information. FL is one such method that allows the sharing of sensitive data while enabling the deployment of large-scale AI models that have been trained across numerous data centers. Instead of transmitting data between data centers, FL transfers a general model that has been trained on local datasets. FL has been acknowledged as a promising field of study due to its vast range of possible applications in medical practice and research scenarios. The numerous applications of Federated Deep Learning models in the healthcare sector for AD, PD, and cancer are covered in-depth in this chapter.

REFERENCES

1. Sultan, H.H., Salem, N.M. and Al-Atabany, W., 2019. Multi-classification of brain tumor images using deep neural network. *IEEE Access*, 7, pp. 69215–69225.
2. Ge, C., Gu, I.Y.H., Jakola, A.S. and Yang, J., 2020. Enlarged training dataset by pairwise GANs for molecular-based brain tumor classification. *IEEE Access*, 8, pp. 22560–22570.
3. Harerimana, G., Kim, J.W., Yoo, H. and Jang, B., 2019. Deep learning for electronic health records analytics. *IEEE Access*, 7, pp. 101245–101259.
4. McWilliams, A., Beigi, P., Srinidhi, A., Lam, S. and MacAulay, C.E., 2015. Sex and smoking status effects on the early detection of early lung cancer in high-risk smokers using an electronic nose. *IEEE Transactions on Biomedical Engineering*, 62(8), pp. 2044–2054.
5. Sun, C., Shrivastava, A., Singh, S. and Gupta, A., 2017. Revisiting unreasonable effectiveness of data in deep learning era. In *Proceedings of the IEEE International Conference on Computer Vision* (pp. 843–852), Venice, Italy.
6. Cohen, I.G. and Mello, M.M., 2018. HIPAA and protecting health information in the 21st century. *JAMA*, 320(3), pp. 231–232.
7. Makridis, C. and Dean, B., 2018. Measuring the economic effects of data breaches on firm outcomes: Challenges and opportunities. *Journal of Economic and Social Measurement*, 43(1–2), pp. 59–83.
8. Voigt, P. and Von dem Bussche, A., 2017. *The EU General Data Protection Regulation (GDPR). A Practical Guide*, 1st Ed., Cham: Springer International Publishing, 10(3152676), pp. 10–5555. https://doi.org/10.1007/978-3-319-57959-7
9. Hard, A., Rao, K., Mathews, R., Ramaswamy, S., Beaufays, F., Augenstein, S., Eichner, H., Kiddon, C. and Ramage, D., 2018. Federated learning for mobile keyboard prediction. *arXiv* preprint arXiv:1811.03604.
10. Sethi, M., Rani, S., Singh, A. and Mazón, J.L.V., 2022. A CAD system for Alzheimer's disease classification using neuroimaging MRI 2D slices. *Computational and Mathematical Methods in Medicine*, 2022, p.Article 8680737.
11. Sethi, M., Ahuja, S., Singh, S., Snehi, J. and Chawla, M., 2022, March. An intelligent framework for Alzheimer's disease classification using efficient net transfer learning model. In *2022 International Conference on Emerging Smart Computing and Informatics (ESCI)* (pp. 1–4). IEEE, Pune, India.
12. Lakhan, A., Grønli, T.M., Muhammad, G. and Tiwari, P., 2023. EDCNNS: Federated learning enabled evolutionary deep convolutional neural network for Alzheimer disease detection. *Applied Soft Computing*, 147, p. 110804.

Applications of Federated Deep Learning Models in Healthcare Era   57

13. Khalil, K., Khan Mamun, M.M.R., Sherif, A., Elsersy, M.S., Imam, A.A.A., Mahmoud, M. and Alsabaan, M., 2023. A federated learning model based on hardware acceleration for the early detection of Alzheimer's disease. *Sensors*, 23(19), p. 8272.

14. Huang, Y.L., Yang, H.C. and Lee, C.C., 2021, November. Federated learning via conditional mutual learning for Alzheimer's disease classification on T1w MRI. In *2021 43rd Annual International Conference of the IEEE Engineering in Medicine & Biology Society (EMBC)* (pp. 2427–2432). IEEE, Virtual Conference.

15. Li, J., Meng, Y., Ma, L., Du, S., Zhu, H., Pei, Q. and Shen, X., 2021. A federated learning based privacy-preserving smart healthcare system. *IEEE Transactions on Industrial Informatics*, 18(3), pp. 2021–2031.

16. Ouyang, X., 2023, June. Design and deployment of multi-modal federated learning systems for Alzheimer's disease monitoring. In *Proceedings of the 21st Annual International Conference on Mobile Systems, Applications and Services* (pp. 612–614). Helsinki, Finland, June 18–22, 2023.

17. Sethi, M., Ahuja, S., Rani, S., Bawa, P. and Zaguia, A., 2021. Classification of Alzheimer's disease using Gaussian-based Bayesian parameter optimization for deep convolutional LSTM network. *Computational and Mathematical Methods in Medicine*, 2021, pp. 1–16.

18. Greenspan, H., Van Ginneken, B. and Summers, R.M., 2016. Guest editorial deep learning in medical imaging: Overview and future promise of an exciting new technique. *IEEE Transactions on Medical Imaging*, 35(5), pp. 1153–1159.

19. Shin, H.C., Roberts, K., Lu, L., Demner-Fushman, D., Yao, J. and Summers, R.M., 2016. Learning to read chest x-rays: Recurrent neural cascade model for automated image annotation. In *Proceedings of the IEEE Conference on Computer Vision and Pattern Recognition* (pp. 2497–2506). Las Vegas, NV.

20. Kaushal, C., Bhat, S., Koundal, D. and Singla, A., 2019. Recent trends in computer assisted diagnosis (CAD) system for breast cancer diagnosis using histopathological images. *IRBM*, 40(4), pp. 211–227.

21. Lilhore, U.K., Poongodi, M., Kaur, A., Simaiya, S., Algarni, A.D., Elmannai, H., Vijayakumar, V., Tunze, G.B. and Hamdi, M., 2022. Hybrid model for detection of cervical cancer using causal analysis and machine learning techniques. *Computational and Mathematical Methods in Medicine*, 2022, p.Article 4688327.

22. Li, L., Xie, N. and Yuan, S., 2022. A federated learning framework for breast cancer histopathological image classification. *Electronics*, 11(22), p. 3767.

23. Ogier du Terrail, J., Leopold, A., Joly, C., Béguier, C., Andreux, M., Maussion, C., Schmauch, B., Tramel, E.W., Bendjebbar, E., Zaslavskiy, M. and Wainrib, G., 2023. Federated learning for predicting histological response to neoadjuvant chemotherapy in triple-negative breast cancer. *Nature Medicine*, 29(1), pp. 135–146.

24. Hashmani, M.A., Jameel, S.M., Rizvi, S.S.H. and Shukla, S., 2021. An adaptive federated machine learning-based intelligent system for skin disease detection: A step toward an intelligent dermoscopy device. *Applied Sciences*, 11(5), p. 2145.

25. Bdair, T., Navab, N. and Albarqouni, S., 2021. Semi-supervised federated peer learning for skin lesion classification. *arXiv* preprint arXiv:2103.03703.

26. Yaqoob, M.M., Alsulami, M., Khan, M.A., Alsadie, D., Saudagar, A.K.J. and AlKhathami, M., 2023. Federated machine learning for skin lesion diagnosis: An asynchronous and weighted approach. *Diagnostics*, 13(11), p. 1964.

27. Li, Y., He, Y., Fu, Y. and Shan, S., 2023, January. Privacy preserved federated learning for skin cancer diagnosis. In *2023 IEEE 3rd International Conference on Power, Electronics and Computer Applications (ICPECA)* (pp. 27–33). IEEE, Shenyang, China.

28. Dipro, S.H., Islam, M., Nahian, M.A.A. and Azad, M.S., 2022. A federated learning approach for detecting Parkinson's disease through privacy preserving by blockchain (Doctoral dissertation, Brac University).
29. Jorge, J., Barros, P.H., Yokoyama, R., Guidoni, D., Ramos, H.S., Fonseca, N. and Villas, L., 2022, December. Applying federated learning in the detection of freezing of Gait in Parkinson's disease. In *2022 IEEE/ACM 15th International Conference on Utility and Cloud Computing (UCC)* (pp. 195–200). IEEE, Vancouver, WA.
30. Sarlas, A., Kalafatelis, A., Alexandridis, G., Kourtis, M.A. and Trakadas, P., 2023, August. Exploring federated learning for speech-based Parkinson's disease detection. In *Proceedings of the 18th International Conference on Availability, Reliability and Security* (pp. 1–6), Benevento Italy.

5 Machine Learning for Healthcare
Review and Future Aspects

Aadrita Nandy, Jyoti Choudhary, Joanne Fredrick,
T. S. Zacharia, Tom K. Joseph, and Veerpal Kaur

5.1 INTRODUCTION: BACKGROUND AND DRIVING FORCES

Artificial intelligence (AI) and machine learning (ML) are related but distinct fields. The development of computer systems that can do activities that usually require human intelligence, such as pattern recognition, natural language understanding, and decision-making, is referred to as AI. A subfield of AI called "ML" focuses on developing statistical models and methods that enable computers to "learn" from data. ML algorithms can be divided into two main categories: supervised learning and unsupervised learning.

Figure 5.1 shows the relationship between all the AI-ML learnings. Reinforcement learning is a third new category that has been added. It is a form of ML technique where a smart agent interacts with its environment and picks up on how to behave in it. Data acquisition, analysis, and utilization are critical components of modern medical science. AI technology has the potential to transform how medical data is managed and used. It can help to organize patient records, recommend treatments for illnesses, monitor drug efficacy, and personalize medical treatments. It can also be used to analyze medical images, allowing for faster, more accurate, and cost-effective detection and diagnosis of diseases. AI can also be used to detect patterns in medical data that would otherwise go unnoticed. Furthermore, AI has the potential to reduce medical errors and increase patient safety. AI-powered systems can monitor a wide range of variables in a patient's medical history and alert medical professionals when something is out of the ordinary.

Figure 5.2 shows the types of classification of algorithms rooted on unsupervised and supervised learning which are utilized in the medical field as predictions, diagnosis, and other important things. In supervised learning, the algorithms are trained on labeled data with the aim of classifying or predicting new data based on the associations discovered from the training set. The algorithms learn to map the input features to the proper output labels by studying the input features and their matching output labels in the training data. The benefits of supervised learning include:

- Disease diagnosis and prediction: With a high volume of medical data, including genetics, imaging, and medical information, supervised learning can be used to diagnose and forecast diseases such as cancer and Alzheimer's

DOI: 10.1201/9781032694870-5

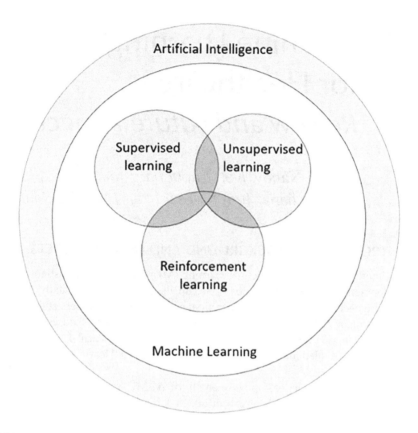

FIGURE 5.1 Relationship between machine learning, supervised learning, unsupervised learning, and reinforcement learning.

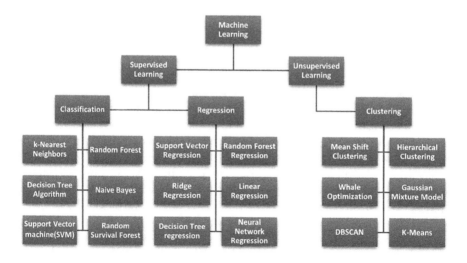

FIGURE 5.2 Classification of algorithms used in medical field.

disease (AD). Continuous training and validation can increase the accuracy of these models.

- Personalized medicine: Based on a patient's medical history, genetic information, and responsiveness to treatment, supervised learning can be used to produce personalized treatment regimens. This can result in improved patient outcomes, fewer side effects, and lower expenses.
- Medical imaging analysis: Supervised learning can be used to evaluate medical images such as CT (computerized tomography) scans and MRI (magnetic resonance imaging) to aid in the diagnosis and treatment of medical illnesses such as heart disease and cancer. These models can identify structures and characteristics.
- Risk prediction: Supervised learning algorithms can determine a patient's chances of developing certain medical illnesses such as heart disease, cancer, or stroke, allowing for early intervention and safety precautions.
- Flexibility: Supervised learning can be applied to a wide range of issues, including both regression and classification, and time-series forecasting. As a result, it is a versatile method to ML.

Unsupervised learning involves training the algorithm using data that has not been labeled, therefore the result variable is unknown. After that, the algorithm finds patterns and connections in the data, which may be applied to several operations including clustering and dimensionality reduction. Some common applications of unsupervised learning in the medical field include:

- Drug discovery: Unsupervised learning can be used in drug development to identify new drug targets as well as analyze and interpret enormous amounts of data generated throughout the drug discovery process.
- Electronic health record (EHR) analysis: Unsupervised learning can be used to discover hidden patterns in EHR data, such as disease prevalence and patient risk factors. This has the potential to enhance patient outcomes while also lowering expenditure.
- Disease diagnosis and clustering: Unsupervised learning can be used to detect patterns in medical data that can be utilized to aid in disease detection and clustering. Clustering algorithms, for example, can classify patients based on clinical criteria, resulting in tailored treatments and improved patient outcomes.
- Dimensionality reduction: To reduce the dimensionality of the data and find the most crucial aspects, unsupervised learning methods can be utilized. This makes the data simpler to analyze and interpret. Principal component analysis (PCA) is a common tactic utilized for this purpose.

Overall, supervised and unsupervised learning are all important tools for exploring and analyzing medical data. They allow us to quickly identify correlations between variables and make accurate predictions, which are essential for delivering effective patient care. The diagnosis and treatment of depression is complicated both ML and AI have been utilized to enhance the outcomes. AI algorithms can be used to discover novel treatments, reuse existing drugs, forecast the likelihood of someone acquiring depression, build individualized treatment regimens, follow patient behavioral patterns, and employ chatbots to provide support and therapy to depression patients. Cancer detection and treatment using ML is an active topic of research, and numerous methods, including Neural Networks, Support Vector Machines (SVMs), Random Forests (RF), and Decision Trees, have been utilized for this purpose.

The study being presented aims to answer research questions related to the deployment of ML methods in the healthcare field.

- Number of publications utilized from 2010 to 2022.
- How many studies or reviews have been published in the relevant field.
- What are types of supervised algorithms used in the recent health-oriented academic papers.
- What are types of unsupervised algorithms used in the recent health-oriented academic papers.
- Which recent algorithms have been created with the intention of advancing healthcare?

5.2 LITERATURE REVIEW

This section of literature survey focuses on the papers published from 2010 to 2022. The papers are considered from the Scopus database, mix of journal and conference publications, and are focused on the deployment of ML algorithms in healthcare. Yadahalli et. al [1] have proposed a technique based on ridge regression with edge detection to identify the bone fractures using the x-ray images of the patients. The benefit of using the proposed model is the consideration of multiple fractures at the same body part. The authors quoted the future work of the paper as deploying the functional model into the x-ray machines directly which is yet missing.

Yu and Xiaowei [2] have come up with a new algorithm formulated from Iterative Dichotomiser 3 (ID3) algorithm which can analyze continuous medical image data. This new algorithm is capable of accurately classifying the MRI images. It can aid in improving diagnostic accuracy and lowering medical error and overlooked diagnoses of pre-natal or postnatal asphyxia. Authors indicated this algorithm does not work in a high-noise atmosphere, and it will be researched more extensively further. Charles Delahunt et al. [3] have introduced the Autoscope, a low automated digital microscope. The Autoscope is connected to computer vision and classification algorithms in addition to automating images. In Thailand, the Autoscope had satisfactory preliminary field trials for the detection of malaria. The authors have created a thorough ML framework using SVMs and convolutional neural networks. The authors have targeted to diagnose other larger parasites in coming time.

Dai et al. [4] acknowledge that the outcomes of multiple weak classifiers can be merged using the RF algorithm to generate precise and reliable classification results on breast cancer. Utilizing the combined findings of numerous decision trees result in high prediction accuracy. The author will discover some additional algorithms for various types of medical issues in the future.

Machine Learning for Healthcare

Gutierrez-Caceres et al. [5] have presented a method for categorizing irregularity and regularity in medical brain scans to facilitate medical diagnosis. In the end K-Nearest Neighbors (KNN) query provides series of related photos as conclusion. A high percentage of classification accuracy when Gabor filter was applied. The author thinks that this is a handy instrument for doctors that can be performed before diagnosing. A more complex filter could be used in future.

Kooptiwoot [6] has constructed GAJA2 (Genetic Algorithm-based J48 Algorithm, version 2), a data mining algorithm using medical dataset from University of California (UCI) repository which gives better results than GAJA. The algorithm was employed to identify severe inflammation in the urinary system. While using the classification algorithm, GAJA can only create one classification whereas using the GAJA2 technique, one can define many characteristics simultaneously. GAJA2 can also be used to identify the connections between class attributes and other associated traits.

Ashraf et al. [7] have delineated use of 26 classification algorithms to predict Cardiovascular Disorders. The authors employed the dataset "Myocardial infarction complications Database", University of Leicester, which has wide range of classes known to have links to myocardial infarction. Incorporating the data and findings, they concluded that ensemble classifiers are ideal for categorizing cardiac problems into various groups. The method that worked the finest was eXtreme Gradient Boosting (XGB) classifier. This model can be applied in healthcare system in upcoming years.

Rochmawati et al. [8] have suggested the use of decision tree algorithm to categorize COVID indicators. Dataset COVID-19 Symptoms Checker from Kaggle was used to compare Hoeffding and J48 algorithm. The idea is to transform the information into decision trees. J48's outcomes marginally outperformed the Hoeffding tree in terms of accuracy. It is also possible to employ additional cross-validation variations and separate percentages of training and testing data in future.

Mhaske and Phalke [9] have proposed use of Neural networks and SVM to identify Melanoma skin cancer. K-means, an unsupervised method, was also employed. In supervised learning, trained information is supplied to predict the outcome; however, in unsupervised learning, existing data is not supplied; instead, the classifier must determine the class or category to which the data belongs on its own. The result showed that SVM achieves the maximum accuracy, i.e., 80%–90%. K-means clustering algorithm's accuracy is lower than that of Neural Network and SVM.

Seixas and Mantovani [10] have proposed a strategy for focusing on seeds since some region expanding techniques have strong grouping outcomes but are sensitive to seed. Medical photos of skin lesions in the bottom body parts were segmented using ML to construct the seed and decision tree algorithms were employed for ML. An average accuracy of 97.21% was attained by binary classification test utilizing Wcka's J48 algorithm. In future, pattern recognition job can also be done using additional ML techniques, or even a hybrid model.

Lakshmi and Naik [11] have developed a strategy utilizing the SVM and KNN classifier. It is a computer-controlled classification system that can detect cancerous and non-cancerous cells in acute myeloid leukemia (AML) and acute lymphoblastic leukemia (ALL) samples, as well as distinguish between the various subcategories of AML and ALL cells. The suggested model's accuracy is 94.39%. The authors cited the upcoming future study as they will try to attain high accuracy by updating test dataset for SVM and taking into consideration both cytoplasm and nuclei.

Rabeh et al. [12] presented a method for detecting AD in its initial stages. The classification method is based on SVM. The methodology has a 90.66% prediction accuracy for detecting AD in its initial stages. According to the researchers, they plan to attach a monitoring application to this one in the future to identify and monitor the growth of AD.

Islam et al. [13] have proposed a method with various data mining and ML techniques that can detect heart disease at early stage. In this paper, Researchers have used UCI heart disease dataset. PCA has been used to reduce attributes. Apart from a hybrid genetic algorithm with k-means utilized for final clustering. The proposed method can predict early heart disease with an accuracy of 94.06%.

Princy et al. [14] presented a model that utilizes ML. Using precisely applied supervised ML methods for disease prediction, a cardiovascular dataset is classified. Based on the findings, Decision Tree classification model outperformed Logistic Regression, SVM, and KNN-based methods in capability to predict cardiovascular problems.73% accuracy rate has been achieved by decision tree. This methodology might help doctors anticipate the onset of heart illnesses and offer the appropriate treatment in advance. In the future, they intend to evaluate and create a better disease prediction model.

Mir et al. [15] have used WEKA tool to construct a classifying model that could predict diabetes disease using Naive Bayes, SVM, RF, and the Simple Classification and Regression Tree (CART) algorithm. The National Institute of Diabetes and Digestive and Kidney Diseases' Pima Indians Diabetes Dataset was utilized in this study. When it is used to forecast the progression of diabetes, SVM outshines Naive Bayes, RF, and Simple CART.

Qin et al. [16] developed a method using ML for detecting cancer severity. RF, SVM, and Multilayer Perceptron (MLP) are three different ML algorithms used in this work. For each algorithm, training and testing sets were divided 70/30. The maximum accuracy when employing a Radial Basis Function (RBF)-based SVM classifier.

Gambhir et al. [17] used multiple ML algorithms to evaluate the current trend or pattern of COVID-19 spread in India. The dataset, which spans 154 days, or from January 22, 2020, to June 24, 2020, is collected from MoHFW [Ministry of Health and Family Welfare (India)]. Polynomial Regression algorithm and SVM algorithm were the two ML models employed. They reached the conclusion that, while predicting the growth in cases over the following 60 days, the Polynomial Regression algorithm surpassed the SVM algorithm with an accuracy of almost 93%. Two ML models were utilized, according to authors, but in the future, Deep Learning models or hybrid models could be used to forecast the same.

Shanmugarajeshwari and Ilayaraja [18] proposed an approach for identifying an early identification of chronic renal disease (CKD). It includes three phases, just like pre-processing, selection of attributes, and classification methods. The goal of this work is to construct a machine-based diagnostic approach utilizing ML methods. Using RF, SVM, and ANN (Artificial Neural Network) algorithms, the early diagnosis of CKD patients was investigated in this study. The RF Decision-Tree Classification Method resulted in a cataloguing efficiency of 98.97% with a minimal time complexity.

Habib et al. [19] designed a healthcare system to examine the relation between quality of life and depression. In the first section, a Secure Hash Algorithm-based data consolidation technique is explained. The second portion introduced a model using both supervised and unsupervised ML algorithms. The National Health and Nutrition Examination Survey (NHANES) data are being used. SVM is used to investigate classification problems and evaluate the degree of correlation between the data. The authors stated the future studies will focus on enhancing the dataset with a variety of characteristics and predicting the severity levels of depression based on a variety of parameters.

Terrada et al. [20] have proposed a medical support Decision System model to detect atherosclerosis, that really can take preventive actions based on the patient's symptoms. An established database is also utilized to forecast individuals with or without atherosclerotic disease using ANN and KNN. The simulation results on four databases indicated that the developed ANN algorithm's highest accuracy was 96.4%. The proposed system will integrate different techniques and features for additional cardiac conditions to enhance prediction accuracy, according to authors' descriptions of the future work.

Wang et al. [21] have suggested a reliable technique for three-dimensional picture categorization that also not retains the benefits of the two types of strategies of lessons, but also overcomes their drawbacks through efficiently blending unsupervised and supervised learning. The suggested model's flexibility and robustness are significant advantages. The challenge of the paper for additional investigation is how to attain such an outcome.

Ono et al. [22] have proposed to use unsupervised cluster analysis based on mutual information maximization to categorize abnormal photos of pancreatic cancer into explicit groups. They concluded that updates would serve as the strongest classified into 16 clusters after assessing the assessment of both data and categorization of trends of tumor materials. In the future, they will use vector quantized variational autoencoder (VQVAE) to execute the duties of decoding and encoding for this work.

Nanyue et al. [23] have proposed to develop a suitable method for analyzing heartbeat signals using an integration of unsupervised and supervised learning. Pursuing the selection of heartbeat waves of Chronic Obstructive Pulmonary Disease (COPD) patients and healthy volunteers, they performed pre-treatment, parameter extraction based regarding rhythmic convenient, modeling, and recognition using unsupervised learning. For analysis, Supervised learning, and PCA Least-squares Regression (LS), as well as Least Absolute Shrinkage and Selection Operator (LASSO), are step-by-step used. They gathered information from 70 healthy individuals and 46 COPD patients. In the future, the study will provide some essential data for the empirical application of heartbeat diagnostic for TCM (Traditional Chinese Medicine) medical assessment.

Bosoni et al. [24] have proposed using unsupervised learning to uncover potential subclasses and supervised learning to develop models for better forecasting a variety of different health outcomes in people suffering from systemic sclerosis, a rare chronic connective tissue illness. They demonstrated that not only does subcategory discovery increase prediction, but that the discovered rules integrate subcategory information that can be directly analyzed to better comprehend the significance of the new illness subtypes.

Wosiak et al. [25] have recommended developing a suitable categorization system for the problem of intrauterine growth restriction types. There are two types of (Intrauterine Growth Restriction) IUGR: symmetrically impaired and asymmetrically impaired. The first type of fetus has a decline in all dimensions of the body and internal organs and is more likely to have a loss in growth potential. The second form, asymmetrical, accounts for 75%–80% of all IUGR cases, causing aberrant cell development. KNN, C4.5, Nave Bayes, random tree, and sequential minimal optimization were the algorithms used. The intrauterine growth-restricted fetuses were identified using fetal heart rate (FHR) variability measurement during the antepartum phase. The results attained 82.4% of accuracy.

Sasubilli et al. [26] have proposed analyzing human illness patterns and utilizing RF or other ML models, we can forecast the actual technique that a person must follow to achieve exceptional health and avoid the various health-damaging behaviors that people engage in on a regular basis. There were several methods utilized, including RF, Decision Tree, K-Neighbors, SVM, Gradient Boosting, and others. RF has the highest implementation accuracy. The two categories employed in this investigation were the modern technological world and ancient medical methods. In today's technological world, diabetes, heart rate, forecasting what will happen in the future according to the current pulse rate, as well as survivorship based on bodily data are all predicted. Ancient Methodology is concerned with the ancient methods of resolving health issues.

Feng et al, [27] have suggested employing Deep Gaussian Processes (DGPs) to offer supervised and unsupervised learning for analysis of FHR tracings. They utilized data from 552 cardiotocography (CTG) recordings, clinical data from women, and biomarkers such as pH levels assessed at delivery collected from the Universite´ Hospital's Maternity Department in Czech Republic, during the trials. They obtained outstanding results using supervised learning, which demonstrated that the DGP beat SVM-based reach on actual data. Yet, it studies on unsupervised models was in its early stages.

Azaria and Azaria [28] have presented a ML-based approach for determining the day of ovulation. They employed five separate datasets in this study: basal body temperature (BBT), salivary electrical resistance (SER), vaginal electrical resistance (VER), ovulation prediction kit (OPK), and ovarian discomfort. This ML model developed therefore it might be very valuable for women attempting to conceive who are having difficulty recognizing their ovulation period, especially when certain measures are missing. In the future, they are attempting to anticipate ovulation in advance to assist couples in conceiving or avoiding pregnancy by detecting ovulation before it occurs.

Das et al. [29] proposed the Velocity Enhanced Whale Optimization Algorithm (VEWOA) as a classification method for predicting three categories of medical datasets: heart disease, echocardiography, and hepatitis. The technique is validated using Root mean square error (RMSE) and time, and seven categorization algorithms have been created: SVM, KNN, RF, Logistic Regression, Artificial, Neural Network Naive Bayes, and Decision Tree. Feature selection approaches have been created, such as LASSO, with low duplication. Maximum Relevance Minimum Redundancy (mRMR) and relief were obtained using K-fold cross-validation. The accuracy obtained for VEWOA-NN in heart disease dataset, Hepatitis dataset, echocardiogram dataset is 97.2%, 92.5%, and 96%, respectively. To attain better results, future research should entail larger medical databases.

Machine Learning for Healthcare

Nair et al. [30] have suggested a method for extracting variables from gait data in order to build a classifier to identify DIP (drug-induced parkinsonism) as soon as possible. Data was acquired from 6 patients and 16 participants using a triaxial accelerometer affixed to the individuals' dominant leg and hand. The use of algorithms such as K-means, which divides the given data into K distinct groups (Unsupervised condition). In the case of supervised algorithms, there is logistic regression. The suggested model has the advantage of being able to detect the early stages of Parkinson Syndrome. In the future, the authors stated that merging data from DIP and Parkinson's Disease for analysis might aid in the potential of distinct diagnoses between the two at the outset.

Chauhan et al. [31], worked on the PIDD (Pima Indians Diabetes Database) dataset, and suggested that the cluster approach provides 90.36% efficiency. The best feature selection technique was suggested as an early diabetes screening tool. Delirium tremens, rheumatoid factor, and nota bene were used, and the NB (Naive Bayes) classifier had the higher precision of 82.3%. Using the suggested model has the advantage of detecting diabetes early on before it progresses to a vulnerable place. In future deep learning-based technology would be used by the author. The precision of diabetes prediction is likely to increase by techniques like ANN, CNN (convolution neural network), etc.

Mazlan et al. [32] established an approach for diagnosing cancers using ML. The benefit of implementing the suggested model is the categorization of tumor into several categories using ML and AI using various forms of healthcare data. As stated by the author, improvements in hybridization and imaging equipment can solve and enhance existing problems like high dimensions and tremendous amounts of data.

Yang and Yang [33] established a test to determine the structural information of a protein employing two different methods, such as a microarray technology experiment and protein phylogenetic analyses. To identify the functions of the enzymes in an RMCT (Recursive maximum contrast tree), the proposed model's use is beneficial. The benefit of applying this proposed approach is to more precisely and properly understand how proteins function. In comparison to a variety of existing classifiers, such as decision trees, SVMs, and closest neighbor classifiers, the author quoted with in future RMCT classifier performs brilliantly.

Stiglic et al. [34] used a substantial quantity of information to suggest a microarray approach to comprehending cell functions and determining cellular behavior related for particular diseases, by evaluating cellular genes, this technology has the advantage of raising the diagnostic techniques to a greater degree. Further to decrease the intellectual complexity of choosing and categorizing features in big transcriptome research, the author also uses implement the proposed and empirical evaluation of these as well as additional impedance mapping methods.

Firdaus et al. [35] developed imaging modalities using CT object tracking for the lung cancer diagnosis. The suggested method has the benefit of offering a solution to the issue of identifying lung cancer based on both benign and malignant types that can appear on the scanning report. The writer additionally suggests that the tomography machine's x-ray tubes and photons detectors might be modified to increase accuracy of the system for the assessment.

Ali et al. [36] suggested a technique that will enhance understanding of human viral species and reveal their historical link (Human adenoviruses, HAdVs). The use of HAdVs for specific treatments and as vaccine delivery vans is a benefit of this research. Future HAdV offers a more accurate and flexible basis for identifying various serovars as opposed to classifying them at a certain ideological level, such as the structural or functional protein expression, as the author also stated in future.

Osman et al. [37] proposed using knowledge on entire genome to identify genetic diseases The advantage of the proposed technique is to evaluate a person based on his genetics to estimate the probability of diseases that he may be afflicted by and about the various foods and drugs that his body reacts faster. The writer additionally suggested that this method's possible future uses include identifying a person's physiological parameters, which could prove useful in forensics.

Latha and Vetrivelan [38] proposed a technique to predict heart disease using Markov process with partial observations. The benefit of this proposed approach is its ability to send the necessary services to the sportsman and alert the doctor the about particular patient on his cardiac function using fog computing. The writer is also mentioned in a future paper that discusses the growth of risk predictions utilizing intravascular volume to give immediate, truthful data about a patient's situation.

Adnan et al. [39] presented a model for how to obtain and show on a phone the probability of AD from a database, with the advantage of identifying AD in its initial phases. In the coming, the authors are also acknowledged. Although this application does not interpret the genetic diversity of probably AD patients, the function can be improved to also include security mechanisms and to instantly forecast the likelihood of AD.

Zhang and Chang [40] created an approach to discover patient similarities employing customer data from of the hospital's medical report. The recommended model's advantages is that it uncovers common symptoms among patients, allowing for a quicker diagnosis of each patient's medical condition. The authors additionally said that, in the future, auxiliary diagnoses' impact and trustworthiness will increase along with the sharing and combining of required data. Healthcare information and ML methods coupled.

Haq et al. [41] put forth a novel Blood Culture (BC) identification technique. In the suggested method, related features from the dataset have been picked using Relief and Autoencoder and PCA algorithms, which were utilized for the training and testing of the SVM. The strategy put forward has been examined using BC dataset. Supervised method's accuracy was 99.91% whereas autoencoder and PCA were poor. In the future, combining multiple datasets with different features selection techniques will help to enhance BC detection with higher accuracy.

Mazlan et al. [42] compared supervised methods such as SVM, Decision Tree, Naive Bayes, and KNN for categorizing breast cancer. When combined with other classifiers, the K-means clustering algorithm under unsupervised learning had demonstrated promising results for classification purposes. These newly created algorithms have demonstrably improved in terms of greater classification accuracy and manageable calculation times. However, there are still several problems with the classification of cancer, including the presence of noisy data, high dimensionality, and an enormous volume of details.

Gao et al. [43] compiled the initial model results into a team graph structure, maximizing the agreement by encouraging consistent labeling allocation across the graph and smooth label presentation. The datasets used were 20 Newsgroup categorization, DBLP (Digital Bibliography & Library Project) data, sentiment data, and

Cora [44]. Experimenting on these datasets, the proposed technique improves by 2%–10%.

Gadermayr et al. [45] proposed and investigated stain translation methods using Generative Adversarial Networks (GANs) without requiring paired training data, aiming to improve segmentation applications in digital pathology and enhance adaptability in supervised training. Also employed a similar method to do a immediate (totally unsupervised) label interpretation from picture. These two techniques are finally integrated. Using a suitable, simple to-segment intermediate representation can improve segmentation results for both supervised and unsupervised methods.

Afrin et al. [46] predicted death based on Current Procedural Terminology (CPT) readings, the period of ICU treatments, and the visits that occurred according to gender as well as age. To assess the results, the authors used Keras Classifier, Neural Network, Recurrent Neural Network, and K-fold cross-validation. The K-fold did well in predicting the number of visits and the outcome of deaths. For all the research topics, the Keras classifier provided very high area under curve predictions (90%). Future studies will focus on improving multiclass categorization and the effectiveness of the selected methodologies based on fewer classes.

Zhu et al. [47] offer a deep learning framework that preserves the temporal characteristics of EHRs when building patient representations for similarity measurement. The authors proposed Contextual Embedding of Medical Concepts, Temporal Patient Representation, Unsupervised Patient Similarity and Measure Similarities with Supervision. The experimental results demonstrate that the used approach greatly outperforms the baselines, allowing for more precise patient cohort discovery. Their future plans call for implementing these techniques in other fields, such as health visualization, in the interest of resolving the problem of data irregularity. Additionally, the studies show that unsupervised systems were successful in matching patients who had comparable conditions.

In this research, Pereira and Silveira [48] suggested a representation learning and latent space-based detection-based unsupervised technique to anomaly detection. Results demonstrated that anomaly identification can be done even in the absence of labels. The totally unsupervised strategy produced results comparable to a traditional (SVM) and superior to newly proposed supervised and unsupervised models from previous publications. Additionally, authors believe there is still much work to be done to improve anomaly identification using unsupervised learning.

In this study, Xie et al. [49] put forth a technique for classifying different types of heartbeats that blends eigenvalues with decision tree algorithm. The technique passed the test with sensitivity, specificity, and accuracy of 97.3%, 99.5%, and 99.6% in the published MIT-BIH Arrhythmia Database. In our future efforts, multicategory research and database validation will require excessive time to accomplish as a result.

Liu et al. [50] introduce a special sample relation consistency (SRC) paradigm that directly maintains the stability of the relations between different specimens under disruptions in to obtain significant semantic features from the unstructured data. In the analysis, two sizable, openly accessible benchmark medical picture datasets were examined, specifically Chest X-ray14 for thoracic disease classification. The results show that our system uses the best cutting-edge semi-supervised learning techniques.

Korkmaz et al. [51] present an innovative unsupervised MRI reconstruction technique based on zero-shot learned adversarial transformers (SLATER). Zero-shot learned adversarial transformers (SLATER) is a model that combines the concepts of zero-shot learning and adversarial training with transformers. For the purpose of mapping noise and regression coefficients onto mains MR images, cross attention transformers and a deep adversarial network are used. Demonstrations were performed on single-coil brain MRI data and multi-coil brain MRI data from. Future applications of SLATER could include structural and dynamic MRI in other anatomies or other imaging modalities like CT.

5.3 RESULTS AND DISCUSSIONS

Fifty research papers and two reviews in all are cited in this review study as shown in Figure 5.3.

Many supervised, unsupervised, and hybrid procedures have been employed. The VEWOA, GAJA2, and hybrid genetic algorithm are just a few of the new algorithms that have been introduced. Supervised approaches have been proposed more frequently, with a count of 33. The number of users for unsupervised and hybrid approaches is 14 as illustrated in Figure 5.4.

With reference to Figure 5.5, Although there are other supervised algorithms for cancer detection, SVM takes the top spot with a total of 19. The Decision Tree and RF algorithms are helpful for the same with counts of 11 and 10, respectively. Several unsupervised algorithms have been employed in various research articles [52–55].

However as shown in Figure 5.6, with a count of seven, the K-means approach is used more successfully in unsupervised algorithms.

Moreover, several hybrid techniques [56–60] were applied as seen in Figure 5.7. Because hybrid techniques are still in the exploratory stage, there are less research articles on them. It can be utilized expertly and successfully in the future to give cancer patients more precise information.

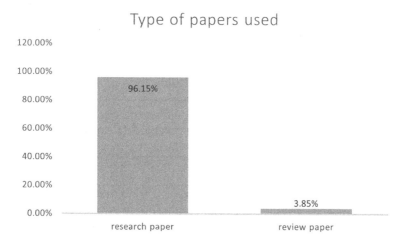

FIGURE 5.3 Graph representing comparison of research paper and review paper used.

Machine Learning for Healthcare

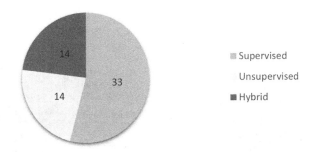

FIGURE 5.4 Count of research publications with different learning methods.

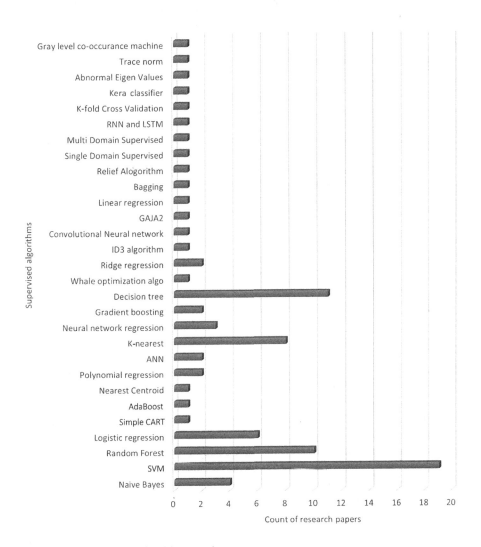

FIGURE 5.5 Count of algorithms used.

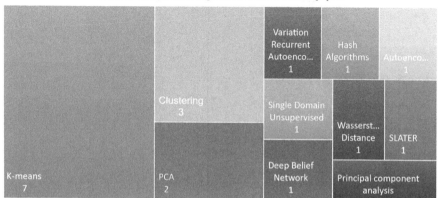

FIGURE 5.6 Count of unsupervised algorithms used.

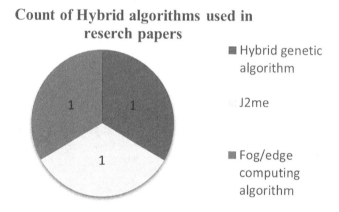

FIGURE 5.7 Count of hybrid algorithms used.

5.4 CONCLUSION

This paper can be concluded by stating that ML is an eminent field for research that aims to create a system that mimics human intellect.it can be utilized in healthcare sector. It can never replace human doctors, but it is offering the best solutions to healthcare problems. It is the most essential part for automatically constructed computational methods. In this paper, an evaluation of 50 research papers from IEEE database that are published between 2008 and 2022 has been presented. The literature demonstrates the degree to which ML and AI techniques could really improve the healthcare system. As mentioned in the preceding sections, a variety of ML algorithms, including supervised, unsupervised, and hybrid ML techniques were utilized to enhance the efficiency of diagnosis. The methods are proposed for prognosis, diagnosis, and ideal plan for the identified disease, such as RF, SVM, Naive Bayes, logistic regression, simple CART algorithm, decision tree, linear regression, k-means, and

Machine Learning for Healthcare 73

PCA. These algorithms can provide precise, productive, and cost-effective forecasting models for making decisions. However, there are intentional drawbacks, complexities, and possibilities in healthcare domain. Considering the current pandemic era, learning techniques are undoubtedly assisting the medical field in making substantial contributions to humanity by improving the entire diagnosis process, which assist in early identification and treatment of diseases, thus also limiting the number of deaths and increasing the probability of survival rate of patients. Each country is concerned about it now, each year they invest more in its intent for the advancement of healthcare systems with the use of methods such as big data and ML. Undoubtedly, ML and AI strategies have now been identified as the most powerful assets that can aid in improving our nation's healthcare systems; however, these techniques must be more accurate and reliable to make the healthcare systems more efficient.

REFERENCES

1. Yadahalli, S., Parmar, A., Zambare, P., & Sawant, R. (2021, May). Bone deformity identification using machine learning. In *2021 5th International Conference on Intelligent Computing and Control Systems (ICICCS)* (pp. 1355–1358). IEEE, Madurai, India.
2. Yu, W., & Xiaowei, Y. (2016, August). Application of decision tree for MRI images of premature brain injury classification. In *2016 11th International Conference on Computer Science & Education (ICCSE)* (pp. 792–795). IEEE, Nagoya, Japan.
3. Delahunt, C. B., Mehanian, C., Hu, L., McGuire, S. K., Champlin, C. R., Horning, M. P., ... Thompon, C. M. (2015, October). Automated microscopy and machine learning for expert-level malaria field diagnosis. In *2015 IEEE Global Humanitarian Technology Conference (GHTC)* (pp. 393–399). IEEE, Seattle, Washington, DC.
4. Dai, B., Chen, R. C., Zhu, S. Z., & Zhang, W. W. (2018, December). Using random forest algorithm for breast cancer diagnosis. In *2018 International Symposium on Computer, Consumer and Control (IS3C)* (pp. 449–452). IEEE, Taichung, Taiwan.
5. Gutierrez-Caceres, J., Portugal-Zambrano, C., & Castañón, C. B. (2014, May). Computer aided medical diagnosis tool to detect normal/abnormal studies in digital mr brain images. In *2014 IEEE 27th International Symposium on Computer-Based Medical Systems* (pp. 501–502). IEEE, New York.
6. Kooptiwoot, S. (2010, July). Mining acute inflammations of urinary system using GAJA2: a new data mining algorithm. In *2010 3rd International Conference on Computer Science and Information Technology* (Vol. 3, pp. 278–281). IEEE, Chengdu.
7. Ashraf, F. B., Siam, T. R., Nayen, Z., & Zaman, F. U. (2022, February). Identification of cardiovascular disorders using machine learning classification algorithms. In *2022 International Conference on Advancement in Electrical and Electronic Engineering (ICAEEE)* (pp. 1–6). IEEE, Gazipur, India.
8. Rochmawati, N., Hidayati, H. B., Yamasari, Y., Yustanti, W., Rakhmawati, L., Tjahyaningtijas, H. P., & Anistyasari, Y. (2020, October). Covid symptom severity using decision tree. In *2020 Third International Conference on Vocational Education and Electrical Engineering (ICVEE)* (pp. 1–5). IEEE, Surabaya, Indonesia.
9. Mhaske, H. R., & Phalke, D. A. (2013, December). Melanoma skin cancer detection and classification based on supervised and unsupervised learning. In *2013 International Conference on Circuits, Controls and Communications (CCUBE)* (pp. 1–5). IEEE, Bengaluru, India.
10. Seixas, J. L., & Mantovani, R. G. (2016, December). Decision trees for the detection of skin lesion patterns in lower limbs ulcers. In *2016 International Conference on Computational Science and Computational Intelligence (CSCI)* (pp. 677–681). IEEE, Las Vegas, NV.

11. Lakshmi, K. G., & Naik, N. M. (2019, July). Automated detection of white blood cells cancer disease. In *2019 1st International Conference on Advances in Information Technology (ICAIT)* (pp. 24–28). IEEE, Chikmagalur, India.

12. Rabeh, A. B., Benzarti, F., & Amiri, H. (2016, March). Diagnosis of Alzheimer diseases in early step using SVM (support vector machine). In *2016 13th International Conference on Computer Graphics, Imaging and Visualization (CGiV)* (pp. 364–367). IEEE, Beni Mellal, Morocco.

13. Islam, M. T., Rafa, S. R., & Kibria, M. G. (2020, December). Early prediction of heart disease using PCA and hybrid genetic algorithm with k-means. In *2020 23rd International Conference on Computer and Information Technology (ICCIT)* (pp. 1–6). IEEE, Dhaka, Bangladesh.

14. Princy, R. J. P., Parthasarathy, S., Jose, P. S. H., Lakshminarayanan, A. R., & Jeganathan, S. (2020, May). Prediction of cardiac disease using supervised machine learning algorithms. In *2020 4th International Conference on Intelligent Computing and Control Systems (ICICCS)* (pp. 570–575). IEEE, Madurai, India.

15. Mir, A., & Dhage, S. N. (2018, August). Diabetes disease prediction using machine learning on big data of healthcare. In *2018 Fourth International Conference on Computing Communication Control and Automation (ICCUBEA)* (pp. 1–6). IEEE, Pune, India.

16. Qin, A., Hasan, M. R., Ahmed, K. A., & Hossain, M. Z. (2022, June). Machine learning for predicting cancer severity. In *2022 IEEE 10th International Conference on Healthcare Informatics (ICHI)* (pp. 527–529). IEEE, Rochester, MN.

17. Gambhir, E., Jain, R., Gupta, A., &Tomer, U. (2020, September). Regression analysis of COVID-19 using machine learning algorithms. In *2020 International Conference on Smart Electronics and Communication (ICOSEC)* (pp. 65–71). IEEE, Trichy, India.

18. Shanmugarajeshwari, V., & Ilayaraja, M. (2021, January). Chronic kidney disease for collaborative healthcare data analytics using random forest classification algorithms. In *2021 International Conference on Computer Communication and Informatics (ICCCI)* (pp. 1–14). IEEE, Coimbatore, India.

19. Habib, M., Wang, Z., Qiu, S., Zhao, H., & Murthy, A. S. (2022). Machine learning based healthcare system for investigating the association between depression and quality of life. *IEEE Journal of Biomedical and Health Informatics*, 26(5), 2008–2019.

20. Terrada, O., Cherradi, B., Raihani, A., & Bouattane, O. (2020, April). Atherosclerosis disease prediction using supervised machine learning techniques. In *2020 1st International Conference on Innovative Research in Applied Science, Engineering and Technology (IRASET)* (pp. 1–5). IEEE, FS Meknes, Morocco.

21. Wang, X., Guo, C., & Zhou, X. (2020, September). Robust segmentation of 3D brain MRI images in cross datasets by integrating supervised and unsupervised *learning*. In *2020 10th International Conference on Information Science and Technology (ICIST)*. *IEEE*, London.

22. Rumman, M. I., Ono, N., Ohuchida, K., Huang, Md. A. A. M., & Kanaya, S. (2023, 18 January). *Feature extraction and unsupervised clustering of histopathological images of pancreatic cancer using information maximization*. In *2022 IEEE 11th Global Conference on Consumer Electronics (GCCE)*. *IEEE*, Osaka, Japan.

23. Nanyue, W., Dawei, H., Yanping, C., Youhua, Y., Zengyu, S., Liyuan, X., ... Ying, H. (2012, October). Signals analysis of pulse-diagnosis in TCM by the combination of unsupervised learning and supervised learning. In *2012 IEEE International Conference on Bioinformatics and Biomedicine Workshops* (pp. 295–298). IEEE, Philadelphia, PA.

24. Bosoni, P., Tucker, A., Bellazzi, R., Nihtyanova, S. I., & Denton, C. P. (2016, June). Combining unsupervised and supervised learning for discovering disease subclasses. In *2016 IEEE 29th International Symposium on Computer-Based Medical Systems (CBMS)* (pp. 225–226). IEEE, Dublin and Belfast.

Machine Learning for Healthcare

25. Wosiak, A., Zamecznik, A., & NiewiadomskaJarosik, K. (2016, 7 November). Supervised and unsupervised machine learning for improved identification of intrauterine growth restriction types. In *2016 Federated Conference on Computer Science and Information Systems (FedCSIS)*. IEEE, Gdansk, Poland.

26. Sasubilli, S. S., Kumar, A., & Dutt, V. (2020, 4 August). Machine learning implementation on medical domain to identify disease insights using TMS. In *2020 International Conference on Advances in Computing and Communication Engineering (ICACCE)*. IEEE, Las Vegas, NV.

27. Djuric, P. M., Quirk, J. G., & Feng, G. (2018, 23 December). *Supervised and unsupervised learning of fetal heart rate tracings with deep gaussian processes*. In *2018 14th Symposium on Neural Networks and Applications (NEUREL)*. IEEE, Belgrade, Serbia.

28. Azaria, A., & Azaria, S. (2020, 13 February). *Semi-supervised ovulation detection based on multiple properties*. In *2019 IEEE 31st International Conference on Tools with Artificial Intelligence (ICTAI)*. IEEE, Portland, Oregon.

29. Das, S., Nayak, M., Senapati, M. S., & Satapathy, J. (2022, 27 July). *Medical data classification using velocity enhanced whale optimization algorithm*. In *2021 First International Conference on Advances in Computing and Future Communication Technologies (ICACFCT)*. IEEE, Meerut, India.

30. Nair, P., Trisno, R., Baghini, M. S., Pendharkar, G., & Chung, H. (2020, 27 August). *Predicting early-stage drug induced parkinsonism using unsupervised and supervised machine learning*. In *2020 42nd Annual International Conference of the IEEE Engineering in Medicine & Biology Society (EMBC)*. IEEE, Montréal, Québec, Canada.

31. Chauhan, T., Rawat, S., Malik, S., & Singh, P. (2021, March). Supervised and unsupervised machine learning based review on diabetes care. In *2021 7th International Conference on Advanced Computing and Communication Systems (ICACCS)*. IEEE, Coimbatore, India.

32. Mazlan, A. U., Sahabudin, N. A., Remli, M. A., Ismail, N. S. N., Mohamad, M. S., & Warif, N. B. A. (2021, June). Supervised and unsupervised machine learning for cancer classification: Recent development. In *2021 IEEE International Conference on Automatic Control & Intelligent Systems (ICACIS)*. IEEE, Malaysia.

33. Yang, J. Y., & Yang, M. Q. (2006, October). Assessing protein function using a combination of supervised and unsupervised learning. In *Sixth IEEE Symposium on BioInformatics and BioEngineering (BIBE'06)*. IEEE, Arlington, VI.

34. Stiglic, G., Kocbek, S., & Kokol, P. (2009, August). Unsupervised variance based preprocessing of microarray data. *2009 22nd IEEE International Symposium on Computer-Based Medical Systems*. IEEE, Albuquerque, NM.

35. Firdaus, Q., Sigit, R., Harsono, T., & Anwar, R. (2020, September). Lung cancer detection based on CT-scan images with detection features using gray level co-occurrence matrix (GLCM) *and support vector machine (SVM) methods*. In *2020 International Electronics Symposium (IES)*. IEEE, Indonesia.

36. Ali, M., & Seto, D. (2011, December). Phylogenetic analysis of hexon and DNA polymerase genes from selected serotypes of human adenoviruses, using bioinformatics tools. *2011 IEEE 14th International MultitopicConference*. IEEE, Karachi, Pakistan.

37. Osman, A., Al-Alwawi, A., & Abdelbagi, O. (2017, August). Using DNA sequencing in diagnosis of hereditary diseases in Al-Unfeudal, *KSA*. In *2017 Joint International Conference on Information and Communication Technologies for Education and Training and International Conference on Computing in Arabic (ICCA-TICET)*. IEEE, Sudan.

38. Latha, R., & Vetrivelan, P. (2019, January). Blood viscosity based heart disease risk prediction model in edge/fog computing. In 2019 *11th International Conference on Communication Systems & Networks (COMSNETS)*. IEEE, Bengaluru, India.

39. Adnan, S. F. S., & Hashim, H. (2011, December). Implementation of MIDlet application on probability of Alzheimer' disease via mobile phone. In *2011 IEEE International Conference on Computer Applications and Industrial Electronics (ICCAIE)*. IEEE, Malaysia.

40. Zhang, J., & Chang, D. (2019, June). Semi-supervised patient similarity clustering algorithm based on electronic medical records. *IEEE Access*, 7. IEEE. DOI:10.1109/ACCESS.2019.2923333.

41. Haq, A. U., Li, J. P., Saboor, A., Khan, J., Wali, S., Ahmad, S., ... Zhou, W. (2021). Detection of breast cancer through clinical data using supervised and unsupervised feature selection techniques. *IEEE Access*, 9, 22090–22105.

42. Mazlan, A. U., bintiSahabudin, N. A., Remli, M. A., Ismail, N. S. N., Mohamad, M. S., & AbdWarif, N. B. (2021, June). Supervised and unsupervised machine learning for cancer classification: recent development. In *2021 IEEE International Conference on Automatic Control & Intelligent Systems (I2CACIS)* (pp. 392–395). IEEE, Malaysia.

43. Gao, J., Liang, F., Fan, W., Sun, Y., & Han, J. (2011). A graph-based consensus maximization approach for combining multiple supervised and unsupervised models. *IEEE Transactions on Knowledge and Data Engineering*, 25(1), 15–28.

44. McCallum, A., Nigam, K., Rennie, J., & Seymore, K. (2000). Automating the construction of internet portals with machine learning. *Information Retrieval Journal*, 3, 127–163.

45. Gadermayr, M., Gupta, L., Appel, V., Boor, P., Klinkhammer, B. M., & Merhof, D. (2019). Generative adversarial networks for facilitating stain-independent supervised and unsupervised segmentation: a study on kidney histology. *IEEE Transactions on Medical Imaging*, 38(10), 2293–2302.

46. Afrin, R., Haddad, H., &Shahriar, H. (2019, July). Supervised and unsupervised-based analytics of intensive care unit data. In *2019 IEEE 43rd Annual Computer Software and Applications Conference (COMPSAC)* (Vol. 2, pp. 417–422). IEEE, Milwaukee, WI.

47. Zhu, Z., Yin, C., Qian, B., Cheng, Y., Wei, J., & Wang, F. (2016, December). Measuring patient similarities via a deep architecture with medical concept embedding. In *2016 IEEE 16th International Conference on Data Mining (ICDM)* (pp. 749–758). IEEE, Barcelona, Spain.

48. Pereira, J., & Silveira, M. (2019, February). Learning representations from healthcare time series data for unsupervised anomaly detection. In *2019 IEEE International Conference on Big Data and Smart Computing (BigComp)* (pp. 1–7). IEEE, Kyoto, Japan.

49. Xie, T., Li, R., Zhang, X., Zhou, B., & Wang, Z. (2019, October). Research on heartbeat classification algorithm based on CART decision tree. In *2019 8th International Symposium on Next Generation Electronics (ISNE)* (pp. 1–3). IEEE, Zhengzhou, China.

50. Liu, Q., Yu, L., Luo, L., Dou, Q., & Heng, P. A. (2020). Semi-supervised medical image classification with relation-driven self-ensembling model. *IEEE Transactions on Medical Imaging*, 39(11), 3429–3440.

51. Korkmaz, Y., Dar, S. U., Yurt, M., Ozbey, M., & Cukur, T. (2022). Unsupervised MRI reconstruction via zero-shot learned adversarial transformers. *IEEE Transactions on Medical Imaging*.

52. Institute of Health Metrics and Evaluation. (2019). Global Health Data Exchange (GHDx), retrieved on August 4, 2022 from https://ghdx.healthdata.org/gbd-results-tool?params=gbd-api-2019-permalink/d780dffbe8a381b25e1416884959e88b

53. Kaur, V., & Kaur, R. (2022). *An Elucidation for Machine Learning Algorithms Used in Healthcare*. Machine Learning for Edge Computing, Taylor Francis Group.

54. Takkar, S., Kakran, A., Kaur, V., Rakhra, M., Sharma, M., Bangotra, P., & Verma, N. (2021). Recognition of imagebased plant leaf diseases using deep learning classification models. *Nature Environment and Pollution Technology*, 20, 2137–2147.

Machine Learning for Healthcare

55. Kaur, V., & Singh, A. (2021). *Role of Machine Learning in Communication Networks. Intelligent Communication and Automation Systems*, 1st Edition, Taylor & Francis Group. Boca Raton.
56. Kaur, V., Kaur, G., Dhiman, G., Bindal, R., Mishra, M. K. (2020). Adaptability of machine learning in cryptography. *Solid State Technology*, 63(4), 2874–2880.
57. Kaur, V., & Singh, A. (2015). An encryption scheme based on AES and SHA-512. *International Journal of Applied Engineering Research*, 10(10), 25207–25218.
58. Kaur, V., & Singh, A. (2013). Review of various algorithms used in hybrid cryptography. *International Journal of Computer Science and Network*, 2(6), 157–173.
59. Kaur, G., Goyal, S., & Kaur, H. (2021, December). Brief review of various machine learning algorithms. In *Proceedings of the International Conference on Innovative Computing Communication (ICICC)*. Delhi, India.
60. Kaur, G., Kaur, H., & Goyal, S. (2022). Correlation analysis between different parameters to predict cement logistics. *Innovations in Systems and Software Engineering*, 19(1), 117–127.

6 Federated Multi-Task Learning to Solve Various Healthcare Challenges

Seema Pahwa and Amandeep Kaur

6.1 INTRODUCTION

6.1.1 BACKGROUND OF HEALTHCARE CHALLENGES

Numerous issues, especially in developing nations, affect the healthcare industry, including inadequate accessibility. This has an impact on patient outcomes, service providers, and the global economy by delaying diagnosis and treatments, deteriorating health conditions, and lowering life expectancy.

Affordability: High treatment costs, pricey medications, and chronic illnesses frequently cause poverty, preventing individuals and families from accessing essential healthcare, and perpetuating a cycle of poverty and ill health [1]. As a result, affordable healthcare is a major issue in nations without universal healthcare systems.

Quality of Care: Healthcare quality is still a major problem in industrialized countries, where discrepancies in patient outcomes are caused by inconsistent standards, poor training, antiquated facilities, and a lack of established procedures, and they impact people from all walks of life.

Healthcare Workforce Shortages: Global shortages of healthcare workers arise when demand outpaces supply, leading to overworked personnel and poor patient care. To address this, deliberate expenditures in training, education, and bettering working conditions are needed to attract and retain qualified individuals [2].

Chronic conditions including diabetes, heart disease, and mental health issues are becoming more common, placing a burden on healthcare systems, necessitating ongoing, long-term treatment, and placing a substantial demand on healthcare resources.

Modern technological integration and data security issues include patient data privacy and possible sensitive information abuse [3]. To create a strong healthcare system that can satisfy the demands of a varied population via strategic investments, policy changes, and preventative care, cooperation between governments, healthcare providers, researchers, and technology specialists is essential.

6.1.2 SIGNIFICANCE OF FEDERATED LEARNING IN HEALTHCARE

Federated learning is a critical piece of technology for the healthcare industry since it revolutionizes data-driven procedures and upholds confidentiality and privacy [4]. It allows for cooperation without centralizing private healthcare information,

Federated Multi-Task Learning to Solve Various Healthcare Challenges 79

protecting patient privacy. By combining information from several sources, federated learning improves the accuracy of diagnostic evaluations and treatment predictions. It enhances research by using a variety of datasets, resulting in medicinal advancements. This decentralized method expedites medical research, encourages innovation, and improves patient outcomes in a safe and morally responsible way.

6.1.3 History

Through collaborative and decentralized learning, Federated Multi-Task Learning (FMTL), a potent tool in healthcare, solves a variety of difficulties [5]. It is especially useful in the industry where data sensitivity is crucial since it makes use of data from several sources while maintaining privacy and security. The origins of FMTL may be found in the early 2010s, when it became clear that effective, team-based, and privacy-preserving machine learning techniques were needed [6]. Collaborative learning from networked healthcare data, however research originally concentrated on creating algorithms that could learn from decentralized data sources.

FMTL picked more steam as the need for customized treatment and predictive analytics grew the potential of FMTL in generating precise and tailored healthcare models without centralizing sensitive information by introducing a federated learning technique for predicting illness development based on patient data from different institutions. A deep federated multi-task learning framework for medical image analysis [7], allowing several hospitals to cooperatively train deep neural networks for jobs like tumor identification and classification while maintaining data privacy.

The development of safe and private federated learning protocols has further hastened the deployment of FMTL in the healthcare industry. In order to ensure that patient data remained anonymous while aiding in the model's training, Bonawitz et al. introduced the idea of federated learning with differential privacy [8].

FMTL has recently been used to address a number of healthcare issues, including as illness prediction, medication development, and healthcare resource optimization. FMTL algorithms are still being improved by researchers, who use methods like transfer learning and meta-learning to improve model performance across various tasks and datasets.

6.2 DEFINITION AND CORE CONCEPTS OF UNDERSTANDING FEDERATED LEARNING

A machine learning approach called federated learning allows models to be trained across a number of decentralized edge devices or local data samples without having to exchange them. Machine learning models may be taught across several devices or servers thanks to this collaborative training approach, which protects privacy and minimizes the need to send vast volumes of data to a single place.

6.2.1 Core Concepts of Federated Learning

a. **Decentralized Data:** Federated learning includes distributing data among a number of servers or devices, including local servers located inside an enterprise, IoT (the Internet of Things) devices, and individual smartphones [9,10].

b. **Privacy Preservation:** Federated learning protects user privacy by guaranteeing that only model changes are transferred to the central server for aggregation and that raw data remains local [11].

c. **Model Updates:** Instead of delivering raw data, local devices construct gradients from their data and send them to a central server, which combines these changes to improve the overall model [12].

d. **Aggregation:** The central server collects and aggregates the model updates from various devices or servers. This aggregation can be done using techniques like averaging or weighted averaging, depending on the specific federated learning algorithm being used [13].

e. **Iterative Learning:** Federated learning uses several iterations of model updates and aggregation to improve the model's accuracy using local device information [13].

f. **Heterogeneous and Non-Independently and Identically Distributed (Non-IID) Data:** Due to the important nature and spread of the data, federated learning systems often manage non-identically distributed data that might differ dramatically among devices, making it difficult to aggregate meaningful updates [14].

g. **Communication Efficiency:** Federated learning algorithms often use methods like model compression and scarification in order to manage huge model updates, which may be expensive owing to bandwidth and time constraints [15].

h. **Security Concerns:** Federated learning systems need security precautions, such as the deployment of methods to thwart attacks like model poisoning and inference assaults and the encryption of model changes during transmission [15,16].

i. **Real-time Adaptation:** Federated learning allows real-time model adaptation on edge devices, enabling applications to swiftly respond to changing data patterns without relying on a centralized infrastructure.

Understanding fundamental ideas is essential for creating and implementing successful federated learning systems, especially in situations where data protection, effective communication, and real-time adaptability are required.

6.3 COMPARISON BETWEEN CENTRALIZED MACHINE LEARNING AND FEDERATED LEARNING

Processing of Data and Storage: In centralized machine learning data is saved and processed locally on various devices, as opposed to centralized machine learning data, which is stored and processed on a single server [17].

Sharing of Data: Centralized machine learning transfers data to a central server for training, while federated learning keeps data on the user's device, reducing privacy concerns [18].

Confidentiality: Due to the centralized nature of the data, centralized machine learning causes privacy issues, while federated learning enhances privacy by keeping the data on local devices and avoiding direct sharing [19].

Federated Multi-Task Learning to Solve Various Healthcare Challenges 81

Transmission: While federated communication decreases transmission between the server and individual devices, centralized machine learning requires constant communication between the central server and client devices. This reduces bandwidth use [18,20,21].

Ease of Use: As the number of devices grows, centralized machine learning may become a bottleneck but federated learning is extremely scalable and can support many devices without taxing the server.

Data Security: Federated learning improves security by lowering the danger of network transmission interception while centralized machine learning necessitates strong security measures for data protection.

6.4 MULTI-TASK LEARNING (MTL) IN HEALTHCARE

A method called "multi-task learning" (MTL) is used in machine learning to train a single model to do multiple tasks simultaneously [22]. Now, algorithms can diagnose illnesses, evaluate patients' risks, and prescribe treatments, among other medical tasks. The model improves with each task through learning. Since healthcare data is often expensive and difficult to obtain, MTL is a lifesaver. By training on numerous tasks at once, MTL increases model efficiency and makes it easier to generalize to new tasks or patients. Its versatility makes it a promising approach to developing individualized healthcare solutions.

6.4.1 RELEVANCE TO HEALTHCARE DATA

MTL is a machine learning paradigm where a model is trained to perform multiple tasks simultaneously. In the context of healthcare data, MTL has several important applications and advantages:

6.4.1.1 Data Efficiency

Healthcare data is often scarce and costly to acquire, but MTL enables shared patterns across tasks, making the learning process more efficient. Models can learn from related tasks to improve performance on primary tasks.

6.4.1.2 Improved Generalization

By learning many tasks simultaneously, MTL improves the generalization of machine learning models and more accurately detects underlying patterns in data. Better performance on unseen data is a result of this, which is essential in healthcare applications since it directly affects patient outcomes.

6.4.1.3 Transfer Learning

With the use of MTL, learnings from medical data analysis may be applied to related tasks like CT scans without requiring a model to be completely retrained, boosting performance on the first task.

6.4.1.4 Disease Diagnosis and Prognosis

MTL in healthcare can forecast numerous illness-related outcomes from the same patient data, giving healthcare providers a complete picture, including the existence, severity, and propensity for a disease to return.

6.4.1.5 Clinical Decision Support

By including activities pertaining to patient health, such as illness risk prediction, ideal treatment plans, and drug response, MTL assists in building reliable clinical decision support systems, improving healthcare practitioners' decision-making and patient care.

6.4.1.6 Personalized Medicine

By taking into account genetic information, lifestyle choices, and environmental variables, MTL supports personalized medicine by providing customized treatment recommendations and healthcare actions for specific patients.

6.4.1.7 Feature Learning and Representation

By simultaneously learning tasks and extracting pertinent characteristics for various activities, MTL helps in the learning of meaningful data representations. These similarities advance our comprehension of biology and disease processes by shedding light on the connections between various healthcare factors.

Enhancing prediction accuracy, facilitating transfer learning, and improving patient care and outcomes via well-informed decision-making processes are all benefits of MTL in healthcare data analysis.

6.4.2 BENEFITS OF MULTI-TASK LEARNING (MTL) IN ADDRESSING DIVERSE HEALTHCARE CHALLENGES

Healthcare organizations are increasingly turning to the MTL paradigm to solve their many complex problems. It permits the learning of many tasks simultaneously, such as illness prediction, patient risk stratification, and therapy suggestion, improving the predictive accuracy and generalizability of machine learning models. The creation of individualized healthcare options is also made easier by MTL since patients' reactions to medicines vary depending on their genetic makeup, way of life, and environment. MTL can forecast illness progression, suggest customized therapies, and evaluate the efficacy of therapy by taking into account different activities connected to specific patient profiles. This allows for the development of more individualized and successful healthcare plans [23].

MTL enables healthcare workers to concentrate on preventative actions for certain illnesses by combining various jobs into a single model, which helps to ensure effective use of healthcare resources. By minimizing pointless tests and treatments, this tailored strategy improves patient outcomes while also contributing to cost savings.

6.5 CHALLENGES IN FEDERATED MULTI-TASK LEARNING

Federated Multi-Task Learning (FMTL) is a dynamic area that integrates federated learning with MTL, bringing advantages including privacy protection and resource efficiency. It does, however, also provide certain difficulties, such as the need to strike a balance between the effective use of resources and the efficient use of resources [24].

Federated Multi-Task Learning to Solve Various Healthcare Challenges

1. **Data Heterogeneity:**
   Task Heterogeneity: Managing tasks with various needs might be difficult because of jobs with different levels of complexity and data dispersion.
   Device Heterogeneity: Because devices' processing, memory, and network bandwidth vary, federated learning environments struggle to train models effectively.

2. **Communication Efficiency:**
   Bandwidth Limitations: Transporting model updates between the central server and participating devices can be bandwidth-intensive, particularly if the model size is large.
   Communication Overhead: The system's overall efficiency might be significantly impacted by frequent communication between the central server and devices.

3. **Privacy and Security:**
   Privacy Concerns: Federated learning presents a big problem to protecting privacy when learning across several devices since it often contains sensitive data.
   Data Leakage: Since even small model changes might divulge private training data information, the learning process necessitates strict information leakage avoidance.

4. **Model Complexity:**
   Training Complex Models in federated settings can be challenging due to limited computational capacity of individual devices.
   Model Aggregation involves combining updates from multiple devices without loss of information or biases.

5. **Non-IID Data:**
   Non-IID Data: Due to variances in data distribution across various devices, traditional machine learning models may have trouble developing a global model that works effectively across all devices.

6. **Dynamic and Asynchronous Environments:**
   Federated systems require algorithms that can handle dynamic device participation and adapt to changing data distributions, as devices may join or leave dynamically, requiring adaptive learning algorithms to handle these changes.

7. **Evaluation and Benchmarking:**
   Lack of Standard Metrics: The absence of standardized evaluation metrics and benchmarks for federated multi-task learning makes it challenging to effectively compare different algorithms.
   Model Generalization: The difficult element is making sure the learnt models generalize well to unknown data from other devices, especially when working with non-IID data.

8. **Resource Constraints:**
   Computational Resources: The quality of learnt models may be impacted by the complexity of trained models being constrained by the limited processing capabilities of devices.

Energy Efficiency: Federated Multi-Task Learning is being improved on devices with limited resources by researchers and practitioners using energy-efficient algorithms, communication protocols, privacy-preserving strategies, and model designs.

6.6 ADDRESSING COMMUNICATION CHALLENGES (E.G., COMPRESSION, EDGE COMPUTING)

Federated deep learning tackles issues with edge computing and compression in communications for effective distributed machine learning across several devices. In addition to protecting privacy and lowering transmission costs, it enables model training without transmitting raw data. The following strategies are proposed to tackle these issues [25].

1. **Model Compression:**
   Quantization and knowledge distillation are techniques used to reduce model size and speed up communication by representing weights and activations with fewer bits.
   Sparsification: Pruning unnecessary weights in a model encourages sparsity, which reduces its size and improves transmission effectiveness.
   Differential Privacy: Noise addition to gradients can enhance privacy and function naturally as compression before transmission.
2. **Edge Computing:**
   On-Device Training uses local model updates on hardware with enough capacity, such edge AI (artificial intelligence) chips, to reduce the amount of data transmitted back to the main server.
   Edge Servers: By processing data closer to the source, installing local servers or edge nodes adjacent to devices may reduce latency and communication overhead.
   Federated Averaging: Federated averaging approaches can decrease communication costs by allowing devices to calculate partial model updates based on local data and only communicate these changes to the central server.
   Adaptive Learning: According to device capabilities, the learning process may be modified, for example, by providing smaller updates or simpler models to devices with constrained resources.
   Dynamic Aggregation: The frequency of aggregation can be adjusted based on network conditions and device availability to decrease communication overhead.
3. **Optimized Communication:**
   Devices may asynchronously update the central model, cutting waiting times and increasing productivity. Algorithms that are aware of the network may change their communication plans in response to changes in the network. Communication may be optimized by using hybrid strategies that combine federated learning with conventional distributed learning methods. Data integrity is ensured by error correction algorithms, which

also reduce the need for retransmission and boost communication effectiveness. Both initial training and fine-tuning may be accomplished using these techniques.

4. **Security and Privacy:**
   Federated deep learning systems use secure protocols to protect data while it is being sent, ensure differential privacy to protect sensitive information, and securely aggregate model updates using cryptographic approaches. The solution to these problems calls for algorithmic advancements, system enhancements, and privacy and security concerns. The efficiency and efficacy of federated deep learning systems will be improved through further research and development in these fields.

6.7 FUTURE TRENDS AND INNOVATIONS

6.7.1 EVOLUTION OF FEDERATED LEARNING IN HEALTHCARE

6.7.1.1 Personalized Medicine

Federated learning allows the creation of highly personalized AI models. In healthcare, this means tailoring treatments and interventions based on individual patient data. These models can adapt to the unique biological and genetic makeup of patients, leading to more effective and personalized healthcare strategies [26].

6.7.1.2 Decentralized Clinical Trials

Federated learning facilitates the conducting of clinical trials across diverse demographics and geographies without centralizing sensitive patient data. This can lead to more representative and inclusive trials, accelerating the drug discovery process and making healthcare solutions accessible to a broader population.

6.7.1.3 Real-Time Disease Surveillance

Federated learning enables real-time analysis of healthcare data from various sources. This is invaluable in monitoring disease outbreaks, understanding epidemiological trends, and deploying timely interventions. Early detection and response can significantly impact public health outcomes.

6.7.2 POTENTIAL TECHNOLOGICAL ADVANCEMENTS

6.7.2.1 Enhanced Security Protocols

Future advancements in federated learning will likely focus on robust encryption methods and privacy-preserving algorithms. Ensuring data security and privacy will be paramount, especially in highly regulated fields like healthcare.

6.7.2.2 Edge Computing Integration

Integration with edge computing devices will enhance the efficiency of federated learning algorithms. This integration will reduce latency, making real-time analysis and decision-making possible in remote or resource-constrained environments.

6.7.2.3 Federated Transfer Learning

Combining federated learning with transfer learning techniques can allow models trained on one task to be adapted efficiently for related tasks across different healthcare domains. This would significantly reduce the computational resources needed for training new models from scratch.

6.7.3 ETHICAL IMPLICATIONS AND RESPONSIBLE AI IN HEALTHCARE

6.7.3.1 Privacy Preservation

To preserve patient trust and confidence, the ethical use of federated learning requires stringent privacy protection, open data use standards, and healthcare-specific data utilization.

6.7.3.2 Bias Mitigation

AI models' quality relies on trained data, and federated learning should remove biases in healthcare data to prevent gaps in outcomes.

6.7.3.3 Regulatory Compliance

Federated deep learning has a bright future in healthcare, but to stay out of trouble and uphold moral standards, healthcare organizations must abide by constantly changing laws like General Data Protection Regulation (GDPR) and Health Insurance Portability and Accountability Act (HIPAA). To fully use this technology in healthcare, it is essential to strike a balance between innovation, ethical issues, and legal requirements.

6.8 CONCLUSION OF FEDERATED MULTI-TASK LEARNING IN HEALTHCARE

6.8.1 THE SUMMARY PROVIDES A COMPREHENSIVE OVERVIEW OF THE KEY FINDINGS

A potential strategy in the healthcare industry is federated multi-task learning (FMTL), which enables different institutions to train machine learning models without disclosing private patient information. FMTL makes it possible to create reliable and precise prediction models for a range of medical activities, including illness diagnosis, prognosis, and therapy suggestion. Via guaranteeing that data remains in its original place and is secured via encryption and secure communication methods, it allays privacy concerns.

Machine learning algorithms are more effective and efficient thanks to the collaborative model training process. FMTL also exhibits impressive scalability, allowing for the daily generation of an increasing amount of healthcare data. The magnitude of medical datasets is difficult for traditional centralized learning algorithms to manage, but FMTL spreads the learning process to guarantee real-time updates and ongoing model development.

6.8.2 The Article Explores the Probable Effects on Healthcare Solutions in the Future

By encouraging cooperative research and development, FMTL is revolutionizing healthcare by enabling medical institutions all over the world to pool resources and knowledge, resulting in the development of more precise diagnostic tools and quicker scientific discovery, ultimately improving patient outcomes and enhancing treatments.

FMTL enables personalized medicine by training models across diverse datasets, providing healthcare practitioners with insights into disease variations. This allows for personalized treatments and interventions based on individual patient profiles, maximizing efficacy and minimizing adverse effects. FMTL also integrates genomic, clinical, and imaging data, promoting a holistic approach to healthcare analytics.

6.8.3 Researchers and Practitioners Are Urged to Act Right Once to Solve the Problems That Have Been Highlighted

Federated multi-task learning (FMTL), which enables seamless cooperation and interoperability across institutions, has the potential to change the healthcare industry. To enable smooth cooperation, researchers must create standardized procedures, and practitioners must invest in safe data-sharing infrastructures that follow stringent privacy and security guidelines. The goal of research and development should be to improve the accuracy, scalability, and efficiency of federated learning algorithms. With FMTL, healthcare solutions undergo a paradigm change that balances data-driven insights with patient privacy. The future of healthcare promises more precise diagnosis, individualized treatments, and better patient outcomes as academics and practitioners collaborate to develop and use FMTL technology.

REFERENCES

1. Goudge, J., Gilson, L., Russell, S., Gumede, T., & Mills, A. (2009). Affordability, availability and acceptability barriers to health care for the chronically ill: Longitudinal case studies from South Africa. *BMC Health Services Research*, 9(1), 1–18.
2. World Health Organization. (2024). *Global Spending on Health: A World in Transition.* Retrieved https://www.who.int/health-topics/health-workforce#tab=tab_1.
3. Chernyshev, M., Zeadally, S., & Baig, Z. (2019). Healthcare data breaches: Implications for digital forensic readiness. *Journal of Medical Systems*, 43, 1–12.
4. Ali, A., Al-Rimy, B. A. S., Tin, T. T., Altamimi, S. N., Qasem, S. N., & Saeed, F. (2023). Empowering precision medicine: Unlocking revolutionary insights through blockchain-enabled federated learning and electronic medical records. *Sensors*, 23(17), 7476.
5. Shaheen, M., Farooq, M. S., Umer, T., & Kim, B. S. (2022). Applications of federated learning; Taxonomy, challenges, and research trends. *Electronics*, 11(4), 670.
6. Kumaresan, M., Kumar, M. S., & Muthukumar, N. (2022). Analysis of mobility based COVID-19 epidemic model using federated multitask learning. *Mathematical Biosciences and Engineering*, 19, 9983–10005.
7. Goncharov, M., Pisov, M., Shevtsov, A., Shirokikh, B., Kurmukov, A., Blokhin, I., ... Belyaev, M. (2021). CT-based COVID-19 triage: Deep multitask learning improves joint identification and severity quantification. *Medical Image Analysis*, 71, 102054.

8. Bonawitz, K., Ivanov, V., Kreuter, B., Marcedone, A., McMahan, H. B., Patel, S., ... Kurosawa, K. (2017). Practical secure aggregation for privacy-preserving machine learning. In *Proceedings of the 2017 ACM SIGSAC Conference on Computer and Communications Security* (pp. 1175–1191).

9. Kourtellis, N., Katevas, K., & Perino, D. (2020, December). Flaas: Federated learning as a service. In *Proceedings of the 1st Workshop on Distributed Machine Learning* (pp. 7–13).

10. Kumar, A., Sharma, S., Goyal, N., Singh, A., Cheng, X., & Singh, P. (2021). Secure and energy-efficient smart building architecture with emerging technology IoT. *Computer Communications, 176*, 207–217.

11. Shen, S., Zhu, T., Wu, D., Wang, W., & Zhou, W. (2022). From distributed machine learning to federated learning: In the view of data privacy and security. *Concurrency and Computation: Practice and Experience, 34*(16), e6002.

12. Lim, W. Y. B., Luong, N. C., Hoang, D. T., Jiao, Y., Liang, Y. C., Yang, Q., ... Miao, C. (2020). Federated learning in mobile edge networks: A comprehensive survey. *IEEE Communications Surveys & Tutorials, 22*(3), 2031–2063.

13. Zhang, C., Xie, Y., Bai, H., Yu, B., Li, W., & Gao, Y. (2021). A survey on federated learning. *Knowledge-Based Systems, 216*, 106775.

14. Luo, M., Chen, F., Hu, D., Zhang, Y., Liang, J., & Feng, J. (2021). No fear of heterogeneity: Classifier calibration for federated learning with non-iid data. *Advances in Neural Information Processing Systems, 34*, 5972–5984.

15. Kishor, K. (2022). Communication-efficient federated learning. In *Federated Learning for IoT Applications*, (ed.) Imrich Chlamtac (pp. 135–156). Cham: Springer International Publishing.

16. Guendouzi, B. S., Ouchani, S., Assaad, H. E., & Zaher, M. E. (2023). A systematic review of federated learning: Challenges, aggregation methods, and development tools. *Journal of Network and Computer Applications, 220*, 103714.

17. Shen, S., Zhu, T., Wu, D., Wang, W., & Zhou, W. (2022). From distributed machine learning to federated learning: In the view of data privacy and security. *Concurrency and Computation: Practice and Experience, 34*(16), e6002.

18. AbdulRahman, S., Tout, H., Ould-Slimane, H., Mourad, A., Talhi, C., & Guizani, M. (2020). A survey on federated learning: The journey from centralized to distributed on-site learning and beyond. *IEEE Internet of Things Journal, 8*(7), 5476–5497.

19. Xu, J., Glicksberg, B. S., Su, C., Walker, P., Bian, J., & Wang, F. (2021). Federated learning for healthcare informatics. *Journal of Healthcare Informatics Research, 5*, 1–19.

20. Agrawal, S., Sarkar, S., Aouedi, O., Yenduri, G., Piamrat, K., Alazab, M., ... Gadekallu, T. R. (2022). Federated learning for intrusion detection system: Concepts, challenges and future directions. *Computer Communications*,195, 346–361.

21. Konečný, J., McMahan, H. B., Yu, F. X., Richtárik, P., Suresh, A. T., & Bacon, D. (2016). Federated learning: Strategies for improving communication efficiency. *arXiv preprint arXiv:1610.05492*.

22. Ruder, S. (2017). An overview of multi-task learning in deep neural networks. *arXiv preprint arXiv:1706.05098*.

23. Huang, Z. A., Hu, Y., Liu, R., Xue, X., Zhu, Z., Song, L., & Tan, K. C. (2022). Federated multi-task learning for joint diagnosis of multiple mental disorders on MRI scans. *IEEE Transactions on Biomedical Engineering, 70*(4), 1137–1149.

24. Farahani, B., & Monsefi, A. K. (2023). Smart and collaborative industrial IoT: A federated learning and data space approach. *Digital Communications and Networks, 9*(2), 436–447.

25. Xia, Q., Ye, W., Tao, Z., Wu, J., & Li, Q. (2021). A survey of federated learning for edge computing: Research problems and solutions. *High-Confidence Computing, 1*(1), 100008.

26. Moingeon, P., Kuenemann, M., & Guedj, M. (2022). Artificial intelligence-enhanced drug design and development: Toward a computational precision medicine. *Drug Discovery Today, 27*(1), 215–222.

7 Smart System for Development of Cognitive Skills Using Machine Learning

Rashmi Aggarwal, Uday Devgan, Sandhir Sharma, Tanvi Verma, and Aadrit Aggarwal

7.1 INTRODUCTION

The present paper relates generally to the devices specially built to assist people in task management and maintenance. More specifically, it relates to electronic devices and methods for assisting people in developing and maintaining cognitive skills. A device for developing cognitive skills is provided according to one aspect of the present work, the device comprising a user interface, imaging sensor, speaker system, microphone, communication interface, processor, and memory unit operably linked with the processor. The memory unit of the system contains instructions that can be read by the processor. These instructions enable the processor to perform various tasks, including receiving the scheduling command from the user interface, which includes a specific date and time for an event; displaying a keyboard on the user interface based on an application that is stored in the memory unit; receiving input via the displayed keyboard; receiving visual input from the imaging sensor; receiving data through the communication interface; receiving audio input from the microphone; generating different audio outputs by way of a speaker system, each one corresponding to separate audio input (such as scheduling command, input via displayed keyboard, visual input, as well as information from the communication interface); and producing visual output that corresponds with the audio input received from the microphone.

7.2 OBJECTIVES OF THE STUDY

- To provide a device that allows a user to develop and maintain their cognitive skills
- To provide a device that allows the user to better organise their activities
- To provide a device that promotes user engagement with their activities and events
- To provide a device that incorporates the capabilities of several distinct devices into a single device thereby offering better economy and less complexity to the user

DOI: 10.1201/9781032694870-7

7.3 LITERATURE REVIEW

Attention deficit hyperactivity disorder (ADHD) is a neurodevelopmental disorder that is frequently present and characterised by impulsivity, hyperactivity, and inattention. The prevalence of this condition is higher among males compared to females, and it often persists into adulthood [1]. The functional connectivity of the brain system can be altered by a variety of illnesses, including diseases such as Alzheimer's, anxiousness, epilepsy of the temporal lobe, and ADHD, to name just a few of them. Cognitive deficit disorders are another condition that can have this effect [2]. Since ADHD is a diverse disorder, a thorough medical evaluation of the condition should always include an in-depth analysis of the patient's physical condition, a review of their medical history, and a careful evaluation of all potential illnesses and related comorbidities [3]. The neurodevelopmental disorder ADHD is frequently co-occurring with other health issues [4]. The high prevalence of comorbidities makes it more challenging and complicated. A risk factor for various mental health illnesses, resulting in adverse outcomes such as poor performance in school, career and relationship problems, and criminality, ADHD usually persists into adulthood. Children with symptoms similar to ADHD should be promptly identified and treated in order to enhance long-term outcomes [5]. Diagnostic and treatment processes may become simpler and more effective with the use of technology. With the comfort of their own devices, digital treatments, for example, the provision of an effective strategy for individuals with ADHD can facilitate the management of their symptoms, reduce financial burden, and enhance outcomes [6].

Primary concerns for parents of children with ADHD include their children's academic achievement, their own social surroundings, and their difficulty navigating the healthcare and educational systems [7]. There are various programmes available to assist youngsters diagnosed with ADHD, such as organisational and homework skills programmes, as well as targeted academic interventions are moderately helpful in enhancing academic achievements [8]. The suboptimal educational achievements among individuals diagnosed with ADHD impose constraints on their employment prospects, and income potential, and further exacerbate the substantial financial burden associated with managing ADHD. In Australia alone, the economic costs attributed to ADHD amount to over $20 billion annually [9,10]. A system was introduced to assist children with ADHD, including a toy apparatus with a speech detection module and a text reading module, however, it does not disclose a reminder module, and an arithmetic calculation module [11]. A system was patented to assist children with ADHD, including a mobile device (e.g., tablet) with a speech detection module to detect and analyse speech inputted by the child, however, it does not disclose a reminder module, an arithmetic calculation module, and a text reading module [12]. Despite the fact that medication is the primary method of treatment for kids with ADHD, alternative intervention modalities must be developed in order to optimise care for these patients. The use of a mobile device to deliver a digital treatment intervention by optimising the user experience and ensuring the therapy is convenient and pleasant to utilise within a residential environment, it is possible to improve the availability of treatment, reduce the financial burden associated with care, and increase adherence to the prescribed regimen [13]. The cognitive benefits

Smart System for Development of Cognitive Skills Using Machine Learning   **91**

derived from cognitive training through the use of digital gadgets and video games necessitate replication in real-world contexts and practical application in everyday activities. Other mental health conditions may benefit from the use of digital therapy [14,15]. It is imperative for practitioners to prioritise the consideration of comorbid conditions in children diagnosed with ADHD, as these conditions have significant implications for their academic performance and overall behavioural and psychological well-being [16,17]. Pharmacological intervention and behaviour management strategies have been found to be correlated with a decrease in the primary symptoms of ADHD and an increase in academic productivity. However, it is important to note that these interventions do not appear to have a significant impact on enhanced standardised test scores or long-term educational achievements [18–20].

Therefore, no cited references disclose all the aspects/features of the current device in the paper, that is, a system to assist a person with ADHD to improve their skills and confidence.

7.4   DETAILED DESCRIPTION AND PROPOSED SOLUTION

The device described is designed for the purpose of enhancing cognitive skills. It consists of various components, including a user interface, an image sensor, a speaker system, a microphone, a communication interface, a processor, and a memory unit. The memory unit contains machine-readable instructions that enable the processor to perform certain tasks. These tasks include receiving the scheduling command from the user interface, which specifies a date and time for an event. The device is also capable of displaying a keyboard on the user interface, based on an application that is stored in the memory unit, and receiving input from this displayed keyboard. Additionally, the device is able to receive visual input from the imaging sensor, data through the interface for communication, and audio input from the microphone, produce multiple audio outputs through the speaker system, corresponding to the scheduling command, the input received on the displayed keyboard, the visual input, and the data received from the communication interface, respectively, and generate a visual output corresponding to audio input received from the microphone.

It is envisaged that a device is provided for the development of cognitive skills in an individual and for making learning and other activities more engaging. In that regard, the device is envisaged to include several hardware features such as an imaging sensor, speakers, microphone, and communication interface, which can convert one kind of signal into another kind, for example, visual information to aural signals, to make the learning more interactive. The device is envisaged to include computing capabilities such as a processor, a memory unit, and a communication interface. The several components of the device may be integrated into a single housing or may be assembled and connected with each other through wired or wireless means. Referring to the figures, the device will now be described in further detail.

Figure 7.1 presents instrument 100 designed for the enhancement of cognitive abilities, as per an embodiment of the current innovation. The Gadget 100 is equipped with a user interface 102. User interface 102 has the capability·to function as either a capacitance or a resistive touch screen. Additionally, user interface 102 has the potential to be a touch screen that utilises TFT (thin film transistor), LCD (liquid

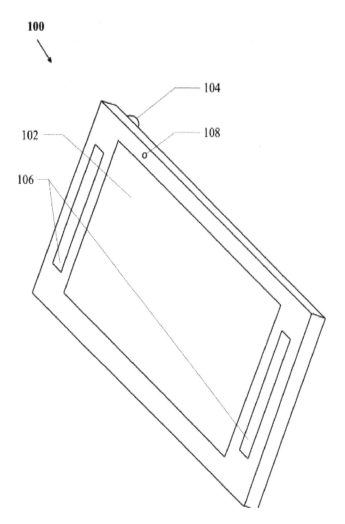

FIGURE 7.1 Perspective view of a device for the development of cognitive skills.

crystal display), or LED (light-emitting diode) technology. The touch screen has the potential to be integrated within the physical structure of the device 100, or alternatively the device 100 might have separate modules for its user interface 102 and the processing unit. The Gadget 100 is equipped with imaging sensors 104. In multiple variations of the innovation, the positioning of the imaging sensors 104 is situated on the side that is opposed to the user interface 102. In several alternative configurations of the innovation, the imaging sensors 104 may be situated at multiple positions on the device 100, encompassing both the front and rear sides of the device 100. In numerous other examples of the invention, the imaging sensors 104 may not be physically integrated into the body of device 100. Instead, it may be connected to the device 100 using wired or wireless methods, such as Bluetooth. Additionally, the device 100 is equipped with the speaker system 106. The speaker system 106 has the

Smart System for Development of Cognitive Skills Using Machine Learning

capability to function as either the stereo or mono speaker system. Speaker system 106 might include one or two speakers, situated either on the front, back, or lateral surfaces of the gadget 100, contingent upon its arrangement. In addition, the Gadget 100 is equipped with a microphone. The device is designed to be set up in a manner that allows it to accept audio inputs from either a user or other external devices. It should be acknowledged that device 100 comprises multiple components that might not be externally observable but are internally included within the device's casing. Overall logical diagram of device is shown in Figure 7.2.

In addition to the components, the device also comprises a non-volatile storage device, a communication interface, a CPU (central processing unit), and a memory unit. The storage device 110 is anticipated to function as a non-volatile memory device, specifically a solid-state drive (SSD), electrically erasable programmable read-only memory (EEPROM), erasable programmable read-only memory (EPROM), or flash memory. Memory unit 116 is intended to function as a volatile memory unit, such as Random Access Memory (RAM). The memory unit 116 is designed to contain

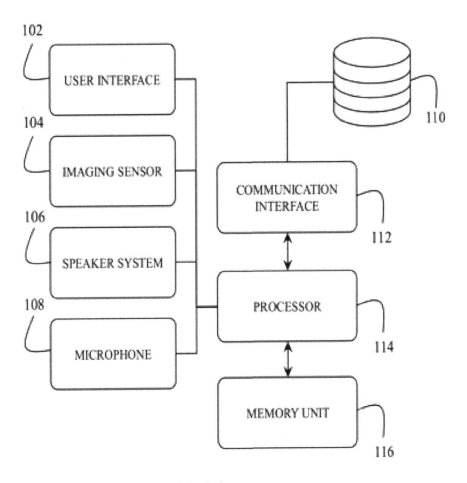

FIGURE 7.2 Logical diagram of the device.

machine-readable instructions that, when processed by the processor 114, allow the processor 114 to carry out various commands. However, it should be noted that a person with expertise in this field would recognise that the Gadget 100 is not constrained to the architecture outlined previously and has the potential to incorporate various other architectures while remaining within the boundaries of the invention. The flow of scheduling command is shown in Figure 7.3.

In various iterations of the innovation, the enhancement of cognitive abilities involves the user issuing a scheduling command to the processor 114 via the user interface 102. The scheduling function in question involves specifying both a date and a time for an event, with the purpose of setting up a reminder for the user. Processor 114 is responsible for storing the scheduling details, including the date, time, and location of the event, in storage device 110. As the event's date and time draw near, processor 114 has the capability to generate audio output in the form of alarms and notifications, which are then transmitted through speaker System 106. Multiple alerts and notifications can be implemented in various embodiments, occurring at distinct time periods. As an illustration, the alerts and notifications can be scheduled to be delivered in advance of the event, such as 1 week prior, 1 day prior, 1 hour prior, or at intervals of 15 minutes commencing 1 hour prior to the event. Furthermore, it should be noted that the audio output, namely in the form of alarms and notifications, has the

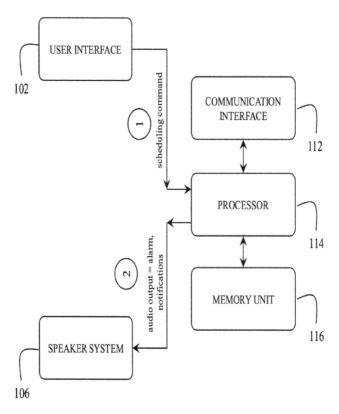

FIGURE 7.3 Flow diagram for the handling of a scheduling command.

Smart System for Development of Cognitive Skills Using Machine Learning 95

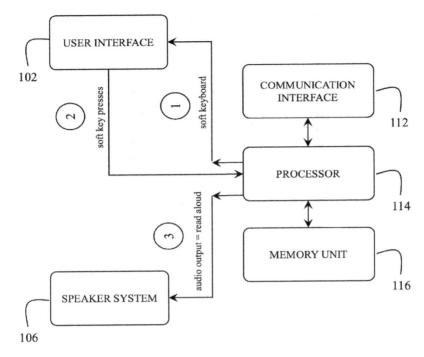

FIGURE 7.4 Flow diagram for generating and responding to a soft keyboard.

potential to increase in volume and duration as the event draws nearer. This feature enables users to receive continuous reminders regarding events or activities, hence minimising the likelihood of missing out on significant engagements. Consequently, users experience less cognitive burden associated with memorisation and recollection of these events or activities, ultimately leading to improved productivity. The flow diagram for generating and responding to a soft keyboard is shown in Figure 7.4. The processor 114 has the capability to present a virtual keyboard that corresponds to a certain application stored within the memory unit 116. Additionally, it is able to accept input from this virtual keyboard.

The user interface 102 shows a soft keyboard from processor 114. The soft keyboard may represent a calculator or qwerty keyboard app. The processor 114 may generate numerous musical tones from the speaker system 106 for each key push. The audio output may be a read-aloud of the key hit, text written on a word processor, or the user's math result. Aural feedback will let the user know if they pushed the proper key. It will also assist users in learning fundamental calculations. The processor 114 also outputs audio to help users read and understand books, periodicals, magazines, as well as other textual material is shown in Figure 7.5. When the user has short attention span or is cooking, driving, and visually monitoring other activities, audio output is vital. In such a situation, the individual would struggle to read material from a book or electronic device.

Imaging sensor 104 may receive book and journal images. Imaging sensor 104 might photograph books, journals, and any other textual data and save them in

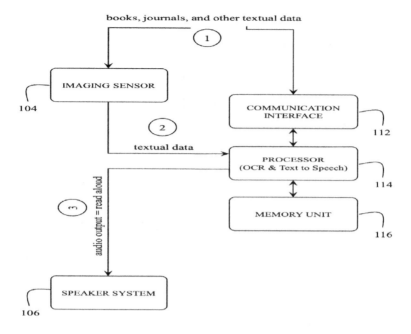

FIGURE 7.5 Flow diagram of the handling of books, journals, and other textual data.

a storage device 110. Books, journals, and other types of textual content may also be received through communications interface 112, such as on a flash drive connected to the device 100's universal serial bus (USB) port. Optical Character Recognition (OCR) would then be performed by the processor 114 on visual data from the imaging sensor 104 or books and journals received over the communication link 112. After OCR, text-to-speech processing would enable the processor 114 to produce audio through the speaker's system 106. Reading books and journals aloud will be audio output. Thus, the user can conduct other tasks without always staring at the gadget 100. The processor 114 may perform natural language processing (NLP) on user-provided audio speech input is shown in Figure 7.6.

Through NLP, the user's spoken words would appear on the interface 102 as they are input via the microphone 108. The user might use this to check for typos in his grammar, spelling, phonetics, and punctuation as he speaks. The device 100 is novel in this sense since it performs the functions of multiple devices simultaneously is shown in Figure 7.7.

At step 210, one or more of these occur: the system receives a scheduling command with a date and time, a keyboard for an application, visual input from the imaging sensor 104, and textual data from the communication interface 112 (e.g., images of books, journals, etc.). To respond to step 210, step 220 does one or more of the following: In reaction to both the scheduling command and keyboard input, audio output is generated as alarms and notifications and the flowchart is shown in Figure 7.8. OCR and/or text-to-speech conversion are performed on the visual input obtained

Smart System for Development of Cognitive Skills Using Machine Learning

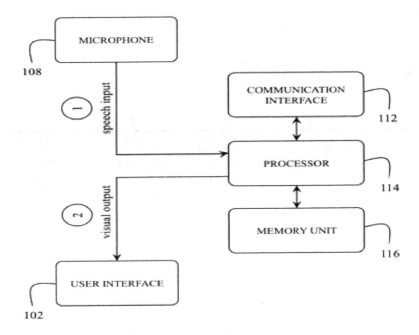

FIGURE 7.6 Flow diagram for the handling of speech input.

from the imaging sensor 104 as well as textual data received via the communication interface 112, and NLP is performed on the audio input from the microphone 108 to generate a visual output.

The system 300 has input 310, display 320, audio 330, and processing engine 340. The communications interface 112, processor 114, and memory unit 116 comprise the processing engine 340. The input module 310 receives scheduling commands, keyed-in input, visual input, communication interface data, and audio input from the microphone 108. Display module 320 displays a keyboard on the user's interface 102 and displays audio input from a microphone 108. The audio module 330 generates audio outputs through the speakers' system 106 for the scheduling command, keyboard input, visual input, and communication interface 112 data. The input module 310, display module 320, and audio module 330 communicate via the processing engine 340. The principles associated with the various embodiments described herein may be applied to other embodiments. Thus, the invention is expected to include all other alternatives, changes, and variations within its breadth and appended claims.

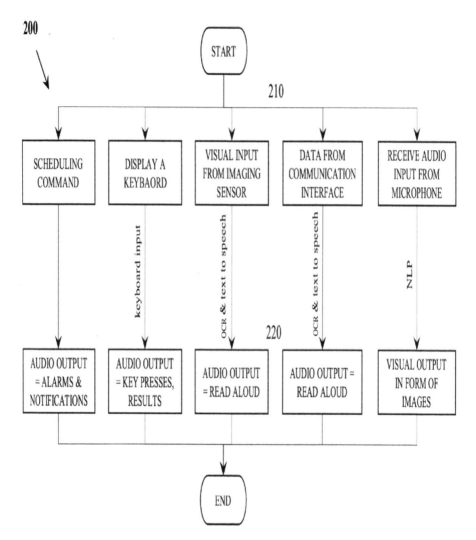

FIGURE 7.7 Method for the development of cognitive skills in accordance with an embodiment.

7.5 CONCLUSION

The proposed device provides a single device with several capabilities combined for the development of cognitive skills of the user, such as speech, and visual capabilities. The device promotes the engagement of the user with their events and activities thereby assisting people who have relatively short attention spans. The device provides economy and ease of usage as the construction of the device is simple and relatable to the user. The device proposed for the enhancement of cognitive abilities in the present investigation comprises a memory unit that is functionally linked to a processor. This memory unit contains instructions that can be read by a machine and, once executed by a processor, will enable it to receive the scheduling command from a user interface. The scheduling command comprises a specific date and time for an

Smart System for Development of Cognitive Skills Using Machine Learning

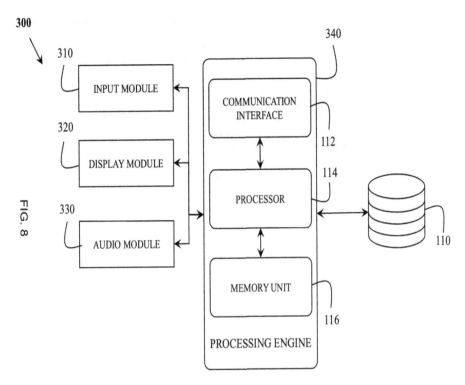

FIGURE 7.8 System for the development of cognitive skills in accordance with an embodiment.

event. Furthermore, the processor is capable of displaying the keyboard on the user interface, based on an application that is stored in a memory unit, and receiving input from the displayed keyboard. Furthermore, the processor can receive visual input from an imaging sensor, data through a communication interface, and audio input from a microphone. It is also capable of generating multiple audio outputs and a visual output.

REFERENCES

1. Vahia, V. N. (2013). Diagnostic and statistical manual of mental disorders 5: A quick glance. *Indian Journal of Psychiatry*, 55(3), 220–223.
2. Khullar, V., Salgotra, K., Singh, H. P., & Sharma, D. P. (2021). Deep learning-based binary classification of ADHD using resting state MR images. *Augmented Human Research*, 6(1), 5.
3. Bélanger, S. A., Andrews, D., Gray, C., & Korczak, D. (2018). ADHD in children and youth: Part 1-Etiology, diagnosis, and comorbidity. *Paediatrics & Child Health*, 23(7), 447–453.
4. Mohammadi, M.R., Zarafshan, H., Khaleghi, A., Ahmadi, N., Hooshyari, Z., Mostafavi, S.A., Ahmadi, A., Alavi, S.S., Shakiba, A., Salmanian, M. (2021). Prevalence of ADHD and its comorbidities in a population-based sample. *Journal of Attention Disorders*, 25(8), 1058–1067.

5. Sayal, K., Prasad, V., Daley, D., Ford, T., & Coghill, D. (2018). ADHD in children and young people: Prevalence, care pathways, and service provision. *The Lancet Psychiatry*, 5(2), 175–186.

6. Mishra, S. K., Sharma, A., & Khullar, V. (2023, February). Technological intervention system for attention deficit hyperactivity disorder. In *2023 3rd International Conference on Innovative Practices in Technology and Management (ICIPTM)* (pp. 1–6). IEEE, Uttar Pradesh, India.

7. Pajo, B., & Cohen, D. (2012). The problem with ADHD: Researchers' constructions and parents' accounts. *International Journal of Early Childhood*, 45(1), 11–33.

8. Langberg, J. M., Molina, B. S. G., Arnold, L. E., Epstein, J. N., Altaye, M., Hinshaw, S. P., Swanson, J. M., Wigal, T., & Hechtman, L. (2011). Patterns and predictors of adolescent academic achievement and performance in a sample of children with attention-deficit/hyperactivity disorder. *Journal of Clinical Child and Adolescent Psychology*, 40(4), 519–531.

9. Zendarski, N., Guo, S., Sciberras, E., Efron, D., Quach, J., Winter, L., Bisset, M., Middeldorp, C. M., & Coghill, D. (2022). Examining the educational gap for children with ADHD and subthreshold ADHD. *Journal of Attention Disorders*, 26(2), 282–295.

10. DuPaul, G. J., Eckert, T. L., & Vilardo, B. (2012). The effects of school-based interventions for attention deficit hyperactivity disorder: A meta-analysis 1996-2010. *School Psychology Review*, 41(4), 387–412.

11. Cohen, M., & Sege, A. (2015). U.S. Patent No. 9,039,482. Washington, DC: U.S. Patent and Trademark Office.

12. Celenk, U. (2019). Eurpoean Patent No. 3,867,894. Interactive artificial intelligence controlled education system.

13. Davis, N. O., Bower, J., & Kollins, S. H. (2018). Proof-of-concept study of an at-home, engaging, digital intervention for pediatric ADHD. *PLoS One*, 13(1), e0189749.

14. Pandian, G. S. B., Jain, A., Raza, Q., & Sahu, K. K. (2021). Digital health interventions (DHI) for the treatment of attention deficit hyperactivity disorder (ADHD) in children-a comparative review of literature among various treatment and DHI. *Psychiatry Research*, 297, 113742.

15. Kollins, S. H., DeLoss, D. J., Cañadas, E., Lutz, J., Findling, R. L., Keefe, R. S., ... Faraone, S. V. (2020). A novel digital intervention for actively reducing severity of paediatric ADHD (STARS-ADHD): A randomised controlled trial. *The Lancet Digital Health*, 2(4), e168–e178.

16. Barnard-Brak, L., Sulak, T. N., & Fearon, D. D. (2011). Coexisting disorders and academic achievement among children with ADHD. *Journal of Attention Disorders*, 15(6), 506–515.

17. Crawford, S. G., Kaplan, B. J., & Dewey, D. (2006). Effects of coexisting disorders on cognition and behavior in children with ADHD. *Journal of Attention Disorders*, 10(2), 192–199.

18. Loe, I. M., & Feldman, H. M. (2007). Academic and educational outcomes of children with ADHD. *Journal of Pediatric Psychology*, 32(6), 643–654.

19. Mechler, K., Banaschewski, T., Hohmann, S., & Häge, A. (2022). Evidence-based pharmacological treatment options for ADHD in children and adolescents. *Pharmacology & Therapeutics*, 230, 107940.

20. Adamo, N., Seth, S., & Coghill, D. (2015). Pharmacological treatment of attention-deficit/hyperactivity disorder: Assessing outcomes. *Expert Review of Clinical Pharmacology*, 8(4), 383–397.

8 Patient-Driven Federated Learning (PD-FL)
An Overview

A. Menaka Devi and V. Megala

8.1 INTRODUCTION

Healthcare is experiencing a transformative phase, driven by advancements in artificial intelligence (AI) and machine learning (ML). Deep Learning, in particular, has shown remarkable promise in diagnosing diseases, predicting patient outcomes, and personalizing treatment plans. Deep learning applications in healthcare, however, face significant obstacles, particularly with regard to data security, privacy, and compliance with legal frameworks like the General Data Protection Regulation (GDPR) in Europe and the Health Insurance Portability and Accountability Act (HIPAA) in the United States.

Federated Deep Learning (FDL) has emerged as a solution to these challenges. FDL enables the training of ML models across decentralized data sources, such as multiple healthcare institutions, without the need to centralize sensitive patient data. This chapter serves as a practical guide to understanding FDL in the context of healthcare, outlining its implementation steps, highlighting potential opportunities, and addressing the associated challenges.

With the recent incorporation of cutting-edge technology like AI and ML, the healthcare sector has recently undergone a significant shift. FDL, one of these breakthroughs, stands out as a potent strategy with a lot of potential for real-time healthcare applications. To address the specific difficulties and possibilities in healthcare, FDL combines the strengths of federated learning with the capabilities of deep learning. In this chapter, we examine how FDL is used in real-world healthcare settings and the effects it has on patient care and scientific investigation.

8.2 REAL-TIME USAGE

8.2.1 PERSONALIZED TREATMENT PLANS

Healthcare professionals may now design individualized treatment regimens for patients in real time thanks to FDL. FDL may create patient-specific models by combining data from many sources, such as electronic health records (EHRs), medical imaging, and genetic data. To suggest customized treatment plans, these models take into consideration a patient's particular medical history, genetic predispositions, and present state of health. This degree of customization might enhance the effectiveness of the therapy and lessen unfavourable side effects, which will eventually improve patient outcomes.

DOI: 10.1201/9781032694870-8

8.2.2 Predictive Analytics for Disease Management

The treatment of diseases benefits greatly from the real-time capabilities of FDL. FDL can continually analyse patient-generated data, such as glucose levels, blood pressure, and lung function, for chronic illnesses including diabetes, heart disease, and asthma. By doing this, it can offer timely insights and suggestions to patients and healthcare professionals to help them manage these disorders better. For instance, depending on the patient's real-time health data, FDL may recommend lifestyle modifications, medication reminders, or adjustments to insulin dose.

8.2.3 Rapid Drug Discovery and Clinical Trials

In pharmaceutical research, FDL shows a vital role in accelerating drug discovery and clinical trials. Researchers can collaborate across institutions and share insights without sharing sensitive patient data directly. Real-time data analysis permits for the identification of potential drug candidates, monitoring of drug responses in real-world patient populations, and adapting clinical trial protocols on the fly. This agility leads to faster drug development and reduced time to market for new treatments.

8.2.4 Ethical Considerations and Data Security

While the benefits of real-time FDL in healthcare are evident, ethical considerations and data security remain paramount. To ensure patient privacy and compliance with regulations such as HIPAA and GDPR, FDL employs privacy-preserving techniques like federated learning with secure aggregation. These techniques allow model updates to be shared securely without exposing sensitive patient information.

8.2.5 The Traditional Healthcare Data Landscape – An Overview

FDL has begun as an innovative technology in healthcare, enabling collaboration and data-driven insights while maintaining data privacy and security. This chapter discovers a unique approach to FDL for healthcare called Patient-Driven Federated Learning (PD-FL). PD-FL places patients at the centre of the healthcare data ecosystem, empowering them to actively participate in research, diagnostics, and treatment decisions while safeguarding their sensitive health information.

Traditionally, healthcare data has been siloed within institutions, creating barriers to research and limiting the potential for personalized medicine. Healthcare providers and researchers faced challenges accessing diverse patient data and leading to generalized treatments and slower medical discoveries. Moreover, patients often limited control over the health data and lack transparency regarding its use.

8.3 PD-FL: A PARADIGM SHIFT IN HEALTHCARE DATA SHARING

PD-FL introduces a paradigm shift by putting patients in control of their health data while promoting collaborative research and personalized healthcare. Here's how it works:

Patient-Driven Federated Learning

8.3.1 PATIENT DATA OWNERSHIP AND CONSENT

In the PD-FL model, patients own their health data and have the right consent to its use for research and treatment. Patients can choose to share their data strongly with healthcare providers, research institutions, and pharmaceutical companies for specific purposes, such as clinical trials or disease research.

8.3.2 FEDERATED LEARNING FRAMEWORK

A federated learning framework is established, connecting healthcare providers, researchers, and patients. This framework consists of secure communication channels and data anonymization techniques to safeguard patient confidentiality. Patients' data remains decentralized and under their control.

8.3.3 PATIENT-MANAGED HEALTH PROFILES

Patients maintain their health profiles, which include medical records, diagnostic reports, wearable device data, and treatment histories. These profiles are stored in secure, patient-controlled repositories. Patients can grant access to their profiles to healthcare providers and researchers when needed.

8.3.4 CUSTOMIZED MACHINE LEARNING MODELS

Healthcare providers and researchers can request access to specific patient data profiles or cohorts for research or diagnostic purposes. Upon patient consent, ML mockups are trained on the patient's data within the federated learning framework. These models are tailored to individual patient.

8.3.5 PATIENT COLLABORATION IN RESEARCH

Patients become active participants in research initiatives. They can choose to collaborate with researchers on disease studies, treatment optimization, or clinical trials. Patients benefit from personalized treatment recommendations constructed on the models trained on their data.

8.3.6 DATA MONETIZATION AND INCENTIVES

Patients can opt to monetize the usage of their data for research and development efforts. Pharmaceutical companies and research institutions compensate patients for data sharing, creating an ecosystem of incentives for patients to subsidize to medical advancements.

8.4 BENEFITS OF PD-FL IN HEALTHCARE

PD-FL offers a variety of unique benefits that have the likely to revolutionize healthcare:

8.4.1 Patient-Centric Care

Patients re-claim control over their health data, ensuring their privacy and security. They actively participate in treatment decisions and research initiatives, leading to more patient-centric healthcare.

8.4.2 Personalized Medicine

PD-FL enables the creation of highly personalized ML mockups that study each patient's unique health profile. Treatment recommendations are tailored to individual needs and responses.

8.4.3 Accelerated Research

By granting researchers access to their data, patients accelerate the pace of medical research. Collaborative efforts lead to faster disease understanding, drug development, and treatment breakthroughs.

8.4.4 Data Monetization

Patients have the option to monetize their data contributions, creating a new revenue creek while auxiliary healthcare advancements. This incentivizes patients to actively participate in the healthcare data ecosystem.

8.4.5 Enhanced Transparency

Patients gain full transparency into how their facts is used and who accesses it. This transparency builds trust and empowers patients to make informed assessments about data sharing.

8.4.6 Ethical Data Use

PD-FL prioritizes ethical data use. Patients have the final say in how their data is used, ensuring that it aligns with their values and preferences.

8.5 CHALLENGES AND CONSIDERATIONS

While PD-FL presents a promising approach to healthcare data sharing, several challenges and considerations must be addressed:

8.5.1 Data Standardization

Ensuring that patient data from various cradles adheres to common standards is crucial for actual ML model training. Data standardization efforts need to be coordinated.

Patient-Driven Federated Learning

8.5.2 DATA SECURITY

Maintaining the security of patient data repositories is paramount. Robust encryption, authentication, and access control mechanisms are necessary to avoid data breaches.

8.5.3 INFORMED CONSENT

Clear and understandable informed consent processes must be in place to ensure that patients fully comprehend the implications of sharing their data for research and treatment.

8.5.4 DATA QUALITY

Ensuring the quality and accuracy of patient-contributed data is essential for the reliability of ML models.

8.5.5 REGULATORY COMPLIANCE

PD-FL must comply with existing healthcare regulations, such as HIPAA and GDPR. Legal frameworks must be adapted to accommodate this patient-centric model.

8.5.6 PATIENT EDUCATION

Patients need to be educated about the benefits and risks of PD-FL. Healthcare providers and researchers must communicate effectively to build patient trust.

PD-FL represents a groundbreaking approach to healthcare data sharing and AI-driven medicine. By placing patients at the centre of the data ecosystem, PD-FL empowers individuals to take control of their health data, participate in research, and benefit from personalized treatments. While challenges exist, the potential for accelerated medical advancements, enhanced data privacy, and a patient-centric healthcare system make PD-FL a promising paradigm for the future of healthcare. As the healthcare industry continues to embrace data-driven approaches, PD-FL stands as a beacon of patient empowerment and collaboration in the pursuit of better health outcomes.

8.6 PRACTICAL IMPLEMENTATION OF FEDERATED DEEP LEARNING IN HEALTHCARE

Data Preparation and Preprocessing: The success of FDL in healthcare hinges on the availability of diverse, high-quality data. Healthcare organizations must ensure that data is clean, well-structured, and compliant with privacy regulations. This section provides insights into data collection, preprocessing, and anonymization techniques.

Federated Learning Frameworks: Understanding the technical underpinnings of federated learning frameworks is crucial. We discuss popular frameworks like TensorFlow Federated (TFF) and PySyft and provide practical guidance on how to set up and configure these frameworks for healthcare applications.

Secure Communication: Maintaining data security during the federated learning process is paramount. We delve into secure communication protocols, encryption techniques, and best practices for safeguarding data while it is in transit.

Model Architecture: Designing the right deep learning architecture for healthcare tasks is essential. We explore various architectures suitable for tasks such as medical image analysis, clinical text processing, and predictive modelling.

Model Aggregation and Evaluation: Federated learning involves aggregating model updates from multiple participants. We discuss aggregation techniques like Federated Averaging and Federated Stochastic Gradient Descent (FSGD). Additionally, we address methods for evaluating federated models' performance and ensuring model fairness.

8.7 CHALLENGES IN FEDERATED DEEP LEARNING FOR HEALTHCARE

Data Heterogeneity: Healthcare data is highly heterogeneous, varying across institutions, modalities, and formats. This section explores strategies to handle data diversity within the federated learning framework.

Privacy and Security: Protecting patient data is of utmost importance. We discuss privacy-preserving techniques, secure model aggregation, and the role of trusted aggregators in FDL.

Regulatory Compliance: Complying with healthcare regulations is a non-negotiable requirement. We cover the challenges of adhering to HIPAA, GDPR, and other regional data protection laws while implementing FDL.

Communication Overhead: Federated learning involves frequent communication between participants, which can result in significant overhead. We address ways to minimize communication costs and optimize the federated learning process.

Bias and Fairness: Ensuring fairness in healthcare AI models is crucial to avoid perpetuating biases. We explore methods for detecting and mitigating bias in federated learning.

8.8 OPPORTUNITIES IN FEDERATED DEEP LEARNING FOR HEALTHCARE

Collaborative Research: FDL facilitates collaborative research among healthcare institutions, enabling the pooling of knowledge and resources for tackling complex healthcare challenges.

Data Sharing without Data Leakage: Healthcare organizations can share insights and improve patient care without compromising sensitive data, fostering trust and cooperation.

Personalized Medicine: FDL enables the development of personalized treatment plans by leveraging data from multiple sources, resulting in more effective healthcare interventions.

Real-time Monitoring: The ability to update models without centralizing data allows for real-time monitoring and early detection of disease outbreaks and adverse events.

Reduced Costs: FDL can potentially reduce the computational and infrastructure costs associated with healthcare AI, making it more accessible to smaller institutions and resource-constrained regions.

8.9 CONCLUSION

FDL holds great promise for revolutionizing healthcare by harnessing the power of deep learning while respecting privacy and security concerns. This chapter has provided a comprehensive guide to implementing FDL in healthcare, addressing the practical steps, challenges, and opportunities in this domain. As the healthcare industry continues to embrace AI and ML, FDL emerges as a vital tool for ensuring ethical, secure, and collaborative advancements in patient care. However, healthcare organizations must remain vigilant in addressing privacy, security, and regulatory compliance to fully realize the potential benefits of FDL. With careful planning and adherence to best practices, the future of healthcare looks brighter than ever, thanks to FDL.

BIBLIOGRAPHY

Cheng, V.S., Hung, P.C., 2006. Health insurance portability and accountability act (hippa) compliant access control model for web services. *International Journal of Healthcare I nformation Systems and Informatics (IJHISI)* 1(1), 22–39.

Ghassemi, M., Oakden-Rayner, L., Beam, A.L., 2021. The false hope of current approaches to explainable artificial intelligence in health care. *The Lancet Digital Health* 3(11), e745–e750

Healthcare Information and Management Systems Society - **HIMSS (www.himss.org)**

Kaissis, G., Ziller, A., Passerat-Palmbach, J., Ryffel, T., Usynin, D., Trask, A., Lima, I., Mancuso, J., Jungmann, F., Steinborn, M.M., et al., 2021. End-to-end privacy preserving deep learning on multi-institutional medical imaging. *Nature Machine Intelligence* 3(6), 473–484.

Li, Q., Wen, Z., Wu, Z., Hu, S., Wang, N., Li, Y., Liu, X., He, B., 2021. A survey on federated learning systems: vision, hype and reality for data privacy and protection. *IEEE Transactions on Knowledge and Data Engineering.* https://doi.org/10.1109/TKDE.2021.3124599

Long, G., Shen, T., Tan, Y., Gerrard, L., Clarke, A., Jiang, J., 2022. Federated learning for privacy-preserving open innovation future on digital health. In: Chen, F., Zhou, J. (eds), *Humanity Driven AI*, pp. 113–133. Springer. https://doi.org/10.1007/978-3-030-72188-6.

Muhammad, G., Alshehri, F., Karray, F., El Saddik, A., Alsulaiman, M., Falk, T.H., 2021. A comprehensive survey on multimodal medical signals fusion for smart healthcare systems. *Information Fusion* 76, 355–375.

Peng, Y., Zhang, Y., Wang, L., 2010. Guest editorial: Artificial intelligence in biomedical engineering and informatics: An introduction and review. *Artificial Intelligence in Medicine* 48(2–3), 71–73.

Rahman, K.J., Ahmed, F., Akhter, N., Hasan, M., Amin, R., Aziz, K.E., Islam, A.M., Mukta, M.S.H., Islam, A.N., 2021. Challenges, applications and design aspects of federated learning: A survey. *IEEE Access* 9, 124682–124700.

Sarker, S., Jamal, L., Ahmed, S.F., Irtisam, N., 2021. Robotics and artificial intelligence in healthcare during covid-19 pandemic: A systematic review. *Robotics and Autonomous Systems* 146, 103902

Shickel, B., Tighe, P.J., Bihorac, A., Rashidi, P., 2017. Deep EHR: A survey of recent advances in deep learning techniques for electronic health record (EHR) analysis. *IEEE Journal of Biomedical and Health Informatics* 22(5), 1589–1604.

Truong, N., Sun, K., Wang, S., Guitton, F., Guo, Y., 2021. Privacy preservation in federated learning: An insightful survey from the GDPR perspective. *Computers & Security* 110, 102402

Warnat-Herresthal, S., Schultze, H., Shastry, K.L., Manamohan, S., Mukherjee, S., Garg, V., Sarveswara, R., Händler, K., Pickkers, P., Aziz, N.A., et al., 2021. Swarm learning for decentralized and confidential clinical machine learning. *Nature* 594(7862), 265–270.

Yang, Q., Liu, Y., Chen, T., Tong, Y., 2019. Federated machine learning: Concept and applications. *ACM Transactions on Intelligent Systems and Technology (TIST)* 10(2), 1–19.

Yu, K.H., Beam, A.L., Kohane, I.S., 2018. Artificial intelligence in healthcare. *Nature Biomedical Engineering* 2(10), 719–731.

Zhang, C., Xie, Y., Bai, H., Yu, B., Li, W., Gao, Y., 2021. A survey on federated learning. *Knowledge-Based Systems* 216, 106775.

9 An Explainable and Comprehensive Federated Deep Learning in Practical Applications

Real World Benefits and Systematic Analysis Across Diverse Domains

Khalid Aziz, Sakshi Dua, and Prabal Gupta

9.1 INTRODUCTION

Shaheen et al. (2022) (Figure 9.1) explain in detail the applications of Federated Deep Learning (FDL); it has a great impact on healthcare, IoT (Internet of Things), banking and finance, and much more. FDL, a dynamic and innovative paradigm of distributed machine learning (ML), has emerged as a beacon of progress in recent years. Its remarkable ability to empower model training across decentralized data sources, without necessitating centralized data aggregation, has unlocked transformative potential across various domains. This chapter embarks on an extensive exploration of FDL, unveiling its manifold benefits and profound impact across a diverse spectrum of fields. FDL stands as a powerful enabler, fostering innovation and progress across diverse domains. Its capacity to leverage data from multiple sources while preserving privacy and security has propelled it to the forefront of technological advancement (Darzidehkalani et al., 2022). This chapter mainly examines its applications and techniques, illuminating the pivotal role it plays in healthcare, privacy preservation, advanced data analytics, and beyond. In the healthcare sector, FDL emerges as a beacon of hope, enhancing diagnostic accuracy, improving patient care, and facilitating predictive modeling (Darzidehkalani et al., 2022). This chapter delves into its utilization in medical imaging, where it drives advancements in image recognition, interpretation, and analysis. In an era marked by data-driven decisions, FDL addresses the critical concerns of privacy and security. This chapter delves deep into the strategies and techniques employed to safeguard sensitive information in FDL scenarios. This chapter explores its intersection with IoT security, telemedicine, and the integration of blockchain technologies to fortify data privacy. To build a robust

DOI: 10.1201/9781032694870-9

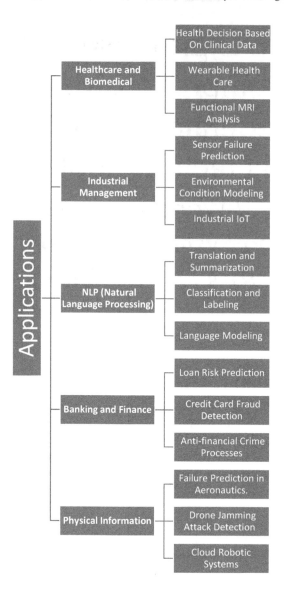

FIGURE 9.1 Applications of federated learning.

foundation, this chapter embarks on an in-depth analysis of the core principles, methodologies, and innovations that shape FDL. The journey spans a diverse array of topics, from swarm-based frameworks for IoT devices to decentralized data evaluation techniques. It tackles the formidable challenge of addressing data imbalance and non-IIDness commonly encountered in federated settings. Moreover, this chapter explores practical aspects, including federated model deployments, hyper-parameter optimization (HPO), and communication-efficient frameworks in smart grids. This chapter provides a meticulously structured framework to navigate the expansive

Comprehensive Federated Deep Learning in Practical Applications

landscape of FDL. As readers embark on this multifaceted journey, they will gain a profound understanding of this revolutionary ML paradigm and its transformative potential. FDL is poised to reshape data utilization and protection across diverse fields, fostering innovation and progress in today's data-centric world. The application of federated learning is shown in Figure 9.1.

9.2 RELATED WORK

Federal Learning (FL) is a development method for solving data distribution problems. A lot of research has been done to develop new models to develop this new learning machine, but there is some work to evaluate the methods, new ones and studies showing the methods. In this section, these studies are reviewed.

Wang et al. (2023) introduced a Swarm-Federated Deep Learning framework in the IoV (Internet of Vehicles) system IoV-SFDL (Internet of Vehicles-Swarm Federated Deep Learning), which integrates SL (Swarm Learning) and FDL (Federated Deep Learning) framework. IoV-SFDL prepares vehicles and adjacent vehicles to build a local SL model based on blockchain-powered SL, and then combines the global FDL model of different SL groups with trust weight estimation to learn how to change the number of N cars in the background. different situations. The main characters used in this study are as follows. Onboard (Global Positioning System) GPS, radar systems, cameras, and other onboard sensors can record vehicles in real time. This allows each vehicle to be represented as (V, P, E).

$$V = \left\{ vi \mid i \in \{1,2,3,...\} \right\} \tag{9.1}$$

The representation of all vehicles on the road, where "vi" denotes automobile i on the road. The symbol $N = |V|$ is used to denote the total automobiles present on the road.

$$P = \left\{ Pi \mid vi \in V \right\} \tag{9.2}$$

It describes the private information associated with a vehicle, encompassing details such as speed, acceleration, orientation, and position.

$$E = \left\{ ei \mid vi \in V \right\} \tag{9.3}$$

Regarding a matrix utilized for storing road environmental data around a vehicle, specifically details concerning the vehicle's surroundings from four directions within a visual radius. This data, represented as "ei" within the road environment matrix, is formally described as follows:

$$\begin{bmatrix} Ir & \cdots & Ie \\ \vdots & \ddots & \vdots \\ Ip & \cdots & Iv \end{bmatrix}$$

$$
I(Vi,Vj) = \begin{cases} 0 \ d(Vi,Vj) > R \\ 1 -(d(Vi,Vj))^2 \ d(Vi,Vj) > R \end{cases} \tag{9.4}
$$

In this context, $d(Vi, Vj)$ signifies the Euclidean distance measurement between Vi and Vj, while R appears as the vision range parameter for vehicles.

The unemployment $fi(w)$ expression of the instrument Vi is as follows:

$$
fi(w) = \frac{\sum_b^B \left| y_{predict}^b - y_{observe}^b \right|^2}{B} \tag{9.5}
$$

Average weight is defined as:

$$
Rm(i) = \frac{\sum_{k=1}^i \left(r^2 \times L_m(k) \right)}{i \times \sum_{k=1}^i r^2} \tag{9.6}
$$

Therefore, the unemployment of the SL group is defined accordingly:

$$
FSL(w) = \frac{1}{|SL|} \sum_{i \in SL} \left[fi(w) + f1 - 1(w) \right] \tag{9.7}
$$

The objective function is defined as the unemployment reduction of the global $F(w)$ model:

$$
\min F(w) = \min \left[\frac{1}{H} \sum_{i \in H} \lambda i \ FSLi \ (w) \right] \tag{9.8}
$$

Chen et al. (2023) explore a scenario involving N participants, stand as $P_1, P_2, P_3, \ldots, P_n$, who collaboratively train an expert learning model without the need to upload their individual datasets, which are labeled as $D_1, D_2, D_3, \ldots, D_n$. Each participant, represented as P_k, possesses a local dataset referred to as D_k. The central goal of this is to jointly train a model, named "w," with multiple participants while ensuring that the actual facts remains decentralized on the respective participants' devices. The formal definition of the impartial function in federated learning is as follows:

$$
\arg \min f(w) = \sum_{k=1}^N \frac{n_k}{n} f_k w \tag{9.9}
$$

In this context, where $f_k(w)$ represents the practical loss function of P_k, N signifies the overall count of clients engaged in the learning process, and n represents the aggregate data volume contributed by all clients. Meanwhile, n_k designates the data volume specific to the kth client.

Xu et al. (2021) focus on the advancement of public education in the field of medical knowledge. They describe general statistical problems and their solutions, competition problems and special problems in this field. They hope to provide a valuable resource for ML research for detailed management of information without paying attention to it and health information. However, the information used in health and information systems also needs to be discussed.

These recommendations by Government Security Research (Q. Yang et al., 2019) propose a security training system that includes vertical learning, horizontal learning, and change in government. They explain the structure and use of public education. They also provide detailed information about current research in this field. They are also required to create a network of organizations that will share information without affecting customers' privacy, according to government policy. However, they did not mention details about where this technology could be used.

9.3 WORKING

Zhou et al. (2021) (Figure 9.2) propose a strategic direction for public education. At each stage t, the central server broadcasts the global shared model Gt to all participants and selects a match St from among n participants from all N clients.

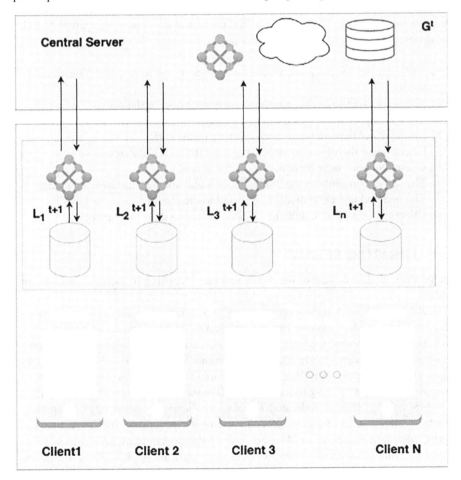

FIGURE 9.2 Federated learning flow chart model.

Each user chooses I to optimize the global model Gt to obtain the local model $(Lt + 1)$ for time $t + 1$, while using the private information set Di. Client I then sends the updated model $\Delta t + 1 = (Lt + 1 - Gt)$ back to the central server. Finally, the server is in the process of receiving updates to receive a new model:

$$G^{t+1} = G^t + \frac{n}{n} \sum_{i \in s^t} \Delta_i^{t+1} \tag{9.10}$$

where η is the learning rate and Δ^{t+1} denotes model updates.

A decentralized instructions that facilitates the collaboration of many participants in the development of deep learning (DL) models. It requires expert system algorithms such as deep neural networks to be trained on many independent datasets without directly exchanging data. The concept revolves around building local models to capture data patterns from different sources and then combining these models to create global models that can be shared across the hole. This approach involves abandoning local limitations, such as the weight and complexity of deep neural networks, to build better and more accurate models. According to Zhou et al. (2021), the strategic plan can define the educational process at the central and national level. The different users forward their local models to the main Hub (Server).

- The main server consolidates the local models and refreshes the universal model.
- The server transmits the refreshed universal model to the clients.
- Clients employ the updated universal model to enhance their local models.
- Flowchart of the federated meta-learning framework.
- Clients train their local models using their individual datasets.
- Clients forward their local models to the server.
- The server consolidates the limited models and updates the universal model.
- The updated universal model is reverted to the clients.
- Clients utilize the updated global model to refine their local models.

9.4 LITERATURE REVIEW

The percentage distribution of the use of federated learning in various industries or fields:

Healthcare (25%): A significant emphasis on federated learning is seen in healthcare, where it's applied to tasks like making health decisions based on clinical data, wearable health devices, medical image analysis, and clinical natural language processing (NLP) (Shaheen et al., 2022). Autonomous Vehicles (15%): Federated learning is also making headway in the autonomous vehicle sector, comprising 15% of its applications, contributing to technologies like self-driving cars. Edge Computing (15%): Similarly, 15% of federated learning applications are in edge computing, which involves processing data closer to where it's generated, like in sensor networks. Mobile Service (10%): Around 10% of the applications involve using federated learning to improve mobile services and applications. IoT (10%): Federated learning is applied in about 10% of IoT-related tasks, optimizing various IoT devices

Comprehensive Federated Deep Learning in Practical Applications 115

and networks. NLP (10%): In the realm of NLP, federated learning contributes to 10% of applications, including tasks like language translation and text classification. Recommendation Systems (10%): About 10% of federated learning applications are dedicated to recommendation systems, which suggest movies, products, or content to users. Finance (5%): A smaller proportion, 5%, of federated learning applications is found in the finance sector, used for tasks like predicting loan risks, detecting credit card fraud, and enhancing financial processes. Some of them are discussed below.

9.5 MEDICAL AND HEALTHCARE

Federated Learning in Medical Imaging has gained significant attention due to its ability to harness the power of distributed data while safeguarding patient privacy in the world of medical imaging, where data privacy is paramount. Federated learning algorithms tailored for this domain, emphasizing the need for privacy-preserving methods when dealing with sensitive medical data (Darzidehkalani et al., 2022). This opens up new avenues for improving diagnostic accuracy and predictive modeling in medical imaging while respecting the confidentiality of patient information. In a complementary study, it recognize the challenges of collecting large-scale annotated datasets for digital pathology. Traditional data sharing across institutions can be hindered by privacy and ownership issues. It explores the potential of federated learning as a solution. By distributing the learning process and aggregating outcomes without centralizing data, federated learning emerges as an efficient and privacy-preserving approach for advancing digital pathology (Babu et al., 2022). This study sets the stage for more accurate disease detection and diagnosis while respecting the privacy rights of patients. Privacy and data ownership are pivotal in healthcare applications, especially in the context of telemedicine. "A Systematic Review of Privacy-Preserving Methods Deployed with Blockchain and Federated Learning for Telemedicine" conducts an in-depth analysis of privacy-preserving methods using blockchain and federated learning. Telemedicine's increasing importance, particularly in light of the COVID-19 pandemic, highlights the need for secure data storage, controlled access, and consent-based sharing of health data. The study explores how emerging technologies can enhance healthcare standards when integrated thoughtfully, providing valuable insights for building trustworthy telemedicine systems (Hiwale et al., 2023). Moreover, it presents an innovative solution to address data quality in federated learning scenarios. Ensuring that local training data is of high quality is crucial for maintaining the accuracy of ML models. The methods based on blockchain and smart contracts, validates local models against secret testing datasets. Only models meeting a preset accuracy threshold are aggregated with the global model, improving overall data quality in federated learning settings (Bhatia & Samet, 2023). Predicting medical data, particularly abnormalities and diseases, plays a pivotal role in early diagnosis and effective treatment. In "FedECG" (Fetal electrocardiography) study focus on predicting heart abnormalities using electrocardiogram (ECG). However, ECG data collected from various devices can exhibit variations, and labeling such data is resource-intensive. Additionally, centralizing data for ML poses privacy concerns. To address these challenges, a federated semi-supervised learning framework named FedECG effectively utilizes

ECG data, incorporates data augmentation techniques, and preserves data privacy while achieving high accuracy in abnormal signal prediction (Ying et al., 2023). The study holds the potential to significantly impact the early detection of heart conditions, saving lives and reducing healthcare costs. Similarly, "A Federated Learning Framework for Pneumonia Image Detection Using Distributed Data" tackles the critical issue of pneumonia diagnosis through X-ray images. Pneumonia is a serious lung disease, and early diagnosis is crucial for timely intervention. However, collecting large and diverse datasets is challenging due to privacy regulations and data sharing restrictions. In response, this study leverages federated learning, which allows for privacy-preserving collaboration across multiple sources of data. The results showed that the proposed method provided accuracy in diagnosing pneumonia while complying with confidentiality rules (Kareem et al., 2023). This research showcases the potential of federated learning in revolutionizing disease diagnosis, ensuring patient privacy, and advancing healthcare outcomes.

9.6 PRIVACY AND SECURITY

FedHM (Federated Learning for Heterogenous Model) is introducing new federal training programs designed to use different models to train models for different products. By integrating with the Fully Convolutional Network (FCN) architecture, it facilitates the integration of different local models and enables local representatives to be shown to the world. FedHM reduces computational and communication overhead by sharing dense data between different Deep Neural Network (DNN) models. Experimental results using the two-list image classification function show that FedHM achieves high accuracy while reducing computational and communication costs compared to other methods (Park & Ko, 2023).

Considering the security problem of IoT systems, this work investigates ML, especially formal learning (FL) and DL, to improve fixed IoT security. It provides an overview of various ML algorithms and their limitations in IoT security. This study focuses on FL and DL as solutions for computing privacy and competition. It discusses the use of FL and DL models in IoT security, i.e. sharing information between systems while preserving privacy.

This study provides an overview, comparison, and summary of FL- and DL-based IoT security technologies (Gugueoth et al., 2023). This study provides an in-depth examination of federal education (FL) and its applications in various fields in the context of the Fourth Industrial Revolution. While he talks about the need for big data and computing power in today's technology, he also talks about privacy. FL was introduced as a solution to introduce ML models to data, protecting data privacy and access distribution. This work provides a comprehensive review of FL, including its learning models, materials, methods, and classification, as well as issues in ML classification. It investigates the potential impact of FL on information privacy, distribution, security, and business management business process (Khan et al., 2023). It focuses on the organization of learning (FL) as a delivery system for modeling distributed knowledge-based collaboration. To improve the privacy of FL, the authors introduce the FL method based on the integration of neural network with homomorphic encryption (HE) without any hidden layers.

Comprehensive Federated Deep Learning in Practical Applications

Unlike the FL method, which requires extensive training, this method achieves international standards in a simple and easy-to-manage environment. He tried to make it suitable for the group by trying to prove that HE does not affect the accuracy of the model (Fontenla-Romero et al., 2023). To solve the problem of sharing valuable information while preserving privacy in the IoV, this work proposed an asynchronous Federated Broad Learning (FBL) project. FBL uses the broad contact model (BFCM) for local education and integrates general education (BL) into federal education (FL).

Shared resource allocation and redesigned intelligent resource (RIS) optimization to improve communications and reduce costs. The simulation proves the effectiveness of FBL in sharing information on the IoV. Yuan et al. (2023) investigate a privacy policy for short-term forecasts using smart metered data and explore the combination of FL and privacy-related methods. Simulations of data under load demonstrate the potential for security and accurate load prediction while keeping the data private (Fernández et al., 2022). DEFEAT proposed a cascade attack mitigation decision model to solve the federal level (FL) mid-level problem.

DEFEAT uses a peer-to-peer network for standard communication and collection. It has a good balance between model accuracy and communication cost and shows its effectiveness in mitigating attacks in FL cases (Lu et al., 2023).

9.7 ARTIFICIAL INTELLIGENCE AND MACHINE LEARNING

Zhang et al. (2023). This work introduces FedHPO (Federated Learning, Hyper-parameter Optimization), a federated optimization algorithm that updates the hyperparameters of each user's base model during federated learning. The aim of communication in education is to speed up exchange, reduce total communication time and reduce the communication cycle. The evaluation compares FedHPO to other best-in-class integrations, revealing reduced integration time and communication costs (Kundroo & Kim, 2023). The investigation also investigates secret communications in the government's study of crowdsourced IoT networks. They advocate centralizing and decentralizing confidential communications to solve privacy issues in public education.

Theoretical analysis and simulations demonstrate the performance of this process (Zhang et al., 2023). It discussed the implementation of government training on smart manufacturing and solving communication problems with large-scale models. It highlights the need for compression techniques to ensure effective communication in public education (Nasri et al., 2023). In the context of drug discovery, this study presents privacy-preserving, large-scale distributed federated ML. It introduces the concept of "effectiveness" as a measure for assessing appropriate standards, showing how education can be expanded in government.

The publication shows the evolution of work in privacy management education among various partners (Heyndrickx et al., 2023). This study investigates the reliability of intelligence, especially for future wireless networks (beyond 5G/6G). It introduces the learning field (FL) as a private-autonomous system for the joint education model of many parties. This research focuses on natively integrating FL services into mobile devices to improve the reliability of AI (Bárcena et al., 2023).

9.8 IoT AND EDGE COMPUTING

Abdel-Basset et al. (2022). The privacy issue for IoT systems in smart cities, where shared space creates sensitive data vulnerable to privacy-related cyber attacks, informs the privacy-preserving federated deep learning (PP-FDL) framework that protects data from privacy attacks. Generative Adversarial Networks (GANs). PP-FDL ensures that participants in the learning process cannot access each other's data while ensuring a high level of independence and sharing. Scenario data. The framework uses self-identifiers to represent classroom abilities, and results observed using MNIST and CIFAR-10 data indicate that the framework performs well, outperforming state standards with 3%–8% improvement accuracy (Abdel-Basset et al., 2022).

Researchers focus on self-analysis, evaluating data management, and exploiting data problems in the context of IoT and smart cities. It offers integration of collaboration in a learning organization, eliminating the need to exchange raw data. With model tracking, end devices calculate local model updates and send them to the server for compilation. The method involves training the model using data exchange for low-level hardware. Clustering methods applied to retail data successfully group customers based on purchasing behavior. This method provides the key benefits of Receiver Operating Characteristic curve (ROC) by demonstrating its effectiveness in reducing communication costs while ensuring confidentiality (Ahmed et al., 2022) provides a comprehensive review of advances in the use of education systems in government and the role of these systems in solving data privacy and security issues.

The federal government's training demonstrated its advantages in protecting personal data and expanding educational materials. A. Yang et al. (2023) examine government education practices in various sectors, including telecommunications and healthcare, discussing their implications and benefits. At the same time, it emphasizes the importance of information security and discusses the consequences of security in government applications and the issues that need to be taken into account. The article concludes with a discussion of the future of public education and its changing role in various fields of practice (A. Yang et al., 2023).

9.9 FEDERATED LEARNING IN INTERNET OF VEHICLES

Wang et al. (2023) introduced the concept of DL organizations in the context of the IoV. When using DL to implement ML in connected vehicles, many users must submit model parameters, resulting in communication issues, overload, and disclosure of sensitive information.

To solve these problems, this study develops the IoV-SFDL framework by integrating SL into the FDL model. IoV-SFDL adopts SL distribution method, which is suitable for mobile computing and facilitates blockchain collaboration. The IoV-SFDL framework uses blockchain-driven SL to organize vehicles with nearby vehicles to create a local SL model. It then uses a confidence-weighted estimator to collect FDL samples from a single SL group.

The main results confirmed the effectiveness of the system. Compared to the reference method, IoV-SFDL reduces the client-to-server communication overhead by 16.72% while improving model performance by approximately 5.02% in the same

Comprehensive Federated Deep Learning in Practical Applications

training iteration. Researchers have also studied the application of electronic learning (FL) in automatic guided vehicle (AGV) control. According to the government's learning technology, agents (in this case AGVs) learn while maintaining privacy and reducing communication costs. AGVs are considered smart people operating in the fleet and controlled by the central system. Each AGV runs a parallel reinforcement learning (RL) system. AGV interacts with the system, learns according to the rules of the RL algorithm, follows instructions and shares its findings with the central system. The proposed method, called Federated Discrete Reinforcement Learning (FDRL), controls the order of AGVs and integrates rule change into group rules using collective learning. Various tests comparing FDRL to a Proportional Integral Derivative (PID) controller show significant improvements in tracking accuracy and speed. The FDRL method also outperforms the optimization fuzzy logic controller (FLC) and investigates the impact of traffic on path tracing performance and network transmission (Sierra-Garcia & Santos, 2024).

This work focuses on the application of FL to improve failure prediction of AGVs used in smart manufacturing environments. AGVs play an important role in production lines, and their maintenance involves monitoring their activity and health using ML-based methods. It is important to know the difference in AGV operation. This paper focuses on estimating instantaneous power as a signal to detect abnormality in AGV.

Research shows that FL can improve energy consumption forecasting by communicating the knowledge and experience gained by individual AGVs. This work includes several methods to develop global forecasting models and experiments using real data obtained from AGVs in field operations. The results show that the federal system is better than the centralized system in the AGV operation environment, and the integration of previous experiences can make good predictions again (Shubyn et al., 2023).

The authors present an integrated DL (IoV-SFDL) framework designed for the IoV environment. They address challenges with FDL, which include communication overhead and data confidentiality due to serving test models from multiple clients. To alleviate these issues, this paper incorporates group learning (SL) into the FDL framework. IoV-SFDL leverages decentralized ML from SL to enable cell edge computing and blockchain-based collaboration. The framework leverages blockchain-enabled SL vehicle organization to create local SL models with neighboring vehicles. It then assembles the global FDL model of various SL groups using the confidence-weighted prediction algorithm.

The authors present comprehensive experimental results showing that IoV-SFDL reduces client-to-client communication overhead by 16.72% compared to the baseline. It also improves model performance by approximately 5.02% for the same training iterations.

In their work (Sierra-Garcia & Santos, 2024) the authors investigated the application of FL in the context of fleet management of AGVs. According to the government's education system, AGVs work as intelligent people, learn equally and contribute to the international standard of knowledge. This method increases confidentiality and reduces communication costs. AGVs interact with the hub operating at the edge and manage their information to create global behavioral patterns. Additionally, the study provided RL to this method, allowing the AGV to interact with the system and learn according to RL rules to follow the path. AGVs feed their findings to the central system, which collects these findings and aggregates them into group policies using their learning collection capabilities.

The paper presents simulation results demonstrating the effectiveness of their approach via FDRL. Compared with the PID controller optimized using the genetic algorithm, the true error of FDRL was improved by 78% on average, the root mean square error by 75% on average, and the standard deviation by 73% on average.

The system also accelerates learning by completing up to 50% faster depending on the method. In this work Shubyn et al. (2023) the authors focus on the application of federated learning (FL) to improve failure prediction of autonomous guided vehicles (AGVs) used in a smart manufacturing environment. AGVs play an important role in production lines, and their maintenance involves monitoring their activity and health using ML. Identifying deficiencies in AGV performance is critical to maintaining operational performance. Shubyn et al. (2023) provide an instantaneous power estimate based on the signal indicating abnormal AGV. It has been shown that FL can improve energy consumption forecasting by allowing AGVs to exchange knowledge and experience from their operations.

This work presents several methods for developing global predictive models and includes experiments using real data generated by AGVs in the workplace. The results show that the government's work outperforms the centralized implementation in the field of AGV. Additionally, studies have shown that the integration of AGVs can improve prediction.

9.10 METHODOLOGIES

FL algorithms suitable for medical imaging are cited as important methods for the importance of protecting patient information, along with the specific challenges posed by the use of converged networks in medical facilities, study aims to solve these problems by using the potential of government education in medical imaging (Darzidehkalani et al., 2022). Babu et al. (2022) explore the practical use of state education in digital pathology.

The approach includes a comprehensive review of important data sharing, privacy, and data-related challenges in healthcare. Conducted a real study around the world to demonstrate the feasibility and effectiveness of government training in advancing digital pathology. The authors present a new federal quasi-monitoring (FSSL) framework called FedECG to predict cardiovascular diseases using ECG. The approach involves a prioritization process, improved ResNet-9-based models to obtain accurate fuzzy set estimation, combined pseudo-labeling and data augmentation methods to partially improve the tuning of training, and creating a unified structure to improve the unified structure in a federal education district (Ying et al., 2023).

Lung diagnosis by X-ray imaging using federal studies, including the use of federal studies for confidentiality-collaboration across multiple databases. In addition, this study conducts experiments using state-of-the-art ML models, including pre-trained convolutional neural network (CNN) models, and evaluates their performance using multiple measurement methods, including area under the curve (AUC; Kareem et al., 2023). The approach involved extensive literature and literature review of existing

Comprehensive Federated Deep Learning in Practical Applications

research on privacy-friendly approaches to telemedicine, with a focus on blockchain and government education. This study provides a qualitative analysis of research findings based on architecture, privacy mechanisms, and ML for data storage, management, and analysis. The goal is to identify opportunities to integrate blockchain and government technology to improve telemedicine services while ensuring privacy and security (Hiwale et al., 2023).

Researchers have suggested ethical use of blockchain to improve data quality in public education. The technique involves using miners to verify the accuracy of the local model by comparing it with secret data. During the mining process, smart contracts called miners are used to determine whether the local model meets the actual preset.

The scheme was tested on two databases, including the brain tumor database and the MNIST clinical database, to evaluate its effectiveness in improving the quality of information in the federal system education (Bhatia & Samet, 2023). FedHM provides an FL framework for training models of different devices with different models. It enables the elevation of local representatives to global representatives by facilitating collaborative training through an FCN architecture. Sharing weighted data between different DNN models reduces the computational and communication overhead.

To evaluate the accuracy and functionality of the framework, a test was conducted on two profile (Park & Ko, 2023). It provides an overview of different ML algorithms for IoT security, highlighting advantages and limitations, with a special focus on level learning (FL) and DL as a privacy and competition solution.

This work investigates different models, compares them, and summarizes the security methods of IoT based on FL and DL in terms of preserving privacy when sharing information between systems (Gugueoth et al., 2023). This project provides an overview of federal education (FL) and its impact in various areas, especially in dealing with privacy issues. It includes different FL learning styles, combinations, methods and problems. This study explores the potential of FL by focusing on its impact on business processes related to data privacy, distribution, security, and business management (Khan et al., 2023).

9.11 RESULT

Salmeron et al. (2023) give the results of a federated learning experiment using the Breast Cancer Wisconsin Dataset. The dataset contains information about breast tumors, with some being malignant (cancerous) and others being benign (non-cancerous).

There are a total of 569 patients in the dataset, with 212 having malignant tumors and 357 having benign tumors.

The goal of the experiment was to improve the accuracy of ML models by using federated learning, where the data is kept on the individual devices and not centralized.

The results showed that, in general, federated learning improved the accuracy of the models. However, the way the results were combined (aggregated) had different effects on the accuracy.

Salmeron et al. (2023) give Column names and Definition as: Accuracy in the non-federated case (Acc(Local)), Accuracy of the federated model using fed averaging (Acc Federated), Accuracy of the model using the mean as accuracy (Acc. Accuracy (Fed)), accuracy of the joint model using the mean of accuracy and size (Acc. Size & Acc. (Fed)), using the participant (Prep. Cont. (Fed)).), the reality of the government structure using the cooperation of the participants.

- In the first case, Figure 9.3, where the dataset was evenly split among participants, all accuracy metrics improved after federated learning.
- This means that the global model was better than the individual models.
- In the second case, Figure 9.4, where the dataset was unevenly split with one participant having only 3% of the data, using a method called "contribution aggregation of the difference of the losses" did not improve the performance. In simpler terms, this aggregation method didn't help much when the data distribution was uneven.
- In the third case, Figure 9.5, where the data split was even more extreme with one participant having only 3% of the data and another with 6% and 7%, the standard federated averaging method didn't improve the local models' performance. This means that combining the results in the usual way didn't work well in this scenario.
- In the final case, Figure 9.6, a weighted aggregation method that considered the size of each participant and their accuracy resulted in lower accuracy than the initial local models. This means that the aggregation method made the model worse.

Mabrouk et al. (2023) simulated a scenario with five nodes or hospitals, and each of these nodes had a dataset for training and testing ML models.

However, these datasets were not evenly balanced; they contained different amounts of data related to pneumonia and normal medical images.

They conducted several rounds of federated learning (FL), where they trained eight different CNN models using the training data on each node. After training,

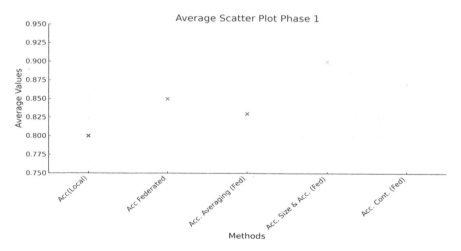

FIGURE 9.3 Average scatter plot phase 1.

Comprehensive Federated Deep Learning in Practical Applications

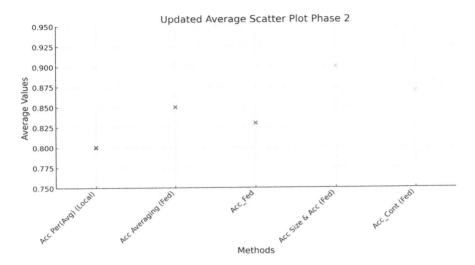

FIGURE 9.4 Average scatter plot phase 2.

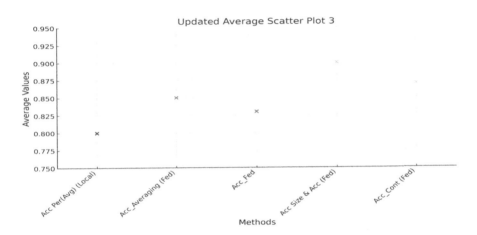

FIGURE 9.5 Average scatter plot phase 3.

they measured how well these models could correctly classify new, unseen data on a separate test dataset.

Here's what they found in the first round (R1) of FL:

- On the first node (N1), Figure 9.7, the "densenet121" model achieved the highest accuracy, correctly classifying 92.74% of the test data.
- This model performed better than the other CNN models on this node.
- The "mobilenetv2" model came in second place with an accuracy of 90.32%.
- Moving to the second node (N2), Figure 9.8, again, the "densenet121" model was the top performer with an accuracy of 90.32%. It outperformed the "resnet152v2" model, which achieved an accuracy of 89.52%.

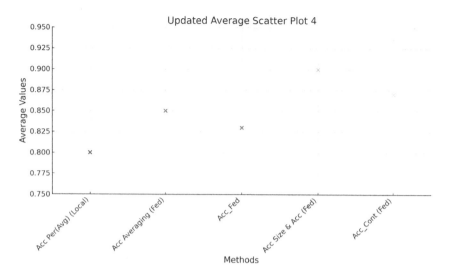

FIGURE 9.6 Average scatter plot phase 4.

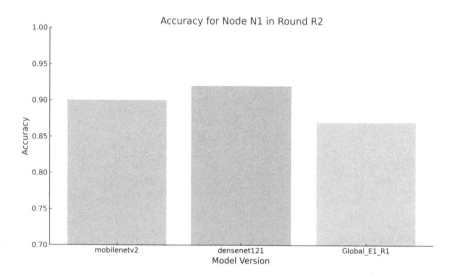

FIGURE 9.7 Accuracy for node 1 in round 2.

- In the third node (N3), Figure 9.9, both the "densenet121" and "inceptionv3" models performed well. The "densenet121" model had an accuracy of 91.13%, while the "inceptionv3" model achieved an accuracy of 89.52%.
- On the fourth node (N4), Figure 9.10, the best-performing model in terms of accuracy was the "densenet121" model, with an accuracy of 91.94%. The "mobilenetv2" model followed closely with an accuracy of 90.32%.
- Lastly, on the fifth node (N5), Figure 9.11, they found that the "densenet121" model achieved the best results in terms of accuracy.

Comprehensive Federated Deep Learning in Practical Applications

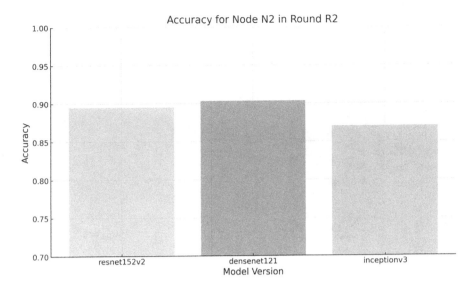

FIGURE 9.8 Accuracy for node 2 in round 2.

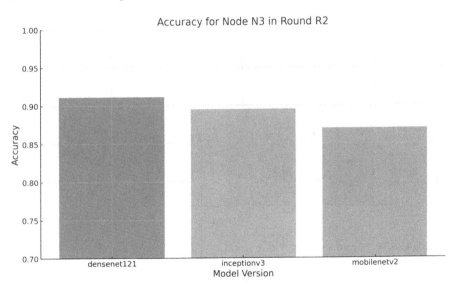

FIGURE 9.9 Accuracy for node 3 in round 2.

Same is applied for other round, and the results show that different CNN models performed differently on each node. "Densenet121" consistently performed well on multiple nodes, while other models like "mobilenetv2" and "inceptionv3" also showed good results on certain nodes. This suggests that the choice of model can impact how well the ML system performs, and it might not be the same for all nodes or hospitals due to variations in their datasets.

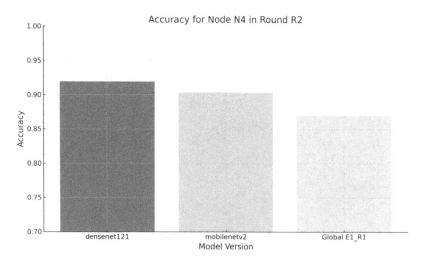

FIGURE 9.10 Accuracy for node 4 in round 2.

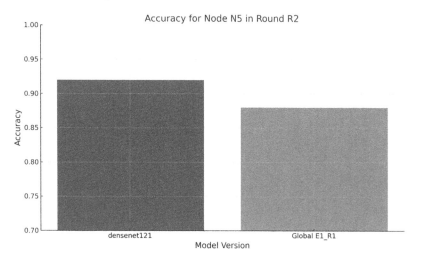

FIGURE 9.11 Accuracy for node 5 in round 2.

Jeong et al. (2023) (Figure 9.12) evaluate the performance of different ML methods for a task called "localization." Localization is about determining where something is located accurately, like classifying items into specific groups or clusters.

They compared four methods: DNN, FedAvg, FedAMP, and FedAMP-F under different data settings. They changed two things during the experiments: the number of regions where data was collected (L) and the number of clients or participants in the ML process (M). Here's what they found:

- When they kept the number of clients (*M*) fixed and increased the number of data collection regions (*L*), the overall performance went down. This happened because each region had less training data, which made it harder for the models to learn accurately.

Comprehensive Federated Deep Learning in Practical Applications

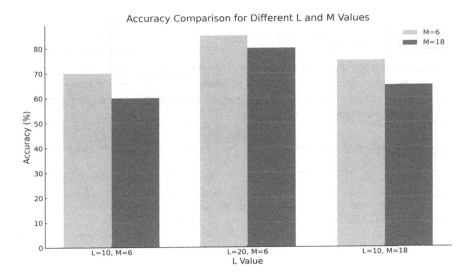

FIGURE 9.12 Accuracy comparison of regions and machine learning.

- Similarly, when they kept the number of data collection regions (L) fixed and increased the number of clients (M), the performance also decreased. Again, this was because each client had less data to train on, which affected the model's accuracy.
- In all cases, the method called FedAMP didn't perform as well as FedAvg. This means that FedAvg was more reliable and accurate for this task.
- However, FedAMP-F showed the best performance among all the methods. FedAMP-F uses a technique involving Bayesian probabilistic classification to improve accuracy. This method was the most accurate at localizing items into clusters.
- It's worth noting that FedAMP, while it did improve localization, required a lot of computational power to work with the global model.
- In practical terms, it wasn't significantly better than FedAvg, which is simpler to use.

So, in simple terms, increasing the number of data regions or clients can make the localization task more challenging. Among the methods tested, FedAMP-F was the most accurate, but FedAvg was often the most practical choice due to its simplicity and reasonable performance.

Above are few results explained from research in different domains; talking broadly the FDL has a great impact on healthcare, IoT, autonomous vehicles, smart homes, and much more.

9.12 CONCLUSION

In summary, public education is a great way to collaborate on education in many areas. It allows multiple parties to train on shared models without sharing information, addressing privacy and security concerns. Although public education faces challenges such as information heterogeneity and communication burden, research in this field is growing rapidly and there are many opportunities for future research. Overall, federated learning has the potential to revolutionize collaborative ML and enable new applications in various domains. Future research can be directed toward enhancing privacy mechanisms, reducing communication overhead, integrating with edge computing, establishing industry standards, and exploring innovative applications, all of which are pivotal for realizing its full potential in our daily lives and driving continued advancements.

REFERENCES

Abdel-Basset, M., Hawash, H., Moustafa, N., Razzak, I., & Abd Elfattah, M. (2022). Privacy-preserved learning from non-iid data in fog-assisted IoT: A federated learning approach. *Digital Communications and Networks.* https://doi.org/10.1016/j.dcan.2022.12.013

Ahmed, U., Srivastava, G., & Lin, J. C. W. (2022). Reliable customer analysis using federated learning and exploring deep-attention edge intelligence. *Future Generation Computer Systems, 127,* 70–79. https://doi.org/10.1016/j.future.2021.08.028

Babu, G. M., Wong, K. W., & Parry, J. (2022). Federated learning for digital pathology: A pilot study. *Procedia Computer Science, 207,* 736–743. https://doi.org/10.1016/j.procs.2022.09.129

Bárcena, J. L. C., Ducange, P., Marcelloni, F., Nardini, G., Noferi, A., Renda, A., Ruffini, F., Schiavo, A., Stea, G., & Virdis, A. (2023). Enabling federated learning of explainable AI models within beyond-5G/6G networks. *Computer Communications.* https://doi.org/10.1016/j.comcom.2023.07.039

Bhatia, L., & Samet, S. (2023). A decentralized data evaluation framework in federated learning. *Blockchain: Research and Applications,* 100152. https://doi.org/10.1016/j.bcra.2023.100152

Chen, S., Jie, Z., Wang, G., Li, K. C., Yang, J., & Liu, X. (2023). A new federated learning-based wireless communication and client scheduling solution for combating COVID-19. *Computer Communications, 206,* 101–109. https://doi.org/10.1016/j.comcom.2023.04.023

Darzidehkalani, E., Ghasemi-rad, M., & van Ooijen, P. M. A. (2022). Federated learning in medical imaging: Part II: Methods, challenges, and considerations. *Journal of the American College of Radiology, 19*(8), 975–982. https://doi.org/10.1016/j.jacr.2022.03.016

Fernández, J. D., Menci, S. P., Lee, C. M., Rieger, A., & Fridgen, G. (2022). Privacy-preserving federated learning for residential short-term load forecasting. *Applied Energy, 326.* https://doi.org/10.1016/j.apenergy.2022.119915

Fontenla -Romero, O., Guijarro-Berdiñas, B., Hernández-Pereira, E., & Pérez-Sánchez, B. (2023). FedHEONN: Federated and homomorphically encrypted learning method for one-layer neural networks. *Future Generation Computer Systems, 149,* 200–211. https://doi.org/10.1016/j.future.2023.07.018

Gugueoth, V., Safavat, S., & Shetty, S. (2023). Security of internet of things (IoT) using federated learning and deep learning – Recent advancements, issues and prospects. In *ICT Express.* Korean Institute of Communication Sciences. https://doi.org/10.1016/j.icte.2023.03.006

Heyndrickx, W., Arany, A., Simm, J., Pentina, A., Sturm, N., Humbeck, L., Mervin, L., Zalewski, A., Oldenhof, M., Schmidtke, P., Friedrich, L., Loeb, R., Afanasyeva, A., Schuffenhauer, A., Moreau, Y., & Ceulemans, H. (2023). Conformal efficiency as a metric for comparative model assessment befitting federated learning. *Artificial Intelligence in the Life Sciences, 3,* 100070. https://doi.org/10.1016/j.ailsci.2023.100070

Hiwale, M., Walambe, R., Potdar, V., & Kotecha, K. (2023). A systematic review of privacy-preserving methods deployed with blockchain and federated learning for the telemedicine. In *Healthcare Analytics* (Vol. 3). Elsevier Inc. https://doi.org/10.1016/j.health.2023.100192

Jeong, M., Choi, S. W., & Kim, S. (2023). A tutorial on Federated Learning methodology for indoor localization with non-IID fingerprint databases. In *ICT Express*. Korean Institute of Communication Sciences. https://doi.org/10.1016/j.icte.2023.01.009

Kareem, A., Liu, H., & Velisavljevic, V. (2023). A federated learning framework for pneumonia image detection using distributed data. *Healthcare Analytics, 4*. https://doi.org/10.1016/j.health.2023.100204

Khan, M., Glavin, F. G., & Nickles, M. (2023). Federated learning as a privacy solution - An overview. *Procedia Computer Science, 217*, 316–325. https://doi.org/10.1016/j.procs.2022.12.227

Kundroo, M., & Kim, T. (2023). Federated learning with hyper-parameter optimization. *Journal of King Saud University - Computer and Information Sciences*, 101740. https://doi.org/10.1016/j.jksuci.2023.101740

Lu, G., Xiong, Z., Li, R., Mohammad, N., Li, Y., & Li, W. (2023). Defeat: A decentralized federated learning against gradient attacks. *High-Confidence Computing*, 100128. https://doi.org/10.1016/j.hcc.2023.100128

Mabrouk, A., Díaz Redondo, R. P., Abd Elaziz, M., & Kayed, M. (2023). Ensemble federated learning: An approach for collaborative pneumonia diagnosis. *Applied Soft Computing, 144*, 110500. https://doi.org/10.1016/j.asoc.2023.110500

Nasri, S. A. E. M., Ullah, I., & Madden, M. G. (2023). Compression scenarios for federated learning in smart manufacturing. *Procedia Computer Science, 217*, 436–445. https://doi.org/10.1016/j.procs.2022.12.239

Park, J. Y., & Ko, J. G. (2023). FedHM: Practical federated learning for heterogeneous model deployments. *ICT Express*. https://doi.org/10.1016/j.icte.2023.07.013

Salmeron, J. L., Arévalo, I., & Ruiz-Celma, A. (2023). Benchmarking federated strategies in peer-to-peer federated learning for biomedical data. *Heliyon, 9*(6). https://doi.org/10.1016/j.heliyon.2023.e1692

Shaheen, M., Farooq, M. S., Umer, T., & Kim, B. S. (2022). Applications of federated learning; taxonomy, challenges, and research trends. *Electronics (Switzerland), 11*(4). https://doi.org/10.3390/electronics11040670

Shubyn, B., Kostrzewa, D., Grzesik, P., Benecki, P., Maksymyuk, T., Sunderam, V., Syu, J. H., Lin, J. C. W., & Mrozek, D. (2023). Federated learning for improved prediction of failures in autonomous guided vehicles. *Journal of Computational Science, 68*. https://doi.org/10.1016/j.jocs.2023.101956

Sierra-Garcia, J. E., & Santos, M. (2024). Federated discrete reinforcement learning for automatic guided vehicle control. *Future Generation Computer Systems, 150*, 78–89. https://doi.org/10.1016/j.future.2023.08.021

Xu, J., Glicksberg, B. S., Su, C., Walker, P., Bian, J., & Wang, F. (2021). Federated learning for healthcare informatics. *Journal of Healthcare Informatics Research, 5*(1). https://doi.org/10.1007/s41666-020-00082-4

Yang, A., Ma, Z., Zhang, C., Han, Y., Hu, Z., Zhang, W., Huang, X., & Wu, Y. (2023). Review on application progress of federated learning model and security hazard protection. *Digital Communications and Networks, 9*(1), 146–158. https://doi.org/10.1016/j.dcan.2022.11.006

Yang, Q., Liu, Y., Chen, T., & Tong, Y. (2019). Federated machine learning: Concept and applications. *ACM Transactions on Intelligent Systems and Technology, 10*(2). https://doi.org/10.1145/3298981

Ying, Z., Zhang, G., Pan, Z., Chu, C., & Liu, X. (2023). FedECG: A federated semi-supervised learning framework for electrocardiogram abnormalities prediction. *Journal of King Saud University - Computer and Information Sciences*, *35*(6). https://doi.org/10.1016/j.jksuci.2023.101568

Yuan, X., Chen, J., Zhang, N., Ye, Q., Li, C., Zhu, C., & Sherman Shen, X. (2023). Low-cost federated broad learning for privacy-preserved knowledge sharing in the RIS-aided internet of vehicles. *Engineering*. https://doi.org/10.1016/j.eng.2023.04.015

Zhang, H., Zou, Y., Yin, H., Yu, D., & Cheng, X. (2023). CCM-FL: Covert communication mechanisms for federated learning in crowd sensing IoT. *Digital Communications and Networks*. https://doi.org/10.1016/j.dcan.2023.02.013

Zhou, X., Xu, M., Wu, Y., & Zheng, N. (2021). Deep model poisoning attack on federated learning. *Future Internet*, *13*(3). https://doi.org/10.3390/fi13030073

10 Federated Deep Learning System for Application of Healthcare in Pandemic Situation

Vandana and Chetna Kaushal

10.1 INTRODUCTION OF FEDERATED DEEP LEARNING

A machine learning (ML) method known as Federated Learning (FL) enables numerous participants to train an ML model together without sharing their personal information [1]. In classical ML, the model is trained using all of the data gathered and consolidated in one place, such as has been gathered and consolidated in one place, such a server or data centre. However, with FL, the data is still saved locally on gadgets like smartphones or IoT (Internet of Things) devices and is still decentralized [2]. In FL, the model is initially trained using a small sample of data from each device, and the updated model is then sent back to the devices to improve accuracy. Each device privately trains the model using its own private data before submitting the updated model weights to the main server. Using data from several sources, FL aims to integrate ML models. FL consists of two operations: model inference and model training. Although data cannot be shared throughout the model training phase, information may. The dialogue does not divulge any sections of the data that are privately protected at any site. The skilled model is able to exist at one party or is shared by several parties.

FL is an algorithmic framework for developing ML models, where a model links data from one party to an output. At least two parties collaborate to develop the model, each retaining data during the training process. The model may be partially shared using encryption to prevent third parties from re-engineering the data. The final model's performance closely matches the ideal model constructed with all data from a single party. The model is applied to a fresh data instance at inference time, such as in a business-to-business scenario where a federated medical imaging system forecasts a new patient. The profit generated should be distributed fairly, and sustainability should be considered when designing the mechanisms [3].

10.1.1 PRACTICE OF EFFECTIVE FEDERATED LEARNING IN MEDICAL DOMAIN

Healthcare organizations used FL to develop an ML model for calculating the risk of patient death using clinical data from electronic health records (EHRs). Stanford was able to train the ML model utilizing data from several healthcare providers while

DOI: 10.1201/9781032694870-10

maintaining the security and privacy of the data thanks to the FL technique. Due to the model's high accuracy in predicting the chance of patient mortality, it has been used to improve patient outcomes [4].

10.2 FEDERATED LEARNING CONCEPTS AND FRAMEWORK IN THE MEDICAL DOMAIN

The principles of trust, cooperation, effectiveness, and scalability serve as the foundation for training complicated ML algorithms in a distributed medical setting [5]. Under this paradigm, instead of storing all patient information on a single server, data about specific healthcare institutions is still available for training servers at a nearby medical facility.

10.2.1 ADVANTAGES

1. Individual healthcare data is still decentralized, which always worries about data privacy and ownership. This is especially important in medical settings where maintaining patient privacy is of the utmost importance.
2. Data ownership remains intact, which is essential in delicate industries like healthcare. Patients, clinics, and hospitals all retain control of their unique data sources.
3. The absence of a central server means that bandwidth and latency problems are minimized, which makes it perfect for real-time applications like immersive augmented reality and the meta verse in healthcare.
4. Energy effectiveness. By utilizing local computing power and participating in model training, healthcare devices can reduce the requirement for large-scale data transfers.
5. Due to the lack of a central server, which lessens bandwidth and latency issues, it is ideal for real-time applications in healthcare such as immersive augmented reality and the metaverse.
6. FL uses decentralized data sources to function, guaranteeing that private medical data stays where it originated, minimizing the possibility of illegal access.
7. By combining model updates or gradients from several devices, FL preserves individual healthcare data while obtaining overall insights. This is done instead of releasing raw healthcare data [6].
8. To prevent the reconstruction of individual healthcare data, techniques like differential privacy can be implemented into FL by introducing noise to aggregated updates.
9. FL makes it possible to train models without explicitly disclosing data, allowing healthcare organizations to anonymize patient data while still making a contribution to model improvement.
10. To reduce the possibility of eavesdropping, communication lines between devices and the central server are encrypted [5,6].

10.2.2 Framework

The clients of the FL network get the AI/ML model parameters through broadcast from a single, central global server, either at random or using a client selection approach. After receiving the global model parameters, selected customers train the model using their localized data. The overall model is subsequently created by the server by compiling and combining the local model parameters from various clients. With the reference of fuzzy logic, FedAvg is a fundamental algorithm that iteratively averages the local parameters of several clients. Although it performs well with non-IID data, there are no theoretical certainties on how it will perform in non-IID data circumstances. Figure 10.1 illustrates a similar framework for FL in the context of medicine. FL may be used for home healthcare, hospital healthcare, and mobile healthcare, all of which may have different data distributions. According to the data characteristics, FL must be applied to many domains in order to address difficulties with security, privacy, healthcare systems, and gadgets. Mobile healthcare requires intelligent medical devices, energy efficiency, communication, computation, and privacy considerations, whereas hospital healthcare necessitates larger organizations with significant resources and computational capabilities to mitigate problems like client dropouts and straggler issues. Last but not least, home healthcare refers to medical treatments delivered in residential settings, frequently using a variety of smarthealthcare gadgets. Remote under a single roof of home healthcare, offering patient-specific care in a comfortable setting [7].

Here, Figure 10.1 highlights the crucial part FL aggregation plays in coordinating collaborative convergence from many data sources while protecting the confidentiality of private medical data. Locally improved model updates or gradients from several decentralized devices or data sources are combined during the aggregation phase.

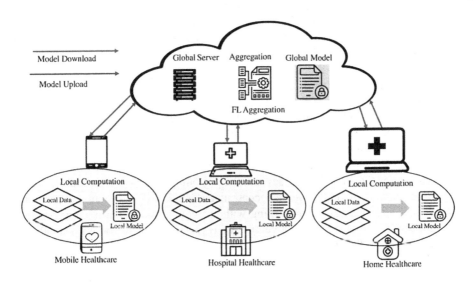

FIGURE 10.1 Federated learning frameworks for the medical domain.

This crucial step is essential to creating a more accurate global model while stubbornly protecting data privacy and security. FL aggregation has several purposes, particularly in the medical field where patient anonymity is of the utmost importance [8].

10.3 FL AND ITS APPLICATIONS

FL is a special form of ML that enables the development of reliable and accurate representations without the need for sharing raw data. It might be used in many different fields, including banking, transportation, and natural language processing. Preserving the privacy and security of medical information in the age of networked IoT devices is a difficult task. In industrial and medical AI applications, FL methods have become essential tools for maintaining anonymity. Compared to conventional data-driven medical applications, they are more resilient and effective and provide efficiency advantages and alleviation to international healthcare systems. By working together with other cutting-edge technologies [9], FL may broaden its scope and speed up the group training of ML and deep learning models without centralized data sharing. Without necessitating centralization of data exchange, this synergy speeds up collectively training ML and deep learning models.

10.3.1 FL IN HEALTHCARE BASED ON BLOCKCHAIN

Implementing FL, a distributed and safe deep learning technique is an effective technique to train a shared model without endangering patient privacy. Additionally, FL has created a technique for obtaining data from several sources or hospitals without risking the privacy of the hospitals. The benefit of FL is that it increases training model quality while lowering participant resource usage (memory, power, etc.). FL, in other words, spreads the learned model among the local machines after jointly learning the model. To train the global shared model, each user uploads their local model to the blockchain distributed ledger. Then, for upgrading the global model, the users or hospitals submit fresh data, such as weights or gradients [9].

Information from a range of sources should be gathered without compromising user privacy or authentication in order to create a more effective AI model for Industry 4.0. The updating of the global AI model is a result of FL and the distributed ledger on the blockchain. The data model that is gained via the blockchain combines the local and global models from several nodes. The smart contract updated the models and submitted the weights. The suggested architecture combines FL with blockchain for complete decentralization and improved security. Decentralization also increases the model's accuracy and the poisoning-attack-proof is enabled.

Blockchain is fundamentally a decentralized, public ledger system that promotes cross-device collaboration in learning without relying on a centralized aggregator. Healthcare is one of several data-centric industries that benefit from its adaptability. Although blockchain was first designed to manage Bitcoin transactions and other cryptocurrencies, its applications are incredibly broad. Numerous industries, including business, transportation, logistics, and healthcare, have seen considerable change as a result. Blockchain technology's possibilities in the healthcare industry provide safe administration of electronic health information and have sparked a lot of study. The combination of FL with blockchain offers a way to deploy FL applications in the healthcare industry effectively and store health data in a safe manner. In this mutually beneficial partnership, blockchain improves FL's security and privacy.

The combination of decentralized data and cooperative FL methods meshes with blockchain's decentralized nature and can hasten the creation of AI solutions for healthcare. The presented architecture secures multi-agent systems for the Internet of Medical Things (IoMT) by combining blockchain and FL and promoting cooperation among individual agent units. The results are quite promising, with a categorization of skin diseases that is 80% accurate. Clinical trials and precision medicine are two areas where blockchain technology has potential. With FL and transfer learning, it provides a distributed parallel computing platform for precision medicine [10]. The decentralized processing of large amounts of medical data is made possible by this breakthrough. Blockchain may also be used to diagnose diseases; for instance, Health-Chain offers a decentralized, cross-institutional illness categorization framework that is privacy-preserving and blockchain-based. Issues with data privacy are efficiently handled by using differential privacy and pseudo-identity techniques. In summary, the sector has a lot to gain from the symbiotic integration of blockchain-based FL. Here are some crucial details emphasizing its significance [11]:

- **Optimized Information Security:** The built-in security of blockchain characteristics like immutable and decentralized ledgers enhances the confidentiality and reliability of healthcare data. This pairing assures patient safety when paired with FL Information is kept in strict confidence.
- **Data Accountability and Transparency:** Due to the transparency of blockchain, patients may exert more control over who can access their health data and how. FL simultaneously upholds data privacy and gives a clear and auditable record of the model updates and access requests, strengthening relationships between stakeholders.
- **Cooperatively:** Interoperability is facilitated via blockchain among various healthcare facilities and systems. This interoperability is expanded by FL's federated strategy enabling smooth integration of ML models exchanging information and cooperating in the healthcare sector with suppliers and academics.
- **Handling of Authorization:** Blockchain-based intelligent contracts can control patient data sharing permission and training models. Thus, FL can guarantee only the use of patient data by authorized parties, adapting to changing data privacy laws.
- **Commercializing Information:** Patients may gain from providing their health data in exchange for incentives or tokens based on the blockchain. FL protects data privacy while giving patients discretion over how their information is used, which can result in new revenue-sharing structures.
- **Developments in Research:** By enabling safe and cooperative model training across institutions and locations, the combination of blockchain and FL quickens the creation of more precise diagnostic and therapeutic tools.
- **Adherence to Regulations:** The healthcare industry is highly regulated, and blockchain-based FL can help by offering a strong foundation for data management and privacy. This can help organizations comply with data protection rules like HIPAA (Health Insurance Portability and Accountability Act) or GDPR (General Data Protection Regulation).

10.3.2 Healthcare Monitoring Implemented by IoT and FL

The emergence of IoT technology has organized a new environment that integrates seamless connection, smart gadgets, and increased productivity. The integration of various scattered smart devices and sensors, which controls the real-time generation of user data across numerous applications, has directed this development. Healthcare is one of the many industries that has been greatly touched by the IoT revolution [12].

IoT and FL integration in healthcare combines real-time data from IoT devices with privacy-preserving FL model training. Notably, the research described explores the complexities of this fusion and clarifies how IoT and healthcare applications interact. An excellent examination of the security issues raised by this convergence and potential solutions to them complements this research [13].

The IoMT paradigm, which enables local data assessment at edge devices, represents a significant leap in IoT and healthcare technologies. Data privacy for IoT devices is ensured by this decentralized strategy, a tenet of FL, especially in delicate industries like healthcare. By balancing data value and confidentiality, FL sets itself apart from traditional centralized ML algorithms. Using FL, differential privacy, and blockchain, ground-breaking project [14] enables manufacturers to safely and effectively evaluate IoT-derived data, aligning with improved healthcare monitoring.

IoT and FL have the potential to change several industries, including healthcare.

- **Processing of Data in Real Time:** IoT devices continually gather and transmit patient health data, giving medical professionals access to up-to-date data. With the protection of patient privacy, FL may be used to evaluate this data collectively, producing immediate insights and treatments.
- **Monitoring of a Patient Remotely:** The vital signs and chronic problems of patients can be remotely monitored by IoT devices. FL enables this data to be combined and collectively analysed, allowing healthcare practitioners to make knowledgeable decisions about patient care without jeopardizing the privacy of specific individuals.
- **Early Disease Detection and Prediction:** Healthcare professionals may anticipate and identify illnesses at an early stage by evaluating IoT-generated data using FL models. This may result in prompt treatments and better patient outcomes.
- **Saved Money for Healthcare:** The combination of IoT and FL can assist in lowering healthcare expenses by preventing hospital readmissions through continuous monitoring, improving treatment strategies, and removing pointless procedures medical procedures.
- **Flexibility:** The IoT ecosystem is constantly growing and FL may expand to handle an increasing amount It is appropriate for use with IoT devices and data streams because of applications in healthcare on a broad scale.
- **Enhanced Participation of Patients:** IoT gadgets may interact by giving them resources to assist people in their healthcare and useful information about their state of health. FL can customize this engagement and make it even more effective suggestions and criticism.

Federated Deep Learning System for Application of Healthcare

10.3.3 Edge Computing Assisted FL for Healthcare

Deep learning is being used in the medical industry to tackle difficult pattern identification problems. The accuracy of trained models is limited when applied to unseen data. To fix the issue and adhere to HIPAA rules, edge FL may be utilized to train models without revealing patient data. Edge FL is being used to train a chest X-ray image classification model for COVID-19 and FL is being used to construct an image semantic segmentation model for brain scans [15]. The final model selection technique enables each medical institution to pick the best locally validated model for global model aggregation, hence improving the performance of medical image learning models. In addition to medical facilities, edge federated transfer learning is employed on personal health monitoring equipment, including as blood pressure monitors and activity recognition devices. These devices are crucial parts of smart health systems. Users must train a personalized model that is regularly updated by their physical conditions starting with a ready-made model. Federated Health, Federated learning with personalization layers, and Federated learning in medicine may be used in conjunction to jointly create a model at the network edge while recording customization. By include model training in this security measure, FL ensures that patient data is always safeguarded [15].

- **Diagnostic Edge AI:** Edge computing and FL combined allows for AI-powered diagnostic and decision assistance there. In situations like the study of medical imaging, this may result in a quicker and more precise diagnosis.
- **Diverse Edge Devices:** From sophisticated medical equipment to wearable fitness monitors, healthcare depends on a wide variety of gadgets. FL that is built on the edge can adjust to this variety and offer a versatile platform for healthcare applications.
- **Economicalness:** Costs related to data transport and centralized cloud infrastructure can be decreased through edge computing. Decentralized training offered by FL further improves resource efficiency.

10.4 HEALTHCARE EDGE COMPUTING APPLICATIONS

- **Aboard Ambulances:** Paramedics are typically only able to provide emergency doctors a quick overview of the patient under the current emergency care system. As a result, these individuals can only obtain the necessary diagnostic procedures after the ambulance gets to the hospital. This might lead to challenges and hold up patient transfers to the appropriate wards, delaying patient diagnosis. Such delays, particularly in emergency situations, might be lethal. Due to its low latency, mobility, and data-processing capabilities, edge computing at the network edge (in conjunction with 5G) can enable better and more precise treatment by on-site paramedics as well as send more particular facts on the state and location of patients arriving at the hospital [16].
- **Operation Theatres:** Edge computing and AI in operation theatres (OTs) have also ushered in a change in the operating room with AI-assisted surgery. For instance, nurses are expected to record each activity taken during

procedures, starting with the time a patient enters the OT until the room is cleaned. In the span of using this method may require hitting hundreds of touchscreen buttons. However, AI systems can automatically track and classify surgical procedures when used in conjunction with AI. Cameras and edge computing devices are used for every OT action information from many identical. Afterwards, data from surgeries may be collated and examined, enabling more effective procedures and better care for the patient.

- **Hospitals:** A central cloud link is frequently absent from monitoring devices, raising questions about patient and facility security. By combining data from several hospital sources while protecting patient privacy, on-site edge technologies on the hospital's campus can assist in resolving this problem. AI-enabled edge solutions offer real-time notifications concerning aberrant patient habits and securely store sensitive data on a cloud platform. This strategy can boost output, resource effectiveness, and patient billing, ultimately resulting in lower expenses per patient [16].

10.5 AUTHENTIC USE OF FL IN THE MEDICAL INDUSTRY AS IN PANDEMIC SITUATION

Medical data streams are collections of steadily growing sets of medical data produced during patient monitoring and care. In telemedicine and patient monitoring, these data streams—like temperature, heart rate, and blood pressure—are utilized to notify doctors of changes in patients' conditions. The objective is to create an analytical model that can quickly identify significant patterns or risk factors. FL and medical data streams can improve training tasks and security performance by removing disparities in changing medical datasets and data transmission between FL coordinators and participant nodes. Due to the fast, massive, and dynamic nature of medical data streams, it is crucial to develop a successful FL step-by-step implementation in order to achieve high accuracy, little overall memory use, and quick processing times.

10.5.1 COVID-19

The coronavirus pandemic exposed significant FLaws in current healthcare systems, increasing the need for medical facilities globally. Healthcare facilities, however, struggle to provide the continual care that is required because of the expanding population and per capita income. The epidemic has also brought attention to the industry's narrow margins of error, underscoring the necessity of adopting digital healthcare for cooperation and efficiency [17]. FL, which is renowned for its capacity to protect privacy, has emerged as a potent weapon in the war against the infection. To help the investigation of the COVID-19 epidemic, researchers have taken use of FL's capabilities, which has resulted in a variety of creative applications. The Unified Computed Tomography (CT)-COVID AI Diagnostic Initiative (UCADI), which enables international collaboration in the development of a clinic CT-COVID AI application, is one of the ground-breaking FL applications in healthcare. By coordinating efforts globally, FL uses a variety of data sources for improved diagnostic precision while protecting privacy [18].

Federated Deep Learning System for Application of Healthcare **139**

FL has also shown promise in predicting death among hospitalized COVID-19 patients by merging patient data from several institutions within a health system. By integrating vital signs, laboratory results, and chest X-rays, FL models outperformed locally trained models in predicting outcomes; this demonstrates the feasibility of developing effective prediction tools without invading patient privacy. The EMR Chest X-ray AI model (EXAM), another ground-breaking project, uses FL to predict future oxygen needs for COVID-19 patients with symptoms. Medical facilities can filter COVID-19 from chest X-ray pictures using collaborative FL frameworks without disclosing patient information [18].

Numerous studies have suggested and supported the use of FL in COVID-19 X-ray data training and deployment trials. Additionally, an examination into a hybrid architecture for COVID-19 prediction utilizing federated ML models is recommended together with an asynchronously updated FL model for portable and deployable resource nodes. The newly created idea of clustered FL (CFL) was used for automated diagnosis of COVID-19 at the edge by creating a multi-modal ML model that can distinguish COVID-19 in both X-ray and ultrasound imaging [20]. Safeguarded global informatics A 5G-enabled architecture of auxiliary COVID-19 diagnostics based on FL for multiple institutions and central cloud cooperation is offered. FL infrastructure has been established to investigate COVID-19. To solve the privacy issue for COVID-19 data, the SCOR (secure international informatics infrastructure to investigate COVID-19) cooperation has been developed to provide a ready-to-deploy secure FL infrastructure based on privacy and security technologies [19,20].

10.5.2 MONKEYPOX

A global notice has been issued in response to the development of the monkeypox virus during the 2019 pandemic, and the virus has undergone a scientific review. Healthcare infrastructure has been considerably changed by ML and federated deep learning algorithms, which make it possible to find hidden data, monitor patient health, and issue life-threatening situation alerts. These algorithms use mathematical and scientific methods to extract new information from data, producing reliable and accurate diagnosis systems [20]. Pathologists and radiologists have benefited from Fl, which has produced incredibly precise and effective diagnostic models for a variety of ailments, including cancer, neurological disorders, fractures, and cardiovascular problems. Drug and vaccine development also makes use of FL models. Recent research has focused on the pathogenesis, etiology, transmission, clinical features, diagnosis, and treatment of monkeypox infection, as well as the science of monkeypox disease prevention and therapy, including prospective antiviral drugs and immunological strategies. Monkeypox defences are progressively being developed using AI-based methods, and a number of methods, including image recognition, immunodiagnostics, nucleic acid, and whole-particle detection, have been suggested.

10.6 CHALLENGES OF FL IN HEALTHCARE

- Current FL studies only take into account non-Inactive Ingredient Database (IID) features like label skew or data imbalance. However, there are no exhaustive studies that look at a variety of non-IID's attributes in the medical dataset. Additional methods will be found in the future view to deal with the problems posed by hybrid non-IID characteristics.

- The second limitation and issue is the quest for FL's hyperparameter framework. A crucial yet time-consuming stage in the ML pipeline is hyperparameter tweaking. When models are trained across a distributed network of diverse data silos using FL, optimizing hyperparameters becomes noticeably more challenging. Future research therefore urgently needs an automated technique or framework to choose the best hyperparameters in the FL model.

- Multiple rounds of communication between players are necessary for FL, which puts a burden on bandwidth resources. Particularly for rural institutions, geographic discrepancies and unstable network connectivity might hinder the procedure. Geographical inequalities can lead to unstable connections, while bandwidth limitations might put a burden on the available resources. Real-time decision-making can be hampered by latency problems, particularly in time-sensitive applications like telemedicine. Data privacy issues are extremely important, and securing sensitive data requires the use of encryption and data integrity. To maintain data security and privacy while implementing FL in healthcare, certain communication procedures are needed.

- Data distribution across clients is the statistical difficulty of federated optimization (FL) in healthcare systems, notably in EHR data. Healthcare data is varied and vulnerable to differences across facilities and geographical areas. Data heterogeneity, bias, and generalizability, data sparsity, and non-IID data distribution are all difficulties. Healthcare data may be found in EHRs, medical imaging, wearable tech, and genomics, among other places. The generalizability of ML models might be hampered by training them on data from a particular hospital or clinic. Smaller clinics could only have a limited amount of EHR data, which makes ML challenging to use.

- There are considerable computational hurdles as a result of the expanding usage of edge devices in healthcare. Over 80% of newly generated data will be handled at network edges by 2030, opening up possibilities for on-device AI. These issues include scalability, data discrepancy in cross-silo FL, lightweight models, device dependability, and edge device proliferation. Although edge devices, including wearable medical devices and IoT sensors, provide a sizable amount of healthcare data, they differ greatly in terms of their processing power, storage capacity, and energy consumption. In healthcare FL, balancing model performance with resource restrictions is still difficult.

- FL systems enable remote clients to work together and train ML and DL models. However, sending gradient changes to a central server might invite reverse engineering assaults, jeopardizing the FL system as a whole. Given that medical information is sensitive and confidential, this could be against the GDPR. Although it could hinder the speed of the global model, encrypting global gradients shared throughout the distributed network could aid in preventing backdoor assaults. Data privacy breaches can also be avoided using other technological methods like additive homomorphic encryption.

10.7 CONCLUSION

FL is an ML technique used in the healthcare industry to calculate the likelihood of patient mortality using clinical data from EHRs. Patients, medical facilities, and clinics can preserve control over their own data sources thanks to the preservation of data privacy and ownership. Decentralized data sources are used by FL to ensure that confidential medical data remains where it was created and to reduce unauthorized access. With various data distributions, it may be utilized in healthcare settings such as home healthcare, healthcare in hospitals, and healthcare on the go. In the healthcare sector, FL techniques are critical for protecting patient privacy and delivering productivity gains. Without depending on a single aggregator, blockchain, a decentralized public ledger technology, encourages cross-device learning collaboration. By combining FL with blockchain, healthcare AI solutions such the IoMT architecture, clinical trials, and precision medicine may be developed more quickly. Local data evaluation at edge devices is made possible by the IoMT paradigm, enabling real-time data processing, remote patient monitoring, early illness identification, cost savings, flexibility, and improved patient involvement. Edge computing, which combines deep learning and FL, enhances model training without transferring patient data, guaranteeing the privacy of patient data. With applications like the UCADI and EXAM, FL has emerged as a potent weapon in the fight against COVID-19. The non-IID characteristics, hyperparameter framework search, several communication rounds, data dissemination among clients, computational difficulties brought on by edge devices, and distant client cooperation are obstacles to FL implementation in the healthcare industry.

REFERENCES

1. Kaissis, G., Ziller, A., Passerat-Palmbach, J., Ryffel, T., Usynin, D., Trask, A., ... Braren, R. (2021). End-to-end privacy preserving deep learning on multi-institutional medical imaging. *Nature Machine Intelligence*, 3(6), 473–484.
2. Farooq, K., Syed, H. J., Alqahtani, S. O., Nagmeldin, W., Ibrahim, A. O., & Gani, A. (2022). Blockchain federated learning for in-home health monitoring. *Electronics*, 12(1), 136.
3. Han, H., Shiwakoti, R. K., Jarvis, R., Mordi, C., & Botchie, D. (2023). Accounting and auditing with blockchain technology and artificial intelligence: A literature review. *International Journal of Accounting Information Systems*, 48, 100598.
4. Vaid, A., Jaladanki, S. K., Xu, J., Teng, S., Kumar, A., Lee, S., ... Glicksberg, B. S. (2020). Federated learning of electronic health records improves mortality prediction in patients hospitalized with COVID-19. *MedRxiv*, 241, 1–19.
5. Rahman, A., Hossain, M. S., Muhammad, G., Kundu, D., Debnath, T., Rahman, M., ... Band, S. S. (2023). Federated learning-based AI approaches in smart healthcare: Concepts, taxonomies, challenges and open issues. *Cluster Computing*, 26(4), 2271–2311.
6. Mahlool, D. H., & Abed, M. H. (2022). A comprehensive survey on federated learning: Concept and applications. In: *Mobile Computing and Sustainable Informatics: Proceedings of ICMCSI 2022*, Tribhuvan University, Nepal, pp. 539–553.
7. Yang, Q., Liu, Y., Chen, T., & Tong, Y. (2019). Federated machine learning: Concept and applications. *ACM Transactions on Intelligent Systems and Technology (TIST)*, 10(2), 1–19.

8. Myrzashova, R., Alsamhi, S. H., Shvetsov, A. V., Hawbani, A., & Wei, X. (2023). Blockchain meets federated learning in healthcare: A systematic review with challenges and opportunities. *IEEE Internet of Things Journal*, 10(16), 14418–14437. DOI:10.1109/JIOT.2023.3263598

9. Antunes, R. S., André da Costa, C., Küderle, A., Yari, I. A., & Eskofier, B. (2022). Federated learning for healthcare: Systematic review and architecture proposal. *ACM Transactions on Intelligent Systems and Technology (TIST)*, 13(4), 1–23.

10. Estrela, V. V., Deshpande, A., Stutz, D., de Assis, J. T., Laghari, A. A., da Silva, H. H., ... Tavares, J. M. R. S. 6G in healthcare-anticipating needs and requirements. In Vania V. Estrela (Ed), *Intelligent Healthcare Systems* (pp. 159–181). CRC Press.

11. Jabarulla, M. Y., & Lee, H. N. (2021, August). A blockchain and artificial intelligence-based, patient-centric healthcare system for combating the COVID-19 pandemic: Opportunities and applications. In: Marco P. Soares dos Santos (Eds), *Healthcare* (Vol. 9, No. 8, p. 1019). MDPI.

12. Ma, C., Li, J., Wei, K., Liu, B., Ding, M., Yuan, L., ... Poor, H. V. (2023). Trusted AI in multiagent systems: An overview of privacy and security for distributed learning. *Proceedings of the IEEE*, 111(9), 1097–1132.

13. Kumar, A., Sharma, S., Goyal, N., Singh, A., Cheng, X., & Singh, P. (2021). Secure and energy-efficient smart building architecture with emerging technology IoT. *Computer Communications*, 176, 207–221

14. Srivastava, G., K, D. R., Yenduri, G., Hegde, P., Gadekallu, T. R., Maddikunta, P. K. R., & Bhattacharya, S. (2023). Federated learning enabled edge computing security for internet of medical things: Concepts, challenges and open issues. In: Srivastava, G., Ghosh, U., Lin, J. C-W. (Eds), *Security and Risk Analysis for Intelligent Edge Computing* (pp. 67–89). Springer International Publishing.

15. Xia, Q., Ye, W., Tao, Z., Wu, J., & Li, Q. (2021). A survey of federated learning for edge computing: Research problems and solutions. *High-Confidence Computing*, 1(1), 100008.

16. Wang, S. (2019). Edge computing: Applications, state-of-the-art and challenges. *Advances in Networks*, 7(1), 8–15.

17. Ortiz-Barrios, M., Borrego-Areyanes, A. A., Gómez-Villar, I. D., De Felice, F., Petrillo, A., Gul, M., & Yucesan, M. (2021). A multiple criteria decision-making approach for increasing the preparedness level of sales departments against COVID-19 and future pandemics: A real-world case. *International Journal of Disaster Risk Reduction*, 62, 102411.

18. Tiwari, S., Kumar, S., & Guleria, K. (2020). Outbreak trends of coronavirus disease-2019 in India: A prediction. *Disaster Medicine and Public Health Preparedness*, 14(5), e33–e38.

19. Rauniyar, A., Hagos, D. H., Jha, D., Håkegård, J. E., Bagci, U., Rawat, D. B., & Vlassov, V. (2022). Federated learning for medical applications: A taxonomy, current trends, challenges, and future research directions. *arXiv* preprint arXiv:2208.03392.

20. Thilakarathne, N. N., Muneeswari, G., Parthasarathy, V., Alassery, F., Hamam, H., Mahendran, R. K., & Shafiq, M. (2022). Federated learning for privacy-preserved medical internet of things. Intelligent Automation & Soft Computing, 33(1), 157–172.

11 The Integration of Federated Deep Learning with Internet of Things in Healthcare

Hirak Mondal, Md. Mehedi Hassan,
Anindya Nag, and Anupam Kumar Bairagi

11.1 INTRODUCTION

The healthcare industry is now on the edge of significant and revolutionary instability, which is being driven by the confluence of two notable technology advancements: Federated Deep Learning (FDL) and the Internet of Things (IoT). In the current epoch characterized by the prevalence of data-driven decision-making and the persistent quest for tailored healthcare interventions, the convergence of these advanced advancements provides an exceptional prospect to surpass the conventional confines of medical practice. The integration of FDL's sophisticated machine learning capabilities with the widespread use of IoT devices has positioned the healthcare industry on the verge of a transformative change that will have significant consequences for the treatment of diseases, provision of patient care, and advancement of medical research [1]. The recent progress achieved via FDL has shed light on a potential trajectory for using decentralized data sources while maintaining the fundamental values of individual privacy. The union of power and privacy has the utmost importance in the realm of healthcare, particularly when it comes to safeguarding the confidentiality of patient data. Simultaneously, the rapid and widespread use of IoT devices has facilitated access to a substantial amount of real-time health data [2]. A wide range of technologies, including wearable fitness trackers and advanced medical sensors, effectively gather a substantial amount of data. This data encompasses vital signs, lifestyle information, and biometric data, all of which have the potential to significantly transform the delivery and management of healthcare [3]. However, within the context of the healthcare ecosystem, the process of integrating FDL and IoT is accompanied by several difficulties and obstacles.

One of the foremost obstacles in this context is the intricate matter of data heterogeneity arising from the diverse array of formats and origins of healthcare data. The existence of these differences poses a significant problem in establishing a unified and compatible data environment. Furthermore, healthcare systems are also facing the significant challenge of managing the immense amount of data produced by IoT devices [4]. This situation raises substantial issues about the scalability of

DOI: 10.1201/9781032694870-11

143

healthcare systems, the security of the data, and the overall operational effectiveness. This study undertakes an academic investigation to examine the potential synergies that may arise from the integration of FDL and IoT technologies in the healthcare sector's transformation. Central to this investigation is the widespread use of wearable gadgets, which is a defining characteristic of the IoT revolution. This study extensively examines the function of these devices as means for acquiring real-time patient data, their potential impact on the construction of FDL models by combining diverse data sources, and their importance as tools for continuous health monitoring. Furthermore, we carefully examine the complex incorporation of FDL into Electronic Health Records (EHRs), specifically emphasizing its capacity to improve healthcare quality via the augmentation of diagnostic accuracy and treatment efficacy [5]. This study examines the significant impact of FDL on the analysis of medical imaging, the anticipation of illness initiation, and the customization of treatment protocols. This research aims to emphasize the importance of clarity, accuracy, and creativity in exploring the possibility of integrating FDL and IoT technologies. Additionally, it acknowledges and addresses the significant hurdles associated with this fusion. As we confront the challenges posed by data security, heterogeneity, scalability, and operational efficiency, we will not hesitate to put up novel and inventive solutions. These include the use of sophisticated procedures such as differential privacy (DP), cutting-edge encryption techniques, and innovative approaches to data harmonization. In conclusion, it is important to recognize the significant potential that exists in the integration of FDL and IoT in the healthcare sector [6]. As we begin on this revolutionary path, we are aware of the latent opportunities that may be unlocked via this convergence. This journey acknowledges the urgent need for a healthcare future in which the amalgamation of FDL and IoT acts as a catalyst, leading to an age distinguished by exceptional healthcare, a steadfast focus on patient needs, and continuous innovation driven by data. While the route may be complex, the ultimate outcome has the potential for significant and transformative change [7].

11.2 RELATED WORK

A detection model at the edge has been proposed to safeguard the cloud against potential attacks by effectively stopping data from reaching its gateway [2]. Utilizing this methodology has several benefits, including a decrease in the time required for detection, a reduction in computing and processing demands, and the capacity to effectively manage smaller datasets, which is made possible by implementing Federated Learning (FL). The evaluation of the BoT-IoT dataset involved the assessment of two models, namely the Artificial Neural Network (ANN) and Xtreme Gradient Boosting (XGBoost). The results suggest that ANN models have significantly higher accuracy, achieving a 99.99% level of precision. Furthermore, these models showcase superior performance in handling the varied characteristics of data in IoT devices, specifically in the setting of intensive care units (ICUs) within healthcare systems.

The study by authors used a technique of FL to analyze cardiac activity data obtained via the use of smart bands, with the aim of assessing stress levels [3].The technique of monitoring across several occurrences. The research successfully implemented FL and used an MLP classifier, resulting in an impressive accuracy rate of 87.55%.

The study by Chen et al. [4] introduced FedHealth, a novel federated transfer learning (FTL) system designed specifically for wearable healthcare. The platform aims to address the aforementioned issues in the field. Fed-Health uses FL for data collection and then employs transfer learning to construct somewhat personalized models. The effectiveness of Fed-Health in achieving accurate and personalized healthcare while maintaining privacy and security has been assessed via tests on wearable activity identification and its use in the auxiliary diagnosis of Parkinson's disease. The performance of the model demonstrated that FedHealth attains the highest level of classification accuracy, surpassing the top-performing comparison approach by a substantial margin of 21.6% and 16.6% in two distinct datasets. Additionally, FedHealth earns the highest mean-F1 score across all users.

Liu et al. [7] proposed that the use of computer vision and deep learning methodologies has the potential to aid in the identification and diagnosis of COVID-19 infection via the analysis of Chest X-ray images. This research proposes the use of FL as a means to facilitate COVID-19 data training. Furthermore, tests are conducted to validate the efficacy of this approach. Additionally, this study aims to evaluate the performances of four widely used models, namely MobileNet, ResNetXt, ResNet18, and COVID-Net, both with and without the use of the FL framework. The ResNet18 model has the most rapid convergence speed and achieves the greatest accuracy rates of 96.15% and 91.26% on the training and testing sets, respectively.

The research by Qayyum et al. [8] explores the use of collaborative FL in the healthcare domain, specifically focusing on the multi-modal diagnosis of COVID-19 at the edge. The effectiveness of the proposed framework was assessed across multiple experimental setups utilizing two benchmark datasets. The results obtained from both datasets show promising outcomes, indicating a performance that is comparable to the central baseline. The customized models, which were trained using centralized data, demonstrate enhancements of 16% and 11% in overall F1-Scores in comparison to the model developed in the CFL (Client Federated Learning) configuration utilizing multi-modal COVID-19 data on X-ray and Ultrasound datasets, correspondingly. Table 11.1 presents a comprehensive summary of literature reviews.

TABLE 11.1
Summary of Literature Reviews

Authors	Dataset	Model Used	Best Performing Model	Outcome (%)
Ashraf et al. [2]	BoT-IoT dataset	ANN, XGBoost	ANN	99.99
Can et al. [3]	Dataset 1, Dataset 2, and Dataset 3	SVM, MLP, FL	FL	87.55
Chen et al. [4]	UCI smartphone dataset	KNN, SVM, RF, NoFed, FedHealth	FedHealth	99.4
Liu et al. [7]	COVIDx dataset	CovidNet, ResNeXt, MobileNet-v2, and ResNet18	ResNet18	91.26
Qayyum et al. [8]	Chest X-ray, chest ultrasound images	CFL (multi-modal), FL (multi-modal), FL (specialized)	FL (specialized)	97

11.3 FEDERATED DEEP LEARNING

The concept of "FDL" commonly denotes learning methodologies that rely on a variety of neural networks, such as RNN, CNN, and DNN. The network model is commonly divided into three distinct levels, namely the input layer, the hidden layer, and the output layer. Every layer is comprised of many neurons. The objective of deep learning is to optimize the connection weights between adjacent layers of neurons in a network model, so that the output of the model minimizes the error with respect to the original label [9].

Let HM denote a dataset of m samples, expressed as HM = {(cr, dr), d_k = 1, 2, ..., n}. In this context, "cr" denotes the feature vector of the r-th sample, while "d_k" represents the matching label. In light of the basic information provided, to calculate the output function, we begin by determining the weight vector, denoted as w. First, we need to determine the function f(cr, w) of the neural network. Once we have established this function, we may proceed to compute the error. There exists a relationship between the output function and the label. The imprecision under consideration pertains to the loss function, referred to as $\mathcal{L}_f$, which is mathematically expressed by a specific equation.

$$\mathcal{L}_f(\text{HM}, w) = \frac{1}{|\text{HM}|} \sum_{\langle \text{cr,dk} \rangle \in \text{HM}} \|f(\text{cr}, w) - \text{dr}\|_2 \tag{11.1}$$

Within this particular framework, the notation "HM" denotes the magnitude of the dataset, whereas "$\|\bullet\|2$" signifies the L2-norm of a vector. Forward propagation refers to the computational process within a neural network that involves calculating from the output function to the loss function. To minimize the loss function, it is imperative to make constant adjustments to the model parameters. The procedure described is often known as backward propagation, which typically uses the stochastic gradient descent (SGD) algorithm to calculate the ideal parameters for the model. The formula represents the specific model change in each iteration.

$$w^{t+1} = w^t - \beta. \, \nabla \mathcal{L}_f\left(\text{HM}, w^t\right) \tag{11.2}$$

In this context, the variable t represents the number of iterations, whereas β represents the learning rate, which indicates the magnitude of adjustment made to the model in each iteration. The expression $\nabla \mathcal{L}_f\left(\text{HM}, w^t\right)$ represents the gradient of the model.

This necessitates the calculation of the partial derivative of the loss function, within each dimension of the model. In the context of a d-dimensional model, let w be a vector represented as $p = (p_1, p_2 ..., p_d)$. The gradient may be computed according to the formula. According to the prescribed formula,

$$\nabla \mathcal{L}_f\left(\text{HM}, w^t\right) = < \frac{\partial \mathcal{L}}{\partial p_1}, \frac{\partial \mathcal{L}}{\partial p_2}, ..., \frac{\partial \mathcal{L}}{\partial p_d}, \tag{11.3}$$

CNN is commonly considered the preferred choice for training models on extensive medical images. To decrease the dimensionality of the image and extract significant characteristics, various techniques can be employed. Subsequently, the aforementioned features undergo a flattening process and are subsequently fed into fully connected layers in order to facilitate the categorization task. During the earliest phases of the image processing pipeline, the utilization of the convolutional layer and pooling layer is employed to sample and compress the image. The primary objective of this process is to decrease the number of dimensions in the image while identifying and isolating important elements. Afterward, the retrieved features are flattened and then sent through fully connected layers, which are responsible for carrying out the classification process [10]. To achieve the goal of reducing the number of models for the purpose of optimizing computational complexity and addressing potential challenges, it is crucial to define certain characteristics. The subject under consideration pertains to the phenomenon of overfitting. Following a prior training session, the flatten layer is connected to the fully connected layer in the traditional neural network for subsequent training. In the domain of FL, it is postulated that a collection of N clients is present. To facilitate collaborative learning, we designated the individuals involved as {Pi}. Let i be an element belonging to the set {1, 2, ..., N}. The responsibility for teaching the local model, referred to as w_i, lies with each individual client. The HM_i dataset was acquired through multiple iterations. The utilization of the SGD technique is employed. Afterward, the regional model is transmitted to the server. The server aggregates all of the local models that have been uploaded by the users. The arithmetic mean is employed to integrate the contributions of N customers into a comprehensive model [11]. The subject of discourse pertains to the choice between two algorithms: the conventional approach and the weighted average technique. Based on the information provided, the aggregation weight αi represents the weight attributed to the client P_i inside the global model context. The concept of w_g can be developed using formula (11.4) and thereafter implemented. The allocation of the distribution is made to each individual consumer.

$$w_g = \sum_{i=1}^{N} \alpha_i \cdot W_i, \qquad (11.4)$$

Subsequently, each client proceeds with iterative training until the model achieves convergence or the termination condition is met. Throughout the whole of the procedure, the initial dataset is situated. The client does not share information with the server, but rather submits a subset. The act of submitting the model parameters, hence maintaining the integrity of the data [8].

In Figure 11.1, we observe the intricate architecture of the Federated Deep Healthcare IoT (FDH-IoT) System, accompanied by its corresponding communication mechanism, which accommodates a diverse array of client devices. Presently, the IoT device and the aggregation server coexist within the same physical location, specifically at the service access point. During the initial phase of system initialization and device selection, the aggregator assumes the crucial role of selecting specific IoT activities, such as activity detection and predicting future events.

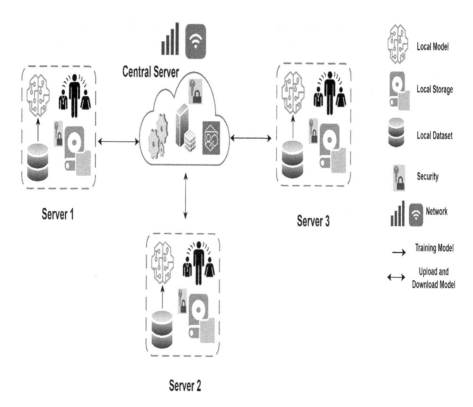

FIGURE 11.1 Block diagram of FDH-IoT system.

Additionally, the aggregator is tasked with determining the learning parameters associated with these activities, encompassing details like the required number of communication rounds and learning rates for achieving an optimal global model. As the server completes its initial setup, it progresses to the phase of local model training and update. In this stage, a novel model is generated and disseminated to FDH-IoT clients, initiating distributed training. Consequently, each client employs its unique dataset to train the local model, minimizing the loss function for computing the update. In the final phase of model aggregation and download, a fresh global model emerges by amalgamating all modifications made to the local client models. The server then resolves the optimization issue, concluding the intricate process of creating an updated and refined global model. This comprehensive approach ensures the effective coordination and enhancement of the FDH-IoT System, contributing to its overall efficiency and performance [12].

11.3.1 FDL with Fine-Grains

FDL with Fine-Grains (FDLFG) represents a nuanced approach within the realm of FL, characterized by its focus on precision, specificity, and meticulous data handling. Let's delve into the formal concept of FDLFG, unraveling its goals, constraints, and specifications.

11.3.1.1 Problem Statement

The standard FDL is a device-centric approach, whereby data owners use the computational capabilities available on edge devices to train their local learning models. This measure guarantees the preservation of privacy in the context of collaborative learning. Following this, the researchers employ privacy-preserving methodologies to send the alterations made to the local models to centralized cloud servers. The servers carry out federated aggregation processes in order to combine the modifications and update the global learning models. One instance of such a tactic involves employing the SGD techniques to modify the weights within DNN [13]. To enhance the local learning models, the edge devices receive updates of the global model. The FDL systems must confront several challenges, which encompass:

- **The Presence of Diverse Devices and Servers:** Devices and servers in FDL systems often vary widely in terms of computational power, storage capacity, and network bandwidth. Heterogeneity can lead to uneven contributions to model training, potentially causing slower convergence or bias in the learned model. Adaptive FL algorithms that dynamically adjust the learning process based on device capabilities can help mitigate this challenge.
- **Data and Model Improvements with a High-Dimensional Dependence:** High-dimensional data and model updates pose challenges in terms of communication bandwidth and computational resources [14]. Transmitting and processing large volumes of data and updates can lead to increased latency and resource consumption. Techniques like model compression, quantization, and sparsity-inducing methods are employed to reduce the dimensionality of data and updates without compromising accuracy.
- **Bias in Data, Algorithms, and Model Training:** Bias can arise from variations in data distributions, algorithms used, and model training methodologies across different devices. Biases can result in models that are skewed toward certain subsets of the population, impacting the generalizability of the learned models. FL algorithms need to account for and mitigate biases by incorporating fairness-aware techniques and regularizing methods.
- **Centrality in Model Training:** Despite the distributed nature of FDL, model training often involves a centralized server, posing a risk of central points of control. Centralized training may hinder scalability, and it can be susceptible to security and privacy concerns. Decentralized or edge-based training approaches can distribute the training process, reducing reliance on a single central server and enhancing scalability [15].
- **Centralized Points of Failure:** Relying on centralized cloud servers introduces a vulnerability to single points of failure. Server downtimes or attacks can disrupt the entire FDL system, impacting the availability and reliability of services. Implementing distributed architectures, redundancy, and fault-tolerant mechanisms can enhance the resilience of FDL systems.

Despite their clear execution technique and advantages in terms of latency, bandwidth efficiency, and privacy protection, standard FDL schemes are subject to restrictions. Moreover, conventional FL systems provide centralized global model updates, which may be beneficial for broader-level applications [16]. For instance, they can facilitate the creation of a collaborative social health platform that identifies general activity patterns among all users of an application. To achieve customization, particularly within a specific subset of the population, it is essential to consider the individuality of each mobile user, which encompasses distinct patterns of behaviors like as running, sitting, and walking, as well as variations in pace.

11.3.2 Classification of FDL

FDL can be categorized into two primary classifications, namely data partitioning and network design. Based on an analysis of the distribution of training data in both the sample and feature space, the data partition can be categorized into three unique classifications: Vertical FL(VFL), Horizontal FL (HFL), and FTL [17].

- **Vertical Federated Learning (VFL):** Consider seeing the VFL as a choreographer who skillfully coordinates a dance routine, whereby the dancers symbolize data entities. In this analogy, the dancers execute their movements in a synchronized manner, ensuring a cohesive performance while concealing their individualized sequences. The VFL framework demonstrates exceptional proficiency in facilitating cooperation at the feature level. This allows various organizations to exchange valuable insights obtained from certain features while maintaining the confidentiality of their whole datasets. Envision it as a choreographed dance of privacy, whereby the safeguarding of sensitive information is pursued with utmost dedication. The VFL framework has emerged as a safeguard for privacy, enabling FL models to acquire shared knowledge while upholding the principles of uniqueness and secrecy for each participant [17].
- **Horizontal Federated Learning (HFL):** Within the dynamic realm of data cooperation, HFL serves as a vibrant marketplace where merchants, in the form of entities, convene to present their distinct offerings, namely data samples while refraining from disclosing the full of their inventory. The HFL serves as a central hub where various datasets from different sources are interconnected, therefore contributing to the development of a common model. The situation may be likened to a vibrant town square, where each institution contributes to the collective knowledge without compromising the confidentiality of its data repositories. HFL may be seen as a commemoration of collective cooperation at the level of individual data samples, promoting a collective intelligence that surpasses individual limitations.
- **Federated Transfer Learning (FTL):** Enter the world of FTL which serves as a significant conduit between two distinct realms, akin to a scholar imparting knowledge from one field of study to another. FTL has exceptional proficiency in the realm of knowledge transfer, enabling the use of insights acquired in one area to provide light on the trajectory in another. The transmission of intellectual legacy serves as a crucial technique in sectors characterized by limited availability of labeled data. FTL, or Faster-than-Light, serves as a cognitive guide, facilitating the transfer of

Integration of Federated Deep Learning with Internet of Things 151

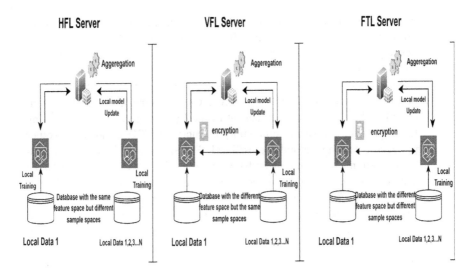

FIGURE 11.2 Three types of Federated Deep Learning approaches: (a) Horizontal federated learning (HFL). (b) Vertical federated learning (VFL). (c) Federated transfer learning (FTL).

information across different domains, hence enhancing comprehension and expediting advancements. This process promotes flexibility and effectiveness within the context of FL [18].

Figure 11.2 represents the configuration of HFL, VFL, and FTL. In the context of CFL, the client uses their individual dataset to simultaneously train the FDL model within a singular training iteration. The technique described above involves the use of a central server to facilitate cooperation. Once the client has transferred the acquired parameters to the central server, the server proceeds to aggregate them using a weighted average process. Consequently, upon completing the training procedure, every customer will get both a global and individualized model. The central server is widely recognized as a fundamental component of the CFL network. The primary objectives of this system encompass disseminating model updates to client participants and preserving the security and integrity of training data. In contrast, the FDL solution incorporates a network architecture that eliminates the need for a central server.

11.3.3 Popular Method for Studying Federated Deep Learning

This section provides an overview of the technologies that are most often used to put into action FL applications in the medical field.

- **TensorFlow Federated (TFF):** TFF is an open-source framework that has been created by Google. This technique enhances the functionalities of TensorFlow by enabling machine learning on data that is dispersed across several decentralized sources. The TFF framework provides conceptual frameworks for the construction of FL models and the execution of simulations to investigate various algorithms. The system has been purposefully developed to cater to scenarios whereby data is distributed across multiple devices or servers.

- **PySyft:** PySyft is a versatile and robust software library designed for the purpose of encrypted and privacy-preserving machine learning. The mentioned tool is an integral component of the PyTorch ecosystem, facilitating the implementation of FL, homomorphic encryption (HE), and several other privacy-preserving methodologies. The PySyft framework facilitates the construction of models that may undergo training using data derived from many sources while ensuring the privacy of the original data is maintained [19].
- **Flower:** The Flower framework is a tool that facilitates the construction of FL systems by using the capabilities of TensorFlow. The use of this technology streamlines the procedures involved in the creation and implementation of FL models. The Flower framework offers a comprehensive application programming interface (API) that facilitates the creation of FL configurations and encompasses a range of optimization techniques. FL may be effectively deployed on a vast array of devices, facilitating its scalability [20].
- **FederatedAI/FATE:** FATE, an acronym for Federated AI Technology Enabler, is an open-source initiative that offers a framework for FL. The primary objective of this research is to facilitate the use of machine learning techniques that provide both security and privacy. FATE encompasses the capability to provide both HFL and VFL, along with including tools for data pretreatment, feature engineering, and model training.
- **PyVertical:** PyVertical is a specialized framework for VFL situations, offering a comprehensive solution for this particular domain. VFL is a collaborative approach whereby many parties work together on distinct elements of the same dataset while ensuring that the data remains localized. The primary objective of PyVertical is to streamline the process of creating and implementing VFL models [20].
- **PaddleFL:** The PaddlePaddle association has developed PaddleFL, a library for FL. This platform offers a comprehensive suite of tools and algorithms designed specifically for the purpose of training models in a federated way. PaddleFL offers support for a range of FL situations and can be seamlessly connected with the wider Paddle Paddle ecosystem, which is renowned for its deep learning capabilities.

11.4 FDL DIGITAL HEALTH ACTIVITIES

The FDL framework is a comprehensive learning framework that efficiently reduces the necessity for data pooling in the development of artificial intelligence models. Consequently, its usefulness extends to all facets of AI implementation in the field of healthcare. The potential for revolutionary advancements in the future might be facilitated by the expansion of data collection and the inclusion of patients from diverse demographic groups in FDL research. The current use of the aforementioned item is already underway [21].

Integration of Federated Deep Learning with Internet of Things

153

11.4.1 CLINICAL STAFF

In general terms, primary care services were rendered to patients. The utilization of machine learning methodologies, particularly FDL, within the global market, holds the capacity to augment clinical assessments irrespective of the therapy setting. Specifically, persons who require medical treatment in geographically isolated regions may derive benefits from the utilization of advanced machine learning-supported diagnostic tools, akin to the delivery of these services in institutions that serve a large number of patients. The aforementioned statement holds true for illnesses that are rare or unusual in certain regions. In such cases, the consequences are expected to be less severe if prompt and accurate diagnosis can be made. The utilization of FDL has the potential to reduce the barriers associated with being a data provider. This is due to the assurance patients have that their data will remain inside their designated healthcare facility and can be revoked at their discretion.

11.4.2 HOSPITALS AND MEDICAL PROCEDURES

The implementation of a comprehensive data access system enables hospitals and healthcare practitioners to exert full control over patient data, so effectively reducing the risk of cyberbullying from external entities. To provide uninterrupted training and assessment of machine learning models, organizations must allocate resources toward the procurement of physical on-premises computer infrastructure or the implementation of private cloud service delivery holds significant importance. In addition, adhering to defined and publicly accessible data formats is of utmost significance. The inquiry concerns the degree of engagement of a specific area in a particular activity. The determination of assessment and testing activities, as well as involvement in training efforts, will be ascertained. The requisite level of computer capability. Even institutions that possess limited resources have the chance to engage and acquire membership. One can derive advantages from the community models that have been constructed [21].

11.4.3 THE CLINICAL OVERTURE

For the clinical virtuosos, FDL offers a maestro's wand, elevating diagnostic tools to an unparalleled crescendo of sophistication. Imagine a realm where complex deep learning models collaboratively refine themselves without the need for central data repositories. This not only expedites diagnostics but also opens doors to a new era of predictive and preventive healthcare. The personnel responsible for overseeing the conductor's operations are also employed by the IoT device, ensuring that patients' vital signs are not only monitored but intricately incorporated into the diagnostic symphony, so providing a holistic understanding of health.

11.4.4 EMPOWERING THE PATIENT PROTAGONIST

In the narrative of healthcare, patients, especially those in remote realms, become the protagonists empowered by the saga of FDL and IoT. Wearable devices and IoT-enabled healthcare tools transform patients into active contributors, securely sharing their health data. FDL ensures that these individual contributions aren't isolated notes but harmonious chords that resonate with the collective intelligence, steering healthcare toward a participatory and patient-centric future [22].

11.4.5 Hospitals Guardians of Data Sanctity

Within the hallowed halls of hospitals, FDL and IoT usher in a new era of data governance and cybersecurity. The decentralized nature of FDL mitigates the risk of cyberbullying, providing a shield against unauthorized access to sensitive patient information. Standardized data formats create a common language, fostering seamless communication and collaboration between disparate healthcare entities. It's a fortification of data sanctity, where hospitals wield the power of advanced technology while upholding the sacred trust of patient confidentiality.

11.4.6 Surgical Suites and Beyond

The integration of IoT functionalities extends beyond diagnostics into the very fabric of medical procedures. Connected devices in surgical suites enhance the precision of surgeries, while post-operative care is monitored in real time through IoT sensors. Each procedure becomes a synchronized dance of data, enriching the understanding of patient responses and paving the way for personalized treatment plans.

11.5 FDL DATA PRIVACY ATTACKS

FDL is vulnerable to two types of potential data privacy breaches. The model inversion (MI) attack is an example of the initial assault, which involves attempting to recreate the supplied data. The following assault, as exemplified by the membership inference attack, seeks to reveal the training data.

11.5.1 Model Inversion Attack

The occurrence is commonly referred to as Model Inversion (MI) attack. The MI attack is a technique utilized to launch an offensive against a given model. The process of replicating the dataset used for training a machine learning model. When considering the concept of federated systems, the acquisition of knowledge for healthcare applications has the potential to inadvertently expose confidential patient information that is utilized in these contexts. The training phase of the model. The ability to produce the genetic markers of the patient could be facilitated. The attack specifically capitalizes on the anticipated the machine learning model and provides a probability confidence score as output for making predictions [22]. The class was provided with the dataset including various features. When considering a machine learning model, it can be conceptualized as a function. The equation y-hat equals f of w and x_1 through x_n, where y-hat, w, and X, represented as $\{x_1, x_2, ..., x_n\}$, denote the predicted probability class, the weight vector, and the set of input variables, respectively. The input for machine learning consists of parameters and a feature vector. The aforementioned model the objective of an inversion attack is to exploit a vulnerable attribute, such as attribute x_1, under certain circumstances. Details regarding the additional characteristics $x_2, ..., x_n$ and the estimated likelihood of the

Integration of Federated Deep Learning with Internet of Things   155

output y are provided. One potential approach to mitigating this hazard involves the implementation of a DP mechanism, which has the capability to address this issue. The integration of certain measures within the learning process is implemented with the aim of safeguarding the data against potential inversion assaults, including but not limited to. The process of deducing or deriving the values of model weights.

11.5.2 The Membership Inference Attack

The subject of inquiry pertains to the membership inference attack. Given a machine learning model denoted as f $(w; x_1, \ldots, x_n)$ and, in certain exemplifications, the objective of the membership inference attack is to ascertain whether the presence or absence of the instance in the training dataset is being considered. Membership inference attacks present a significant concern. The disclosure of personal information through membership poses a notable concern about privacy. For example, the process of ascertaining an individual's inclusion in the clinical trial training dataset of a hospital. This statement suggests that the individual in question had previously received medical care at the institution. The individual receiving medical care and the medical facility the two primary stakeholders invested in safeguarding against membership inference are the Tal organization and the key parties involved. Acts of aggression. The patients perceive their memberships as confidential and articulate a preference for the preservation of their information's privacy, the dissemination of sensitive information to the broader populace. Initially, the assailants strive to create a shadow dataset D_0 that closely resembles the training dataset D of the target model. Additionally, the assailant generates a shadow model by utilizing the shadow dataset D_0, which effectively replicates the behavior of the target model. During this phase, the assailant carefully monitored the shadow model's reactions to occurrences that were included in its training data and those that were not. This behavior is employed to construct a dataset for the purpose of capturing various instances in both the training data and previously unseen data. The assault dataset is ultimately utilized in the creation of a binary classifier, which aims to forecast if a given instance has been previously employed in the output of the target model [22].

11.6   DATA PRIVACY PROTECTIONS FOR FEDERATED DEEP LEARNING

In the FDL context, two techniques may be used to safeguard data privacy against potential threats such as data leakage and attackers: perturbation and encryption. In contrast, the encryption technique used in the FDL framework effectively safeguards sensitive data and model confidentiality. The encryption of parameters and gradients shared throughout the aggregation process is accomplished through the utilization of techniques such as the HE algorithm [23].

11.6.1 DP Protection Method

This study explores the application of data privacy safeguards through the utilization of the DP approach. The incorporation of a deep learning model with privacy preservation has emerged as a major field of research. For example, numerous researchers employ DP strategies in order to augment the security of deep learning models. The acquisition of knowledge and skills via a structured educational framework. Motivated by the effective use of dynamic programming in centralized learning, Numerous academics have successfully used DP techniques in the context of distributed training, with a particular emphasis on FDL investigations. In the context of medical applications. The method dynamic programming (DP) is achieved through the implementation of statistical rigorously controlled. The introduction of noise to the input or output of the machine learning model. While the inclusion of noise the use of this measure guarantees the concealment of unique individual data inputs, while also offering valuable insights. Ensuring the privacy of the whole population while maintaining data integrity [24]. The magnitude of the additional noise is the privacy budget, represented as epsilon (ϵ), is referred to as such. Gaussian and Laplace are two often used probability distributions in the field of statistics. Various noise methods are used in the context of DP for the purpose of preserving privacy in FL research conducted in the medical domain. The subject matter under consideration pertains to applications. The use of the Gaussian noise mechanism in DP is a prevalent approach.

11.6.2 HE PRIVACY PROTECTION METHOD

The implementation of the HE scheme was employed in order to guarantee the confidentiality of data by encrypting the parameters that are transmitted throughout the gradient aggregation process. A considerable amount of recent scholarly research has been undertaken in the healthcare domain, with a specific emphasis on the utilization of FDL in training healthcare applications. There exist two main categorizations of HE, namely Fully Homomorphic Encryption (FHE) and Additively Homomorphic Encryption (AHE). The phrase "Fully FHE strategy" refers to an encryption technique that enables the execution of computational operations on encrypted data, resulting in an encrypted output that is equal to the outcome achieved by performing the same operations on unencrypted data [25]. Fundamentally, the act of deciphering the encoded text through the utilization of addition or multiplication operations is equivalent to the outcome achieved by using these identical processes to the original, unencoded data. In contrast, AHE is a cryptographic technique that facilitates the direct computation of a single operation on encrypted data, resulting in an encrypted output that is equivalent to the result obtained by applying the same operation to the plaintext. The AHE method has been specifically designed to cater to applications that necessitate basic arithmetic operations, such as addition or multiplication.

11.7 CONCLUSION

According to the framework of scientific and technological improvement, the convergence of FDL with the IoT presents a multitude of potential opportunities, specifically in the highly regarded domain of healthcare. The exploration of this interconnected association uncovers not just gradual progressions, but rather the emergence of a transformative epoch. The combination of FDL and IoT surpasses the traditional limits of medical innovation, presenting a paradigm shift that has the capacity to rethink the fundamental nature of healthcare. As we conclude this investigation, we encounter significant obstacles that mark the journey toward advancement. These include apprehensions regarding data security, the intricate diversity of data, the complexity introduced by this diversity, the substantial challenge of scalability, and the constant need for operational efficiency. However, our expedition is not just focused on recognizing barriers; rather, it serves as evidence of the unwavering will of the human spirit to overcome difficulties and fully use the capabilities of technological integration. Within the ever-evolving healthcare domain, where the utmost importance is placed on the preservation of patient welfare, the integration of FDL and IoT emerges as a promising and potentially transformative prospect. The utilization of wearable gadgets, the prompt synchronization of patient data, and the complex progression of FDL models indicate not only a convergence of technology but also a noteworthy shift in the delivery of healthcare services. The integration of FDL into EHRs is seen as a significant driver for change, with the potential to improve healthcare quality and align with the principles of compassionate and customized patient care. The effective use of DP and encryption methods indicates the onset of a paradigm shift, wherein the integration of FDL and the IoT is not merely a possible consequence but a necessary requirement for a more resilient and enduring future. Given the dynamic nature of the healthcare industry, we assert with certainty that the combination of FDL and the IoT represents more than just a merging of technologies. Instead, it serves as a compelling catalyst for a fundamental change in approach. This statement serves as a rallying cry to promote the improvement of patient care, enhance diagnostic techniques, and construct a fresh narrative about the quality of healthcare. By strategically addressing obstacles and adopting inventive strategies, the integration discussed has the potential to not only improve the current state of affairs but also initiate a significant and transformative era in healthcare. This era would witness the convergence of FDL and IoT not only as a remarkable technological achievement but also as a guiding force toward a healthier and more empathetic future.

REFERENCES

1. Alazzam, M. B., Alassery, F., & Almulihi, A. (2022). Federated Deep Learning Approaches for the Privacy and Security of IoT Systems. *Wireless Communications and Mobile Computing*, 2022, 1–7. https://doi.org/10.1155/2022/1522179.
2. Ashraf, E., Areed, N. F. F., Salem, H., Abdelhay, E. H., & Farouk, A. (2022). FIDChain: Federated Intrusion Detection System for Blockchain-Enabled IoT Healthcare Applications. Healthcare, 10(6), 1110. https://doi.org/10.3390/healthcare10061110.
3. Can, Y. S., & Ersoy, C. (2021). Privacy-Preserving Federated Deep Learning for Wearable IoT-Based Biomedical Monitoring. *ACM Transactions on Internet Technology*, 21(1), 1–17. https://doi.org/10.1145/3428152.
4. Chen, Y., Qin, X., Wang, J., Yu, C., & Gao, W. (2020). FedHealth: A Federated Transfer Learning Framework for Wearable Healthcare. *IEEE Intelligent Systems*, 35(4), 83–93. https://doi.org/10.1109/MIS.2020.2988604.
5. Dhiman, G., Juneja, S., Mohafez, H., El-Bayoumy, I., Sharma, L. K., Hadizadeh, M., Islam, M. A., Viriyasitavat, W., & Khandaker, M. U. (2022). Federated Learning Approach to Protect Healthcare Data over Big Data Scenario. *Sustainability*, 14(5), 2500. https://doi.org/10.3390/su14052500.
6. Lim, W. Y. B., Garg, S., Xiong, Z., Niyato, D., Leung, C., Miao, C., & Guizani, M. (2021). Dynamic Contract Design for Federated Learning in Smart Healthcare Applications. *IEEE Internet of Things Journal*, 8(23), 16853–16862. https://doi.org/10.1109/JIOT.2020.3033806.

7. Liu, B., Yan, B., Zhou, Y., Yang, Y., & Zhang, Y. (2020). *Experiments of Federated Learning for COVID-19 Chest X-ray Images* (arXiv:2007.05592). arXiv. https://arxiv.org/abs/2007.05592.

8. Qayyum, A., Ahmad, K., Ahsan, M. A., Al-Fuqaha, A., & Qadir, J. (2022). Collaborative Federated Learning for Healthcare: Multi-Modal COVID-19 Diagnosis at the Edge. *IEEE Open Journal of the Computer Society, 3*, 172–184. https://doi.org/10.1109/OJCS.2022.3206407.

9. Liu, D., Miller, T., Sayeed, R., & Mandl, K. D. (2018). FADL: *Federated-Autonomous Deep Learning for Distributed Electronic Health Record* (arXiv:1811.11400). arXiv. https://arxiv.org/abs/1811.11400.

10. Neranjan Thilakarathne, N., Muneeswari, G., Parthasarathy, V., Alassery, F., Hamam, H., Kumar Mahendran, R., & Shafiq, M. (2022). Federated Learning for Privacy-Preserved Medical Internet of Things. *Intelligent Automation & Soft Computing, 33*(1), 157–172. https://doi.org/10.32604/iasc.2022.023763.

11. Yasmin, F., Hassan, M. M., Hasan, M., Zaman, S., Bairagi, A. K., El-Shafai, W., Fouad, H., & Chun, Y. C. (2023). GastroNet: Gastrointestinal Polyp and Abnormal Feature Detection and Classification with Deep Learning Approach. *IEEE Access, 11*, 97605–97624. https://doi.org/10.1109/access.2023.3312729.

12. Nag, A., Hassan, M. M., Das, A., Sinha, A., Chand, N., Kar, A., Sharma, V., & Alkhayyat, A. (2023, November 11). Exploring the Applications and Security Threats of Internet of Thing in the Cloud Computing Paradigm: A Comprehensive Study on the Cloud of Things. *Transactions on Emerging Telecommunications Technologies.* https://doi.org/10.1002/ett.4897.

13. Siniosoglou, I., Sarigiannidis, P., Argyriou, V., Lagkas, T., Goudos, S. K., & Poveda, M. (2021). Federated Intrusion Detection in NG-IoT Healthcare Systems: An Adversarial Approach. In *ICC 2021—IEEE International Conference on Communications*, 1–6. Montreal, QC, Canada. https://doi.org/10.1109/ICC42927.2021.9500578.

14. Wassan, S., Suhail, B., Mubeen, R., Raj, B., Agarwal, U., Khatri, E., Gopinathan, S., & Dhiman, G. (2022). Gradient Boosting for Health IoT Federated Learning. *Sustainability, 14*(24), 16842. https://doi.org/10.3390/su142416842.

15. Wu, Q., Chen, X., Zhou, Z., & Zhang, J. (2022). FedHome: Cloud-Edge Based Personalized Federated Learning for In-Home Health Monitoring. *IEEE Transactions on Mobile Computing, 21*(8), 2818–2832. https://doi.org/10.1109/TMC.2020.3045266.

16. Xu, J., Glicksberg, B. S., Su, C., Walker, P., Bian, J., & Wang, F. (2021). Federated Learning for Healthcare Informatics. *Journal of Healthcare Informatics Research, 5*(1), 1–19. https://doi.org/10.1007/s41666-020-00082-4.

17. Yuan, B., Ge, S., & Xing, W. (2020). *A Federated Learning Framework for Healthcare IoT devices* (arXiv:2005.05083). arXiv. https://arxiv.org/abs/2005.05083.

18. Zhang, L., Xu, J., Vijayakumar, P., Sharma, P. K., & Ghosh, U. (2023). Homomorphic Encryption-Based Privacy-Preserving Federated Learning in IoT-Enabled Healthcare System. *IEEE Transactions on Network Science and Engineering, 10*(5), 2864–2880. https://doi.org/10.1109/TNSE.2022.3185327.

19. Ahsan, M. M., Ali, M. S., Hassan, M. M., Abdullah, T. A., Gupta, K. D., Bagci, U., Kaushal, C., Soliman, N. F. (2023). Monkeypox Diagnosis with Interpretable Deep Learning. *IEEE Access, 11*, 81965–81980. https://doi.org/10.1109/access.2023.3300793.

20. Yasmin, F., Hassan, M. M., Hasan, M., Zaman, S., Kaushal, C., El-Shafai, W., & Soliman, N. F. (2023). PoxNet22: A Fine-Tuned Model for the Classification of Monkeypox Disease Using Transfer Learning. *IEEE Access, 11*, 24053–24076. https://doi.org/10.1109/access.2023.3253868.

21. Nag, A., Das, A., Sil, R., Kar, A., Mandal, D., & Das, B. (2023). Application of Artificial Intelligence in Mental Health. In *Intelligent Systems Design and Applications*, 128–141. https://doi.org/10.1007/978-3-031-27440-4_13.

22. Nag, A., Hassan, M. M., Das, A., Sinha, A., Chand, N., Kar, A., ... Alkhayyat, A. (2023). Exploring the Applications and Security Threats of Internet of Thing in the Cloud Computing Paradigm: A Comprehensive Study on the Cloud Of Things. *Transactions on Emerging Telecommunications Technologies*. https://doi.org/10.1002/ett.4897.
23. Haque, R., Sultana, A., & Haque, P. (2023). Ensemble of Fine-Tuned Deep Learning Models for Monkeypox Detection: A Comparative Study. *2023 4th International Conference for Emerging Technology (INCET)*. https://doi.org/10.1109/incet57972.2023.10170232.
24. Rieke, N., Hancox, J., Li, W., Milletari, F., Roth, H. R., Albarqouni, S., ... Cardoso, M. J. (2020). The Future of Digital Health with Federated Learning. *NPJ Digital Medicine*, *3*(1), 119.
25. Lim, W. Y. B., Luong, N. C., Hoang, D. T., Jiao, Y., Liang, Y. C., Yang, Q., ... Miao, C. (2020). Federated Learning in Mobile Edge Networks: A Comprehensive Survey. *IEEE Communications Surveys & Tutorials*, *22*(3), 2031–2063.

12 FireEye
An IoT-Based Fire Alarm and Detection System for Enhanced Safety

Md. Moynul Islam, Nahida Fatme, Md AL Mahbub Hossain, and Muhammad Fiazul Haque

12.1 INTRODUCTION

Fire safety is a critical concern in any building, and an effective fire alarm system can play a crucial role in protecting life and property. Fires can spread quickly and can be difficult to control, leading to injuries, fatalities, and significant damage to buildings and infrastructure. Additionally, fires can cause financial and emotional distress to those affected, and they can have long-lasting effects on the environment [1]. By being cautious and taking steps to prevent fires, individuals can reduce the risks associated with this hazard and ensure the safety of themselves and those around them. According to the National Fire Protection Association, in 2019, there were approximately 1.3 million fires reported in the USA, resulting in 3,704 civilian deaths, 16,600 civilian injuries, and $14.8 billion in property damage [2]. In this project, we have developed a fire alarm system that is equipped with advanced sensors, communication technologies, and intelligent algorithms to detect, respond, and mitigate the risk of fire. Our system is designed to automatically detect the presence of fire and alert the building occupants through a sound buzzer and notifications to devices such as mobile phones and computers. The system can also automatically activate a water or gas-based extinguishing system to suppress the fire and minimize property damage. The development of this system is based on the integration of various technologies, including microcontrollers, sensors, wireless communication, mobile application, and firebase. Our system uses a combination of flame sensors to detect the presence of fire. It is also designed to be easy to install, operate, and maintain, making it an ideal solution for both residential and commercial applications. It can be customized to meet specific needs and requirements, and it can be integrated with other building automation systems to enhance its functionality.

The following report provides a comprehensive overview of our fire alarm system, including its design, development, and testing. We describe in detail the hardware and software components of the system, its operation, and its performance under various scenarios.

160

DOI: 10.1201/9781032694870-12

12.2 LITERATURE REVIEW

Listyorini has developed a novel gadget utilizing fuzzy logic and the Internet of Things (IoT) to detect fire hotspots in Riau's peatlands, Indonesia. The device, powered by the WEMOS ESP8266 microprocessor, effectively coordinates servo motors, buzzers, fire and temperature sensors, and security cameras. Fuzzy logic determines flame intensity, minimizing false alarms. Testing has shown that this IoT-connected fire detection device expedites monitoring while reducing false alarms. It has the potential to revolutionize fire detection in critical areas like peatlands and serves as an educational tool for high school students studying computer engineering and networking. This innovation combines environmental significance with practical application, providing valuable insights into IoT technology and fuzzy logic for future engineers and technologists [3].

Jadon proposes a novel neural network called "FireNet" to overcome the performance-size compromise in existing solutions. FireNet is a lightweight network that outperforms previous alternatives, aiming to be deployed on embedded platforms like Raspberry Pi. Extensive evaluations using conventional and customized fire datasets demonstrate promising results. The project article explores FireNet's capabilities, incorporating Convolutional Neural Networks (CNNs), Embedded Systems, Fire Detection, IoT, Neural Networks, and Smoke Detection. This comprehensive examination highlights FireNet's potential in bridging the gap between efficient model design and high-performance outcomes in fire detection and embedded systems [4].

Altowaijri presents a novel fire detection approach that upholds high detection accuracy while prioritizing privacy. Instead of transmitting complete video footage, this method transmits derived features extracted from IoT device videos. It employs CNNs and binary video descriptors for feature extraction and data classification. The proposed technique outperforms existing methods using raw video data, achieving an impressive 97.5% classification accuracy. The study also demonstrates the suitability of the suggested video descriptors for real-time processing on the Raspberry Pi 4 platform, known for its average processing speed of 100 milliseconds per frame. This combination of innovative approaches enhances fire detection accuracy and enables efficient and privacy-conscious processing in IoT environments [5].

Basu proposes a NodeMCU-based IoT-based fire indication and monitoring system. It communicates with a variety of parts, such as temperature and smoke sensors, and it uses an Arduino-connected buzzer to sound an alarm in case of a fire. Clear system status presentation is made possible by NodeMCU integration with an LCD display, and user transmission of status messages is facilitated by an Ethernet module. When a fire occurs, the system automatically detects it and immediately alerts the user via alarms delivered to an Android mobile app or website. This ground-breaking approach makes advantage of NodeMCU's capabilities to build a user-centric fire monitoring system that bridges the gap between distant alarms and real-time detection. The system's efficacy and usability are improved since its functioning continues even when the user is geographically separated [6].

Giacomo Peruzzi presents a prototype Video Surveillance Unit (VSU) that incorporates two embedded Machine Learning (ML) algorithms for timely forest fire detection. ML models run on a low-power device with input from audio samples and photos.

Together, the ML models achieve 96.15%, 92.3%, 100.00%, and 96.0% accuracy, precision, recall, and F1 score, respectively. The LoRaWAN protocol smoothly transmits incident detection, ensuring prompt notification to accountable parties. The prototype VSU is recognized as a novel solution for accurate and timely forest fire detection because of the integration of embedded ML algorithms and cutting-edge communication protocols. This enables quick and efficient actions in reaction to probable fire occurrences [7].

Ren proposes a multi-information fusion-based integrated detection technology to address electric fires in environment-friendly buildings. By applying fuzzy logic reasoning and membership functions within the framework of fuzzy set theory, a comprehensive system model is established to tackle the complex interplay of problems and symptoms related to electric fires. The study focuses on identifying arc faults, a common cause of electrical fires in green buildings. Through multi-information fusion, arc faults are effectively detected, with simulation results validating the model's reliability. The research highlights the efficacy of this approach in preventing electrical fires, offering a more precise solution compared to traditional methods relying on single criteria. The empirical findings contribute to enhancing fire safety in green buildings by leveraging advanced fusion techniques to accurately identify and prevent potential arc-related fire hazards [8].

Mahzan et al. (2018) have proposed an Arduino-based home fire alarm system with a GSM (Global System for Mobile communication) module. They used the Arduino microcontroller which is connected to the fire sensor and the alarm buzzer. They had to add a GSM module which is connected to the Arduino microcontroller. In this chapter, they must have GSM system in order to use it at its best and there is a possibility of false alarm [9].

Dosani et al. have proposed a NodeMCU-based fire detection system. They described the use of NodeMCU, a microcontroller board, as the main component of the fire detector system. It is connected to a smoke sensor and a buzzer to detect and alert about the presence of smoke or fire. The NodeMCU collects data from the smoke sensor and sends it to the ThingSpeak server through the cloud system. Having a smoke sensor and fire sensor can cause false detection in few circumstances [10].

Khalaf et al. have proposed an IoT fire detection system using Arduino. They discussed the use of IoT technology, specifically temperature sensors (flame sensors) connected to an Arduino device, to detect and measure the intensity of fire outbreaks in various locations. The sensors serve as an early alarm system, sending email notifications to mobile phones, fire stations, and hospitals to alert them of any fire outbreaks and prevent significant damage. They utilized an IoT system consisting of temperature sensors (flame sensors) connected to an Arduino device to detect fire outbreaks and measure the intensity of heat generated by the fire. The sensors are connected to a central hub called a gateway, which collects and processes the data from the sensors. They aimed to have lower cost which made it less secure and efficient in terms of service [11].

12.3 PROPOSED SYSTEM

Upon detecting a fire, FireEye, an IoT-based fire alarm and detection system for enhanced safety, immediately activates an alarm to alert the homeowner. The system is an efficient, cost-effective, and reliable solution for home fire safety, designed to provide quick and accurate detection and response to fires while also providing the

FireEye

user with easy control and monitoring through both the central control unit and the mobile app. The proposed system is shown in Figure 12.1. As well the operational flowchart is shown in Figure 12.2.

12.4 SYSTEM ARCHITECTURE

To create the FireEye: An IoT-based fire alarm and detection system

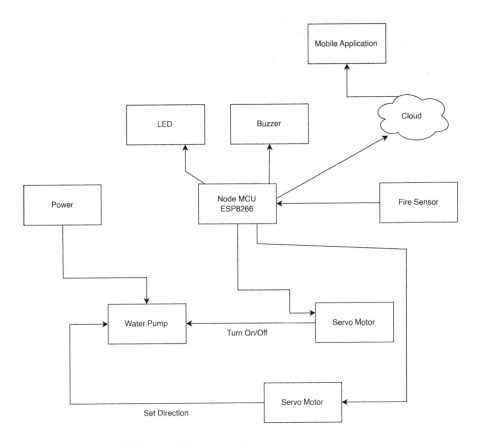

FIGURE 12.1 Block diagram of the proposed system.

12.5 HARDWARE

- NodeMCU ESP8266
  Fire Sensor
- Servo motor
- LED
- Buzzer
- Water Pump
- Jumper wire
- Type-B USB cable

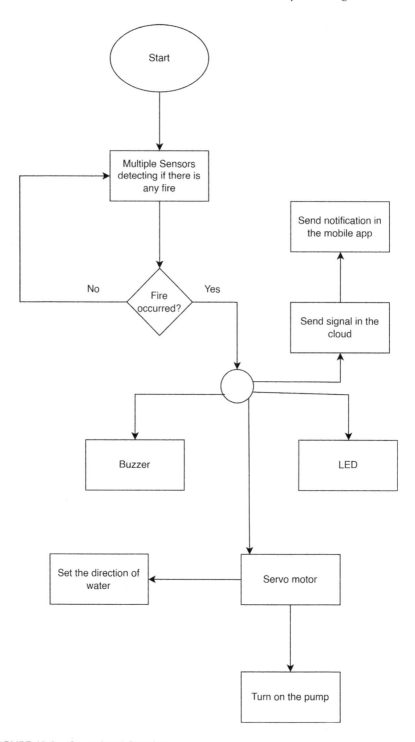

FIGURE 12.2 Operational flowchart.

FireEye 165

12.6 FLOWCHART

The fire alarm system is designed to operate automatically when power is supplied to it. The system's sensors continually monitor the environment for signs of fire. When a fire is detected, the system initiates a set of pre-programmed steps that include activating visual and auditory alarms such as LED and buzzer, as well as notifying the fire department and building occupants through cloud-based communication. Additionally, the system employs servo motors to detect the direction of the fire and activate a water pump. These steps are crucial in mitigating the spread of the fire and ensuring the safety of building occupants. Overall, the system provides a reliable and automated response to potential fire hazards, minimizing damage and saving lives.

12.7 METHODOLOGY

Certainly, the development of FireEye, an IoT-based fire alarm and detection system, was a comprehensive process that involved research, hardware and software design, and testing.

The hardware components of FireEye included a variety of sensors and actuators. Sensors are devices that detects and responds to some type of input from the physical environment [12] and Actuators convert electrical signals into movement, enabling IoT devices to interact with the real world. We included multiple flame sensors as sensor and servo motors as actuators [13]. There is a water pump for watering the fire. The flame sensor is responsible for detecting the presence of fire, while the servo motors are used to control the direction of water flow to the room where the fire is detected. That servo motor is also responsible for turning on the switch. The water pump is responsible for pumping water into the room to extinguish the fire.

In addition to these components, we explored the possibility of adding a gas-releasing system to the design, which can be triggered in case of a fire. This would provide an additional layer of protection in the event that the fire cannot be extinguished by water alone.

The software components of FireEye enable real-time monitoring and notifications. The system sends notifications to the user's device as soon as a fire is detected, providing the homeowner with immediate information about the potential threat. The mobile app allows users to monitor the system remotely and receive notifications even when they are not at home.

Throughout the development process, we conducted extensive testing of the FireEye system to ensure its reliability, efficiency, and safety. We tested the system in various simulated fire scenarios and made necessary adjustments to the hardware and software components to optimize its performance.

Overall, the development of FireEye was a comprehensive process that involved research, hardware and software design, and testing. The system utilizes a variety of sensors and actuators to detect and respond to fires in a home environment, with the option to add a gas-releasing system for added protection. The software components provide real-time monitoring and notifications to ensure the homeowner can respond quickly in the event of a fire.

12.8 IMPLEMENTATION

FireEye is an IoT-based fire alarm and detection system designed to enhance safety in buildings. The system is designed to detect fire, activate a buzzer and LED lights, dispense water to the affected area, and notify users on their devices. The project has been completed and undergone testing and improvements to ensure its effectiveness in detecting fires and providing early warning to users. The FireEye team identified potential risks and implemented mitigation strategies, resulting in a highly effective and efficient system for enhanced safety.

The FireEye fire alarm and detection system is built using the NodeMCU configuration with specific pins for each of the system's components. The flame sensors are connected to D6 and D7 pins, allowing for accurate detection of fires. The D4 and D5 pins are used to activate the buzzer and LED, respectively, providing an immediate alert to occupants of the building. The servo motor, which is used to dispense water to the affected area, is connected to D2 and D3 pins, allowing for precise control over the direction and intensity of the water flow. The water pump, which is powered individually from a separate power source, is activated when a fire is detected, ensuring the immediate suppression of the fire. This NodeMCU configuration has proven to be highly effective in detecting fires and activating the necessary responses for enhanced safety. The complete project is shown in Figures 12.3–12.5.

In addition to the hardware components of FireEye, an Android app was developed to provide real-time notifications to users in the event of a fire. The app was built using Kotlin programming language and Android Studio development environment. Firebase was used as the database for storing and updating information related to the system's status, allowing users to receive notifications in real time. The app provides a user-friendly interface, displaying the system's status and allowing users to configure and monitor the system's settings remotely. The app's real-time update

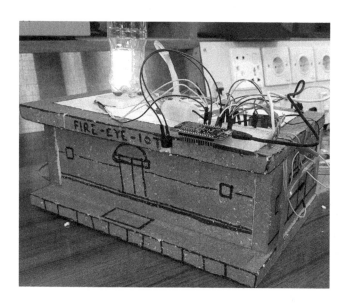

FIGURE 12.3 Complete project of the proposed system.

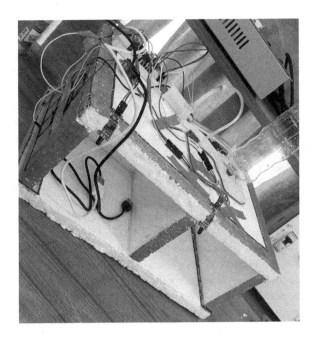

FIGURE 12.4 Complete project.

FIGURE 12.5 NodeMCU ESP8266 configuration.

feature ensures that users are immediately alerted in the event of a fire, enabling them to take swift and effective action to ensure their safety. Overall, the Android app is an essential component of the FireEye system, providing a crucial layer of safety and peace of mind for building occupants.

12.9 RESULT ANALYSIS

FireEye fire alarm and detection system is highly effective in detecting fires and providing early warning to building occupants. The system's flame sensors are highly sensitive, detecting even small fires and activating the necessary responses within seconds. The servo motor, which dispenses water to the affected area, was highly effective in controlling the direction and intensity of the water flow, suppressing the fire within seconds of activation. Our device quickly detects any fire occurrence using a highly effective sensor, causing immediate water dispersion within a split second of discovery. The system then instantly notifies the user, and this notification cycle repeats every 30 seconds. This efficient procedure makes sure that user alerting, water dispersion to put out the fire, and fire detection all happen in a couple of seconds. Moreover, there is no delay in the system's response after a fire occurs, which makes our project unique. The system takes immediate action, which is crucial for containing fires and reducing their potential impact.

Additionally, our project incorporated several unique features that made it stand out from other fire alarm and detection systems. We used a different servo motor as a switch to turn on the water pump, making the system faster to respond and able to water fires more quickly. We also added LED lights and a buzzer both inside and outside of the house to alert neighbors and building occupants in the event of a fire.

In conclusion, the FireEye system is an excellent choice for building owners and property managers looking to improve the safety of their occupants and assets. Our project's unique features, along with the system's effectiveness and efficiency, make it a superior fire alarm and detection system. The system's ability to provide early warning and enable swift and effective action can mean the difference between a minor incident and a devastating loss.

12.10 CONCLUSION AND FUTURE WORK

In conclusion, fires pose significant risks to both property and human life, making prevention and early detection crucial. Smoke and toxic fumes produced during a fire can be just as dangerous as the flames themselves, and the damage caused can be devastating. Measures such as keeping flammable materials away from heat sources, maintaining electrical appliances, and installing smoke detectors can reduce the risks associated with fires. Additionally, investing in a reliable fire alarm system, such as the FireEye system, can provide early warning and enable swift action in case of a fire, minimizing damage and protecting property and occupants.

Looking to the future, we aim to develop this system even further. This could include exploring new technologies or developing more accessible and cost-effective methods for suppressing fires in existing properties along with implementing ML. By pursuing these avenues, we can improve overall fire safety and reduce the risks associated with fires, helping to protect both property and lives. Continuous research and development are essential to ensure that we are always adapting to new challenges and improving our ability to prevent and detect fires.

REFERENCES

1. G. Eason, B. Noble, and I. N. Sneddon, On certain integrals of Lipschitz-Hankeltype involving products of bessel functions, *Phil. Trans. Roy. Soc.*, volume A247, April 1955, 529–551.
2. J. C. Maxwell, *A Treatise on Electricity and Magnetism*, 3rd ed., volume 2. Oxford, UK: Clarendon, 1892, 68–73.

3. T. Listyorini and R. Rahim, A prototype fire detection implemented using the Internet of Things and fuzzy logic, *World Trans. Eng. Technol. Educ.*, volume 16, 2018, 42–46.

4. A. Jadon, Md. Omama, A. Varshney, M. S. Ansari, and R. Sharma, FireNet: A specialized lightweight fire & smoke detection model for real-time IoT applications, *arXiv preprint arXiv:1905.11922*, 2019.

5. A. H. Altowaijri, M. S. Alfaifi, T. A. Alshawi, A. B. Ibrahim, and S. A. Alshebeili, A privacy-preserving iotbased fire detector, *IEEE Access*, volume 9, 2021, 51393–51402.

6. M. T. Basu, R. Karthik, J. Mahitha, and V. L. Reddy, IoT based forest fire detection system, *Int. J. Eng. Technol.*, volume 7, 2018, 124–126.

7. G. Peruzzi, A. Pozzebon, and M. Van Der Meer, Fight fire with fire: Detecting forest fires with embedded machine learning models dealing with audio and images on low power IoT devices, *Sensors*, volume 23, 2023, 783.

8. X. Ren, C. Li, X. Ma, F. Chen, H. Wang, A. Sharma, G. S. Gaba, and M. Masud, Design of multi-information fusion based intelligent electrical fire detection system for green buildings, Sustainability, volume 13, 2021, 3405.

9. N. N. Mahzan, N. I. M. Enzai, N. M. Zin, and K. S. S. K. M. Noh, "Design of an Arduinobased home fire alarm system with GSM module," *1st International Conference on Green and Sustainable Computing (ICoGeS)*, Kuching, Malaysia, 2017.

10. J. Dosani, N. Makwana, and A. Chaugule, NodeMCU based fire detector system, *Recent Trends Cloud Comput. Web Eng.*, volume 2, issue 3, 2020, 1–6.

11. O. I. Khalaf, G. M. Abdulsahib, and N. A. K. Zghair, IOT fire detection system using sensor with Arduino. *Aust. J. Educ.*, volume 26, 2019, 74–78.

12. *Sensor*, https://www.techtarget.com/whatis/definition/sensor (accessed on June 2023).

13. *Actuator*, https://www.geeksforgeeks.org/actuators-in-iot/ (accessed on June 2023).

13 Safeguarding Data Privacy and Security in Federated Learning Systems

Wasswa Shafik, Kassim Kalinaki,
Khairul Eahsun Fahim, and Mumin Adam

13.1 INTRODUCTION

Machine learning (ML) model training and application in our increasingly digital world have undergone a substantial paradigm shift due to the big data era and advancements in digital technologies (Cheng et al., 2020; Shafik, 2023a). Federated learning (FL), a technology approach at the forefront of this transition, is decentralized and privacy-focused. With the promise of collaborative model training across geographically dispersed data sources without compromising security and data privacy, it has already shown tremendous potential across various industries, including healthcare, smart farming, marketing, finance, and beyond (Zhang et al., 2023; Wang et al., 2023). This exceptional promise, however, also raises serious concerns and challenges for preserving data security and privacy.

The rise of FL has highlighted issues on data security and privacy. The potential for cooperative model training across diverse data sources is coupled with intrinsic challenges that necessitate a complex and comprehensive approach (Nguyen et al., 2021a, 2021b). These insights assist practitioners and academics in weighing the advantages and disadvantages of the currently available solutions by shedding light on the practical usefulness of various platforms in upholding data security and privacy (Ma et al., 2022a; Shafik, 2023a). Describe the innovative techniques and enhancements made to the FL environment and give a glimpse into the future of private and secure collaborative ML.

FL enters this market as a strategy that ensures both the benefits of cutting-edge ML and data privacy protection with the knowledge and skills required to navigate the challenges of data privacy and security, paving the way for trust and resilience in FL systems in light of the quick expansion of decentralized data sources and FL's ascendancy (Nguyen et al., 2021). Instead of supplying raw data, collaborative model training involves trading model updates to reduce privacy hazards. Even these model improvements may be able to identify particular data sources. FL makes it very challenging to pinpoint the precise contribution of any one input source by using

170

DOI: 10.1201/9781032694870-13

Safeguarding Data Privacy and Security in Federated Learning Systems **171**

techniques like differential privacy (DP) to add noise to the model updates (Bonawitz et al., 2019; Shafik, 2023a and Shafik, 2023b). FL minimizes privacy problems by utilizing techniques like DP to safeguard the anonymity of individual data sources during model training.

Under many jurisdictions' tight data privacy regulations, sensitive data must be handled with care and per prescribed privacy principles, for example, the General Data Protection Regulation (GDPR) in Europe. FL aids businesses in abiding by these laws because data can remain localized (Shafik, 2024). By enabling compliance with data regulations, FL helps businesses avoid the financial and legal ramifications of data privacy violations (Wei et al., 2020). Sensitive data must be handled carefully and in accordance with certain privacy rules, as severe data privacy requirements in many regions and businesses require. Businesses can abide by these restrictions due to FL because the data can stay localized. By facilitating compliance with data regulations, FL helps firms avoid data privacy violations' negative financial and legal effects (Wei et al., 2020).

FL has security measures to protect against insider threats, where a staff person can try to misuse or leak sensitive information. Due to encryption, authentication, and access restrictions, only authorized users may access and participate in the FL process (Mo et al., 2021). Insider threat protection is crucial for FL systems to provide data privacy and security. FL incorporates security measures to protect against insider threats, in which an employee of the firm might attempt to misuse or divulge confidential information (Fang and Qian, 2021). Encryption, authentication, and access controls are used to ensure that only people with the right authorization can access and participate in the FL process (Tran et al., 2021). Inside FL systems, security against insider threats is necessary to maintain data privacy and security.

Identifying and reducing attacks is a critical approach; a few examples of the many risks FL systems have put in place are model inversion attacks, membership inference attacks, and poisoning assaults. Using these techniques will protect the integrity of the FL process. Assaults must be discovered and neutralized for FL systems to be strong and secure (Xu et al., 2021). FL systems implement defenses against various dangers, including model inversion, membership inference, and poisoning. These techniques protect the FL process's integrity; attack detection and prevention are crucial for FL systems to be trustworthy and safe.

In the era of data breaches and privacy violations, which routinely make headlines, the importance of protecting personal and sensitive information has never been more apparent. While attempting to use the data for innovation and insight, organizations and institutions must respect the rights and expectations of the individuals who are the data's stewards (Mbonihankuye et al., 2019). Forging a path toward trust and resilience in FL systems in light of the explosive growth of decentralized data sources and the ascendancy of FL, FL enters this space as a methodology that guarantees both the benefits of cutting-edge ML and data privacy protection, techniques necessary to navigate the challenges of data privacy and security (Alabdulatif et al., 2023).

FL's ability to successfully address these problems while maximizing the potential of dispersed data sources for collaborative ML is what determines its success. A complex web of challenges accompanies the potential of FL. The nature of decentralized learning raises several queries, such as how to protect data privacy in FL without sacrificing model performance. How does the distribution of model updates throughout a participant-distributed network affect security? How can we identify and neutralize new threats in this dynamic environment? The main tenets of our literature search are these inquiries.

13.1.1 THE CONTRIBUTION OF THIS CHAPTER

This study presents the following contributions as summarized below.

- An overview of FL's principles and concepts is presented, along with examples of its reasons, its use, and the difficulties and dangers it poses for data security and privacy.
- Examines the critical facets of data privacy in FL, goes in-depth on DP and other privacy-preserving techniques, and provides examples of potential mechanisms and tactics for data privacy protection in FL.
- Scrutinizes the critical elements of data privacy in FL, in-depth explores DP and other privacy-preserving methods, and provides examples of potential mechanisms and tactics for protecting data privacy in FL.
- Provide an overview of popular FL frameworks and platforms, describing how these frameworks address data privacy and security concerns and highlighting notable limitations or vulnerabilities in existing FL platforms.
- The study also shows potential future possibilities for research in data privacy and security and FL. Identifies opportunities for improvement and advancement before offering a concluding suggestion for potential study extensions or applications.

13.1.2 THE ORGANIZATION OF THIS CHAPTER

The remaining sections of the study are structured as follows. Section 13.2 presents the fundamentals of FL, explains its basic principles and concepts, discusses its motivation and applications, and presents the challenges and risks related to data privacy and security in FL. Section 13.3 illustrates data privacy in FL and explores the critical aspects of data privacy in FL with an emphasis on the healthcare domain. Discuss in-depth DP and other privacy-preserving techniques and present strategies and mechanisms for preserving data privacy in FL, analyzing the security threats and vulnerabilities associated with FL systems. Section 13.4 explains the FL frameworks and platforms. Describe how these frameworks address data privacy and security concerns. Highlight any limitations or vulnerabilities in existing FL platforms. Section 13.5 demonstrates the future directions in the field of FL and data privacy and security approaches. Finally, Section 13.6 presents this chapter's conclusion.

13.2 MOTIVATION OF FEDERATED LEARNING

The goals of FL stem from an in-depth understanding of data privacy, security, and collaborative efficacy, as well as the requirement to address current issues in a connected and data-driven society. It is an important advancement in ML because it enables companies and individuals to leverage decentralized data sources while observing data sovereignty and privacy rules. Some of these reasons are discussed in this subsection.

Safeguarding Data Privacy and Security in Federated Learning Systems **173**

13.2.1 Data Privacy and Security

FL is a result of the pressing need to protect data security and privacy in a society that is becoming increasingly digital. When managing sensitive information, such as identifying information, financial data, or medical records, it recognizes the necessity for extra vigilance. FL enables organizations and individuals to keep their data locally and never share it with the outside world, thus reducing the risk of data breaches and unwanted access (Xu et al., 2021). This emphasis on data privacy is in keeping with the regulations and growing concerns about safeguarding personal data.

13.2.2 Regulatory Compliance

FL was developed because it is crucial to protect data security and privacy in a world that is becoming increasingly digital. It is aware of the significance of treating sensitive information, such as private information, financial information, or medical records, with the utmost care. FL significantly decreases the risks associated with data breaches and unauthorized access by enabling organizations and people to keep their data localized and never share it with the outside world (Mo et al., 2021). This focus on data privacy is compatible with regulations and growing concerns about safeguarding personal data.

13.2.3 Data Sovereignty

Particularly in nations with strict rules, data sovereignty is a serious challenge. FL, which allows data to stay inside specific geographic or legal jurisdictional bounds, and does an outstanding job of satisfying these needs. This complies with not only national data regulations but also the principles of data governance and sovereignty that some nations have created as part of their data protection strategies (Fang and Qian, 2021).

13.2.4 Efficient Collaboration

Collaborative model training is becoming increasingly valuable in several sectors. Healthcare organizations, for instance, might wish to enhance a disease prediction model. FL offers a good substitute by enabling cooperative model training without necessitating the disclosure of sensitive patient data (Wei et al., 2020). It promotes collaboration and knowledge sharing between multiple organizations while protecting the privacy of their data.

13.2.5 Edge Devices and the Internet of Things

Due to the proliferation of edge devices and IoT (the Internet of Things) sensors, ML models that can successfully operate in contexts with limited resources are now necessary. Because FL enables edge devices to participate in model training without using up their central processing unit (CPU) capacity, these circumstances are well suited for it (Xu et al., 2021). This ensures that ML may be effectively used at the edge, creating a wide range of new applications and services.

13.2.6 REDUCED COMMUNICATION OVERHEAD

The proliferation of edge devices and IoT sensors necessitates using ML models that perform well in environments with limited resources. FL is a perfect solution for many use cases because it enables edge devices to participate in model training without taxing their computational resources (Fang and Qian, 2021). As a result, when ML is adequately implemented at the edge, a wide variety of new applications and services can be unlocked.

13.2.7 SCALABILITY

Due to the proliferation of edge devices and IoT sensors, ML models that can successfully operate in contexts with limited resources are now necessary. Because FL enables edge devices to participate in model training without using up their CPU capacity, these circumstances are well suited for it (Tran et al., 2021). This ensures that ML may be effectively used at the edge, creating a wide range of new applications and services.

13.2.8 PERSONALIZATION AND ADAPTATION

FL makes it possible to customize and update the overall model to fit each participant's unique data distribution. This personalized approach enhances the effectiveness of the global model for particular participants by offering a customized user experience using pooled knowledge. Therefore, FL is motivated by a deep awareness of data privacy, security, and collaboration and the need to solve contemporary problems in a connected and data data-driven environment (Xu et al., 2021). It is an essential advancement in ML because it enables companies and individuals to leverage decentralized data sources while observing data sovereignty and privacy rules.

13.3 CHALLENGES AND RISKS RELATED TO DATA PRIVACY AND SECURITY IN FEDERATED LEARNING

This section outlines the significant difficulties of integrating technical solutions, stringent security procedures, and continuous monitoring. Data security and privacy must be maintained, and FL must effectively solve these challenges while offering valuable ML insights.

13.3.1 MODEL INVERSION ATTACK

Model inversion attacks pose a severe threat to FL. Attackers seek to retrieve confidential information about particular data sources by looking at the model modifications. FL essentially exchanges model updates, but even so, these updates could contain distinctive quirks and information that are only available from particular data sources (Cheng et al., 2020). Privacy-preserving strategies like DP can assist in lowering this risk by making it very challenging to extract useful information from the model by adding controlled noise to the updates.

Safeguarding Data Privacy and Security in Federated Learning Systems   **175**

13.3.2 Membership Inference Attacks and Model Poisoning Attacks

Assaults on membership inference are still another privacy problem. In this scenario, attackers check the model outputs to see if a certain data piece is part of the training dataset. This may be especially problematic when participants in FL share model modifications (Nguyen et al., 2021). Strategies like adversarial training or privacy amplification can be used to fight off such attacks by introducing ambiguity to the model's responses. Model poisoning attacks by malevolent actors are possible in FL. By giving the central server inaccurate or biased model updates, these assaults jeopardize the integrity of the global model (Zhang et al., 2023). To prevent model poisoning, robust aggregation techniques and secure methods to identify and block malicious participants are required. Cryptographic methods can also be used to verify the integrity of model changes.

13.3.3 DP Challenges

When malevolent actors participate, FL is susceptible to attacks from model poisoning. These attacks send biased or erroneous model updates to the central server, compromising the integrity of the global model. Model poisoning can be avoided using efficient aggregation techniques and secure systems that can identify and omit malicious individuals (Cheng et al., 2020). Cryptographic approaches may be used to verify the accuracy of model updates further.

13.3.4 Data Distribution Variability and Secure Model Aggregation

Aggregating model updates from numerous participants must be done securely to prevent data loss or manipulation. Secure aggregation techniques, such as secure multi-party computation (SMC), must ensure the confidentiality and integrity of the aggregate process demonstrated by SMC (Nguyen et al., 2021). These protocols allow the central server to aggregate without requiring access to every model update. Collecting model updates from various participants must be done securely to avoid data leakage or manipulation. Secure aggregation protocols are essential to guarantee the confidentiality and integrity of the aggregating process, like SMC (Ma et al., 2022a and 2022b). Using these protocols, the central server may aggregate data without access to each model update.

13.3.5 Secure Initialization and Insider Threats

At all costs, user-to-main server communication must be safeguarded. When sending model updates, encryption mechanisms like transport layer security (TLS) or secure sockets should be used to safeguard data confidentiality. These prevent interference and eavesdropping while data is being sent (Cheng et al., 2020). The main server and user communications must always be kept private. Encryption technologies, such as TLS or secure sockets, should be utilized to safeguard data confidentiality while communicating model changes (Nguyen et al., 2021). These prevent listening in and interfering with data transmission.

13.3.6 Communication Security and Data Leakage Prevention

The protection of the user-to-main server connection is essential. The confidentiality of the data should be protected when sending model updates using encryption technologies like TLS or secure sockets. This guards against eavesdropping and interference during data transfer (Mo et al., 2021). To prevent accidental data breaches during the FL process, strict access controls and data sanitization procedures must be implemented (Fang and Qian, 2021). Since data leakage may occur due to model updates or other side channels, it is imperative to implement rigorous data protection procedures.

13.3.7 Regulatory Compliance

To handle these risks and issues, a multifaceted approach is required that combines technology solutions, strong security protocols, regulatory adherence, and ongoing monitoring. The ability of FL to properly negotiate and mitigate these complex difficulties while delivering useful ML insights determines its success in preserving data privacy and security. To deal with these issues and risks, a multidimensional approach that incorporates technical solutions, strong security protocols, regulatory adherence, and ongoing monitoring is required (Mbonihankuye et al., 2019). FL must successfully negotiate and address these complex difficulties to deliver intelligent ML outcomes while safeguarding data privacy and security.

13.4 HEALTHCARE DATA PRIVACY AND SECURITY IN FEDERATED LEARNING

This section presents the critical aspects of data privacy and security measures in FL in healthcare.

Healthcare data often exhibit a pronounced fragmentation owing to the intricacies inherent in the healthcare ecosystem and its associated procedures. As an illustrative instance, individual healthcare institutions may solely possess access privileges to the clinical records of their specific patient cohorts (Xu et al., 2021). These records bear significant sensitivity, housing protected health information (PHI) belonging to distinct individuals. Stringent regulatory frameworks, exemplified by the Health Insurance Portability and Accountability Act (HIPAA; Mbonihankuye et al., 2019), have been meticulously devised to oversee data access and analysis. Consequently, this intricate landscape poses a formidable hurdle for contemporary data mining and AI-powered techniques such as ML and deep learning (DL), which traditionally demand substantial reservoirs of training data for optimal functionality (Alabdulatif et al., 2023).

While FL offers several benefits in transforming the healthcare domain, as highlighted in the introduction section, it poses certain data security and privacy concerns in modern digital healthcare systems, further hampering widespread deployment. FL systems demand sharing and aggregating data from multiple healthcare devices and sources, which raises concerns about privacy and data security (Alabdulatif et al., 2023; Chemisto et al., 2023). Most of these ingenious devices emerged without the armor of security, leaving them tantalizingly vulnerable to the clutches of compromise. As a result, sensitive patient information may be transmitted or stored

Safeguarding Data Privacy and Security in Federated Learning Systems   **177**

across different devices, increasing the risk of data breaches or unauthorized access (Kalinaki et al., 2023).

Attacks such as adversarial attacks, reconstruction attacks, inference and poisoning attacks, evasion attacks, man-in-the-middle attacks, model reversal attacks, gradient leakage attacks, and free-riding attacks have been reported in several FL implementations in digital healthcare systems (Chen et al., 2018; Joshi et al., 2022; Yang et al., 2023a; Wu et al., 2021a, 2021b; Jia et al., 2022). For instance, hackers have attacked healthcare facilities in different countries, like the US's Boston Children's Hospital in 2014, the National Health Service of the UK in 2017, LifeLabs of Canada in 2019 and Düsseldorf University Hospital of Germany in 2020 (Mothukuri et al., 2021; Coelho et al., 2023). Such attacks lead to unauthorized access to patient data, which can lead to loss of life, tarnishing the image of healthcare providers, and blackmail. Additionally, FL suffers from unintentional data leakage due to shared information, which may indirectly expose the private data of participating healthcare institutions (Alabdulatif et al., 2023; Mothukuri et al., 2021). Other studies have indicated the susceptibility of genomic data leakage due to using FL while training genome sequencing algorithms (Dhiman et al., 2022).

13.5 PRIVACY-PRESERVING TECHNIQUES IN FEDERATED LEARNING FOR HEALTHCARE

As the Internet of Health Things (IoHT) advances in processing power and other computing resources, users' expectations and reliance on IoHT systems that require AI capabilities also increase. This growing reliance on AI-driven IoHT systems further amplifies the importance of addressing concerns related to security, privacy, confidentiality, and other related aspects. Accordingly, this section details the different privacy-preserving techniques devised to solve the above concerns.

13.5.1 Differential Privacy

Initially introduced by Abadi et al. (2016), and subsequently integrated into the FL paradigm by Geyer et al. (2017), DP emerges as an indispensable framework for the analysis and construction of privacy-centric algorithms and systems. DP furnishes a rigorous mathematical underpinning and an array of methodologies; all orchestrated to harmonize the preservation of individual privacy and security by extracting valuable insights from data. Its emergence marked a pivotal moment, promising to mitigate the gradient data leakage of sensitive information. The central tenet of DP revolves around the infusion of controlled randomness or noise into the computational processes or output of data analysis algorithms. This cloak of noise effectively obscures any distinctive data point's contribution, rendering it extremely difficult for an adversary of formidable computational prowess to establish connections between specific data inputs and their resultant outputs (Abadi et al., 2016). DP aspires to bestow plausible deniability upon individual data profiles.

This extraordinary promise has galvanized scholarly efforts, delving deeply into differentially private federated learning (DPFL) frameworks, spanning domains from cutting-edge technologies to the domain of smart healthcare solutions. For instance, in a ground-breaking endeavor, a study introduced a novel DPFL framework that adroitly balances task efficiency and privacy considerations by introducing artificial noise into local datasets (Wu et al., 2021a and 2021b). Their meticulous analysis dissects the contributions, privacy, costs, computational overhead, and communication entailed by each data owner, exposing an inherent information asymmetry. They proffered a sophisticated three-dimensional contract approach for incentive mechanism design to optimize the model owner's utility within this asymmetry. Rigorous simulations undertaken in their study validated the efficacy of the proposed mechanism within the DPFL framework and showcased its superiority over various baseline mechanisms.

In another pioneering study (Choudhury et al., 2019), the authors presented an FL framework grounded in DP, meticulously designed to glean a global model from decentralized health data dispersed across various sites. This framework employs two pivotal measures to safeguard patient privacy: one refrains from sharing raw data, and the other employs a DP scheme to fortify the model against privacy breaches. A scrupulous evaluation demonstrated its effectiveness and illuminated a revolutionary revelation; the FL framework upheld the sanctity of privacy while concurrently preserving the utility of the global model. Authors recently introduced an innovative privacy protection framework tailored for the IoHT, aptly named privacy protection framework (BFG). This framework is specially designed for decentralized FL and leverages a synergistic blend of blockchain technology, DP, and the transformative capabilities of Generative Adversarial Networks (GANs).

Notably, their innovative framework tackles the formidable challenge of mitigating singular vulnerabilities and thwarting inference attacks while surpassing projections by constraining the prevalence of poisoning attacks to an astonishingly low threshold of less than 26%. Furthermore, BFG adeptly navigates the storage intricacies of blockchain, striking an optimal balance between the privacy budget and the proficiency of the global model, all while resiliently withstanding the potential repercussions of node withdrawal. Through a meticulously orchestrated series of simulation experiments across various image datasets, the authors affirm the unrivaled effectiveness of the BFG framework, establishing a radical standard for decentralized FL systems by its extraordinary amalgamation of precision, resilience, and privacy safeguarding. Furthermore, the author introduced a cutting-edge FL framework, placing privacy at the forefront within IoHT systems (Nair et al., 2023).

This pioneering paradigm revolves around fortifying privacy through mitigating vulnerabilities in data transfer, incorporating user anonymity, and reducing computational loads, all achieved through the seamless fusion of an edge computing-driven multitier system architecture. Additionally, to bolster the security of transmitted data against potential adversarial attacks, a DP technique employing Laplacian noise has been artfully employed on shared attributes. This approach adds a layer of confidentiality and ensures data protection even in the face of adversarial threats. To address the limitations imposed by privacy concerns in healthcare due to the scarcity of large-scale medical datasets, a novel approach known as differentially private FL was introduced (Adnan et al., 2022).

They conducted a compelling case study employing histopathology images as a testbed, investigating the impact of independent and non-independent data distributions and the number of participating healthcare providers and their dataset sizes,

Safeguarding Data Privacy and Security in Federated Learning Systems

utilizing the publicly available Cancer Genome Atlas (TCGA) dataset. The study unequivocally demonstrates that private, distributed training using the differentially private FL framework attains performance comparable to conventional training methods while delivering robust privacy guarantees. While the studies mentioned above eloquently exemplify the potency of DP in preserving patient information security and privacy within the healthcare sector, it is imperative to acknowledge a limitation: DP's efficacy diminishes when dealing with meager datasets. The rationale behind this limitation lies in the adverse impact of injecting noise into a diminutive dataset during model training. Consequently, when handling colossal datasets, DP indisputably stands as the bastion of privacy within the domain of IoHT.

13.5.2 Homomorphic Encryption

In data security, encryption emerges as a resolute protector of privacy and security through preserving confidentiality. It stands as a bulwark that only duly authorized entities possessing the requisite cryptographic key may access the concealed troves of data. Nonetheless, while robust in its fundamental purpose, traditional encryption grapples with its limitations (Singh and Singh, 2023). The obligatory exchange of cryptographic keys becomes necessary, and the domain of computational possibilities on encrypted data remains uncharted. Moreover, data sensitivity, especially in critical healthcare domains, necessitates a more sophisticated custodial approach (Acar et al., 2018; Alli et al., 2021).

To address the shortcomings of conventional encryption, a transformative paradigm known as homomorphic encryption (HE) emerges. HE bestows upon encrypted data the ability to undergo computations without unveiling their underlying secrets, ushering in a new era of cryptographic innovation (Ogburn et al., 2013). This paradigm beckons applications where data is transmitted across intermediary computational waypoints before arriving at the decryption destination. Addition, multiplication, or a combination of addition and multiplication can be done on encrypted data (Acar et al., 2018; Yang et al., 2023a and 2023b). This singular attribute positions HE as a beacon guiding secure computational offloading, the advancement of ML, and the meticulous manipulation of sensitive data within the healthcare domain.

HE adorns itself in several distinctive forms. Partially Homomorphic Encryption (PHE) extends a limited veil of secrecy, permitting only a curated set of mathematical operations on encrypted values. Somewhat Homomorphic Encryption (SWHE) extends a more flexible but bounded range of computations, including addition and multiplication, up to a specified robustness threshold, albeit with fewer iterations. Fully Homomorphic Encryption (FHE) embodies the dual properties of additive and multiplicative isomorphisms, unlocking an infinite spectrum of operations and empowering the execution of virtually any computable function. FHE, in particular, transcends its counterparts, exhibiting remarkable proficiency in efficiently managing encryption and computation of ciphertexts (Wu et al., 2021a and 2021b; Chen et al., 2021). HE assumes a pivotal role, orchestrating computations across multiple platforms while preserving the bedrock of trust.

Most FL models frequently hinge on directly deploying computational processes and training models onto client devices. The success of such models, in turn, is contingent upon the efficiency of these devices, encompassing battery life, processing capabilities, and storage capacity. Several studies have been deployed to improve patient information security and privacy in healthcare. For instance, a novel approach wherein homomorphic re-encryption takes center stage, orchestrating data collection by IoT devices, model training via fog nodes, and data aggregation on centralized servers was demonstrated (Ku et al., 2022). This ingenious scheme emerges as the guardian of data, alleviating the burdens associated with computational and storage costs, even in the face of faltering fog nodes. To fortify privacy and thwart adversarial incursions in healthcare, cryptographic innovations such as masks and HE come into play (Zhang et al., 2022).

Instead of focusing solely on the magnitude of datasets, the emphasis shifts toward discerning the intrinsic qualities encapsulated within the datasets contributed by diverse participants. This perspective informs the quantification of each local model's contribution to the global model during each training epoch. Additionally, a robust framework, resilient to dropout, ensures the unimpeded progression of FL, even during episodes of dwindling active clients (Adnan et al., 2022). A meticulous examination of data privacy and an analysis of computational and communication costs offer a comprehensive view of this scheme's capabilities. Its effectiveness is underscored through real-world healthcare applications, such as skin lesion classification using the HAM10000 medical dataset's training images, demonstrating promising results while preserving privacy and surpassing existing methodologies.

Furthermore, to guarantee individual participant data and local models' privacy, the authors devised a privacy-preserving FL architecture grounded on HE for the healthcare sector. Moreover, to ensure data privacy conformance, they implemented an encrypted query technology within this architecture, which enables data providers to explore encrypted data in ciphertext, identify encrypted data fulfilling the task criteria, and execute the model training methodology without giving concessions to any requirements of the task originator.

13.5.3 Secure Multi-Party Computation

SMC, nestled within the domain of cryptography, emerges as a guardian of data confidentiality. This cryptographic technique orchestrates collaborative computing without allowing participants to glimpse their peers' information. However, the virtues of SMC do not come without their burdens. The computational overhead and heightened communication costs stem from the essential encryption and decryption operations (Ma et al., 2022a and 2022b). Many studies have arisen to confront the security and privacy challenges inherent in SMC. Consider, for instance, an exemplary framework meticulously crafted to preserve the privacy of sensitive medical data during the diagnostic process (Li et al., 2020). In this scheme, the healthcare data of registered patients undergoes a process of encryption before being transmitted to the healthcare facility server.

The encrypted data takes part in the computation, yielding a correlation coefficient between the patient's medical history and a trait vector intricately connected to hospital ailments. Based on this similarity measure, the server discreetly discloses the appropriate disease diagnosis and treatment to the respective patient. This innovative scheme, rooted in self-serviced medical diagnosis, combines two fundamental privacy-preserving techniques: HE and a privacy-preserving access control mechanism. Together, they forge a bastion of confidentiality around the diagnostic process, emphasizing preserving patient data (Wibawa et al., 2022). To mitigate potential threats from malicious entities, a secure MPC protocol is utilized to protect the integrity of the DL model. In another study (Kalapaaking et al., 2022), the authors proposed a novel FL scheme for the fifth generation and Internet of Medical Things (IoMT), based on a convolutional neural network and incorporating both SMC and Encrypted Inference methods.

Their framework addresses privacy and security challenges by enabling several healthcare facilities consisting of clusters of varied IoMT and edge devices to train locally and encrypt their models before transmitting them for encryption and aggregation in the cloud based on SMC. To optimize the model's efficacy, their innovative approach yields an encrypted global model that is subsequently distributed back to individual healthcare institutions for further refinement through localized training. Moreover, their method enables hospitals to execute encrypted inferences seamlessly on their edge servers or within the cloud, ensuring the utmost confidentiality of data and models throughout the entire procedure. Although these approaches provide an additional layer of data privacy and security, they do come at a cost to communication efficiency and model performance. For instance, DP incorporates random noise into client training data, enhancing privacy, albeit at the potential cost of diminished model proficiency. HE encrypts model parameters exclusively, which safeguards the data but also has performance implications (Dang et al., 2022). SMC maintains client input privacy but is computationally demanding and requires substantial communication among the involved parties.

13.5.4 BLOCKCHAIN TECHNOLOGY

The advent of decentralized networks, leveraging blockchain technology, has significantly enhanced the privacy of IoT networks (Ali et al., 2021). The underlying principles of blockchain networks align seamlessly with the requisites of data privacy, trustworthy security, and decentralization, as envisioned by FL. FL merged with blockchain, leading to a promising avenue for swift enhancement in the IoHT (Stephanie et al., 2023). FL aggregates local model parameters on a central server and distributes a global model to every participating device. However, this centralized server becomes vulnerable to attackers, who may disrupt or manipulate FL training data. To mitigate such risks, blockchain as a protective mechanism offers the potential to manage data access and decentralize the orchestration mechanisms within FL, creating an unchanging and accountable/traceable ledger.

Consequently, recent investigations have embraced the merging of FL and Blockchain, facilitating the realization of a secure and privacy-preserving smart healthcare framework (Chang et al., 2021; Hsu and Huang, 2022). A novel health management framework grounded in healthcare, employing blockchain technology within edge nodes, was presented (Rahman et al., 2023). The authors advocate for replacing the conventional blockchain-based gradient aggregator solution, specifically a consensus-driven distributed aggregator. Such an innovative approach effectively mitigates the concerns of bias and privacy breaches associated with a centralized aggregation entity. A notable example that aligns with these principles is the fog-IoT-based approach for medical services (Baucas et al., 2023), which integrates a private blockchain mechanism to regulate access rights, guaranteeing interactions between trusted devices and the local training and the global knowledge base of the predictive model.

An FL-based system for fraud detection, empowered by blockchain (Lakhan et al., 2023), applies privacy-preserving measures and detection of fraud algorithms across various Fog-Cloud endpoints. Moreover, the pioneering work that introduces an innovative agent architecture for smart healthcare systems, leveraging the combined power of FL and blockchain technology with a primary focus on detecting and classifying skin cancer patients, is proposed (Połap et al., 2021). Their scheme securely encrypts personal data within the dataset utilizing blockchain methodology. In a related study (Kumar et al., 2021), the authors propose a novel approach wherein a modest volume of data is gathered from diverse sources, encompassing various hospitals. This data is subsequently employed to train a global DL model, employing a blockchain-based FL paradigm to effectively identify patients afflicted with coronavirus disease 19 (COVID-19).

Using blockchain technology, the authenticity of the data is diligently upheld, while FL ensures the model's global training, effectively safeguarding the privacy of the organizations involved. Furthermore, an innovative blockchain-empowered FL framework designed specifically for healthcare applications aims to facilitate accurate and reliable FL aggregation results while concurrently incentivizing healthcare facilities such as hospitals to willingly collaborate and share their respective local data purposely for training in FL undertakings (Liu et al., 2022). Thus, merging FL with blockchain in healthcare applications is a paramount strategy to improve the global prediction model, security, and privacy (Rehman et al., 2022). By leveraging the blockchain, decentralized coordination of global models becomes feasible through consensus among participants, thus ensuring a distributed approach. This blockchain-based framework not only fosters seamless cooperation and partnership among healthcare service providers but also establishes an entirely trustworthy, distributed, and adaptable environment (Abou El Houda et al., 2022), propelling it as an emerging area of research.

13.6 FEDERATED LEARNING FRAMEWORKS AND PLATFORMS

In this section, we explore FL frameworks and platforms. Each of these FL frameworks and platforms offers unique features and capabilities, catering to a diverse range of use cases, programming languages, and privacy requirements. The choice of framework depends on specific project needs, technical preferences, and the level of control over FL system components that developers require.

13.6.1 TensorFlow Federated

A thorough open-source framework for FL was created by Google and is called TensorFlow Federated (TFF). It increases TensorFlow's capacity to support FL application scenarios. Developers may define federated data and federated models thanks to TFF's abstractions for federated computing (Liu et al., 2022). It is a useful tool for researchers and developers interested in testing out FL because it comes with pre-implemented FL algorithms (Dang et al., 2022). By offering a high-level interface and TensorFlow model compatibility, TFF makes it easier to construct unique FL applications.

Safeguarding Data Privacy and Security in Federated Learning Systems   **183**

13.6.2 PYSYFT

This is a DL framework constructed using the PyTorch open-source library. It is an essential part of the PySyft ecosystem, which is centered on FL, MPC, and privacy-preserving ML. PySyft provides robust tools for FL implementation, like DP techniques, FL algorithms, and protocols for secure model updates (Chang et al., 2021). It benefits from a thriving and expanding ecosystem of privacy-conscious AI developers as a member of the larger PySyft community.

13.6.3 FEDERATED LEARNING FRAMEWORK (FLOWER)

The Flower framework is an open-source platform that has been specifically created to streamline the process of developing apps for FL. The provided software solution provides a sophisticated interface that effectively conceals numerous intricate aspects often associated with FL. The Flower framework exhibits framework-agnostic characteristics, allowing it to be utilized in conjunction with diverse ML frameworks for example, PyTorch and TensorFlow (Stephanie et al., 2023). The inherent flexibility of this technology renders it highly accessible to a diverse array of developers who are interested in constructing FL systems. The emphasis placed by Flower on usability and seamless integration renders it a valued asset inside the FL domain.

13.6.4 FEDERATED AI TECHNOLOGY ENABLER

Federated AI Technology Enabler (FATE) is an open-source framework for FL that has been created by WeBank and presented to the Linux Foundation. FATE has been specifically developed to offer a broad range of components for the purpose of FL, hence rendering it well suited for enterprises operating in areas such as banking and healthcare, which necessitate stringent privacy and security measures (Alabdulatif et al., 2023). The aforementioned components encompass secure computation protocols, FL algorithms, and a runtime environment. FL projects of significant scale often employ and utilize the FATE framework extensively.

13.6.5 OPENMINED

The present community and platform are dedicated to privacy-preserving AI technologies, encompassing FL, and operate within an open-source framework. The platform provides a comprehensive range of libraries and tools, one of which is PySyft, facilitating the development of ML solutions that prioritize security and privacy (Adnan et al., 2022). OpenMined facilitates cooperation among individuals who prioritize privacy in the field of AI, rendering it a significant asset for anybody seeking to contribute to or utilize privacy-preserving FL systems.

13.6.6 IBM FEDERATED LEARNING

IBM provides a range of FL solutions and tools within its portfolio of AI capabilities. IBM FL is specifically designed to cater to the needs of companies that aim to utilize FL for a wide range of applications. This technology facilitates the training of AI models by businesses using decentralized data sources while ensuring the preservation of privacy and security (Xu et al., 2021). The solution developed by IBM is specifically tailored to fulfill the unique demands and privacy regulations associated with FL applications at the corporate level.

13.7 EDGE MACHINE LEARNING (EDGE ML) AND INTEL OPEN FEDERATED LEARNING (OPENFL)

EdgeML and OpenFL are open-source FL platforms that are specifically designed for edge computing environments. This approach is particularly suitable for situations in which the training of models must take place on edge devices, such as smartphones and IoT devices, without the need to transfer sensitive data to a central server. EdgeML enables real-time inference and low-latency answers, rendering it well suited for edge computing applications that prioritize privacy and efficiency (Xu et al., 2021; Shafik et al., 2020). The OpenFL framework was specifically developed to cater to the requirements of edge devices and IoT platforms. The provided tools enable developers to perform safe model aggregation effectively, hence facilitating the efficient and privacy-centric execution of FL (Acar et al., 2018). The characteristics of OpenFL are especially advantageous for applications that require secure and privacy-preserving ML in edge computing environments.

13.8 PYGRID AND HOROVOD

PyGrid, an open-source initiative created by OpenMined, offers a comprehensive framework for facilitating secure and privacy-preserving FL. The utilization of a grid of nodes enables businesses to implement FL models, thereby facilitating collaborative model training while maintaining the preservation of data privacy and security. PyGrid has been specifically developed to possess the qualities of scalability and robustness, rendering it a highly valuable constituent of FL systems that prioritize privacy (Xu et al., 2021). Although not specifically designed for FL, Horovod is a widely used distributed DL system that may be modified to support FL. Parallel computing across numerous devices and servers is frequently employed for training DL models, making it a viable option for specific FL application scenarios (Xu et al., 2021). The scale and flexibility of Horovod render it a highly important tool for distributed ML, encompassing applications in FL.

13.9 FUTURE DIRECTIONS

Due to its ability to train models using distributed data sources, FL has attracted more attention. It can enable ML while protecting privacy by not releasing raw data. The field is still developing, although various new study trajectories appear.

Safeguarding Data Privacy and Security in Federated Learning Systems   **185**

13.9.1   Privacy Leaks

Model updates can provide details about the data on which they were calculated even when no raw data is shared. This is because there may be an overlap between the updated data-driven models and the real data.

13.9.1.1   Differential Privacy

By adding computed noise to the updates or model parameters, DP has been utilized to address this problem by obscuring individual data points while still enabling practical calculation. Managing the trade-off is difficult in this situation because increased noise assures higher privacy but may also reduce model accuracy (Khalid et al., 2023). The solution to this problem is to select the appropriate noise distribution. Two outstanding distributions, the Laplace distribution, which is frequently employed in DP, describe the functions. The desired level of privacy has an inverse relationship with the Laplace noise scale. Gaussian Noise is the alternative. Gaussian noise could be desirable in some circumstances, particularly when using the moment accountant method.

13.9.1.2   Secure Aggregation

By safely merging their models, secure aggregation protects user privacy in FL. However, many secure aggregation FL systems have issues, such as the possibility of client dropouts. Additionally, they demand a lot of computation and communication. Certain FL systems abuse secure aggregation, creating an illusory feeling of security (Dhiman et al., 2022). Several creative alternatives could be suggested to address the difficulties of current secure aggregation techniques in FL (Shafik, 2023c and Shafik, 2023d). A simple, secure aggregation can be suggested first. Instead of concentrating on the random seed-based regeneration of the dropped users, using an aggregate mask, this technique may order the single-step reconstruction of the active users (Meftah et al., 2021).

13.9.2   Byzantine Fault Tolerance

Decentralized networks are made to continue operating correctly even in the presence of malicious or dysfunctional nodes due to Byzantine fault tolerance (BFT). Modern systems must function even when some of their components fail. BFT encounters difficulties while using FL, a technique for training models across several devices (Li et al., 2020). The privacy methods that protect training data, such as DP, HE, or SMC, frequently clash with current BFT strategies. Because a FL system that does not prioritize privacy risks data disclosure, this incompatibility reduces the utility of BFT (Jun et al., 2021; Zhang et al., 2022).

    The presence of malicious nodes might result in model poisoning, in which bad actors purposefully submit corrupted updates, endangering both the model's accuracy and user privacy. Innovative solutions are needed to address BFT restrictions in FL, especially when combined with tools that protect privacy. As threats evolve, adaptive algorithms that dynamically adjust based on the level of Byzantine activity observed can easily switch between strict BFT approaches and less strict alternatives

(Kalapaaking et al., 2022). Utilizing layered security protocols can also provide subtle protection, with each tier focusing on a different issue, such as node dependability or data privacy.

13.9.2.1 Adversarial Attacks

FL encounters difficulties from adversarial assault, in which nefarious individuals try to corrupt the aggregated model by introducing contaminated data or harmful updates. These assaults may cause model performance to suffer or may add backdoors. Future directions in FL will probably concentrate on creating strong defenses against such assaults (Mothukuri et al., 2021). Researchers should investigate strategies like robust aggregation, model auditing, and anomaly detection to recognize and lessen the consequences of hostile contributions.

13.9.2.2 Personalized Federated Learning

As a promising future avenue for FL, personalized learning addresses the particular difficulties brought on by varied data distributions among nodes in decentralized systems. Real-world data is frequently non-IID (non-independently and identically distributed). Hence, it is becoming more critical to customize global models to specific users or devices to ensure that everyone benefits from the collective learning process (Shaheen et al., 2022). This customization maintains the network's natural data heterogeneity while improving model accuracy for specific nodes.

13.10 CONCLUSION

In conclusion, this chapter has shed light on the critical importance of safeguarding data privacy and security in FL systems. We began with a comprehensive introduction that underscored the pressing need for such safeguards in today's data-driven world. Throughout this chapter, we delved into the multifaceted challenges faced when seeking to protect data privacy and security in FL environments. Our exploration extended to a real-world case study within the healthcare domain, where the sensitivity and confidentiality of patient data make these concerns particularly acute. We examined the unique challenges faced by FL in healthcare and proposed innovative privacy-preserving techniques to fortify the protection of healthcare data while still reaping the benefits of collaborative learning. Additionally, we provided a detailed overview of FL platforms, showcasing the technologies and tools available to implement data privacy and security measures effectively. As we look to the future, it is evident that safeguarding data privacy and security in FL systems will remain an ongoing, evolving endeavor. The path forward involves continued research, collaboration, and the development of robust, adaptable solutions to ensure that the promise of FL can be fully realized without compromising the integrity of sensitive data.

REFERENCES

Abadi, M., Chu, A., Goodfellow, I., McMahan, H. B., Mironov, I., Talwar, K., & Zhang, L. (2016). Deep learning with differential privacy. *Proceedings of the ACM Conference on Computer and Communications Security*, 308–318, doi: 10.1145/2976749.2978318.

Safeguarding Data Privacy and Security in Federated Learning Systems 187

Abou El Houda, Z., Hafid, A. S., Khoukhi, L., & Brik, B. (2022). When collaborative federated learning meets blockchain to preserve privacy in healthcare. *IEEE Trans. Netw. Sci. Eng.*, doi: 10.1109/TNSE.2022.3211192.

Acar, A., Aksu, H., Uluagac, A. S., & Conti, M. (2018). A survey on homomorphic encryption schemes: Theory and implementation. *ACM Comput. Surv.*, 51(4), doi: 10.1145/3214303.

Adnan, M., Kalra, S., Cresswell, J. C., Taylor, G. W., & Tizhoosh, H. R. (2022). Federated learning and differential privacy for medical image analysis. *Sci. Rep.*, 12(1), 1–10, doi: 10.1038/s41598-022-05539-7.

Alabdulatif, A., Thilakarathne, N. N., & Kalinaki, K. (2023). A novel cloud enabled access control model for preserving the security and privacy of medical big data. *Electronics*, 12(12), 2646, doi: 10.3390/electronics12122646.

Ali, M., Karimipour, H., & Tariq, M. (2021). Integration of blockchain and federated learning for Internet of Things: Recent advances and future challenges. *Comput. Secur.*, 108, 102355, doi: 10.1016/J.COSE.2021.102355.

Alli, A. A., Kassim, K., Mutwalibi, N., Hamid, H., & Ibrahim, L. (2021). Secure Fog-Cloud of Things: Architectures, Opportunities and Challenges. In *Secure Edge Computing*, M. Ahmed and P. Haskell-Dowland (Eds.), 3–20. doi: 10.1201/9781003028635-2.

Baucas, M. J., Spachos, P., & Plataniotis, K. N. (2023). Federated learning and blockchain-enabled Fog-IoT platform for wearables in predictive healthcare. *IEEE Trans. Comput. Soc. Syst.*, 1–10, doi: 10.1109/TCSS.2023.3235950.

Bonawitz, K., Eichner, H., Grieskamp, W., Huba, D., Ingerman, A., Ivanov, V. … Roselander, J. (2019). Towards federated learning at scale: System design. *Proc. Mach. Learn. Syst.*, 1, 374–388, doi: 10.48550/arXiv.1902.01046.

Chang, Y., Fang, C., & Sun, W. (2021). A blockchain-based federated learning method for smart healthcare. *Comput. Intell. Neurosci.*, doi: 10.1155/2021/4376418.

Chemisto, M., Gutu, T. J., Kalinaki, K., Mwebesa Bosco, D., Egau, P., Fred, K., Tim Oloya, I., & Rashid, K. (2023). Artificial Intelligence for Improved Maternal Healthcare: A Systematic Literature Review. In *2023 IEEE AFRICON*, 1–6, doi: 10.1109/AFRICON55910.2023.10293674.

Chen, H., Iliashenko, I., & Laine, K. (2021). When HEAAN Meets FV: A New Somewhat Homomorphic Encryption with Reduced Memory Overhead," In *Lecture Notes in Computer Science (Including Subseries Lecture Notes in Artificial Intelligence and Lecture Notes in Bioinformatics)*, 13129 LNCS, 265–285, doi: 10.1007/978-3-030-92641-0_13/TABLES/11.

Chen S., Xue, M., Fan, L., Hao, S., Xu, L., Zhu, H., & Li, B. (2018). Automated poisoning attacks and defenses in malware detection systems: An adversarial machine learning approach. *Comput. Secur.*, 73, 326–344, doi: 10.1016/J.COSE.2017.11.007.

Cheng, Y., Liu, Y., Chen, T., & Yang, Q. (2020). Federated learning for privacy-preserving AI. *Commun. ACM*, 63, 33–36, doi: 10.1145/3387107.

Choudhury, O., Gkoulalas-Divanis, A., Salonidis, T., Sylla, I., Park, Y., Hsu, G., & Das, A. (2019). Differential Privacy-Enabled Federated Learning for Sensitive Health Data, Accessed: September 17, 2023. Available: https://arxiv.org/abs/1910.02578v3.

Coelho, K. K., Nogueira, M., Vieira, A. B., Silva, E. F., & Nacif, J. A. M. (2023). A survey on federated learning for security and privacy in healthcare applications. *Comput. Commun.*, 207, 113–127, doi: 10.1016/J.COMCOM.2023.05.012.

Dang, T. K., Lan, X., Weng, J., & Feng, M. (2022). Federated learning for electronic health records. *ACM Trans. Intell. Syst. Technol.*, 13(5), 72, doi: 10.1145/3514500.

Dhiman, G., Juneja, S., Mohafez, H., El-Bayoumy, I., Kumar Sharma, L., Hadizadeh, M., … Zhang, L. (2022). Federated learning approach to protect healthcare data over big data scenario. *Sustainability*, 14, 2500, doi: 10.3390/SU14052500.

Fang, H., & Qian, Q. (2021). Privacy preserving machine learning with homomorphic encryption and federated learning. *Future Internet*, 13, 94, doi: 10.3390/fi13040094.

Geyer, R. C., Klein, T., Nabi, M., Se, S., & Zurich, E. (2017). Differentially Private Federated Learning: A Client Level Perspective. Accessed: September 17, 2023. Available: https://arxiv.org/abs/1712.07557v2.

Hsu, R. H., & Huang, T. Y. (2022). Private Data Preprocessing for Privacy-Preserving Federated Learning. In *Proceedings of the 2022 5th IEEE International Conference on Knowledge Innovation and Invention, ICKII*, 173–178, doi: 10.1109/ICKII55100.2022.9983518.

Jia, B., Zhang, X., Liu, J., Zhang, Y., Huang, K., & Liang, Y. (2022). Blockchain-enabled federated learning data protection aggregation scheme with differential privacy and homomorphic encryption in IoT. *IEEE Trans. Industr. Inform.*, 18(6), 4049–4058, doi: 10.1109/TII.2021.3085960. '

Joshi, M., Pal, A., & Sankarasubbu, M. (2022). Federated learning for healthcare domain—Pipeline, applications and challenges. *ACM Trans. Comput. Healthc.*, 3(4), doi: 10.1145/3533708.

Jun, Y., Craig, A., Shafik, W., & Sharif, L. (2021). Artificial intelligence application in cybersecurity and cyberdefense. *Wirel. Commun. Mob. Comput.*, 1–10, doi: 10.1155/2021/3329581.

Kalapaaking, A. P., Stephanie, V., Khalil, I., Atiquzzaman, M., Yi, X., & Almashor, M. (2022). SMPC-based federated learning for 6G-enabled internet of medical things. *IEEE Netw.*, 36(4), 182–189, doi: 10.1109/MNET.007.2100717.

Kalinaki, K., Thilakarathne, N. N., Mubarak, H. R., Malik, O. A., & Abdullatif, M.(2023). Cybersafe Capabilities and Utilities for Smart Cities. In *Cybersecurity for Smart Cities*, Cham, Switzerland: Springer, 71–86, doi: 10.1007/978-3-031-24946-4_6.

Khalid, N., Qayyum, A., Bilal, M., Al-Fuqaha, A., & Qadir, J. (2023). Privacy-preserving artificial intelligence in healthcare: Techniques and applications. *Comput. Biol. Med.*, 158, 106848, doi: 10.1016/J.COMPBIOMED.2023.106848.

Ku, H., Susilo, W., Zhang, Y., Liu, W., & Zhang M. (2022). Privacy-preserving federated learning in medical diagnosis with homomorphic reencryption. *Comput. Stand. Interfaces*, 80, 103583, doi: 10.1016/J.CSI.2021.103583.

Kumar, R., Khan, A. A., Kumar, J., Zakria, Golilarz, N. A., Zhang, S., ... Wang, W. (2021). Blockchain-federated learning and deep learning models for COVID-19 detection using CT imaging. *IEEE Sens. J.*, 21(14), 16301–16314, doi: 10.1109/JSEN.2021.3076767.

Lakhan, A., Mohammed, M. A., Nedoma, J., Martinek, R., Tiwari, P., Vidyarthi, A., ... Wang, W. (2023). Federated-learning based privacy preservation and fraud-enabled blockchain IoMT system for healthcare. *IEEE J. Biomed. Health Inform.*, 27(2), 664–672, doi: 10.1109/JBHI.2022.3165945.

Li, D., Liao, X., Xiang, T., Wu, J., & Le, J. (2020). Privacy-preserving self-serviced medical diagnosis scheme based on secure multi-party computation. *Compute Secur.*, 90, 101701, doi: 10.1016/J.COSE.2019.101701.

Liu, Y., Yu, W., Ai, Z., Xu, Zhao, G. L., & Tian, Z. (2022). A blockchain-empowered federated learning in healthcare-based cyber physical systems. *IEEE Trans. Netw. Sci. Eng.*, doi: 10.1109/TNSE.2022.3168025.

Ma, X., Liao, L., Li, Z., Lai, R. X., & Zhang, M. (2022a). Applying federated learning in software-defined networks: A survey. *Symmetry*, 14(2), 195, doi: 10.3390/SYM14020195.

Ma, X., Zhou, Y., Wang, L., & Miao, M. (2022b). Privacy-preserving Byzantine-robust federated learning. *Comput. Stand. Inter.*, 80, 103561, doi: 10.1016/j.csi.2021.103561.

Mbonihankuye, S., Nkunzimana, A., Ndagijimana, A., & García-Magariño I. (2019). Healthcare data security technology: HIPAA compliance. *Wirel. Commun. Mob. Comput.*, doi: 10.1155/2019/1927495.

Meftah, S., Tan, B. H. M., Mun, C. F., Aung, K. M. M., Veeravalli, B., & Chandrasekhar, V. (2021). DOReN: Toward efficient deep convolutional neural networks with fully homomorphic encryption. *IEEE Trans. Inf. Forensics Sec.*, 16, 3740–3752, doi: 10.1109/TIFS.2021.3090959.

Mo, F., Haddadi, H., Katevas, K., Marin, E., Perino, D., and Kourtellis, N. (2021). PPFL: Privacy-Preserving Federated Learning in Trusted Execution Environments. In *Proceedings of the 19th Annual International Conference on Mobile Systems, Applications, and Services*, 94–108, doi: 10.1145/3458864.3466628.

Mothukuri, V., Parizi, R. M., Pouriyeh, S., Huang, Y., Dehghantanha, A., & Srivastava, G. (2021). A survey on security and privacy of federated learning. *Future Gener. Comput. Syst.*, 115, 619–640, doi: 10.1016/J.FUTURE.2020.10.007.

Nair, A. K., Sahoo, J., & Raj, E. D. (2023). Privacy preserving Federated Learning framework for IoMT based big data analysis using edge computing. *Comput. Stand. Interfaces*, 86, 103720, doi: 10.1016/J.CSI.2023.103720.

Nguyen, D. C., Ding, M., Pathirana, P. N., Seneviratne, A., Li, J., & Poor, H. V. (2021a). Federated learning for internet of things: A comprehensive survey. *IEEE Commun. Surv. Tutor.*, 23, 1622–1658, doi: 10.1109/COMST.2021.3075439.

Nguyen, D. C., Ding, M., Pham, Q.V., Pathirana, P. N., Le, L. B., Seneviratne, A., ... Poor, H. V. (2021b). Federated learning meets blockchain in edge computing: Opportunities and challenges. *IEEE Internet Things J.*, 8, 12806–12825, doi: 10.1109/JIOT.2021.3072611.

Ogburn, M., Turner, C., & Dahal, P. (2013). Homomorphic encryption. *Procedia Comput. Sci.*, 20, 502–509, doi: 10.1016/J.PROCS.2013.09.310.

Połap, D., Srivastava, G., & Yu, K. (2021). Agent architecture of an intelligent medical system based on federated learning and blockchain technology. *J. Inf. Secur. Appl.*, 58, 102748, doi: 10.1016/J.JISA.2021.102748.

Rahman, M. A., Shamim Hossain, M., Islam, M. S., Alrajeh, N. A., & Muhammad, G. (2020). Secure and provenance enhanced internet of health things framework: A blockchain managed federated learning approach. *IEEE Access*, 8, 205071–205087, doi: 10.1109/ACCESS.2020.3037474.

Rehman, A., Abbas, S., Khan, M. A., Ghazal, T. M., Adnan, K. M., & Mosavi, A. (2022). A secure healthcare 5.0 system based on blockchain technology entangled with federated learning technique. *Comput. Biol. Med.*, 150, 106019, doi: 10.1016/J.COMPBIOMED.2022.106019.

Shafik, W. (2023a). A Comprehensive Cybersecurity Framework for Present and Future Global Information Technology Organizations. In *Effective Cybersecurity Operations for Enterprise-Wide Systems*, 56–79, 2023, IGI Global, doi: 10.4018/978-1-6684-9018-1.ch002.

Shafik, W. (2023b). Cyber Security Perspectives in Public Spaces: Drone Case Study. In *Handbook of Research on Cybersecurity Risk in Contemporary Business Systems*, 79–97, IGI Global, doi: 10.4018/978-1-6684-7207-1.ch004.

Shafik, W. (2023c). IoT-Based Energy Harvesting and Future Research Trends in Wireless Sensor Networks. In *Handbook of Research on Network-Enabled IoT Applications for Smart City Services*, 282–306, doi: 10.4018/979-8-3693-0744-1.ch016.

Shafik, W. (2023d). Making Cities Smarter: IoT and SDN Applications, Challenges, and Future Trends. In *Opportunities and Challenges of Industrial IoT in 5G and 6G Networks*, 73–94, IGI Global, doi: 10.4018/978-1-7998-9266-3.ch004.

Shafik, W. (2024). Wearable Medical Electronics in Artificial Intelligence of Medical Things. In *Handbook of Security and Privacy of AI-Enabled Healthcare Systems and Internet of Medical Things*, 21–40, doi: 10.1201/9781003370321-2.

Shafik, W., Matinkhah, M., Etemadinejad, P., & Sanda, M. N. (2020). Reinforcement learning rebirth, techniques, challenges, and resolutions. *Int. J. Inform. Vis.*, 4(3), 127–35, doi: 10.30630/joiv.4.3.376.

Shaheen, M., Farooq, M.S., Umer, T., & Kim, B. S. (2023). Applications of federated learning: Taxonomy, challenges, and research trends. *Electronics*, 11(4), 2022, doi: 10.3390/electronics11040670.

Singh M., & Singh, A. K. (2023). A comprehensive survey on encryption techniques for digital images. *Multimed. Tools Appl.*, 82(8),11155–11187, doi: 10.1007/S11042-022-12791-6/METRICS.

Stephanie, V., Khalil, I., Atiquzzaman, M., & Yi, X. (2023). Trustworthy privacy-preserving hierarchical ensemble and federated learning in healthcare 4.0 with blockchain. *IEEE Trans. Industr. Inform.*, 19(7), 7936–7945, doi: 10.1109/TII.2022.3214998.

Tran, A.T., Luong, T. D. Karnjana, J., & Huynh, V. N. (2021). An efficient approach for privacy-preserving decentralized deep learning models based on secure multi-party computation. *Neurocomputing*, 422, 245–262, doi: 10.1016/j.neucom.2020.10.014.

Wang, Y., Shafik, W., Seong, J. T., Al Mutairi, A., Mustafa, M. S., & Mouhamed, M. R. (2023). Service delay and optimization of the energy efficiency of a system in fog-enabled smart cities. *Alexandria Eng. J.*, 84, 112–125, doi: 10.1016/j.aej.2023.10.034.

Wei, K., Li, J., Ding, M., Ma, C., Yang, H. H., Farokhi, F., ... Poor, H. V. (2020). Federated learning with differential privacy: Algorithms and performance analysis. *IEEE Trans. Inf. Forensics Secur.*, 15, 3454–3469, doi: 10.1109/TIFS.2020.2988575.

Wibawa, F., Catak, F. O., Sarp, S., & Kuzlu, M. (2022). BFV-based homomorphic encryption for privacy-preserving CNN models. *Cryptography*, 6(3), 34, doi: 10.3390/CRYPTOGRAPHY6030034.

Wu, M., Ye, D., Ding, J., Guo, Y., Yu, R., & Pan, M. (2021a). Incentivizing differentially private federated learning: A multidimensional contract approach. *IEEE Internet Things J.*, 8(13), 10639–10651, doi: 10.1109/JIOT.2021.3050163.

Wu, T., Zhao, C., & Zhang, Y. J. A. (2021b). Privacy-preserving distributed optimal power flow with partially homomorphic encryption. *IEEE Trans. Smart Grid.*, 12(5), 4506–4521, doi: 10.1109/TSG.2021.3084934.

Xu, J., Glicksberg, B. S., Su, C., Walker, P., Bian, J., & Wang, F. (2021). Federated learning for healthcare informatics. *J. Healthc. Inform. Res.*, 5(1), 1–19, doi: 10.1007/S41666-020-00082-4/TABLES/2.

Yang, H., Ge, M., Xue, D., Xiang, K., Li, H., & Lu, R. (2023a). Gradient leakage attacks in federated learning: Research frontiers, taxonomy and future directions. *IEEE Netw.*, doi: 10.1109/MNET.001.2300140.

Yang, W., Wang, S., Cui, H., Tang, Z., & Li, Y. (2023b). A review of homomorphic encryption for privacy-preserving biometrics. *Sensors*, 23(7), 3566, doi: 10.3390/S23073566.

Zhang, J., Guo, S., Guo, J., Zeng, D., Zhou, J., & Zomaya A. Y. (2023). Towards data-independent knowledge transfer in model-heterogeneous federated learning. *IEEE Trans. Comput.*, doi: 10.1109/TC.2023.3272801.

Zhang, L., Xu, J., Vijayakumar, P., Sharma, P. K., & Ghosh, U. (2022). Homomorphic encryption-based privacy-preserving federated learning in IoT-enabled healthcare system. *IEEE Trans. Netw. Sci. Eng.*, doi: 10.1109/TNSE.2022.3185327.

14 Diseases Detection System Using Federated Learning

P. Dhiman, S. Wadhwa, and Amandeep Kaur

14.1 INTRODUCTION

During the course of patient consultations and treatments, numerous healthcare facilities and hospitals have amassed enormous volumes of multimodal data. This data includes X-ray images, CT scans, physician diagnoses, and physiological measurements of patients. The multimodal data in question are often closely associated with patient identifiers, which necessitate the implementation of strict privacy protection measures. As a consequence of this, these healthcare institutions have created data islands that are completely separate from one another, which makes it difficult for them to work together directly in terms of cooperative training and data sharing through open databases. Consequently, this gives rise to a number of significant issues in the field of multimodal federated learning (FL). These challenges include activities such as artificial intelligence-assisted diagnosis, medical picture analysis, and the preparation of laboratory reports [1].

In this chapter, the simplicity of techniques was emphasised with the implementation of the FL model for detecting the disease. The significance of this chapter can be summarised as follows:

- To get the most relevant features from the disease image preprocessing techniques were applied described in Section 14.3.1.
- We examine the effectiveness of deep approaches with or without applying image processing methods.
- We investigate the illness detection scheme on skin cancer, Alzheimer's disease, breast cancer, and brain tumour.
- Furthermore, the impact of the input layer size on model performance and network size is evaluated.

This chapter is systematised as follows: Section 14.2 includes the literature review work. In Section 14.3 presents the procedure used, and result analysis is discussed in Section 14.4. And lastly, Section 14.5 concludes up this chapter with some concluding observations.

DOI: 10.1201/9781032694870-14

14.2 LITERATURE REVIEW

In addition, FL has the potential to play a significant role in the healthcare industry since it makes it possible to train models with data that is distributed and decentralised. As long as the patient's privacy is preserved, this can be an effective means of protecting patient privacy while also facilitating the development of models that are more precise and personalised and the examination of a greater quantity of data. Federated machine learning can also make it possible to train models using data that is difficult to gather and consolidate, such as data from rural or underserved areas. In addition, machine learning has the potential to eliminate data islands in the healthcare industry by facilitating the exchange and analysis of data across numerous organisations [2]. The efficiency with which FL is able to learn from data that is dispersed across numerous sites and cannot be integrated into a single dataset, as well as when data are located in multiple clinical systems, has also been improved. To summarise, FL has the potential to greatly enhance the quality of healthcare by adding a greater emphasis on data-driven and personalised care.

The development of FL, however, made it feasible to do analyses on data derived from a wide variety of sources, which bolstered the accuracy and practicability of implementing FL algorithms in cardiology. As a consequence of this, FL has been taking into consideration in a number of different applications for the treatment of cardiac disease. As an illustration, the authors were the pioneers in the field of cardiovascular illness when they brought FL into the picture [3]. They conducted an analysis of a number of electronic health records (EHRs) in order to forecast the number of hospitalisations that patients with heart disease will experience in a specific year based on the medical history that was provided in the EHRs. In order to accomplish this, they developed a federated optimisation method (cPDS) to tackle the sparse support vector machine (sSVM) problem. Additionally, they utilised the electronic health data from the Boston Medical Centre in order to train and test their model. The performance of their model was evaluated based on the area under the curve (AUC), which reached a maximum of 0.78. In addition to ensuring that users' anonymity was preserved, their model demonstrated a high degree of scalability.

A model for the prediction of cardiovascular arrhythmias that is based on FL was proposed in the same area. The authors constructed a centralised federated transfer learning and explainable 1D convolutional neural network (CNN) that was trained with the arrhythmia database that was maintained by the MIT Bureau of Investigation. They were successful in protecting individuals' privacy, enhancing explainability, lowering communication costs, and developing a personalised model that had an accuracy of up to 98.9% in predicting arrhythmias [4].

In comparison to usage in the Internet of Things (IoT) or multimedia fields, medical records are more complicated and varied in terms of both the format and the granularity of the information. As a result of variances in medical equipment, diagnostic methodologies, and data administration practices, the heterogeneity of the data is further increased inside healthcare institutions, which makes federated collaboration [5] more difficult to achieve. There is a significant amount of medical-related MFL

Diseases Detection System Using Federated Learning 193

work that has cropped up. An FL-based strategy was presented by Cobbinah et al. [6] for the purpose of predicting the phase of Alzheimer's disease by utilising MRI data from several centres. For the purpose of AI-assisted disease diagnosis, the authors of [7,8] utilised MFL and achieved performances that were satisfactory.

14.3 MATERIAL AND METHODS

A proposed fruit defect detection approach would start with image processing, then extract texture features, and finally identify the diseases into the appropriate groups. The following algorithm is used in this work.

14.3.1 PROPOSED ALGORITHM

The following steps have been used in the proposed algorithm:

Step 1: Read images
Step 2: Applied Preprocessing
Step 3: Perform Data Augmentation
Step 4: Trained the model
Step 5: Input Layer Resizing and feature extraction
Step 7: Classification of image samples appropriate class
Step 8: Evaluate model performance (confusion matrix, accuracy, precision, specificity, FScore, loss, recall)

14.3.2 DATASET

There is a massive store of information that is stored in the mass archives of clinical data that are retained by hospitals, but the majority of this information is not utilised because of numerous concerns regarding privacy and confidentiality. By using a deep learning approach these diseases can be detected by depending upon the exterior defects. Image samples of skin cancer, breast cancer, Alzheimer, and brain tumour have been collected from the public dataset in this chapter. The dataset contains the image samples of and flawed image samples were accumulated from the publically available dataset. Totally 395 skin cancer, 601 breast cancer, 381 Alzheimer, and 530 brain tumour images were used in this research. The proposed technique has major steps of preprocessing, data augmentation, feature extraction, resizing of input layer, and classification of the disease.

14.3.3 IMAGE PROCESSING

Most commonly used technique in computer vision systems in the agriculture field is image processing. To improve the quality and contrast of input image samples and noise reduction of the images, preprocessing techniques can be applied. All the image samples were initially preprocessed using normalisation and rescaling in order to get the uniform and consistent data for the training process. Furthermore, data augmentation

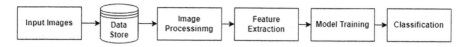

FIGURE 14.1 Steps of disease classification system.

technique is employed to get more image samples from the initial data [9]. It is the technique used for controlling the over-fitting problem of the image data while using a deep learning approach. To implement the data augmentation techniques seven features like width and height shift shearing, zooming, horizontal, and vertical shifting and rotation are used to increase the input samples of the diseases. Figure 14.1 represents the steps for implementing the proposed work.

14.3.4 Feature Extraction Using Federated Learning

The effort to develop an efficient neural network for image recognition and categorisation with seamless feature extraction and interpretation uniformity fuels a novel division of neural networks well-known as CNNs. These networks have a variety of computational multiple layers in the extractor module that learn to extract targeted attributes from the input provided image. The retrieved features are then sent to the classifying segment, which is built in the same way as a Multiple-Layered Neural Network. NN provides the distinct benefit of requiring a few parameters to be trained that permit weight sharing among both across partially linked layers [10].

Deep NNs have made significant progress in applications involving image processing in recent years. These methods have a strong ability to learn and powerful features assertion. Furthermore, it may extract findings layer-wise as of the inceptive cell to the abstraction stage, which will aid in recovering the picture dataset's generic feature and individual data [11]. The purpose of this work is to investigate FL as a paradigm for collaborative learning. In this paradigm, models can be trained across many institutions without explicitly exchanging patient data. Additionally, we demonstrate that the utilisation of FL in conjunction with additional privacy preservation approaches has the potential to enhance the performance of image analysis in comparison to training techniques that do not involve cooperation, and we quantify the privacy. The input size is also an important component in the CNN. When the input image is selected adequately, the model's size decreases substantially [12]. Input layers frequently take the output from antecedent levels; three alternative sizes of input layers: 64×64, 100×100, and 256×256. The subsequent layer comprises a pooling mechanism referred as MaxPooling that utilises the maximum magnitude value. Batch normalisation regulates the data provided to each mini-batch. This strengthens the learning process and expressively reduces the amount of training epochs expected to build complex networks [13]. In the output layer, the output parameters flatten out from a grid arrangement to provide data to the layer in a linear approach in an effort for the layer to retrieve specific features from its previous layer. After that, additional substantial layers are used; the first for excessively hidden layers of the output layer, and the second for the amount of anticipating categories [14]. Figure 14.2 represents the configuration of the proposed CNN model with 100×100 input layer.

Diseases Detection System Using Federated Learning

```
Model: "sequential"

Layer (type)                        Output Shape            Param #
=====================================================================
conv2d (Conv2D)                     (None, 100, 100, 32)    896

batch_normalisation (BatchNo        (None, 100, 100, 32)    128

separable_conv2d (SeparableC        (None, 100, 100, 32)    1344

max_pooling2d (MaxPooling2D)        (None, 50, 50, 32)      0

batch_normalisation_1 (Batch        (None, 50, 50, 32)      128

dropout (Dropout)                   (None, 50, 50, 32)      0

separable_conv2d_1 (Separabl        (None, 50, 50, 64)      2400

separable_conv2d_2 (Separabl        (None, 50, 50, 64)      4736

batch_normalisation_2 (Batch        (None, 50, 50, 64)      256

max_pooling2d_1 (MaxPooling2         (None, 25, 25, 64)      0

dropout_1 (Dropout)                 (None, 25, 25, 64)      0

conv2d_1 (Conv2D)                   (None, 25, 25, 128)     73856

conv2d_2 (Conv2D)                   (None, 25, 25, 128)     147584

batch_normalisation_3 (Batch        (None, 25, 25, 128)     512

max_pooling2d_2 (MaxPooling2        (None, 12, 12, 128)     0

dropout_2 (Dropout)                 (None, 12, 12, 128)     0

flatten (Flatten)                   (None, 18432)           0

dense (Dense)                       (None, 128)             2359424

dropout_3 (Dropout)                 (None, 128)             0

dense_1 (Dense)                     (None, 1)               129
=====================================================================
Total params: 2,591,393
Trainable params: 2,590,881
Non-trainable params: 512
```

FIGURE 14.2 Configuration basic NN implemented model with 100×100 input layer.

14.4 RESULT ANALYSIS

To analyse and compute the model's effectiveness, the 80–20 cross-validations ratio is used. The cross-entropy loss function is used to assess the outcome of the proposed approach. The Adam optimiser is employed to increase the cross-entropy ratio [15]. The Confusion matrix in Table 14.1 depicts the outcomes of the suggested technique on the image dataset for four classes.

TABLE 14.1
Confusion Matrix

Classes	Skin Cancer	Alzheimer	Skin Cancer	Brain Tumour
Skin cancer	**514**	29	32	19
Breast cancer	29	**956**	17	28
Alzheimer	14	16	**1,265**	47
Brain tumour	22	24	28	**1,566**

The proposed work is evaluated on different parameters like precision (P), Recall (R), F1 score (F), and accuracy (Acc). Table 14.2 shows the final outcome of the multi-classification model.

$$P = \left[\frac{\text{Tp}}{\text{Tp} + \text{FP}} \right] \tag{14.1}$$

$$R = \left[\frac{\text{Tp}}{\text{Tp} + \text{FN}} \right] \tag{14.2}$$

$$F = \left[\frac{(2 * \text{PC} * \text{RC})}{\text{PC} + \text{RC}} \right] \tag{14.3}$$

$$\text{Acc} = \left[\frac{\text{Tp} + \text{TN}}{\text{Tp} + \text{FP} + \text{FN} + \text{TN}} \right] \tag{14.4},$$

where Tp - True positive, Fp - False positive, TN - True Negative, and FN - False Negative.

The investigational results in Table 14.3 indicate that in the case of skin cancer highest accuracy, i.e. 96.75%, is achieved by the 256×256 input size, using breast cancer for image dataset highest accuracy, i.e. 94.74%, is achieved by the 256×256 input size, using Alzheimer dataset highest accuracy, i.e. 94.45%, is achieved by the 100×100 input size, and for brain tumour image dataset highest accuracy, i.e.

TABLE 14.2
Evaluation Results of Proposed Model

Classes	Accuracy (%)	Precision (%)	Recall (%)	F1 Score (%)
Skin cancer	97.15	90	94	92
Breast cancer	97.03	93	91	92
Alzheimer	96.94	95	93	94
Brain tumour	96.96	96	96	96

TABLE 14.3

Accuracy Obtained with Different Input Layers

Classes	% Accuracy (64 × 64)	% Accuracy (100 × 100)	% Accuracy (256 × 256)
Skin cancer	92.66	95.86	**96.75**
Breast cancer	94.43	93.82	**94.74**
Alzheimer	92.34	**96.45**	96.05
Brain tumour	94.56	97.06	**97.83**

97.83%, is achieved by the 256 × 256 input size. But the network model sizes in case of 64 × 64, 100 × 100, and 256 × 256 input size obtained are 16, 32.7, and 24.62 MB, respectively.

14.5 CONCLUSION

This research addressed the application of deep learning to the detection of human diseases where FL is applied to the skin cancer, breast cancer, Alzheimer's, and brain tumour. We build a model for categorising different disease dataset using deep neural networks. In the model, max-pooling layers, relu activation function, and the batch normalisation have been used with convolutional layers to enhance the outcome of the model. Simultaneously, the proposed framework with three distinct input layer sizes, 64 × 64, 100 × 100, and 256 × 256, is compared. To get the better quality of the input image samples are preprocessed using normalisation, rescaling, and data augmentation. It is observed that in the case of skin cancer highest accuracy, i.e. 96.75%, is achieved by the 256 × 256 input size, using breast cancer image dataset highest accuracy, i.e. 94.74%, is achieved by the 256 × 256 input size, using Alzheimer image dataset highest accuracy, i.e. 94.45%, is achieved by the 100 × 100 input size, and for brain tumour dataset highest accuracy, i.e. 97.83%, is achieved by the 256 × 256 input size. But the network model sizes in case of 64 × 64, 100 × 100, and 256 × 256 input size obtained are 16 MB, 32.7 MB, and 24.62 MB, respectively. In the future, we will aim to strengthen the dataset and enhance our approach to assure higher levels of accuracy while considering consideration the similarity and ambiguity of some disease parameters.

REFERENCES

1. Moshawrab, M., Adda, M., Bouzouane, A., Ibrahim, H., & Raad, A. (2023). Reviewing federated machine learning and its use in diseases prediction. *Sensors, 23*(4), 2112.
2. Li, J., Chen, T., & Qian, X. (2022). Generalizable pancreas segmentation modeling in CT imaging via meta-learning and latent-space feature flow generation. *IEEE Journal of Biomedical and Health Informatics, 27*(1), 374–385.
3. Zhang, K., Song, X., Zhang, C., & Yu, S. (2022). Challenges and future directions of secure federated learning: A survey. *Frontiers of Computer Science, 16*, 1–8.
4. MIT-BIH Arrhythmia Database v1.0.0. (24 February 2005). PhysioNet. Available online: https://physionet.org/content/mitdb/1.0.0/ (accessed on 1 July 2022).

5. Lakhan, A., Mohammed, M. A., Nedoma, J., Martinek, R., Tiwari, P., Vidyarthi, A., ... Wang, W. (2022). Federated-learning based privacy preservation and fraud-enabled blockchain IoMT system for healthcare. *IEEE Journal of Biomedical and Health Informatics, 27*(2), 664–672.
6. Hossen, M. N., Panneerselvam, V., Koundal, D., Ahmed, K., Bui, F. M., & Ibrahim, S. M. (2022). Federated machine learning for detection of skin diseases and enhancement of internet of medical things (IoMT) security. *IEEE Journal of Biomedical and Health Informatics, 27*(2), 835–841.
7. Chen, S., & Li, B. (2022, May). Towards Optimal Multi-Modal Federated Learning on Non-IID Data with Hierarchical Gradient Blending. In *IEEE INFOCOM 2022-IEEE Conference on Computer Communications* (pp. 1469–1478). IEEE, doi: 10.1109/INFOCOM48880.2022.9796724.
8. Qayyum, A., Ahmad, K., Ahsan, M. A., Al-Fuqaha, A., & Qadir, J. (2022). Collaborative federated learning for healthcare: Multi-modal COVID-19 diagnosis at the edge. *IEEE Open Journal of the Computer Society, 3*, 172–184.
9. Ogier du Terrail, J., Leopold, A., Joly, C., Béguier, C., Andreux, M., Maussion, C., ... & Heudel, P. E. (2023). Federated learning for predicting histological response to neoadjuvant chemotherapy in triple-negative breast cancer. *Nature Medicine, 29*(1), 135–146.
10. Amin, J., Anjum, M. A., Sharif, M., Kadry, S., & Nam, Y. (2022). Fruits and vegetable diseases recognition using convolutional neural networks. *Computers, Materials & Continua, 70*(1), doi: 10.32604/cmc.2022.018562.
11. Ouyang, X. (2023, June). Design and Deployment of Multi-Modal Federated Learning Systems for Alzheimer's Disease Monitoring. In *Proceedings of the 21st Annual International Conference on Mobile Systems, Applications and Services* (pp. 612–614), doi: 10.1145/3581791.3597505.
12. Dhiman, P., Kukreja, V., & Kaur, A. (2021, September). Citrus Fruits Classification and Evaluation using Deep Convolution Neural Networks: An Input Layer Resizing Approach. In *2021 9th International Conference on Reliability, Infocom Technologies and Optimization (Trends and Future Directions) (ICRITO)* (pp. 1–4). Noida, India: IEEE.
13. Yaqoob, M. M., Nazir, M., Khan, M. A., Qureshi, S., & Al-Rasheed, A. (2023). Hybrid classifier-based federated learning in health service providers for cardiovascular disease prediction. *Applied Sciences, 13*(3), 1911.
14. Naeem, A., Anees, T., Naqvi, R. A., & Loh, W. K. (2022). A comprehensive analysis of recent deep and federated-learning-based methodologies for brain tumor diagnosis. *Journal of Personalized Medicine, 12*(2), 275.
15. Luo, G., Liu, T., Lu, J., Chen, X., Yu, L., Wu, J., ... Cai, W. (2023). Influence of data distribution on federated learning performance in tumor segmentation. *Radiology: Artificial Intelligence, 5*(3), e220082.

15 Tailoring Medicine through Personalized Healthcare Solutions

Tejinder Kaur, Madhav Aggarwal, Krish Wason, and Pragati Duggal

15.1 INTRODUCTION

"Tailoring Medicine through Personalized Healthcare Solutions" is a phrase that encapsulates the concept of customizing medical treatment and healthcare services to meet the unique needs and characteristics of each individual patient. This approach to healthcare is often referred to as personalized medicine or precision medicine. Here's a breakdown of the key components of this phrase: This suggests that medical treatments and interventions are not one-size-fits-all but are instead customized or tailored to the specific requirements of each patient (Ashton et al., 2019). It emphasizes the importance of individualized care. This highlights the broader scope of healthcare, including not only medical treatments but also preventive measures, lifestyle recommendations, and other interventions that are personalized to a person's health status, genetics, lifestyle, and preferences (Ashton et al., 2019). The concept of personalized medicine is driven by advancements in genomics, medical technology, and data analysis. By analyzing a person's genetic makeup, medical history, lifestyle, and other factors, healthcare providers can develop treatment plans that are more effective and have fewer side effects. This approach aims to improve patient outcomes, reduce adverse reactions to treatments, and optimize the use of healthcare resources (Ashton et al., 2019).

Some key elements of personalized medicine include: Identifying genetic variations that may impact a person's response to medications or risk for certain diseases (Abrahams and Silver, 2010).

15.1.1 TAILORED TREATMENT PLANS

Developing treatment plans based on individual factors, such as genetics, to ensure the most effective and safest therapies. Offering personalized recommendations for lifestyle changes and preventive measures based on an individual's health risks (Abrahams and Silver, 2009).

DOI: 10.1201/9781032694870-15

15.1.2 Data Analytics

Using data and artificial intelligence to analyze vast amounts of healthcare information to identify trends, predict diseases, and optimize treatment strategies. Empowering patients to take an active role in their healthcare decisions by providing them with personalized information and choices (Abrahams and Silver, 2009)

Overall, the goal of "Tailoring Medicine through Personalized Healthcare Solutions" is to provide patients with the right care, at the right time, and in the right way, ultimately improving their overall health and well-being while optimizing the healthcare system's efficiency. The term "Tailoring Medicine" refers to the practice of customizing or individualizing medical treatments, interventions, and healthcare approaches to meet the specific needs, characteristics, and preferences of individual patients. This approach recognizes that each person is unique, and their medical conditions, genetics, lifestyle, and responses to treatments can vary significantly. In tailoring medicine, healthcare providers consider a range of factors when making treatment decisions (Aarestrup et al., 2020):

Understanding a patient's genetic makeup and molecular profile can help identify genetic mutations, biomarkers, or genetic predispositions that may influence their response to medications or their risk for certain diseases. Taking into account a patient's medical history, including previous illnesses, surgeries, and treatments, to inform current and future medical decisions (Abimbola et al., 2019).

15.1.3 Lifestyle and Environmental Factors

A patient's lifestyle choices (such as diet, exercise, and exposure to environmental toxins) can play a significant role in their health and well-being. Involving patients in healthcare decisions and considering their values, beliefs, and treatment preferences to develop personalized treatment plans that align with (Aarestrup et al., 2020).

Adapting treatment strategies over time based on the evolving nature of a patient's disease or condition and their response to interventions. Leveraging data analytics, medical imaging, genetic testing, and advanced technologies to gather and interpret information crucial for tailoring medical care (Arora and Arora, 2022).

The ultimate aim of tailoring medicine is to optimize patient outcomes, minimize adverse effects and complications, improve treatment efficacy, and enhance patient satisfaction with healthcare services. This approach represents a shift away from one-size-fits-all medical practices toward a more patient-centered and personalized approach to healthcare.

15.1.4 The Evolving Concept of PM

Personalized healthcare allows for treatments that are specifically tailored to an individual's unique genetic makeup, medical history, and current health status. This can significantly enhance the effectiveness of treatments, leading to better health outcomes. By considering a patient's genetic and molecular characteristics, healthcare providers can identify potential risks of adverse reactions to medications or treatments. This leads to safer and more targeted therapies, minimizing the likelihood of negative side effects (Kingma

Tailoring Medicine through Personalized Healthcare Solutions

et al., 2016). Personalized medicine helps identify the most appropriate medications for a patient based on their genetic and biochemical profiles. This reduces the trial-and-error approach in medication selection, saving time and resources. Personalized healthcare solutions enable the identification of an individual's specific health risks. This allows for personalized preventive strategies, such as lifestyle recommendations and screening tests, to reduce the risk of developing certain diseases. Patients are more engaged and informed when they participate in personalized healthcare decisions. They have a better understanding of their health risks and treatment options, leading to improved adherence to treatment plans. Personalized medicine enables the monitoring of disease progression and treatment response over time. Adjustments can be made to treatment plans as needed, ensuring that patients receive the most effective care throughout their healthcare journey. By tailoring healthcare interventions to individual needs, unnecessary tests, treatments, and hospitalizations can be avoided. This optimizes the allocation of healthcare resources and reduces healthcare costs. Personalized healthcare generates vast amounts of data, contributing to medical research and the development of targeted therapies. This can lead to breakthroughs in understanding diseases and discovering new treatments (Kingma et al., 2016).

15.2 DISCUSSION

15.2.1 PERSONALIZED HEALTHCARE

Genetic testing and personalized screening can help identify disease risks at an early stage, allowing for timely interventions and potentially better outcomes. Personalized healthcare extends beyond medical treatments to include psychological and emotional support tailored to a patient's needs, improving overall well-being (Kingma and Dhariwal, 2018). Personalized healthcare has the potential to address health disparities by providing tailored solutions that are accessible to diverse populations, ensuring equitable access to advanced healthcare. In summary, tailoring medicine through personalized healthcare solutions offers numerous advantages, ranging from improved treatment outcomes and patient satisfaction to resource optimization and advancements in medical research. It represents a transformative shift toward more patient-centered and data-driven healthcare practices. While tailoring medicine through personalized healthcare solutions offers numerous advantages, it also comes with some disadvantages and challenges that need to be considered: Personalized healthcare can be expensive due to the need for genetic testing, data analysis, and specialized treatments. This can strain healthcare budgets and may not be accessible to everyone, potentially exacerbating healthcare inequalities (Sloane and Silva, 2020).

15.2.2 COMPLEXITY

Implementing personalized medicine requires sophisticated technology and expertise in genetics and data analysis. It can be challenging for healthcare systems and providers to adapt to these complexities. The collection and storage of genetic and health data raise significant privacy concerns. Ensuring the security and confidentiality of patients' sensitive information is a critical challenge (Bushe, 2013).

For some diseases and conditions, there may be insufficient genetic or molecular data available to enable personalized treatments. This limitation can hinder the application of personalized medicine in certain areas of healthcare. Personalized medicine raises ethical questions about how to use genetic information responsibly, potential discrimination based on genetic predispositions, and the implications of making health decisions based on genetic data (Vaccari et al., 2021).

15.2.3 TREATMENT DELAYS

Personalized medicine often involves additional diagnostic tests and data analysis, which can lead to delays in treatment. In some cases, waiting for personalized treatment plans may not be feasible for patients with urgent medical needs. Focusing too much on genetics can overshadow other important factors that influence health, such as social determinants of health, environmental factors, and lifestyle choices. Patients may have difficulty understanding complex genetic information and treatment options, which can lead to confusion and potentially impact their ability to make informed decisions. The storage and analysis of large volumes of patient data increase the risk of data breaches and cyber attacks, potentially compromising patient privacy and data integrity. While personalized treatments aim to improve effectiveness, individual responses to treatments can still vary, and not all patients may experience the expected benefits. Developing and regulating personalized treatments can be complex due to the unique nature of these therapies. Integrating personalized medicine into existing healthcare systems can be challenging. Healthcare providers and institutions may need to adapt their practices and infrastructure to support personalized care (Zhang et al., 2022).

In conclusion, while tailoring medicine through personalized healthcare solutions holds great promise, it also presents several disadvantages and challenges that need to be carefully addressed to ensure its successful and ethical implementation in healthcare systems. Balancing the potential benefits with these challenges is essential for realizing the full potential of personalized medicine (Parikh et al., 2020).

15.3 RELATED WORK

15.3.1

Personalized medicine plays a significant role in oncology by identifying specific genetic mutations in tumors. This information helps oncologists choose the most effective targeted therapies and immunotherapies for individual cancer patients, minimizing side effects and maximizing treatment success (Thiagarajan et al., 2022).

15.3.2

Pharmacogenomics is the study of how a person's genetic makeup influences their response to medications. Personalized medicine can guide healthcare providers in prescribing the right dosage and type of medication based on a patient's genetic profile, reducing adverse drug reactions.

15.3.3

Personalized healthcare solutions can identify an individual's genetic predisposition to certain diseases, allowing for tailored prevention strategies, such as lifestyle modifications, screening programs, and vaccination plans (Florian, 2002).

15.3.4

Genetic testing and personalized risk assessments can help identify individuals at high risk for cardiovascular diseases. This information can guide interventions, such as medication, dietary changes, and exercise regimens, to reduce the risk of heart disease.

15.3.5

Personalized medicine can benefit patients with rare and genetic diseases by pinpointing the underlying genetic causes and developing tailored treatment approaches, including gene therapy and precision medicine (Florian, 2002).

Genetic factors can contribute to mental health conditions. Personalized healthcare solutions can assist in identifying genetic markers associated with conditions like depression, schizophrenia, or bipolar disorder, informing treatment plans and medication choices. Tailoring medicine is vital in managing infectious diseases, such as HIV and hepatitis C. Personalized treatment plans based on viral genetic profiles can improve the effectiveness of antiviral therapies. Personalized healthcare can aid in the diagnosis and management of neurodegenerative diseases like Alzheimer's and Parkinson's by identifying genetic risk factors and guiding treatment decisions (Durga et al., 2019).

Pediatric patients can benefit from personalized healthcare solutions for conditions like congenital disorders or childhood cancers, where tailoring treatments to a child's specific genetic and medical profile can improve outcomes.

15.4 PROPOSED SYSTEM

The approach of "Tailoring Medicine through Personalized Healthcare Solutions" is characterized by several key features and principles that distinguish it from traditional, one-size-fits-all healthcare approaches (Oh et al., 2019).

15.4.1

Personalized healthcare prioritizes the individual patient, recognizing that each person is unique in terms of genetics, medical history, lifestyle, and preferences. It aims to tailor medical care to the specific needs and characteristics of each patient (Durga et al., 2019).

15.4.2

Personalized medicine often involves genetic and molecular analysis to uncover important information about a patient's health. This includes genetic testing, biomarker identification, and genomic profiling to guide treatment decisions (Durga et al., 2019).

15.4.3

Personalized healthcare relies heavily on data, including patient health records, genetic information, and clinical data. Advanced data analytics and machine learning techniques are used to process and interpret this information to inform treatment plans (Durga et al., 2019).

15.4.4

Personalized healthcare assesses an individual's risk factors for various diseases, adverse reactions to treatments, and other health-related risks. This allows for proactive preventive measures and early interventions.

15.4.5

One of the central features is the customization of treatment plans. Medications, therapies, and interventions are selected and adjusted based on an individual's genetic makeup, medical history, and other relevant factors.

15.4.6

Personalized medicine emphasizes patient engagement a shared decision-making. Patients are actively involved in their healthcare decisions and are provided with information to make informed choices.

These characteristics collectively define the principles and practices of "Tailoring Medicine through Personalized Healthcare Solutions," with a focus on individualized care, data-driven decision-making, and the use of advanced technologies to optimize patient outcomes.

15.5 EXPERIMENTAL RESULTS

Pharmacogenomics studies how an individual's genetic makeup influences their response to drugs. Experimental results in this area have led to the development of genetic tests that can predict how a person will metabolize and respond to medications (Chen et al., 2016).

For example, some studies (Wang et al., 2020) have demonstrated that genetic testing can help determine the most effective antidepressant for a patient or the appropriate dose of warfarin (a blood thinner) (Pan et al., 2019).

15.6 CONCLUSION

This approach allows for more precise and effective medical interventions. This can lead to better health outcomes and reduced healthcare costs. The field has led to the discovery of novel biomarkers for various diseases, aiding in early diagnosis and treatment. Proteomics and metabolomics play a crucial role in identifying these biomarkers. Advanced data analysis techniques, such as artificial intelligence and machine learning, enable the rapid analysis of large datasets, leading to more accurate disease prediction, treatment recommendations, and drug discovery. As personalized medicine relies heavily on genetic and personal data, it raises important ethical and privacy concerns that need to be carefully addressed.

REFERENCES

F. M. Aarestrup, A. Albeyatti, W. J. Armitage, et al., "Towards a European health research and innovation cloud (HRIC)," *Genome Med.*, vol. 12, no. 1, pp. 1–14, 2020.

S. Abimbola, L. Baatiema, and M. Bigdeli, "The impacts of decentralization on health system equity, efficiency and resilience: a realist synthesis of the evidence," *Health Policy Plan.*, vol. 34, no. 8, pp. 605–617, 2019.

E. Abrahams and M. Silver, "The case for personalized medicine," *J. Diabetes Sci. Technol.*, vol. 3, no. 4, pp. 680–684, 2009.

M. Abrahams and E. Silver, *Integrative Neuroscience and Personalized Medicine*. Oxford University Press, 2010.

A. Arora and A. Arora, "Generative adversarial networks and synthetic patient data: current challenges and future perspectives," *Future Healthc. J.*, vol. 9, no. 2, pp. 190–193, July 2022.

J. J. Ashton, E. Mossotto, S. Ennis, and R. M. Beattie, "Personalising medicine in inflammatory bowel disease—current and future perspectives," *Transl. Pediatr.*, vol. 8, no. 1, pp. 56–69, 2019.

G. R. Bushe, "Generative process, generative outcome: the transformational potential of appreciative inquiry," In: D. L. Cooperrider, D. P. Zandee, L. N. Godwin, M. Avital, and B. Boland (Eds.), *Organizational Generativity: The Appreciative Inquiry Summit and a Scholarship of Transformation*, vol. 4, Emerald Group Publishing Limited, 2013, pp. 89–113.

X. Chen, D. P. Kingma, T. Salimans, et al., "Variational lossy autoencoder," *arXiv* [cs.LG], November 8, 2016.

S. Durga, R. Nag, and E. Daniel, "Survey on machine learning and deep learning algorithms used in Internet of Things (IoT) healthcare," In *2019 3rd International Conference on Computing Methodologies and Communication (ICCMC)*, 2019, pp. 1018–1022.

R. Florian, "Named entity recognition as a house of cards: classifier stacking," In *COLING-02: The 6th Conference on Natural Language Learning 2002*, January 2002, Johns Hopkins Center for Language and Speech Processing (CLSP).

D. P. Kingma and P. Dhariwal, "Glow: generative flow with invertible 1x1 convolutions," *Adv. Neural Inf. Process. Syst.*, vol. 31, pp. 1–10, 2018.

D. P. Kingma, T. Salimans, R. Jozefowicz, X. Chen, I. Sutskever, and M. Welling, "Improved variational inference with inverse autoregressive flow," *Adv. Neural Inf. Process. Syst.*, vol. 29, pp. 1–16, 2016.

S. Oh, Y. Jung, S. Kim, and I. Lee, "Deep generative design: integration of topology optimization and generative models," *J. Mech. Des.*, vol. 141, no. 11, p. 1, 2019.

Z. Pan, W. Yu, X. Yi, A. Khan, F. Yuan, and Y. Zheng, "Recent progress on generative adversarial networks (GANs): a survey," *IEEE Access.*, vol. 7, pp. 36322–36333, 2019.

J. Parikh, J. Kozloski, and V. Gurev, "Integration of AI and mechanistic modeling in generative adversarial networks for stochastic inverse problems," arXiv [stat.ML], September 17, 2020.

E. B. Sloane and R. J. Silva, "Chapter 83—Artificial intelligence in medical devices and clinical decision support systems," In *Clinical Engineering Handbook* (Second Edition), E. Iadanza, Ed., Academic Press, 2020, pp. 556–568.

K. Thiagarajan, C. K. Dixit, M. Panneerselvam, C. A. Madhuvappan, S. Gadde, and J. N. Shrote, "Analysis on the growth of artificial intelligence for application security in internet of things," In *2022 Second International Conference on Artificial Intelligence and Smart Energy (ICAIS)*, 2022, pp. 6–12.

I. Vaccari, V. Orani, A. Paglialonga, E. Cambiaso, and M. Mongelli, "A generative adversarial network (GAN) technique for Internet of medical things data," *Sensors*, vol. 21, no. 11, p. 3726, May 2021.

Y. Wang, H. Wang, L. Wei, S. Li, L. Liu, and X. Wang, "Synthetic promoter design in *Escherichia coli* based on a deep generative network," *Nucleic Acids Res.*, vol. 48, no. 12, pp. 6403–6412, July 2020.

J. Zhang, Z. Tang, Y. Xie, M. Ai, and W. Gui, "Generative adversarial network-based image-level optimal setpoint calculation for flotation reagents control," *Expert Syst. Appl.*, vol. 197, p. 116790, July 2022.

16 FedHealth in Wearable Healthcare, Orchestrated Federated Deep Learning for Smart Healthcare

Health Monitoring and Healthcare Informatics Lensing Challenges and Future Directions

Bhupinder Singh and Christian Kaunert

16.1 INTRODUCTION

The notion of wearable healthcare has surfaced as a revolutionary advancement at the nexus of technology and healthcare. As data-driven insights are transforming medical practices in the age of digital health, wearable technology has progressed from being mere accessories to being essential instruments for proactive health management. People may continually and in real time check their physiological indicators using these gadgets since they are furnished with a variety of sensors and data-gathering capabilities [1]. The transition from episodic treatment to ongoing, individualized monitoring represents a revolutionary advance in the provision of patient-centered healthcare.

Wearable healthcare is important because it can collect a wide variety of health data and has the potential to enable people to take control of their own health. Wearables provide a comprehensive perspective of health that goes beyond normal medical visits and easily integrates into everyday activities, beyond the traditional constraints of healthcare facilities. This has significant effects on maintaining general health, preventing illness, and implementing early intervention. Because it helps close the communication gap between patients and healthcare professionals, wearable healthcare has become more popular. Wearable technology enables healthcare practitioners to make well-informed decisions and timely interventions by providing them with an extensive stream of real-time data. In the case of chronic illnesses, when ongoing monitoring might reveal early signs of exacerbations, this becomes extremely important [2].

DOI: 10.1201/9781032694870-16

207

The integration of wearables with digital health platforms and electronic health records fosters a collaborative healthcare ecosystem. Wearable-generated data can be seamlessly transmitted to medical practitioners, enabling remote monitoring, diagnosis, and personalized recommendations. This not only enhances the quality of care but also reduces the burden on healthcare infrastructure by mitigating unnecessary hospital visits. The holistic implications of wearable healthcare extend beyond individual health management. Aggregated and anonymized data from wearables have the potential to drive population health insights and epidemiological research. This wealth of data can uncover trends, patterns, and risk factors on a large scale, informing public health initiatives and preventive measures [3].

FedHealth is the amalgamation of federated deep learning and wearable healthcare. This innovative approach not only addresses the challenges of data privacy and security but also harnesses the wealth of information stored within wearables to revolutionize healthcare informatics. As it navigates this territory, it uncovers the intricacies of orchestrated federated deep learning for smart healthcare, highlighting its applicability to health monitoring and healthcare informatics.

In recent years, the growing interest in federated deep learning has been catalyzed by the pressing need to reconcile the potential of data-driven insights with the paramount concern for data privacy, especially within the realm of health data analysis. Traditional approaches to data sharing often necessitate the centralization of sensitive health information, raising significant concerns about data breaches, unauthorized access, and potential violations of patient confidentiality.

Federated deep learning offers a compelling solution to this conundrum by enabling collaborative model training across decentralized data sources while preserving the data within its originating silos. This approach harnesses the power of collective intelligence without necessitating the aggregation of raw data. This is of particular significance in healthcare, where the sensitivity of patient information demands stringent privacy measures [4].

The architecture of federated learning is elegantly aligned with the distributed nature of health data, emanating from diverse sources such as wearable devices, electronic health records, and medical imaging repositories. By allowing local models to be trained on individual data and updating a global model based on the aggregated learnings, federated deep learning ensures that the raw data remains secure and private at its source. This approach significantly mitigates the risk associated with data breaches and unauthorized access, while still facilitating collaborative insights.

The healthcare domain, characterized by a multitude of stakeholders including patients, clinicians, researchers, and institutions, benefits immensely from this distributed approach. Federated deep learning engenders a collaborative ecosystem where each participant contributes their knowledge, without the need to disclose sensitive data. This democratized approach aligns with the ethos of patient-centered care, empowering individuals to participate actively in medical research while retaining control over their data. Furthermore, the regulatory landscape, characterized by stringent data protection laws such as Health Insurance

Portability and Accountability Act (HIPAA) and General Data Protection Regulation (GDPR), underscores the need for privacy-preserving methodologies in health data analysis. Federated deep learning resonates well with these regulatory frameworks, as it inherently adheres to principles of data minimization, consent, and transparency [5].

As the confluence of healthcare and technology accelerates, federated deep learning stands as a beacon of hope for unlocking the full potential of health data without compromising privacy. The subsequent sections of this chapter delve into the practical implementation and implications of orchestrated federated deep learning in the context of wearable healthcare, particularly focusing on health monitoring and healthcare informatics lensing. Through this exploration, this chapter sheds light on the challenges, opportunities, and future directions of this groundbreaking paradigm [6].

16.2 PURPOSE OF THE PAPER AND ITS STRUCTURE

This research paper aims to explore and elucidate the concept of FedHealth, a pioneering fusion of orchestrated federated deep learning and wearable healthcare [7]. With a specific focus on health monitoring and healthcare informatics lensing, this chapter seeks to demonstrate how this innovative paradigm can revolutionize the landscape of smart healthcare. The central purpose is to dissect the intricate synergy between federated deep learning and wearable healthcare data, highlighting its potential to enhance data-driven health insights while safeguarding individual data privacy. Through a comprehensive analysis of challenges, case studies, and future directions, this chapter aims to contribute to the burgeoning field of privacy-preserving health data analysis [8].

16.3 WEARABLE HEALTHCARE AND FEDHEALTH

FedHealth encapsulates the fusion of two groundbreaking domains: wearable healthcare and orchestrated federated deep learning [9]. The fundamental premise of FedHealth is to harness the insights hidden within wearable healthcare data while preserving the privacy and ownership of individual health information. This paradigm operates on the principle that the power of collective intelligence can be harnessed without necessitating the sharing of raw, identifiable data. In essence, FedHealth paves the way for collaborative learning without compromising the individual's control over their personal health data [10].

This convergence is particularly relevant in the context of health monitoring, where wearable devices generate a continuous stream of data that can offer crucial insights into an individual's health trajectory. FedHealth empowers individuals with the capability to contribute to medical research and insights while ensuring that their sensitive data remains within their control. By aggregating knowledge rather than raw data, FedHealth navigates the ethical and regulatory complexities of healthcare data sharing [11].

16.4 ROLE OF WEARABLE DEVICES IN HEALTHCARE: EMPHASIZING THEIR POTENTIAL TO COLLECT REAL-TIME HEALTH DATA

Wearable devices have emerged as pivotal instruments in redefining healthcare by bridging the gap between personal health management and advanced technology. These devices, ranging from smartwatches and fitness trackers to specialized health monitors, have revolutionized the way individuals interact with their own health and well-being. Their role extends far beyond serving as mere accessories; they are transformative tools that empower users to take proactive control of their health by providing real-time, personalized insights [12]. Central to the appeal of wearable devices is their capacity to seamlessly integrate into the fabric of daily life [13]. For instance, irregularities in heart rate patterns could be indicative of impending cardiac issues, and alterations in sleep patterns might signify underlying stressors. Wearable devices act as vigilant sentinels, alerting users and healthcare providers to potential concerns before they escalate [14].

The convergence of real-time data collection and advanced analytical techniques further magnifies the potential of wearable devices. Deep learning algorithms can mine this treasure trove of data to extract patterns, correlations, and insights that are otherwise elusive. By studying individual and population-level data, wearables contribute to the collective understanding of health trends, risk factors, and preventive strategies.

FedHealth, the amalgamation of wearable healthcare and orchestrated federated deep learning, propels this potential to new heights. It ensures that real-time health data, rich in potential insights, can be harnessed without compromising data privacy. The following sections of this chapter delve into the orchestration, challenges, and opportunities inherent in this paradigm, aiming to illuminate how the synergy of wearables and federated deep learning can revolutionize health monitoring and healthcare informatics [15].

16.5 FEDHEALTH AS THE FUSION OF FEDERATED LEARNING AND WEARABLE HEALTHCARE: ADVANTAGES AND CHALLENGES

FedHealth encapsulates an innovative convergence that marries the transformative potential of federated learning with the insights gleaned from wearable healthcare data. At its core, FedHealth represents a pioneering approach to harnessing the power of collective intelligence while safeguarding the privacy and security of sensitive health information [16]. It emerges as a solution to the dichotomy between data-driven insights and individual data protection, particularly pertinent in the healthcare domain.

Federated learning, a decentralized machine learning paradigm, forms the cornerstone of FedHealth. This methodology allows models to be collaboratively trained across diverse, distributed data sources without necessitating the centralization of raw data. Each data source, often residing on wearable devices, trains a local model on its own data, and the learnings are then aggregated to refine a global model. This ensures that the raw, identifiable data remains within its originating source while contributing to the collective intelligence. The FedHealth brings forth a multitude of advantages that address key challenges in the intersection of wearable healthcare and data-driven health insights.-

Preservation of Privacy: One of the most significant advantages of FedHealth lies in its inherent ability to preserve data privacy. By keeping sensitive health data localized, FedHealth minimizes the risk of data breaches and unauthorized access. It resonates well with data protection regulations such as HIPAA and GDPR, ensuring that individual rights and privacy are upheld.

Enhanced Collaborative Learning: FedHealth empowers collaboration across diverse stakeholders, including patients, healthcare providers, researchers, and institutions. It fosters an ecosystem where each participant contributes their insights without revealing raw data. This synergy advances medical research, diagnostics, and treatment options.

Timely Health Insights: By leveraging wearable healthcare data in real time, FedHealth facilitates the early detection of anomalies and deviations from baseline health parameters. This timely insight is invaluable for proactive interventions and personalized health management.

Empowerment of Individuals: Wearable device users become active participants in their health journeys through FedHealth. They contribute to research and insights while maintaining control over their data, aligning with the principles of patient-centered care.

However, FedHealth is not devoid of challenges:

Technical Complexity: Orchestrating federated learning across distributed devices poses technical challenges, including data synchronization, model aggregation, and communication bottlenecks. Ensuring the seamless operation of FedHealth requires robust infrastructure and protocols.

Heterogeneous Data: Wearable healthcare data varies in format, quality, and reliability across devices and individuals. Integrating and harmonizing this heterogeneous data for effective federated learning demands careful preprocessing and standardization.

Bias and Fairness: Federated models might inadvertently perpetuate biases present in local data sources. Ensuring fairness and unbiased predictions across diverse populations becomes a challenge that requires rigorous attention.

In navigating these challenges and leveraging the advantages, FedHealth emerges as a transformative paradigm that has the potential to reshape the landscape of healthcare informatics. The subsequent sections of this chapter delve into the orchestration, practical implications, and future directions of FedHealth, particularly within the context of health monitoring and healthcare informatics lensing [17].

16.6 FEDERATED LEARNING: DECENTRALIZED APPROACH AND BENEFITS IN HEALTHCARE DOMAIN

Federated learning, a transformative paradigm in machine learning, operates on the principle of decentralized model training across distributed data sources while retaining data privacy. This approach has gained prominence as an ingenious solution to the challenges posed by centralized data analysis, particularly within the sensitive landscape of healthcare [18].

Federated learning leverages the power of distributed intelligence. In the healthcare context, this means that data generated from wearable devices, electronic health records, and other sources remain localized on the devices where they are generated. Instead of sending raw data to a central server, federated learning sends only model updates, ensuring that sensitive health information remains on the device. This decentralized approach shifts the focus from sharing data to sharing knowledge, minimizing the risks associated with data breaches and unauthorized access [19]. The healthcare domain reaps substantial benefits from the decentralized nature of federated learning:

Data Privacy and Security: Healthcare data is characterized by its sensitive nature, containing personal medical histories, diagnoses, and other private information. Federated learning eliminates the need to centralize this data, reducing the risk of privacy breaches and ensuring compliance with data protection regulations. Patient confidentiality is upheld, and the potential consequences of data leaks are mitigated.

Collaborative Insights: Federated learning enables collaboration across diverse stakeholders, including patients, clinicians, researchers, and institutions. Each local model contributes to the refinement of a global model without sharing raw data. This collaborative approach fosters a collective intelligence that advances medical research, diagnostic accuracy, and personalized treatment recommendations.

Real-Time Learning: Wearable devices generate a continuous stream of real-time health data. Federated learning thrives in this dynamic environment by allowing local models to adapt and improve in real time. This real-time learning capability is pivotal for proactive health management and timely interventions.

Data Diversity and Personalization: Healthcare data originates from various sources, capturing different aspects of an individual's health. Federated learning aggregates insights from diverse sources, offering a comprehensive view of an individual's well-being. This enables personalized recommendations and treatments based on an individual's unique health profile.

Ethical Data Utilization: Federated learning aligns with ethical principles by enabling data utilization without data extraction. Patients maintain ownership of their health data, granting explicit consent for its use while ensuring it remains under their control.

However, federated learning is not without challenges. Communication overhead, heterogeneous data sources, and the need for advanced aggregation techniques are technical hurdles that must be overcome. Additionally, the collaborative nature of federated learning demands robust governance and communication protocols to ensure effective collaboration among stakeholders. In the healthcare domain, where patient privacy and data security are paramount, federated learning emerges as a transformative approach that unifies the benefits of data analysis with the demands of ethical data utilization [20]. As the subsequent sections of this chapter delve into the orchestration of federated deep learning for health monitoring and healthcare informatics, the role of federated learning continues to shine as a beacon of hope in reshaping healthcare informatics.

16.7 DEEP LEARNING IN HEALTHCARE: EXPLORING APPLICATIONS IN HEALTHCARE, INCLUDING IMAGE ANALYSIS, DIAGNOSTIC PREDICTIONS, AND PATIENT MONITORING

Deep learning, a subset of machine learning inspired by the structure and function of the human brain's neural networks, has demonstrated remarkable capabilities in revolutionizing healthcare across multiple fronts. Its ability to discern complex patterns and extract meaningful insights from large and heterogeneous datasets has opened new vistas in medical diagnostics, treatment planning, and patient care. Within the healthcare landscape, deep learning applications span diverse domains, with image analysis, diagnostic predictions, and patient monitoring emerging as standout areas of transformative impact [21].

Image Analysis: Deep learning has emerged as a game-changer in medical imaging, significantly enhancing the accuracy and efficiency of image interpretation. Convolutional Neural Networks (CNNs), a class of deep learning models, excel in tasks such as identifying anomalies in X-rays, detecting tumors in MRI scans, and even analyzing histopathological slides for cancer diagnosis. By learning hierarchical features from images, deep learning algorithms can discern intricate details that might elude the human eye, thus bolstering early detection and precise diagnosis. These applications not only expedite diagnostic workflows but also contribute to better patient outcomes by enabling timely interventions.

Diagnostic Predictions: Deep learning's prowess extends to predictive modeling, where it excels in generating insights that aid in early disease detection and prognosis assessment. Recurrent Neural Networks (RNNs) and Long Short-Term Memory (LSTM) networks, designed for sequential data analysis, prove instrumental in analyzing electronic health records and patient histories to predict disease trajectories. Deep learning's predictive capabilities empower clinicians to make informed decisions based on data-driven insights.

The need for large and diverse datasets for training, interpretability of deep models, and addressing bias in algorithms are among the notable hurdles. Additionally, the integration of deep learning models into clinical workflows requires validation and regulatory compliance to ensure patient safety [22]. As the healthcare industry continues to embrace data-driven approaches, deep learning's ability to transform medical imaging, enhance diagnostic precision, and enable continuous patient monitoring underscores its indispensable role in shaping the future of healthcare. This paradigm shift promises improved patient care, better treatment outcomes, and the potential for personalized medicine tailored to individual needs [23].

16.8 CHALLENGES IN FEDERATED DEEP LEARNING FOR WEARABLE HEALTHCARE

While federated deep learning presents a promising paradigm for privacy-preserving and collaborative healthcare data analysis, its implementation within the context of wearable healthcare introduces a unique set of challenges [24]. The decentralized nature of federated learning, coupled with the intricacies of health data generated by wearables, demands careful consideration of technical, ethical, and operational aspects. There are multifarious challenges associated with this.

Data Heterogeneity and Quality: Wearable healthcare data comes from a diverse range of devices, each with varying levels of accuracy, precision, and reliability. Integrating and harmonizing this heterogeneous data to train cohesive models across different devices poses a significant challenge. Variations in data quality can lead to biased or inconsistent models, requiring robust preprocessing techniques and quality control measures.

Communication Overhead: Federated learning necessitates communication between edge devices and a central server for model updates. In the case of wearable devices, which are often resource-constrained and operate on battery power, the communication overhead can impact device performance and battery life. Optimizing communication protocols to minimize overhead while ensuring timely updates is a delicate balance.

Model Aggregation and Bias: Aggregating model updates from different wearable devices introduces challenges in balancing model contributions and mitigating potential biases. Certain devices might contribute disproportionately due to larger user bases, potentially leading to biased global models. Ensuring fair model aggregation that accounts for data diversity and distribution becomes essential to prevent skewed insights.

Privacy-Preserving Techniques: The heart of federated learning lies in privacy preservation, which has become paramount in the healthcare domain. Ensuring that raw health data remains on edge devices while still enabling effective model training demands advanced privacy-preserving techniques. Developing cryptographic protocols, secure aggregation methods, and differential privacy mechanisms adds complexity to the implementation.

Dynamic Data Distribution and Concept Drift: Wearable healthcare data distribution can change dynamically due to variations in user behavior, health conditions, and environmental factors. Traditional federated learning assumes a stationary data distribution, which might not hold true for wearable healthcare. Concepts such as "concept drift," where the data distribution changes over time, challenge the stability of trained models.

Regulatory Compliance and Ethical Considerations: Health data is subject to stringent regulatory frameworks, and wearable healthcare is no exception. Federated deep learning must comply with regulations like HIPAA and GDPR to ensure the protection of patient privacy and data security. Balancing regulatory compliance, ethical data use, and model performance adds an additional layer of complexity.

Lack of Standardization: Wearable devices often lack standardized data formats, communication protocols, and interoperability. This lack of standardization can hinder seamless integration of diverse devices into a federated learning framework. So, developing standardized protocols that accommodate various wearables while maintaining privacy becomes crucial.

Model Interpretability: Interpretable models are vital in healthcare to gain clinicians' and patients' trust. Federated deep learning models, particularly complex ones, might lack transparency and explainability. Ensuring that the insights provided by these models can be understood and interpreted by stakeholders remains a challenge.

In navigating these challenges, the interdisciplinary collaboration of machine learning experts, healthcare professionals, ethicists, and policymakers is vital. The potential benefits of federated deep learning for wearable healthcare are substantial, ranging from personalized health insights to collective intelligence [25]. However, addressing these challenges is essential to unlock this potential and ensure that the integration of federated learning with wearable healthcare aligns with the principles of effective data analysis, privacy protection, and ethical healthcare practices.

The application of federated deep learning to health data collected from wearable devices introduces a constellation of challenges that stem from the dynamic nature of wearable-generated data and the intricacies of privacy preservation. While federated deep learning offers an avenue for collaborative analysis while safeguarding individual data, its integration with wearable health data is not without complexities.

Data Heterogeneity and Variability: Wearable devices gather a diverse array of health data, ranging from heart rate and sleep patterns to activity levels and environmental factors. This heterogeneity poses challenges when aggregating data for model training. Differences in data formats, data quality, and data distribution across wearables require sophisticated approaches to harmonize and standardize the data before it can be used for federated learning. Moreover, the inherent variability in health data collected from different individuals adds another layer of complexity, demanding models that can adapt and generalize across diverse data sources.

Real-Time Processing and Latency: Wearable devices operate in real time, continuously generating streams of health data. Federated deep learning needs to address the latency requirements of real-time data processing while ensuring that model updates are efficiently transmitted without hindering device performance. Striking a balance between real-time processing and communication efficiency is essential to maintain the seamless operation of wearable devices.

Data Privacy and Security: Preserving data privacy is paramount in wearable healthcare, where health data is inherently personal and sensitive. Federated deep learning addresses this challenge by keeping raw data on the device while transmitting only model updates. However, designing privacy-preserving mechanisms that prevent the leakage of sensitive health information during model updates requires advanced cryptographic techniques and secure aggregation protocols.

Scalability and Resource Constraints: Wearable devices often operate with limited computational resources and battery life. Federated learning models must be designed to operate efficiently within these resource constraints. Model complexity, communication overhead, and computational load need to be carefully optimized to ensure that the federated learning framework is viable on wearable devices [26].

Concept Drift and Dynamic Data Distribution: Health data collected from wearables can exhibit dynamic data distribution due to changes in user behavior, health conditions, or external factors. This dynamicity challenges the traditional assumption of stationary data distribution in federated learning. Models trained on previous data might not be optimal for evolving data distributions, necessitating strategies to adapt to concept drift and accommodate changing patterns in wearable health data.

Interpretability and Explainability: The interpretability of federated deep learning models is crucial in healthcare, especially when dealing with wearable-generated health insights. These models might produce accurate predictions, but their complexity can hinder the understanding of the rationale behind their decisions. Ensuring that federated models provide interpretable results is essential for building trust among healthcare professionals and users [27].

So, incorporating federated deep learning into wearable healthcare data analysis is a complex endeavor that requires a multidisciplinary approach. Collaboration between machine learning experts, healthcare practitioners, data privacy experts, and ethicists is necessary to navigate these challenges effectively. By addressing these hurdles, the potential benefits of federated deep learning in wearable healthcare as privacy-preserving insights, personalized health management, and collective knowledge which can be fully realized, transforming the way healthcare data is analyzed and utilized [28].

16.9 ORCHESTRATED FEDERATED DEEP LEARNING FRAMEWORK: SMART HEALTHCARE INFORMATICS

The convergence of orchestrated federated deep learning and smart healthcare informatics represents a groundbreaking paradigm that holds the promise of revolutionizing the landscape of healthcare data analysis. This innovative framework marries the principles of federated learning with the transformative potential of wearable healthcare devices, paving the way for privacy-preserving insights, personalized health management, and collective intelligence [29]. The orchestrated federated deep learning framework in smart healthcare informatics stands as a blueprint for harnessing the power of distributed data while ensuring data privacy, security, and ethical data utilization.

Framework Architecture: The orchestrated federated deep learning framework lies in a distributed architecture that harmonizes the decentralized nature of federated learning with the real-time data generation from wearable devices. Wearable health data, generated by devices such as smartwatches, fitness trackers, and biosensors, remains localized on the devices themselves. Local models are trained on this data, capturing user-specific health patterns, behaviors, and responses. These local models are then aggregated through federated learning mechanisms to refine a global model that captures overarching health trends and insights.

Privacy-Preserving Model Updates: Orchestrated federated deep learning ensures privacy preservation by transmitting only model updates, not raw data, between edge devices and a central server. This approach safeguards sensitive health information, aligning with data protection regulations and ethical considerations. Cryptographic techniques and secure aggregation protocols are employed to ensure that individual health data remains encrypted during transmission.

Real-Time Insights: Wearable devices generate real-time health data, allowing users to monitor their well-being continuously. The orchestrated federated deep learning framework capitalizes on this dynamic data flow, enabling local models to adapt and improve in real time. This responsiveness is crucial for early anomaly detection, timely interventions, and personalized health recommendations, enhancing both individual and population-level health outcomes.

Collective Intelligence and Personalized Insights: The orchestrated framework fosters a collaborative ecosystem where users, healthcare practitioners, researchers, and institutions contribute their insights without sharing raw data. This collective intelligence accelerates medical research, diagnostic accuracy, and treatment optimization. Simultaneously, the framework tailors insights to individuals, recognizing the uniqueness of health patterns and responses across users.

Challenges and Future Directions: The implementation of the orchestrated federated deep learning framework is not devoid of challenges. Addressing data heterogeneity, ensuring communication efficiency, adapting to dynamic data distributions, and ensuring model interpretability are areas that require meticulous attention. Interdisciplinary collaboration between machine learning experts, healthcare professionals, ethicists, and regulators is vital to navigate these challenges effectively.

The orchestrated federated deep learning framework in smart healthcare informatics marks a transformative juncture in the utilization of wearable healthcare data [30]. By synergizing the capabilities of federated learning with the insights derived from wearable devices, this framework opens avenues for data-driven health insights while respecting individual data privacy and ownership. As the journey toward orchestrated federated deep learning in smart healthcare informatics continues, it holds the potential to reshape healthcare informatics, advance medical research, and empower individuals to take charge of their health journeys in unprecedented ways [31].

16.10 CONCEPTUAL FRAMEWORK FOR ORCHESTRATED FEDERATED DEEP LEARNING IN THE CONTEXT OF WEARABLE HEALTHCARE

The conceptual framework of orchestrated federated deep learning in wearable healthcare encompasses a structured approach that synergizes the principles of federated learning with the insights derived from wearable health data [32]. This framework aims to provide privacy-preserving, real-time, and personalized health insights while accommodating the challenges inherent in wearable data analysis. The following components outline the key aspects of this framework.

Data Localization and Collection: Wearable devices, including smartwatches, fitness trackers, and health sensors, collect diverse health data from users in real time. This data remains localized on the devices, eliminating the need for raw data sharing. Users' explicit consent is obtained for data utilization within the orchestrated federated deep learning framework.

Localized Model Training: Each wearable device trains a local deep learning model using the data it collects. These local models capture individual health patterns, behaviors, and responses. Local model training leverages the power of deep neural networks to extract features and learn intricate correlations within the data.

Secure Model Aggregation: Model updates, not raw data, are transmitted to a central server for aggregation. Secure aggregation protocols, including cryptographic techniques and federated averaging, ensure that user data remains encrypted during transmission. Aggregation refines a global model by incorporating insights from diverse wearable devices.

Privacy-Preserving Mechanisms: The framework integrates advanced privacy-preserving mechanisms, such as differential privacy, homomorphic encryption, and federated secure multi-party computation. These mechanisms ensure that health data remains confidential during all stages of the model update and aggregation process.

Real-Time Adaptation: Real-time data generation from wearables allows local models to adapt and improve continuously. This responsiveness ensures timely anomaly detection, intervention, and personalized health recommendations, enhancing user well-being.

Collective Intelligence and Insights: The orchestrated framework fosters a collaborative ecosystem where individuals, healthcare providers, researchers, and institutions contribute their insights. This collective intelligence accelerates medical research, diagnostics, and treatment optimization. The insights are tailored to individual health profiles, accounting for the uniqueness of health patterns.

Ethical and Regulatory Compliance: Ethical considerations and regulatory compliance, including adherence to HIPAA and GDPR, guide the framework's implementation. Transparent communication with users regarding data utilization and privacy ensures informed consent and responsible data handling.

Interdisciplinary Collaboration: Successful implementation of the orchestrated framework requires collaboration between machine learning experts, healthcare practitioners, data privacy specialists, ethicists, and regulators. This collaborative approach addresses technical, ethical, and operational challenges effectively.

Model Interpretability: Ensuring that the insights provided by the federated deep learning models are interpretable and explainable is crucial. Efforts to develop interpretable models that can be understood by healthcare professionals and users foster trust in the framework's outcomes.

The proposed conceptual framework amalgamates the principles of orchestrated federated deep learning with the transformative potential of wearable healthcare data [33]. By embracing data localization, privacy preservation, and real-time insights, this framework paves the way for a new era of healthcare informatics that respects data privacy while unleashing the power of collective intelligence for personalized health management and proactive interventions [34].

16.11 FUTURE DIRECTIONS AND RESEARCH CHALLENGES

By providing creative answers to problems and influencing the course of future developments in health monitoring and healthcare informatics, emerging technologies have the potential to completely transform the FedHealth in Wearable Healthcare and Orchestrated Federated Deep Learning for Smart Healthcare [35]. The quick development of wearable technology, such as fitness trackers, smartwatches, and specialist medical wearables, is one notable technological development [36]. With the ability to gather a wide range of physiological data, including heart rate, ECG signals, sleep patterns, and activity levels, these more advanced gadgets allow for continuous health monitoring and the early diagnosis of medical disorders.

Furthermore, the incorporation of artificial intelligence (AI) and machine learning algorithms is significantly contributing to the derivation of significant insights from the copious amounts of data produced by wearables. AI-powered computers may examine this data and identify patterns, forecast health outcomes, and offer tailored advice, all of which can improve the efficacy of healthcare procedures. Federated deep learning, a cutting-edge approach in machine learning, addresses privacy concerns by allowing multiple institutions to collaboratively train AI models on decentralized data without sharing sensitive information. This technology holds the potential to orchestrate federated learning across a network of wearable devices, enabling the creation of more accurate and adaptable healthcare models [37].

The utilization of 5G technology and edge computing empowers real-time data transmission and processing, ensuring seamless connectivity between wearables and healthcare systems. This not only reduces latency but also enhances the efficiency of remote patient monitoring, telemedicine, and data analysis. Blockchain technology is another emerging trend that could enhance the security and integrity of health data, ensuring that it remains tamper-proof and accessible only to authorized parties. Also, augmented reality (AR) and virtual reality (VR) technologies are poised to transform healthcare education, training, and patient engagement. Healthcare professionals can benefit from immersive simulations and training modules, while patients can use AR/VR for rehabilitation, pain management, and mental health therapy. In healthcare informatics, natural language processing (NLP) and data analytics tools are evolving to extract valuable insights from unstructured clinical notes, research papers, and patient records. This enables more efficient decision support systems, clinical trial optimizations, and evidence-based healthcare policies [38].

As for the future directions, the integration of these technologies into a cohesive ecosystem will foster a new era of proactive and personalized healthcare. Wearable devices will not only monitor health but also facilitate preventive interventions. Federated deep learning will enable a secure and collaborative AI network across devices and healthcare institutions. The adoption of blockchain will ensure data privacy and interoperability. Overall, these emerging technologies are poised to enhance the efficiency and effectiveness of FedHealth in Wearable Healthcare and Orchestrated Federated Deep Learning for Smart Healthcare, shaping a brighter and more patient-centric future for healthcare systems worldwide [39].

16.12 CONCLUSION AND FUTURE SCOPE

The convergence of emerging technologies in the fields of FedHealth, Wearable Healthcare, Orchestrated Federated Deep Learning, and Healthcare Informatics presents a promising and transformative outlook for the future of healthcare. These innovations offer unprecedented opportunities to revolutionize health monitoring, patient care, and medical research. Wearable devices equipped with advanced sensors and powered by 5G connectivity are enabling continuous health tracking and early disease detection, putting the power of personalized healthcare into the hands of individuals. The integration of AI and federated deep learning ensures that the insights derived from this wealth of health data are accurate, secure, and privacy-respecting, allowing for better-informed clinical decisions and treatments. Meanwhile, blockchain technology is paving the way for trust and transparency in healthcare data management, addressing one of the industry's most pressing concerns. As we look ahead, the future direction of FedHealth in Wearable Healthcare and Orchestrated Federated Deep Learning for Smart Healthcare holds the promise of a patient-centric, proactive, and data-driven healthcare system. This transformation will not only improve the efficiency and effectiveness of healthcare delivery but also empower individuals to take charge of their own health and well-being. With AR, VR, NLP, and data analytics enhancing healthcare education, training, and research, the possibilities for innovation and progress in the healthcare sector are boundless. As these technologies continue to evolve, collaboration between healthcare stakeholders, technology developers, and policymakers will be essential to harness their full potential and ensure equitable access to the benefits they offer. Ultimately, the future of FedHealth is bright, with the potential to positively impact the lives of individuals and communities worldwide.

By harnessing the collective intelligence of distributed data sources while respecting privacy concerns, federated deep learning ensures that AI-driven healthcare models become increasingly accurate and adaptable. The adoption of blockchain technology addresses the critical issue of data security and interoperability, creating a trustworthy ecosystem for health information exchange. Looking forward, the future of FedHealth is teeming with possibilities. These innovations are set to redefine not only the way healthcare is delivered but also how it is researched, understood, and experienced. AR and VR are poised to revolutionize medical education and training, while NLP and data analytics will continue to unlock invaluable insights from vast datasets, guiding clinical decision-making and policy formulation.

However, realizing this transformative vision is not without its challenges. The integration of these technologies demands a multidisciplinary approach, close collaboration between healthcare practitioners, technologists, and policymakers, and a vigilant commitment to ethical considerations and data privacy. It also necessitates addressing issues of accessibility to ensure that the benefits of these advancements reach all segments of society, irrespective of socioeconomic factors.

The future of FedHealth in Wearable Healthcare, Orchestrated Federated Deep Learning, and Healthcare Informatics is luminous. It represents a pivotal shift toward patient-centered, data-driven, and preventive healthcare. The synergistic combination of these technologies offers the potential to enhance healthcare outcomes, improve patient experiences, and drive cost efficiencies in the healthcare sector. As these innovations continue to evolve and mature, they have the capacity to redefine the healthcare landscape, making it more efficient, effective, and equitable for all.

REFERENCES

1. Chen, Y., Qin, X., Wang, J., Yu, C., & Gao, W. (2020). Fedhealth: A federated transfer learning framework for wearable healthcare. *IEEE Intelligent Systems, 35*(4), 83–93.
2. Concone, F., Ferdico, C., Re, G. L., & Morana, M. (2022, June). A federated learning approach for distributed human activity recognition. In *2022 IEEE International Conference on Smart Computing (SMARTCOMP)* (pp. 269–274). Helsinki, Finland: IEEE.
3. Zhang, D. Y., Kou, Z., & Wang, D. (2021, May). Fedsens: A federated learning approach for smart health sensing with class imbalance in resource constrained edge computing. In *IEEE INFOCOM 2021-IEEE Conference on Computer Communications* (pp. 1–10). Vancouver, BC, Canada: IEEE.

4. Farooq, K., Syed, H. J., Alqahtani, S. O., Nagmeldin, W., Ibrahim, A. O., & Gani, A. (2022). Blockchain federated learning for in-home health monitoring. *Electronics*, *12*(1), 136.

5. Chen, Y., Lu, W., Wang, J., & Qin, X. (2021). FedHealth 2: Weighted federated transfer learning via batch normalization for personalized healthcare. *arXiv preprint arXiv:2106.01009*.

6. Singh, B. (2023). Blockchain Technology in renovating healthcare: Legal and future perspectives. In *Revolutionizing Healthcare Through Artificial Intelligence and Internet of Things Applications* (pp. 177–186). IGI Global.

7. Raza, A., Tran, K. P., Koehl, L., & Li, S. (2022). Designing ECG monitoring healthcare system with federated transfer learning and explainable ai. *Knowledge-Based Systems*, *236*, 107763.

8. Saha, S., & Ahmad, T. (2021). Federated transfer learning: Concept and applications. *Intelligenza Artificiale*, *15*(1), 35–44.

9. Sharma, A., & Singh, B. (2022). Measuring impact of E-commerce on small scale business: A systematic review. *Journal of Corporate Governance and International Business Law*, *5*(1), https://doi.org/10.37591/jcgibl.v5i1.1087.

10. Dasaradharami Reddy, K., & Gadekallu, T. R. (2023). A comprehensive survey on federated learning techniques for healthcare informatics. *Computational Intelligence and Neuroscience*, 2023, 1–19.

11. Mohammadi, F. G., Shenavarmasouleh, F., & Arabnia, H. R. (2022). Applications of machine learning in healthcare and Internet of Things (IOT): A comprehensive review. *arXiv preprint arXiv:2202.02868*.

12. Shaw, R. (2022). Collaborative machine learning-driven internet of medical things—A systematic literature review. *arXiv preprint arXiv:2207.06416*.

13. Wang, J., Chen, Y., & Hu, C. (2023). Activity recognition. In *Machine Learning for Data Science Handbook: Data Mining and Knowledge Discovery Handbook* (pp. 659–680). Cham, Switzerland: Springer International Publishing.

14. Singh, B. (2022). Understanding legal frameworks concerning transgender healthcare in the age of dynamism. *Electronic Journal of Social and Strategic Studies*, *3*, 56–65.

15. Shaik, T., Tao, X., Higgins, N., Li, L., Gururajan, R., Zhou, X., & Acharya, U. R. (2023). Remote patient monitoring using artificial intelligence: Current state, applications, and challenges. *Wiley Interdisciplinary Reviews: Data Mining and Knowledge Discovery*, *13*(2), e1485.

16. Boumpa, E., Tsoukas, V., Gkogkidis, A., Spathoulas, G., & Kakarountas, A. (2021, November). Security and privacy concerns for healthcare wearable devices and emerging alternative approaches. In *International Conference on Wireless Mobile Communication and Healthcare* (pp. 19–38). Cham, Switzerland: Springer International Publishing.

17. Han, J., Zhang, Z., Mascolo, C., André, E., Tao, J., Zhao, Z., & Schuller, B. W. (2021). Deep learning for mobile mental health: Challenges and recent advances. *IEEE Signal Processing Magazine*, *38*(6), 96–105.

18. Singh, B. (2022). Relevance of agriculture-nutrition linkage for human healthcare: A conceptual legal framework of implication and pathways. *Justice and Law Bulletin*, *1*(1), 44–49.

19. Li, J., & Zhang, J. (2022). Privacy-preserving sports wearable data fusion framework. *Computational Intelligence and Neuroscience*, 2022, 6131971.

20. Prayitno, Shyu, C. R., Putra, K. T., Chen, H.-C., Tsai, Y.-Y., Hossain, K. S. M. T., Jiang, W., & Shae, Z.-Y. (2021). A systematic review of federated learning in the healthcare area: From the perspective of data properties and applications. *Applied Sciences*, *11*(23), 11191.

21. Liu, X., Zhang, M., Jiang, Z., Patel, S., & McDuff, D. (2022). Federated remote physiological measurement with imperfect data. In *Proceedings of the IEEE/CVF Conference on Computer Vision and Pattern Recognition*, New Orleans, LA, USA (pp. 2155–2164).
22. Singh, B. (2022). COVID-19 pandemic and public healthcare: Endless downward spiral or solution via rapid legal and health services implementation with patient monitoring program. *Justice and Law Bulletin, 1*(1), 1–7.
23. Rajendran, S., Pan, W., Sabuncu, M. R., Zhou, J., & Wang, F. (2023). Patchwork learning: A paradigm towards integrative analysis across diverse biomedical data sources. *arXiv preprint arXiv:2305.06217.*
24. Wu, Q., Chen, X., Zhou, Z., & Zhang, J. (2020). Fedhome: Cloud-edge based personalized federated learning for in-home health monitoring. *IEEE Transactions on Mobile Computing, 21*(8), 2818–2832.
25. Mocanu, I., Smadu, R., Dragoi, M., Mocanu, A., & Cramariuc, O. (2021, November). Testing federated learning on health and wellbeing data. In *2021 International Conference on e-Health and Bioengineering (EHB)* (pp. 1–4). Iasi, Romania: IEEE.
26. Alawadi, S., Kebande, V. R., Dong, Y., Bugeja, J., Persson, J. A., & Olsson, C. M. (2021, July). A federated interactive learning iot-based health monitoring platform. In *European Conference on Advances in Databases and Information Systems* (pp. 235–246). Cham, Switzerland: Springer International Publishing.
27. Alawadi, S., Kebande, V. R., Dong, Y., Bugeja, J., Persson, J. A., & Olsson, C. M. (2021, July). A federated interactive learning iot-based health monitoring platform. In *European Conference on Advances in Databases and Information Systems* (pp. 235–246). Cham, Switzerland: Springer International Publishing.
28. Singh, B. (2020). Global Science and Jurisprudential Approach Concerning Healthcare and Illness. *Indian Journal of Health and Medical Law, 3*(1), 7–13.
29. Bhati, N. S., Chugh, G., & Bhati, B. S. (2022). Federated machine learning with data mining in healthcare. In *Federated Learning for IoT Applications* (pp. 231–242). Cham, Switzerland: Springer International Publishing.
30. Arikumar, K. S., Prathiba, S. B., Alazab, M., Gadekallu, T. R., Pandya, S., Khan, J. M., & Moorthy, R. S. (2022). FL-PMI: Federated learning-based person movement identification through wearable devices in smart healthcare systems. *Sensors, 22*(4), 1377.
31. Presotto, R., Civitarese, G., & Bettini, C. (2022, March). Fedclar: Federated clustering for personalized sensor-based human activity recognition. In *2022 IEEE International Conference on Pervasive Computing and Communications (PerCom)* (pp. 227–236). Pisa, Italy: IEEE.
32. Singh, B. (2019). Profiling public healthcare: A comparative analysis based on the multidimensional healthcare management and legal approach. *Indian Journal of Health and Medical Law, 2*(2), 1–5.
33. Ahmed, K. M., Imteaj, A., & Amini, M. H. (2021, December). Federated deep learning for heterogeneous edge computing. In *2021 20th IEEE International Conference on Machine Learning and Applications (ICMLA)* (pp. 1146–1152). Pasadena, CA: IEEE.
34. Campanile, L., Marrone, S., Marulli, F., & Verde, L. (2022). Challenges and trends in federated learning for well-being and healthcare. *Procedia Computer Science, 207,* 1144–1153.
35. Moon, S., & Lee, W. H. (2023, February). Privacy-preserving federated learning in healthcare. In *2023 International Conference on Electronics, Information, and Communication (ICEIC)* (pp. 1–4). IEEE, Singapore.
36. Khoa, T. A., Nguyen, D. V., Dao, M. S., & Zettsu, K. (2021, December). Fed xData: A federated learning framework for enabling contextual health monitoring in a cloud-edge network. In *2021 IEEE International Conference on Big Data (Big Data)* (pp. 4979–4988). IEEE, Orlando, FL, USA.

37. Liu, X., Zhao, J., Li, J., Cao, B., & Lv, Z. (2022). Federated neural architecture search for medical data security. *IEEE Transactions on Industrial Informatics*, *18*(8), 5628–5636.
38. McQuire, J., Watson, P., Wright, N., Hiden, H., & Catt, M. (2021, December). Uneven and irregular surface condition prediction from human walking data using both centralized and decentralized machine learning approaches. In *2021 IEEE International Conference on Bioinformatics and Biomedicine (BIBM)* (pp. 1449–1452). Houston, TX: IEEE.
39. Sabry, F., Eltaras, T., Labda, W., Alzoubi, K., & Malluhi, Q. (2022). Machine learning for healthcare wearable devices: The big picture. *Journal of Healthcare Engineering*, *2022*, 4653923.

17 From Scarce to Abundant
Enhancing Learning with Federated Transfer Techniques

Rezuana Haque, Md. Mehedi Hassan, and Sheikh Mohammed Shariful Islam

17.1 INTRODUCTION

In the fast-changing world of technology, machine learning has become a key tool that opens up many opportunities in different areas. Machine learning is all about teaching computers to recognize patterns and make choices based on data without being directly programmed to do so. This has greatly changed many fields, like medical diagnosis, predicting money trends, voice-operated helpers, and self-driving cars.

A subset of machine learning called transfer learning started to gain popularity as the field developed. Transfer learning is a powerful technique of machine learning that enables the utilization of knowledge from one domain to improve performance in a related domain [1,2]. Instead of starting from scratch, models trained for one task can be adapted for a new one, saving computational time and resources. In scenarios where there is limited labeled data for a particular task, transfer learning can be invaluable. Transfer learning can improve performance and efficiency by employing a model that has been pre-trained on enormous amounts of data and has already learned essential features.

Parallel to these advancements, another paradigm, Federated Learning (FL), started reshaping the way we think about data and model training. FL is a paradigm that allows multiple entities to collaboratively train a machine learning model without centralizing their data, addressing privacy concerns. Google first introduced an FL system for mobile devices [3]. This system allows users to collaboratively train a centralized model while ensuring their data remains securely stored on their local devices. In a world increasingly conscious of data privacy, FL offers a decentralized approach. Instead of pooling data into a central server, models are trained at the source (like a user's device), and only the model updates are shared and aggregated, ensuring data never leaves its origin. FL encompasses various methodologies that allow for decentralized training of machine learning models, ensuring data privacy. Horizontal Federated Learning (HFL) is designed for situations where different entities possess data on distinct users but share identical features. Imagine two hospitals: both record blood pressure and age, but for different sets of patients [4]. Vertical federated learning (VFL) is employed when organizations have varied data types but about

224   DOI: 10.1201/9781032694870-17

the same set of users [4]. For instance, while a hospital might have a patient's health diagnostics, a pharmacy could hold that patient's medication records. However, both HFL and VFL come with constraints. They require either aligned data features (HFL) or common users (VFL), which isn't always feasible in real-world scenarios. This is where Federated Transfer Learning (FTL) steps in, bridging these gaps. Instead of centralizing data, FTL trains models locally on diverse datasets, which might not have significant overlap in terms of features or users [5]. Only the model updates are aggregated, ensuring the data remains private and localized. The FTL framework adds the flexibility of transfer learning to the FL framework. This lets models be trained on datasets that may have different features and users. It's akin to teaching a model a new language by leveraging what it knows from another language, all while ensuring that individual data points never leave their original location. This approach is particularly invaluable in sectors like healthcare or finance, where data is both sensitive and scattered across entities. By leveraging FTL, organizations can collaboratively harness insights from varied datasets, optimizing model performance while maintaining stringent data privacy standards. Figure 17.1 represents the mechanism of FTL. Here, the figure depicts that data X and data Y have minimal overlap in both feature and sample spaces. This kind of overlapping hampers the performance of HFL and VFL due to this limited overlap. Using the power of transfer learning, FTL gets data from areas that do not overlap, making the dataset more complete. Such enriched data fosters improved learning results. Essentially, the incorporation of transfer learning serves to expand the constrained feature and sample domains.

17.2 LITERATURE REVIEW

Chen et al. developed "FedHealth" for wearable healthcare, which combines FL for data aggregation and transfer learning for personalization [6]. Their method beats traditional models like KNN (k-nearest neighbors), SVM (support vector machine), RF (random Forest), and non-federated methods with an impressive average accuracy of 99.4%, using data from three hospitals and the UCI (University of California Irvine) Smartphone dataset.

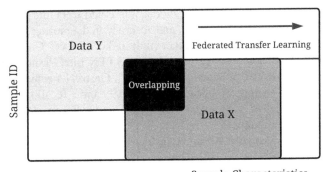

FIGURE 17.1 Federated transfer learning.

Building upon the challenges faced due to limited datasets in EEG classification for Brain–Computer Interface (BCI), Ju et al. introduced a pioneering deep learning method named FTL [7]. This approach addresses the challenge of limited datasets due to privacy concerns. The FTL method, which is based on the FL framework, uses the PhysioNet dataset to classify motor imagery and gets important information from EEG data from multiple subjects without sharing the data directly. There is a 2% increase in the accuracy of classification with subject-adaptive analysis and a 6% increase over other deep learning methods when there is no multi-subject data. The architecture is tailored for EEG data and ensures data privacy.

A paper by Fathima et al. introduces an innovative framework for the analysis and normalization of medical datasets using FL [8]. By mapping data origins and attributes, it offers a multi-layered approach to data acquisition, classification, and optimization. The multi-objective optimal datasets (MooM) are a feature that stands out. They use FL models for feature mapping and cluster categorization. The empirical results are commendable, with a remarkable 97.34% accuracy in telemedicine data clustering.

Tackling the complex challenge of Autism Spectrum Disorder (ASD) detection in children, Lakhan et al. present the FCNN-LSTM (fast convolutional neural network-long short-term memory) framework for enhanced ASD detection in children using multiple datasets [9]. It works in an FL environment and encrypts data for extra safety. It also includes IoT applications and achieves an impressive 99% detection accuracy, which is a great step forward in research into ASD.

Walskaar et al. did a study on a set of COVID-19 X-ray lung scans that used FL and homomorphic encryption to make care data more private [10]. The significant contribution is the novel implementation of an ring learning with errors (RLWE)-based multi-key encryption scheme that offers more secure collaborative model training. The dataset, sourced from Kaggle, provides a balanced distribution of 14,486 images, both COVID and non-COVID, aiding in the comprehensive evaluation of the proposed method.

In their study, Farhana Yasmin et al. focused on using machine learning to quickly identify monkeypox cases [11]. They utilized the "Monkeypox Skin Lesion Dataset (MSLD)" from Kaggle. Their study implemented data augmentation to enhance the dataset and prevent overfitting. Researchers employed transfer learning to assess six pre-trained models. The "PoxNet22" model was found to be the best in the study, demonstrating 100% precision, recall, and accuracy in diagnosing monkeypox

Farhana Yasmin et al. also did another study and developed "GastroNet," a model that uses YOLOv5, MobileNet v2, MobileNet v2 FPN Lite, Resnet50 v1 FPN, and CSPdarknet53 to identify stomach problems [12]. GastroNet achieved notable success, with a mean Average Precision (mAP) of 0.99 and a recall rate of 1.00, highlighting its potential as a significant aid in the early diagnosis and treatment of gastrointestinal conditions.

In a study, Md. Manjurul Ahsan et al. focused on enhancing monkeypox detection using the Kaggle dataset [13]. They significantly improved the performance of models like VGG19 and MobileNetV2, achieving an accuracy rate of up to 99%. The dataset consisted of two parts: one with 76 images and the other with 818, helping to advance quick and effective disease detection techniques.

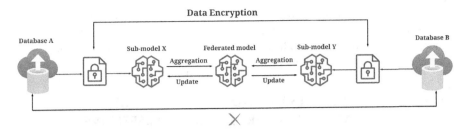

FIGURE 17.2 Data flow diagram of federated transfer learning with data encryption.

17.3 SAFEGUARDING DATA PRIVACY IN FEDERATED TRANSFER LEARNING

FTL places a significant emphasis on ensuring data privacy throughout its learning process. Figure 17.2 represents the overall process of FTL with the encryption process. Here During the model training process, both parties A and B initially compute and encrypt their intermediate outcomes, which include gradients and loss. Subsequently, a third party gathers these encrypted details, decrypts the gradients and loss, and processes them. After this aggregation, parties A and B obtain the consolidated results, allowing them to refine and update their respective models.

One of the primary concerns in machine learning is the potential exposure of sensitive data, and FTL addresses this concern in several innovative ways. One of the foundational principles of FTL is that raw data remains on the user's device. This approach ensures that there's no central repository of data that could be a potential target for breaches. By decentralizing data storage, FTL reduces the risk of mass data leaks. This decentralized approach not only ensures individual data privacy but also reduces the need for massive data storage and transmission infrastructure. Before any data or model parameters are shared or transmitted, they are encrypted [14]. Encryption transforms the original data into code to prevent unauthorized access. This means that even if a malicious actor were to intercept the data during transmission, they would not be able to understand or use it. The encryption standards used in FTL are robust, ensuring that the data remains secure during its entire lifecycle. Homomorphic encryption is a sophisticated form of encryption that allows computations to be carried out on the encrypted data itself without needing to decrypt it first [15]. In the context of FTL, this means that the learning process can occur on the encrypted data, ensuring that the raw, sensitive data is never exposed. This is a significant advancement in the realm of data privacy, as it allows for data utilization without compromising its security. To make data even safer, random masks and polynomial approximations are used, and FTL adds these extra levels of complexity [16]. Random masks are added to the data, ensuring that even if someone tried to reverse engineer the data, they would be met with misleading information. Polynomial approximation introduces a level of complexity to the data computations, making it even harder for someone to deduce the original data from the shared parameters. In traditional machine learning models, raw data might be pooled together for training, which poses a significant privacy risk. FTL, however, ensures that participants in the learning process never directly exchange or share their raw data. Instead, they only share encrypted model parameters, gradients, or losses. This indirect method of sharing ensures that the individual data points remain private while still contributing to the collective learning process.

17.4 THE CHALLENGES IN MODERN HEALTHCARE: A FEDERATED TRANSFER LEARNING PERSPECTIVE

In the modern digital era, artificial intelligence has revolutionized many industries, with healthcare being of paramount importance. Despite its significance, healthcare faces substantial hurdles in data handling and usage. The implications of a single incorrect prediction in this field can be grave. For instance, imagine the repercussions if a diagnostic model wrongly determines a cancer patient to be cancer-free. Such misdiagnoses, known as false negatives, can be fatal.

Additionally, the variability in how diseases present themselves complicates the creation of a universal approach to diagnosis and treatment. Aside from the fact that health data is usually sensitive and hard to get, making safe and useful machine learning models for healthcare is getting harder. Traditional machine learning models, which typically depend on a centralized data system, inadvertently expose sensitive patient data to potential risks and breaches. FTL solves these problems and offers a real solution by spreading out data processing, which protects privacy, and reduces data limitations by sharing knowledge across different areas. This technique also has the potential to minimize false negatives, enhancing the reliability of predictions significantly. In light of this, we introduce "FedFusionNet", a meta-model meticulously designed to uphold data privacy, navigate through data limitations, and reduce the chances of incorrect health predictions, ensuring more reliable and secure healthcare data management and utilization.

17.5 OBJECTIVE

In this framework, data interpretations are leveraged for classification using the FedFusionNet model. The primary objective is to enhance the model's accuracy while safeguarding data privacy. The aim is to minimize misclassifications, ensuring that significant patterns or anomalies are duly recognized.

17.6 PROPOSED FEDERATED TRANSFER LEARNING META-MODEL FEDFUSIONNET

The proposed meta-model is designed to accommodate multiple entities. However, for the sake of clarity and easy comprehension, only two entities are illustrated. The data flow of the suggested model is depicted in Figure 17.3. In this framework, each data source (Database A and Database B) locally trains multiple pre-trained models on its dataset. These models aim to detect specific patterns or anomalies pertinent to various data categories. Given the varied nature of data across centers, each model is attuned to the peculiarities of its local dataset. Pre-trained models (ResNet50, VGG16, and VGG19) have already been trained on large datasets, enabling them to

From Scarce to Abundant

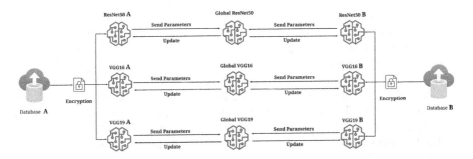

FIGURE 17.3 Data flow diagram of FedFusionNet.

recognize a wide array of features. When an entity has a limited dataset, starting with a model that's already familiar with a broad range of features can be beneficial. By leveraging the knowledge encapsulated in pre-trained models, entities can essentially "bootstrap" their learning process. This means that even with scarce data, the model has a foundational understanding to build upon, which can lead to better performance. To safeguard the confidentiality and privacy of participants' data during the backpropagation process, the FedFusionNet framework employs encryption techniques before the data transfer.

Encryption is utilized to ensure both security and privacy in the transmission and analysis of data. After local model training, the entities (Database A and Database B) periodically send their model parameters to a central server (Global ResNet50, Global VGG16, and Global VGG19) instead of sharing the raw data directly. This methodology safeguards data privacy, as the original patient data never leaves the confines of the local center. By adopting this strategy, centers effectively address data privacy regulations and concerns, ensuring that sensitive patient data remains secure and localized. Moreover, this approach of only transferring model parameters can also be more efficient in terms of bandwidth and transmission costs. In this way, no data is leaving the local environment, thus ensuring patient privacy.

The central server combines the received model parameters to create a unified representation that captures the collective knowledge of similar models across various centers. The server makes sure that each global model (like Global ResNet) keeps the uniqueness of its architecture while taking advantage of the different types of data from different centers by averaging parameters from models that are similar, like ResNetA and ResNetB. Combining different architectures directly might dilute the unique strengths and features of each model. Hence, it's essential to aggregate same-like models separately rather than merging all three types together. This approach enhances the overall accuracy and robustness of each global model. In the next step, each data center will receive these global models. They don't directly use these models for prediction yet. Instead, they fine-tune or adjust these global models using their local dataset. This step ensures that the global models are tailored to the specific characteristics of each center's data. For instance, Global ResNet50 is fine-tuned with the local scans at a particular center. This produces a locally adapted version of Global ResNet50 for that center. The same process occurs for Global VGG16 and Global VGG19.

When assessing a new data entry, all the adapted models within an entity contribute their predictions. These models then engage in a collective decision-making mechanism, essentially a voting system, to determine the final prediction. Using multiple models in concert like this, known as an ensemble method, is pivotal in drastically reducing the chance of incorrect assessments. Consider a scenario where Global ResNet50 interprets the data as Category X, but Global VGG16 and Global VGG19 determine it as Category Y. The overall judgment would favor Category Y because it has the majority—two out of the three models supporting that decision. This decision-making approach is termed hard voting. In this system, every model's prediction counts as a single vote, and the category with the majority of votes is taken as the final verdict.

17.7 FEDFUSIONNET IN HEALTHCARE: DEEP DIVE INTO BENEFITS

FedFusionNet, when applied to healthcare, presents a transformative approach to medical diagnostics. By harnessing the power of pre-trained deep learning models within a federated framework, it offers a synergistic blend of precision, privacy, and adaptability. This innovative integration not only promotes superior diagnostic accuracy but also ensures that patient data remains secure. Moreover, its ensemble-based prediction method is geared toward minimizing diagnostic errors, particularly false negatives.

One of the hallmarks of FedFusionNet is its utilization of pre-trained deep learning models. Pre-trained models have already been trained on extensive datasets, allowing them to have a foundation of knowledge that can be fine-tuned to specific tasks. When applied to healthcare, this pre-existing knowledge aids in identifying subtle patterns or anomalies that might be missed in models trained from scratch. FL (which uses insights from multiple centers) and transfer learning (which makes models fit the unique properties of specific data) work together to make the system as accurate as it needs to be for medical diagnosis.

The sanctity of patient data remains paramount in the healthcare sector. FedFusionNet ensures this by adopting a principle where raw data, especially sensitive patient scans, never leave the confines of their origin. Instead, only model parameters, which are essentially mathematical representations devoid of personal information, are shared. This methodology ensures that while knowledge is disseminated for collective benefit, individual patient privacy remains uncompromised.

False negatives in crucial diagnoses such as cancer can lead to severe repercussions. The beauty of FedFusionNet lies in its ensemble prediction approach. Leveraging multiple models' insights ensures a more rounded and holistic interpretation of the data.

Healthcare is a constantly evolving field, with new centers, technologies, and techniques emerging regularly. FedFusionNet is designed to be inherently scalable. New centers or institutions can seamlessly integrate into the existing federated system. As they contribute their data insights, they also benefit reciprocally from the pooled intelligence of the entire network. This scalability ensures that as the medical community grows and evolves, the FedFusionNet system can adapt and expand accordingly, fostering a collaborative and constantly improving diagnostic environment.

From Scarce to Abundant

17.8 FEDFUSIONNET vs. TRADITIONAL FEDERATED LEARNING: A DEEP DIVE INTO PERFORMANCE AND PRIVACY

In the evolving landscape of data-driven models, both traditional FL and FedFusionNet offer distinct approaches to maintaining data privacy and enhancing model performance. Traditional FL keeps raw data at the local level and only sends model updates or gradients for aggregation. This keeps data where it belongs, at the source. This method provides a consistent framework for data privacy, but it primarily relies on a singular global model structure, which might not always capture the unique characteristics of all local datasets.

FedFusionNet pushes the boundaries of this framework. It not only emphasizes the localization of raw data but also takes a step further by consolidating insights from various pre-trained models. This fusion of both global and local perspectives accentuates the accuracy and reliability of its predictions. FedFusionNet is more flexible and adaptable because it uses more than one model, like ResNet and VGG16. It can handle the subtleties of different datasets. Its method for sending encrypted parameters from these different models also improves data security, giving it an extra layer of defense over what traditional FL provides.

Both approaches put data privacy and model improvement first, but FedFusionNet may be better at performance and adaptability thanks to its multi-model consolidation and advanced encryption. This makes it a strong contender in the field of FL.

17.9 APPLICATION OF FEDFUSIONNET IN HEALTHCARE

FedFusionNet offers transformative applications within the healthcare sector. In medical imaging, for example, hospitals across the world can refine diagnostic tools for diverse conditions, from tumors to cardiovascular issues, without sharing raw patient scans, thus ensuring privacy and boosting diagnostic accuracy. In genomics, different sets of data can be analyzed to find patterns or markers while keeping the genetic information about each person localized. This helps find inherited conditions or possible genetic disorders. In addition, FedFusionNet can help us understand how diseases spread and how common they are in different areas by using information from different local datasets without letting us directly access the data. Similarly, for drug discovery and development, insights from global datasets can be pooled without raw data sharing, fostering a collaborative environment while ensuring data integrity. As the healthcare sector increasingly values both data privacy and collaborative research, FedFusionNet stands out as a promising model for the future.

17.10 CONCLUSION

In the ever-evolving world of data-driven healthcare, the importance of FTL cannot be overstated. It brings together the advantages of data privacy and effective machine learning by keeping information localized while benefiting from insights. Our proposed model, FedFusionNet, is an example of achieving this balance and pushing the boundaries of traditional FL approaches. Better accuracy and dependability can be achieved by combining models that securely send parameters and a method that FedFusionNet adapts to the specifics of local datasets. The need for such a model arises from the growing demand for healthcare solutions that require high levels of accuracy while protecting patient data confidentiality. In summary, FedFusionNet is not an enhancement but a transformative leap forward that bridges global learning to deliver unparalleled outcomes in the field of healthcare.

REFERENCES

1. Zhuang, F., Qi, Z., Duan, K., Xi, D., Zhu, Y., Zhu, H., ... He, Q. (2021). A comprehensive survey on transfer learning. *Proceedings of the IEEE, 109*(1), 43–76. doi:10.1109/jproc.2020.3004555
2. Ardalan, Z., & Subbian, V. (2022). Transfer learning approaches for neuroimaging analysis: A scoping review. *Frontiers in Artificial Intelligence, 5.* doi:10.3389/frai.2022.780405
3. McMahan, H. B., Moore, E., Ramage, D., & y Arcas, B. A. (2016). Federated learning of deep networks using model averaging. *arXiv preprint arXiv:1602.05629, 2, 2.*
4. Yang, Q., Liu, Y., Chen, T., & Tong, Y. (2019). Federated machine learning. *ACM Transactions on Intelligent Systems and Technology, 10*(2), 1–19. doi:10.1145/3298981
5. Razavi-Far, R., Wang, B., Taylor, M. E., & Yang, Q. (2022). An introduction to federated and transfer learning. In *Federated and Transfer Learning* (pp. 1–6). Cham, Switzerland: Springer International Publishing.
6. Chen, Y., Qin, X., Wang, J., Yu, C., & Gao, W. (2020). Fedhealth: A federated transfer learning framework for wearable healthcare. *IEEE Intelligent Systems, 35*(4), 83–93.
7. Ju, C., Gao, D., Mane, R., Tan, B., Liu, Y., & Guan, C. (2020, July). Federated transfer learning for EEG signal classification. In *2020 42nd Annual International Conference of the IEEE Engineering in Medicine & Biology Society (EMBC)* (pp. 3040–3045). Montreal, QC, Canada: IEEE.
8. Fathima, A. S., Basha, S. M., Ahmed, S. T., Mathivanan, S. K., Rajendran, S., Mallik, S., & Zhao, Z. (2023). Federated learning based futuristic biomedical big-data analysis and standardization. *PLoS One, 18*(10), e0291631.
9. Lakhan, A., Mohammed, M. A., Abdulkareem, K. H., Hamouda, H., & Alyahya, S. (2023). Autism spectrum disorder detection framework for children based on federated learning integrated CNN-LSTM. *Computers in Biology and Medicine, 166*, 107539.
10. Walskaar, I., Tran, M. C., & Catak, F. O. (2023). A practical implementation of medical privacy-preserving federated learning using multi-key homomorphic encryption and flower framework. *Cryptography, 7*(4), 48.
11. Yasmin, F., Hassan, M. M., Hasan, M., Zaman, S., Kaushal, C., El-Shafai, W., & Soliman, N. F. (2023). PoxNet22: A fine-tuned model for the classification of monkeypox disease using transfer learning. *IEEE Access, 11*, 24053–24076.
12. Yasmin, F., Hassan, M. M., Hasan, M., Zaman, S., Bairagi, A. K., El-Shafai, W., Fouad, H., & Chun, Y. C. (2023). GastroNet: Gastrointestinal polyp and abnormal feature detection and classification with deep learning approach. *IEEE Access*, doi:10.1109/ACCESS.2023.3312729
13. Ahsan, M. M., Ali, M. S., Hassan, M. M., Abdullah, T. A., Gupta, K. D., Bagci, U., Kaushal, C., & Soliman, N. F. (2023). Monkeypox diagnosis with interpretable deep learning. *IEEE Access, 11*, 81965–81980.
14. Jing, Q., Wang, W., Zhang, J., Tian, H., & Chen, K. (2019). Quantifying the performance of federated transfer learning. *arXiv preprint arXiv:1912.12795.*
15. Saha, S., & Ahmad, T. (2021). Federated transfer learning: Concept and applications. *Intelligenza Artificiale, 15*(1), 35–44.
16. Luo, T., Cai, T., Zhang, M., Chen, S., & Wang, L. (2020). Random mask: Towards robust convolutional neural networks. *arXiv preprint arXiv:2007.14249.*

18 Federated Learning-Based AI Approaches for Predicting Stroke

Satyajit Roy, Fariha Ferdous Mim,
Md. Mehedi Hassan, and
Sheikh Mohammed Shariful Islam

18.1 INTRODUCTION

Stroke is a prevalent and serious health condition. Stroke, also known as a brain attack, occurs when blood flow to the brain is obstructed, depriving it of oxygen and nutrients, leading to the rapid death of brain cells within minutes [1,2]. According to the World Health Organization (WHO), stroke is the second leading cause of death globally, following ischemic heart disease. Each year, 15 million people suffer from strokes, with one in four resulting in death. A person succumbs to a stroke in the affected areas every 4–5 minutes. It is a potentially life-threatening consequence of atrial fibrillation and poses a significant risk of death. Stroke ranks as the sixth leading cause of death in the United States, contributing to around 11% of deaths with a population of approximately 795,000 individuals, the United States witnesses daily disability due to stroke, making it the fourth largest cause of death in India.

There are two primary types of strokes: ischemic and hemorrhagic. Ischemic stroke results from a lack of blood supply, while hemorrhagic stroke occurs when a blood vessel in the brain ruptures. Transient ischemic attack (TIA), also known as a 'ministroke', is caused by temporary blockages, with symptoms disappearing within 24 hours. TIA serves as a warning sign of an impending stroke. Stroke symptoms may include paralysis, impaired speech, vision loss, and more. While some risk factors like family history, age, gender, and race cannot be modified, others, accounting for 60%–80% of stroke risk, can be managed through lifestyle adjustments such as quitting smoking, limiting alcohol consumption, controlling body weight, maintaining healthy blood glucose levels, and ensuring heart and kidney health [3].

Predicting stroke can be a difficult and time-consuming process for healthcare professionals. Machine learning (ML) algorithms offer efficient detection and evaluation capabilities, aiding in timely intervention. This research demonstrates the effectiveness of ML, with Random Forest (RF) outperforming other classification algorithms, achieving higher accuracy. The study utilizes Kaggle's Healthcare

DOI: 10.1201/9781032694870-18

Dataset, encompassing ten attributes including age, gender, hypertension, heart disease, marital status, occupation, residence type, average glucose level, body mass index (BMI), and smoking status, all interconnected in stroke prediction. Employing RF, LightGBM, Extreme Gradient Boost (XGBoost), and an ensemble approach, the research attains impressive accuracy percentages of 96%, 95%, 89%, and 88%, respectively, surpassing previous models' accuracy. These robust findings hold promise for advancing stroke prediction and prevention efforts.

Recognizing the importance of early identification in improving outcomes, we were motivated to explore the prediction of stroke using ML techniques. Early detection can play a pivotal role in stroke prevention and treatment. The main contributions of this work are as follows:

- Gathering data from Kaggle and correctly preparing it.
- Using the SMOTE-ENN approach to balance the dataset.
- Three distinct types of ML algorithms were utilized to predict strokes.
- For each algorithm measure performance based on the confusion matrix.
- Analyze the outcome and compare it to other algorithms.
- Finally, choose the method that has among the most accurate applied algorithms.

18.2 RELATED WORKS

For stroke prediction, several researchers employed ML techniques. This section describes the contributions of certain research investigations.

Emon, M. U. in their paper leveraged clinical data gathered from a Bangladeshi medical clinic, encompassing information on 5,110 individuals, with attributes including age, gender, hypertension, BMI, work type, smoking status, and more [1]. The research aimed to develop predictive models for stroke using ten distinct classifiers, including Logistics Regression, Stochastic Regression, AdaBoost Classifier, Gradient Descent, Decision Tree Classifier, Multilayer Gaussian Classifier, Quadratic Discriminant Analysis, Gradient Boosting Classifier, Perceptron Classifier, K-Neighbor Classifier, and XGBoost Classifier. The classifiers were meticulously evaluated, with the highest accuracy achieved by other classifiers at 97%, followed by GBC (gradient boosting consensus) and XGB classifiers at 96%, and the AdaBoost classifier at 94%. In contrast, the SGD (stochastic gradient descent) classifier had the lowest accuracy, registering at 65%. To enhance accuracy, a weighted voting method was employed by combining the outcomes of these base classifiers, resulting in a 97% accuracy rate in the proposed research, surpassing individual classifier performances. Furthermore, the paper explored additional performance metrics such as False Positive (FP) and False Negative (FN) rates. A higher FN rate signifies more false alarms generated by the model and indicates the relative effectiveness of classifiers in terms of FP and FN. The weighted voting classifier outperformed other methods, exhibiting a significant area under the curve, and lower FP, and FN rates compared to the individual classifiers. Consequently, the weighted voting classifier emerged as a robust predictor for stroke, offering doctors and patients a valuable tool for early detection and identification of potential stroke risk. This research not only delved into stroke prediction but also investigated the link between certain medical conditions and the risk of stroke, emphasizing the importance of early detection and management in reducing stroke risk. In the future, deep learning techniques, such as brain CT scans and MRIs, could be integrated with existing models to further enhance performance metrics.

Ali, A. A. in their study focuses on stroke prediction, comparing various distributed ML approaches using the Healthcare Dataset [4]. The dataset comprises ten independent variables as features and one dependent variable serving as the class label for predicting stroke disease. The attributes include gender, age, hypertension, heart disease, marital status, work type, residence type, average glucose level, BMI, and smoking status. The class label has two values: 0 indicating the absence of stroke disease and 1 indicating its presence. The study leverages Apache Spark, a powerful big data platform, and MLlib, an ML library integrated with Spark. Apache Spark is renowned for its versatility in handling big data and real-time data processing, offering structured and unstructured data support. MLlib provides ML algorithms, including classification, regression, and clustering. The research constructs a stroke prediction model using four distinct ML classification algorithms: Decision Tree, Support Vector Machine (SVM), RF Classifier, and Logistic Regression. Each algorithm is described as follows:

The goal of their 'Logistic Regression' technique is to determine the best fit for describing the relationship between their target variable and the predictive factors that are diagnostically acceptable. The supervised classifier 'Decision Tree' follows a set of rules. A decision tree is divided into two parts: internal nodes that make decisions and leaf nodes that do not have child nodes and are labeled. In classifying occurrences, decision trees support a variety of data kinds.

For modeling outcomes, 'Random Forests' are a collection of trees that are built using randomly selected training datasets and random subsets of predictor variables.

Problems with classification and regression are solved using an 'SVM'. The purpose of SVM is to find the most appropriate hyperplane for dividing the dataset into two classes: 0 and 1. The study employs a confusion matrix to evaluate model performance, considering true positives (TP), true negatives (TN), FP, and FN. Metrics like accuracy, precision, recall, and F-measure are computed based on the confusion matrix. Furthermore, cross-validation and hyperparameter tuning are utilized to enhance model results. The dataset is split into k-folds ($k = 10$ in this research), allowing for comprehensive model evaluation. The results show that the RF classifier achieves the highest accuracy at 90%, followed by Decision Tree at 79%. SVM and Logistic Regression both achieve an accuracy of 77%. This research underscores the effectiveness of ML in stroke prediction, with RF emerging as the top-performing classifier.

In [5] this context, they have developed a model for foreseeing stroke utilizing ML calculations. Later, completely auditing different IEEE papers they chose five unique models which are decision tree, RF, SVM, logistic regression, and K's nearest neighbor. Key attributes were chosen under the direction of clinical experts. Eventually, a higher-performing algorithm for predicting stroke will be chosen, and a simple Graphical User Interface (GUI) will be constructed using Tkinter. The major goal of this research is to develop a stroke prediction model using ML techniques. The dataset was found on the Kaggle website under the heading

'Healthcare dataset stroke data'. A total of 5,110 entries were collected, including 2,995 females and 2,115 males. There are 12 features in total. These are age, gender, hypertension, BMI, work type, smoking status, etc. Categorical feature analysis, Numerical feature analysis, and Multicollinearity analysis are the three forms of data analysis used. Data analysis is carried out to reveal the dataset's hidden correlations and attributes, which aid the ML model's performance. To overcome overfitting difficulties, the effectiveness of all models is tested. Overall evaluation of the model's performance on a separate test dataset. Finally, utilizing the user's input data, the highest-performing model will be utilized to forecast stroke. Python is the programming language utilized in this research. Python is a widely used high-level programming language that is simple to learn, intuitive, object-oriented, and powerful. Python is used in web development, ML, artificial intelligence (AI), operating systems, small application development, and computer games. Python is designed to be extremely easy to understand. It frequently employs English expressions, whereas other languages frequently use the highlight, and it has fewer semantic enhancements than other languages. In this article, the primary goal of data visualization is to allow professionals to represent common patterns and information through graphs, charts, and representations that even data analysts can understand. The libraries pandas, matplotlib, seaborn, and seaborn are used to exhibit data in an informative and appealing manner. On the dataset in this paper, a different model was used. A comparison of the five different models revealed that RF, logistic regression, and K nearest neighbor have 95.5% accuracy, while the decision tree has 91.13% accuracy, and the SVM has 92.43%accuracy. Hence, RF was selected as the most accurate and least FN model. GUI was created using Tkinter to make the application easier to use.

In [6] this research, the researchers have performed stroke disease prediction based on the Healthcare Dataset. The dataset for stroke prediction comes from Kaggle. There are 5,110 rows and 12 columns in this dataset. The main attributes of the columns are 'id', 'gender', 'age', 'hypertension', 'heart disease', 'ever married', 'work type', 'Residence type', 'average glucose level', 'BMI', 'smoking status', and 'stroke'. The value of the output column stroke is either '1' or '0'. The value '0' means there is no risk of stroke, but the value '1' means there is a chance of stroke. The chances of a '0' in the output column ('stroke') outnumber the chances of a '1' in the same column, resulting in a significantly imbalanced dataset. In the stroke column, only 249 rows have the value '1', while 4,861 rows have the value '0'. This research follows a variety of physiological factors and trained six different models for accurate prediction using ML algorithms such as Logistic Regression, Decision Tree Classification, RF Classification, K-Nearest Neighbors, SVM, and Naive Bayes classification. After creating six distinct models, the accuracy measures Accuracy, Precision, Recall, F1 Score, and the Receiver Operating Characteristic (ROC) curve are used to compare them. The dataset used for stroke prediction is extremely unbalanced. There are 5,110 rows in total in the dataset, with 249 columns demonstrating the likelihood of a stroke and 4,861 lines indicating the absence of a stroke. If these unbalanced data are the method of under-sampling is employed for this purpose. Under-sampling equalizes the data by under-sampling the majority class to correspond to the minority class. In this situation, the class with the value '0' is under-sampled in comparison to the class with the value '1'. As a result of the under-sampling, the dataset will have 249 rows with the value '0' and 249 rows with the value '1'. Finally, measuring the reliability of the following algorithm reveals that the Naive Bayes classification approach exceeds the others with an accuracy of 82%.

In [7] this literature, the goal of this study is to use Data Analytics and ML to create a model capable of predicting stroke outcomes based on an unbalanced dataset of 5,110 patients with stroke. Researchers used a variety of ML algorithms in this study, including Decision Tree, Logistic Regression, Naive Bayes, K Neighbors Classifier, RF, Neural Network, SVM, and boost Classifier. After reading this background, they arrived at the following conclusion: the BMI characteristic in the dataset had 201 missing data when it was first created. These fields were completed by calculating the average BMI throughout the entire dataset. Furthermore, it was discovered that more than 30% of the population suffers from mental illness. Smoking status is uncertain, which can also be referred to as there isn't enough data regarding these value characteristics. To avoid omission of this information. Because of the volume, it was recommended to reclassify it. By establishing some predictions about those people. As individuals, younger people have become less likely to start smoking or using tobacco. Smoked, the unidentified values existing in these people were modified from never to never. As a result, the number of okays was lowered. Unknowns between 1,544 and 909, were afterward removed. The researchers used the SMOTE approach for unbalanced data in this research. Unbalanced data becomes balanced after using this procedure. By inserting fake examples along the line segments connecting all of the k minority class's nearest neighbors, this approach oversamples the minority class. Finally, the result was the creation and analysis of many models based on ML techniques with the RF classifier proving to be the most effective which is 91%.

In [8] this research, a stroke occurs when the blood arteries in the brain collapse, resulting in brain damage. Symptoms may appear if the brain's flow of blood and other nutrients is disrupted. To forecast the risk of a stroke happening in the brain, many ML algorithms have been developed. The investigation was done using the stroke prediction dataset. This dataset has 5,110 rows and 12 columns. The stroke value of the output column is either 1 or 0. The number 0 shows that there was no danger of stroke. Result 1 indicates that the danger of stroke was detected. In the output column, the value of 0 in this case, beyond the possibilities of 1 in the same column 249 rows in the stroke column alone contains the value 4,861 rows have the value 0, while 1 has the value 1. This research trains four different models for trustworthy prediction utilizing an assortment of physiological indicators and ML methods such as Logistic Regression (LR), Decision Tree (DT) Classification, RF Classification, and Voting Classifier. The accuracy metrics, such as accuracy score, precision score, recall score, and F1 score, have been used to assess the four alternative models after they have been created. In this work, the usefulness of multiple ML algorithms correctly predicting stroke based on several physiological parameters is explored. The RF algorithm outperforms the other algorithms with a classification rate of 96%. When cross-validation measures are utilized in brain stroke predictions, the RF technique outperforms other methods, according to the study.

18.3 PROPOSED METHOD

Our proposed method is divided into two sections. The first task is the dataset representation and the second part is the classification technique based on the balanced dataset. The overall proposed method is shown in Figure 18.1.

18.3.1 Dataset Representation

The dataset for stroke forecast is from Kaggle. There are 5,110 tuples in this dataset, which is divided into 12 attributes. We included in the study 5,110 patients; 4,861 (95.51%) presented with non-stroke and 249 (4.49%) with stroke patient data. There were 41% males and 59% females among the 5,110 individuals who were eligible for this research. Each tuple of information in Table 18.1 has significant features in the present data about the patient. The sections' primary credits are ID, gender, age, hypertension, heart disease, ever married, work type, residence type, average glucose level, BMI, smoking status, and stroke. The value of the result segment stroke is either '1' or '0'. The number '0' indicates no risk of stroke, but the value '1' suggests there is no risk of stroke, but the value '1' suggests that there is a chance of stroke.

At first, we collected the dataset from Kaggle, which was based on stroke disease. Initially, this dataset was imbalanced, with a significant disparity between the number of positive and negative cases. To address this issue and enhance the robustness of our ML models, we applied the Synthetic Minority Over-sampling Technique combined with the Edited Nearest Neighbors (SMOTE-ENN) technique. This method effectively balanced the dataset by over-sampling the minority class and removing noisy data points, making it suitable for training reliable models. After achieving a balanced dataset, we leveraged three powerful ML classifiers:

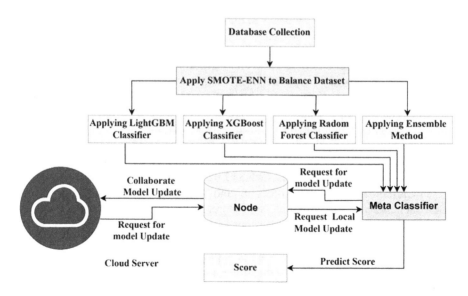

FIGURE 18.1 Diagrammatic depiction of the entire method.

TABLE 18.1
Stroke Dataset Description

SL. No.	Attribute Name	Attribute Type	Description
1	Id	Integer	For each patient, a unique integer value is assigned.
2	Gender	String (male, female)	Indicates the patient's gender.
3	Age	Integer	The patient's age
4	Hypertension	Integer (1,0)	This test determines whether or not the patient has hypertension.
5	Heart disease	Integer (1,0)	Determines whether or whether the patient has cardiac disease.
6	Ever married	String (yes, no)	It determines whether or not the patient is married.
7	Work type	String (children, Govt. job, never worked, private, self-employed)	It divides activities into many categories.
8	Residence type	String literal (urban, rural)	The residence type of the patient is saved.
9	Avg. glucose level	Floating point number	The average blood glucose level is calculated.
10	BMI	Floating point number	The BMI of the patient is calculated.
11	Smoking status	String	It displays the patient's smoking status.
12	Stroke	Binary (1, 0)	The stroke status is displayed in the output column.

LightGBM, XGBoost, and RF. Each of these classifiers brings unique strengths and capabilities to the task of predicting stroke outcomes. Furthermore, we harnessed the strength of ensemble learning by combining the predictions of these three classifiers. This ensemble approach often results in improved overall performance, as it helps mitigate individual model biases and enhances generalization. In addition to model development, we explored Federated Learning, an emerging approach in the field of ML. Federated Learning allows model training across decentralized edge devices while preserving data privacy. This technique is especially relevant when working with sensitive healthcare data, as it ensures that patient information remains secure. Before deploying our framework in production, rigorous testing under realistic conditions is crucial. This process helps verify that the model functions as expected in real-world scenarios, minimizing potential errors due to unexpected conditions or factors beyond normal operating parameters.

18.3.2 Data Preprocessing

Before developing a model, preprocessing data is essential to eliminate undesirable noise and outliers from the dataset, which might cause a divergence from good training. This step takes care of everything that prevents the model from performing as efficiently as possible. Following the collection of the suitable dataset, the data must be cleaned and checked to ensure that it is ready for model creation. As seen in Table 18.1, the dataset used comprises 12 characteristics. To begin, the column 'id' is removed because its presence in model construction makes no impact. The dataset is next searched for null values and, if any are discovered, they are filled. In this scenario, the unfilled values in the column 'BMI' are filled using the column data's mean. The next duty is Label Encoding, which comes after eliminating the null values from the unbalanced dataset. Imbalanced data indicates that the ratio of values for each class label is imbalanced. We use random resample strategies to deal with unbalanced data.

18.3.3 BALANCE DATASET USING SMOTE-ENN

SMOTE (Synthetic Minority Over-Sampling Technique) is an over-sampling technique that generates synthetic samples for the minority class are generated. This approach helps in overcoming the problem of overfitting caused by random over-sampling. It concentrates on the feature space to produce new examples by interpolating between positive instances that are close together. Another hybrid strategy is SMOTE-ENN, which removes a larger number of observations from the sample space. ENN is yet another under-sampling strategy in which the majority class's nearest neighbors are estimated. If the nearest neighbors incorrectly label that particular instance of the majority class, it is eliminated. Integrating this technique with SMOTE's oversampled data allows for considerable data cleaning. Samples from both groups are excluded due to their misclassification [9,10]. As a result, the class separation is more apparent and concise. Let's imagine that, in our taker's detection scenario, only 5 persons out of 100 have a stroke. We want to accurately categorize all malignant patients in this situation since even a very BAD model (predicting everyone as non-stroke) will give us a 95% accuracy (will come to what accuracy is). However, in trying to catch all stroke instances, we may wind up creating a categorization in which a person who is not suffering from a stroke is labeled as a stroke. This may be acceptable because it is less perilous than failing to recognize/capture a malignant patient, as we will be sending the stroke cases for additional investigation and reporting anyhow. Missing a stroke patient, however, would be a tremendous error since they would not be examined further. To additionally see FP, consider an elective situation wherein the model decides if an email is spam. Accept at least for a moment that you're expecting a significant email, for example, a reaction from a selection representative or an acknowledgment letter from a college. Allocate the objective variable a mark, like 1: 'Email is spam' and 0: 'Email isn't spammed'. Suppose the Model classifies the basic email you've been sitting tight for as Spam (instance of False certain). Presently, this is a ton more regrettable than marking a spam email as significant or not significant, since in that occurrence, we can in any case physically eliminate it, and it's anything but nothing to joke about assuming it happens every so often. Subsequently, regarding spam email classification, diminishing misleading up-sides is more fundamental than decreasing bogus negatives.

Federated Learning-Based AI Approaches for Predicting Stroke

18.3.4 Stroke Prediction Using Classification Technique

In the proposed method, the three most popular classifiers used in current research work namely LightGBM, XGBoost, and RF are used. An ensemble method is also applied to check the performance to predict the stroke using the three classifiers mentioned earlier. The characteristics of each classifier are discussed in the following sections.

18.3.4.1 LightGBM

LightGBM is a free and open-source distributed gradient boosting framework for ML that was invented by Microsoft. It is based on decision tree techniques and is used for rankings, classification, as well as other ML applications. Performance and scalability are at the forefront of the development process. While the trees of different calculations grow evenly, the LightGBM calculation develops upward, and that implies it develops leaf-wise while different calculations develop level-wise. To develop, LightGBM chooses the leaves with more grief. While extending a similar leaf, can diminish misfortune over a level-wise strategy [11,12].

18.3.4.2 XGBoost

XGBoost stands for 'Extreme Gradient Boost' which is scalable for tree boosting in ML systems and extensively used in numerous fields to perform on several fronts, cutting-edge findings, and data challenges. XGBoost is used for solving supervised learning problems where trained data are used to predict a target value. XGBoost builds an extraordinary development to the regular algorithm for Gradient Boosted Trees in computer performance, scalability, generalization, and computing speed. It has demonstrated exceptional results in several ways applications, including motion detection, stock sales forecasting, virus classification, consumer behavior analysis, and many others. With efficient data and memory handling, the system runs far quicker on a single machine than any other ML technique. The optimization approaches used by the algorithm improve performance and give speed while using the fewest resources possible [13,14].

18.3.4.3 Random Forest

RF is a well-known ML algorithm that uses the supervised learning method. ML can be utilized for categorization as well as regression issues. It is based on ensemble learning, which is a method of integrating several classifiers to solve a complex problem and increase the model's performance. A classifier joins a few decision trees on various subsets of a dataset and midpoints the outcomes to expand the dataset's anticipated exactness. It further develops the choice tree calculation concerning exactness. It is a valuable apparatus for managing missing information. Without hyper boundary change, it can give a sensible forecast. It beats the issue of decision tree overfitting [15,16].

18.3.4.4 Ensemble

Ensemble approaches are models that are created in multiples and then consolidated to come up with improved results. Ensemble approaches often yield more accurate results than a single model. In several ML contests, the winning solutions employed ensemble approaches. As a result, ensemble-building approaches focus on constructing classifiers that disagree with their predictions. In general, these strategies vary the training process in the hopes of producing alternative predictions from the final classifiers [17].

18.3.5 LIBRARIES IMPORTED INTO A PYTHON PROGRAMMING LANGUAGE

Pandas:
Pandas is now a Python module that is completely free to use. It's utilized in data science, data analysis, and ML applications [18,19].

NumPy:
A Python module called NumPy, adds support for huge, multi-dimensional arrays and matrices, as well as a vast variety of functions of high-level mathematics for experimenting with all these arrays [18,19].

MatplotlibPyplot:
Matplotlib is a Python graphing toolkit that also includes the NumPy numerical math extension. Its API is object-oriented for incorporating charts into general-purpose programs [18,19].

Standard Scaler:
A feature is standardized with StandardScaler eliminating the average before adjusting to random values. To acquire a unit variance, multiply all of the data by the confidence interval. The formal concept of scale that I provided before does not apply to StandardScaler [18,19].

Sklearn:
Sklearn is without a doubt Python's most useful AI library. The Sklearn tool kit for AI and measurable displaying incorporates highlights including characterization, relapse, bunching, and dimensionality decrease [18,19].

Seaborn:
Seaborn is a statistical graphics package for Python. It is based on matplotlib and tightly interacts with pandas' data structures [18,19].

K-Fold:
To split data into train and test sets, K-Fold will offer train/test indices. It will fold the data into k-folds in a row. Fold the remaining k−1 to comprise the training set, after which folds are applied as a testing dataset once [20].

18.4 EXPERIMENTAL RESULTS

A confusion matrix would be a technique for solving problems. that may be used to estimate results. In the sphere of ML, the matrix is said to assess confusion in a classification's efficacy-based ML algorithm.

Additionally, The Confusion matrix may also be thought of as a tabular form that shows the number of accurate and wrong expectations. a classifier's output (or a characterization model) for parallel arrangement undertakings.

Federated Learning-Based AI Approaches for Predicting Stroke

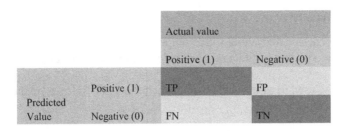

FIGURE 18.2 Confusion matrix.

The anticipated and actual classification is shown in a confusion matrix of dimension $n * n$ connected with a classifier, where the number of possible classes is n. Figure 18.2 displays a confusion matrix for $n = 2$, with the following interpretations for the entries. The following concepts are related to a confusion matrix:

18.4.1 True Positive

- The expected and actual values are identical.
- The model anticipated a positive value, and the actual result was positive.

The term 'true positive' describes the process wherein an individual is experiencing a stroke and the model classifies his case as a stroke [21–24].

18.4.2 False Positive

- The expected value was incorrectly anticipated.
- Although the actual number was negative, the model projected that it would be positive.
- Type 1 mistake is another name for it.

That is when a person has not had a stroke however the model identifies his occurrence as a stroke [21–24].

18.4.3 False Negative

- The expected value was incorrectly anticipated.
- Although the actual number was positive, the model predicted that it would be negative.
- Type 2 mistake is another name for it.

That is FN. When a person experiences a stroke, the model determines that his situation is non-stroke [21–24].

18.4.4 TRUE NEGATIVE

- The expected and actual values are identical.
- The model anticipated a negative value, and the actual value was negative.

That is being used in cases where the patient has not had a stroke yet the model classifies his instance as such.

Here,

- TP denotes the number of correctly predicted positive outcomes.
- The case of negative conjectures is given by FP.
- The case of false-positive conjectures is given by FN.
- TN is the quantity of accurately anticipated adverse results [21–24].

18.4.5 ACCURACY

Accuracy is a phrase that refers to anything being close to its genuine worth or a recognized standard. A system might do complicated mathematical computations that are right based on the data provided, but not the precise value [23–24].

$$\text{Accuracy} = (\mathbf{TP} + \mathbf{TN}) / (\mathbf{TP} + \mathbf{TN} + \mathbf{FP} + \mathbf{FN}) \tag{18.1}$$

18.4.6 PRECISION

Precision is a metric that indicates what percentage of patients diagnosed with stroke truly experienced a stroke. People who are anticipated to have a stroke are TP and FP, whereas those who have a stroke are TP [23,24].

$$\text{Precision} = \mathbf{TP} / (\mathbf{TP} + \mathbf{FP}) \tag{18.2}$$

18.4.7 RECALL

The recall is determined by dividing the total multitude of issues that are positive by the positive quantity of elements accurately categorized as Positive. The recall is a metric that evaluates how well a model can replicate and is recognized. The longer the recall, the better, and the higher the number of affirmative response samples discovered [23,24].

$$\text{Recall} = TP / (TP + FN) \tag{18.3}$$

18.4.8 SPECIFICITY

The fraction of real negatives that were anticipated as negatives is known as specificity (or TN). This means that a part of TN will be forecasted as positives, which might be referred to as FP [23,24].

$$\text{Specificity} = TN / (TN + FP) \tag{18.4}$$

Federated Learning-Based AI Approaches for Predicting Stroke

18.4.9 F1_Score

The F1 rank is the accuracy of a classifier's harmonic mean and recall to create a single statistic. It's mostly used to compare the results of two different classifiers [23,24].

$$F1\_Score = TP / \{TP + 1 / 2(FP + FN)\} \tag{18.5}$$

5,110 patients were included in the study; 4,861 (95.51%) had non-stroke display data, whereas 249 (4.49%) had stroke patient data. Among the 5,110 people who qualified for this study, a male predominance of 41% and a female predominance of 59% was observed. Four supervised ML techniques—XGBoost, RF, Light GBM, and Ensemble—were employed to train the resulting prediction models. We employed ML methods and ten-fold cross-validation adjustments to improve the results. Apply the formula of the accuracy, recall, precision, and f1 evaluate the score were used as five distinct performance of classification models for this particular ten-fold cross-validation.

18.4.10 Results of Applying Light GBM

We use the SMOTE-ENN approach to balance the dataset, even though it is unbalanced. After the dataset has been balanced, the confusion matrix for the LightGBM classifier. The Precision is 93%, the recall is 97%, the specificity is 94%, and the F1 score is 95%. After fine-tuning by roughly 1%, this model attained accuracy. The model's accuracy was 93% before fine-tuning.

18.4.11 Results of Applying XGBoost

Still, we apply SMOTE-ENN techniques to balance the dataset for imbalanced datasets. After the dataset has been balanced. In this case, precision is 83%, recall is 91%, specificity is 87%, and F1 is 95%. After being fine-tuned by around 6%, the accuracy of this model decreased. The model's accuracy was 95% before it was fine-tuned. Again, we use the SMOTE-ENN approach to balance out unbalanced datasets.

18.4.12 Results of Applying Random Forest

In this example, precision is 93%, recall is 98%, specificity is 95%, and F1 is 95%. This model achieved accuracy after being fine-tuned by about 1%. Before it was fine-tuned, the model's accuracy was 95%. This is the final time even if the dataset is imbalanced, we employ SMOTE-ENN techniques to balance it. Following this Precision is 83%, recall is 91%, specificity is 86%, and F1 is 87% in this instance. The accuracy of this model was reduced after being fine-tuned by approximately 6%. Before it was fine-tuned, the model had a 95% accuracy rating.

18.4.13 Results of Applying Ensemble

In this, Precision is 83%, recall is 91%, specificity is 86%, and F1 is 87% in this instance. The accuracy of this model was reduced after being fine-tuned by approximately 6%. Before it was fine-tuned, the model had a 95% accuracy rating.

After applying SMOTE-ENN, here is the final table of performance measures for several methods.

Table 18.2 displays the findings of numerous performance measurement methodologies. In Table 18.2, we examine several terms of the confusion matrix, such as accuracy, precision, recall, specificity, and F1_score for all of the algorithms used in our research. First, we discussed the accuracy of all algorithms. It displays the percentage of the accuracy of all the classifiers that we used in our article. LightGBM has a 95%, RF has a 96%, XGBoost has an 89%, and ensemble (which is a combination of all three algorithms) has an 88% accuracy. When we compared all of these algorithms, we determined that RF has the highest accuracy, at 96%.

Second, all algorithms were examined for precision. Here depicts the percentage of precision for all of the classifiers we used in our study. LightGBM has an accuracy of 94% RF has an accuracy of 94% XGBoost has an accuracy of 84%, and Ensemble (which is a combination of all three techniques) has an accuracy of 83%. When we analyzed all of these algorithms, we discovered that RF has the best accuracy (96%).

Third, all algorithms were compared for recall. The percentage of recall for all of the classifiers employed in our investigation is shown. LightGBM is 97%, RF is 98%, XGBoost is 92%, and the ensemble is 91%. We discovered that RF had the highest accuracy of all of these algorithms, at 98%.

Fourth, all algorithms were put to the test for specificity. The percentage of specificity of all the classifiers we utilized in our paper is shown. LightGBM is 95%, RF is 95%, XGBoost is 87%, and the ensemble is 87%. When we looked at all of these algorithms, we discovered that RF and LightGBM both have a 95% specificity.

Fifth, the F1_score of all algorithms was discussed. The percentage of the F1 score of all the classifiers we used in our paper is shown. LightGBM is 95%, RF is 96%, XGBoost is 88%, and the ensemble is 87%. We can see that RF predicts the best F1 score when we study all of these algorithms. The cross-validation result is shown in Table 18.3.

Table 18.4 provides data on the accuracy of various study findings. Here, we see that the accuracy of Dangamvura Sailasya1, Gorlin L2 Aruna Kumari predictions using the Naive Bayes classification is 82%. After all, it's a decent accuracy. The study then predicts Harshitha K V1, Harshitha P, Gunjan2 Gupta, Vaishak P, and Prajna KB. We can observe that the accuracy rate is 95% in this case. This is a fantastic outcome. The KNN classifier was employed in this study. This classifier, I believe, is one of the finest. Then there's the paper by T M. Geethanjali, Divyashree M. D.,

TABLE 18.2

Performance Measurement of the Various Methods After Applying SMOTE-ENN

Method Name	Accuracy	Precision	Recall	Specificity	F1_Score
LightGBM	95.77	93.62	97.07	94.74	**95.31**
XGBOOST	89.16	83.91	91.79	87.26	**87.67**
RANDOM FOREST	96.26	93.97	97.82	95.02	**95.86**
ENSEMBLE	88.56	83.33	91.06	86.74	**87.02**

Federated Learning-Based AI Approaches for Predicting Stroke

TABLE 18.3
After Cross-Validation from (6–10) Is Given Below in This Table

Method Name	Accuracy of Six-Fold	Accuracy of Seven-Fold	Accuracy of Eight-Fold	Accuracy of Nine-Fold	Accuracy of Ten-Fold
Light GBM	94.57	94.52	94.57	94.55	94.61
XGBOOST	89.45	89.44	89.42	89.36	89.34
Random Forest	94.89	94.97	95.00	94.93	94.93
ENSEMBLE	95.64	95.58	95.78	95.77	95.69

TABLE 18.4
Comparing the Accuracy Based on the Different Classifiers

Method Name	Used Classifier	Accuracy
Machine Learning	Naive Bayes classification	82%
Machine Learning	KNN	95%
Machine Learning	Logistic Regression	95%
Distributed Machine Learning Based on Apache Spark	Random Forest	91%.
Proposed Method	Random Forest	96%

Monisha S. K., and Sahana M. K. I believe this is one of the greatest papers. They use Logistic Regression to forecast their findings. The accuracy rate is 95%. This accuracy rate is similar to Harshitha K V, Harshitha P, Gunjan Gupta, Vaishak P, and Prajna KB's previous study. Then there's a paper utilizing the RF classifier by Hager Ahmed, Sara F. Abd-el Ghani, EmanM.G. Youn, and Nahla.Omran, and Abdelmgeid A. Ali. The accuracy percentage is 95%. Finally, our paper draws to a close. To forecast accuracy, we utilize RF. This is among the most efficient classification systems. Our study is 96%F accurate. This document is superior to all others.

18.5 CONCLUSION

Stroke is the second leading cause of death globally, following heart disease, in terms of years lived. To initiate our study, we acquired a dataset from Kaggle based on healthcare data, comprising records of 5,110 patients and their various health parameters, including stroke incidence. This healthcare dataset was employed to train and test models for predicting stroke. The dataset comprises ten independent attributes: Gender, age, hypertension, heart disease, marital status, occupation, residence type, average glucose level, BMI, and smoking status. The class label contains two values: 0 signifies the absence of stroke disease, while 1 indicates its presence. Initially, the data was imbalanced, prompting us to employ the SMOTE-ENN technique, an improved version of SMOTE, to address this imbalance. We applied ML algorithms for stroke prediction, including RF, XGBoost, LightGBM, and ensemble methods. We utilized metrics such as recall, precision, specificity, F1 score, and accuracy to assess model performance. Among these algorithms, RF outperformed the rest, achieving a 96% accuracy rate, followed by LightGBM at 95%, XGBOOST at 89%, and the ensemble method at 88%. Our findings highlight the RF algorithm as this study's most accurate predictor for stroke disease. In this research. We discovered RF has the best accuracy for predicting stroke disease. However, if we use the RF algorithm to predict another disease, we will either achieve or not get the best accuracy. This is the classifier's limitation, which we observed in our research. In the future, we will try to expand our efforts. We want to see which algorithm is the most accurate and which approach is best for a variety of disease-related datasets.

REFERENCES

1. Emon, M. U., Keya, M. S., Meghla, T. I., Rahman, M. M., Al Mamun, M. S., & Kaiser, M. S. (2020, November). Performance analysis of machine learning approaches in stroke prediction. In *2020 4th International Conference on Electronics, Communication and Aerospace Technology (ICECA)* (pp. 1464–1469). IEEE, Coimbatore, India.
2. Hassan, M. M., Raihan, M., Khan, M. H. B., Dhali, T., Rahman, M. M., & Sneha, Z. H. (2022, March). A hybrid machine learning approach to predict the risk of having stroke. In *Proceedings of the 2nd International Conference on Computing Advancements*, New York (pp. 460–465).
3. Dritsas, E., & Trigka, M. (2022). Stroke risk prediction with machine learning techniques. *Sensors*, 22(13), 4670.
4. Ali, A. A. (2019). Stroke prediction using distributed machine learning based on Apache spark. *Stroke*, 28(15), 89–97.
5. KV, H. H., Gupta, G., & KB, P. (2021). Stroke prediction using machine learning algorithms. *International Journal of Innovative Research in Engineering & Management*, 8(4), 6–9.
6. Sailasya, G., & Kumari, G. L. A. (2021). Analyzing the performance of stroke prediction using ML classification algorithms. *International Journal of Advanced Computer Science and Applications*, 12(6), doi:10.14569/IJACSA.2021.0120662.
7. Rodríguez, J. A. T. *Stroke Prediction through Data Science and Machine Learning Algorithms*. doi:10.13140/RG.2.2.33027.43040.
8. Tazin, T., Alam, M. N., Dola, N. N., Bari, M. S., Bourouis, S., & Monirujjaman Khan, M. (2021). Stroke disease detection and prediction using robust learning approaches. *Journal of healthcare engineering*, 2021, 7633381.
9. Muntasir Nishat, M., Faisal, F., Jahan Ratul, I., Al-Monsur, A., Ar-Rafi, A. M., Nasrullah, S. M., Reza, M. T., & Khan, M. R. H. (2022). A comprehensive investigation of the performances of different machine learning classifiers with SMOTE-ENN oversampling technique and hyperparameter optimization for imbalanced heart failure dataset. *Scientific Programming*, 2022, 1–17.
10. Lamari, M., Azizi, N., Hammami, N. E., Boukhamla, A., Cheriguene, S., Dendani, N., & Benzebouchi, N. E. (2021). SMOTE-ENN-based data sampling and improved dynamic ensemble selection for imbalanced medical data classification. In *Advances on Smart and Soft Computing: Proceedings of ICACIn 2020* (pp. 37–49). Singapore: Springer.
11. Ke, G., Meng, Q., Finley, T., Wang, T., Chen, W., Ma, W., Ye, Q., & Liu, T. Y. (2017). Lightgbm: A highly efficient gradient-boosting decision tree. *Advances in Neural Information Processing Systems*, 30. https://api.semanticscholar.org/CorpusID:3815895.
12. Ju, Y., Sun, G., Chen, Q., Zhang, M., Zhu, H., & Rehman, M. U. (2019). A model combining convolutional neural network and LightGBM algorithm for ultra-short-term wind power forecasting. *IEEE Access*, 7, 28309–28318.

13. Liang, W., Luo, S., Zhao, G., & Wu, H. (2020). Predicting hard rock pillar stability using GBDT, XGBoost, and LightGBM algorithms. *Mathematics, 8*(5), 765.
14. Ramraj, S., Uzir, N., Sunil, R., & Banerjee, S. (2016). Experimenting XGBoost algorithm for prediction and classification of different datasets. *International Journal of Control Theory and Applications, 9*(40), 651–662.
15. Abdulkareem, N. M., & Abdulazeez, A. M. (2021). Machine learning classification based on Radom Forest algorithm: A review. *International journal of science and business, 5*(2), 128–142.
16. Shaik, A. B., & Srinivasan, S. (2019). A brief survey on random forest ensembles in classification model. In *International Conference on Innovative Computing and Communications: Proceedings of ICICC 2018, Volume 2* (pp. 253–260). Singapore: Springer.
17. Dietterich, T. G. (2000, June). Ensemble methods in machine learning. In *International Workshop on Multiple Classifier Systems* (pp. 1–15). Berlin, Heidelberg: Springer.
18. Lemenkova, P. (2019). Processing oceanographic data by Python libraries NumPy, SciPy and Pandas. *Aquatic Research, 2*(2), 73–91.
19. Lemenkova, P. (2020). Python libraries matplotlib, seaborn and pandas for visualization geo-spatial datasets generated by QGIS. *Analele stiintifice ale Universitatii "Alexandru Ioan Cuza" din Iasi—seria Geografie, 64*(1), 13–32.
20. Anguita, D., Ghelardoni, L., Ghio, A., Oneto, L., & Ridella, S. (2012, April). The '*K*' in *K*-fold cross validation. In *ESANN* (pp. 441–446). European Symposium on Artificial Neural Networks, Computational Intelligence and Machine Learning. Bruges (Belgium).
21. Liang, J. (2022). Confusion matrix: Machine learning. *POGIL Activity Clearinghouse, 3*(4).
22. Townsend, J. T. (1971). Theoretical analysis of an alphabetic confusion matrix. *Perception & Psychophysics, 9*, 40–50.
23. Lewis, H. G., & Brown, M. (2001). A generalized confusion matrix for assessing area estimates from remotely sensed data. *International Journal of Remote Sensing, 22*(16), 3223–3235.
24. Zhu, W., Zeng, N., & Wang, N. (2010). Sensitivity, specificity, accuracy, associated confidence interval and ROC analysis with practical SAS implementations. *NESUG Proceedings: Health Care and Life Sciences*, Baltimore, Maryland, 19, 67. http://www.nesug.org/Proceedings/nesug10/hl/hl07.pdf.

Index

AI approaches 141, 233, 235, 237, 239, 241, 243, 245, 247, 249
application 2, 3, 4, 6, 11, 12, 13, 17, 22, 23, 25, 26, 27, 28, 37, 38, 40, 47, 48, 49, 50, 51, 53, 55, 56, 57, 61, 69, 70, 75, 76, 80, 81, 87, 88, 101, 105, 107, 108, 109, 110, 111, 113, 114, 115, 116, 117, 118, 119, 121, 123, 125, 127, 128, 129, 132, 134, 136, 137, 138, 140, 141, 142, 150, 151, 154, 156, 157, 158, 159, 160, 169, 172, 173, 174, 179, 180, 182, 184, 187, 188, 189, 192, 194, 198, 213, 221, 222, 226, 231, 232, 241, 242, 248, 249

cognitive skills 89, 91, 92, 93, 95, 97, 98, 99
collaborative approach 1, 152, 212, 218
computer vision 15, 56, 57, 62, 145, 193, 222

data privacy 4, 7, 10, 12, 17, 18, 22, 26, 31, 32, 36, 41, 42, 43, 47, 55, 78, 79, 88, 102, 105, 107, 109, 115, 116, 118, 121, 132, 134, 135, 136, 140, 141, 154, 155, 170, 171, 172, 173, 174, 175, 176, 177, 179, 180, 181, 183, 184, 185, 186, 187, 189, 208, 209, 210, 211, 212, 215, 216, 217, 218, 219, 220, 224, 225, 226, 227, 228, 229, 231, 239
data security 2, 9, 12, 18, 23, 24, 26, 29, 32, 41, 47, 53, 78, 81, 85, 101, 102, 105, 106, 140, 144, 157, 170, 172, 173, 174, 176, 179, 188, 212, 214, 220, 223, 231
deep learning 2, 4, 6, 8, 9, 10, 12, 13, 14, 16, 18, 20, 22, 24, 26, 28, 30, 31, 32, 33, 34, 35, 36, 37, 38, 39, 40, 41, 42, 43, 44, 45, 46, 47, 48, 49, 50, 51, 52, 53, 54, 55, 56, 57, 58, 60, 62, 64, 66, 68, 69, 70, 72, 74, 76, 80, 82, 84, 85, 86, 88, 90, 92, 94, 96, 98, 100, 101, 102, 104, 105, 106, 107, 108, 109, 110, 111, 112, 113, 114, 115, 116, 117, 118, 119, 120, 121, 122, 123, 124, 125, 126, 127, 128, 129, 130, 131, 132, 133, 134, 135, 136, 137, 138, 139, 140, 141, 142, 143, 144, 145, 146, 147, 148, 149, 150, 151, 152, 153, 154, 155, 156, 157, 158, 159, 162, 164, 166, 168, 172, 174, 176, 178, 180, 182, 184, 186, 188, 190, 192, 193, 194, 196, 197, 198, 200, 202, 204, 205, 206, 207, 208, 209, 210, 212, 213, 214, 215, 216, 217, 218, 219, 220, 221, 222, 226, 228, 230, 232, 234, 235, 236, 238, 240, 242, 244, 246, 248

differential privacy 4, 6, 7, 11, 14, 15, 34, 36, 40, 42, 53, 79, 84, 85, 132, 135, 136, 144, 171, 185, 186, 187, 188, 190, 214, 218
digital health 17, 18, 19, 20, 21, 22, 23, 24, 25, 26, 27, 28, 29, 100, 107, 152, 159, 207, 208

explainable AI 128, 221

federated deep learning 2, 4, 6, 8, 10, 12, 14, 16, 18, 20, 22, 24, 26, 28, 30, 31, 32, 33, 34, 35, 36, 37, 38, 39, 40, 41, 42, 43, 44, 45, 46, 47, 48, 49, 50, 51, 52, 53, 54, 55, 56, 57, 58, 60, 62, 64, 66, 68, 70, 72, 74, 76, 80, 82, 84, 85, 86, 88, 90, 92, 94, 96, 98, 100, 101, 102, 104, 105, 106, 108, 109, 110, 111, 112, 113, 114, 115, 116, 117, 118, 119, 120, 121, 122, 123, 124, 125, 126, 127, 128, 129, 130, 131, 132, 133, 134, 135, 136, 137, 138, 139, 140, 141, 142, 143, 144, 145, 146, 147, 148, 149, 150, 151, 152, 153, 154, 155, 156, 157, 158, 159, 162, 164, 166, 168, 172, 174, 176, 178, 180, 182, 184, 186, 188, 190, 192, 194, 196, 198, 200, 202, 204, 206, 207, 208, 209, 210, 212, 213, 214, 215, 216, 217, 218, 219, 220, 222, 226, 228, 230, 232, 234, 236, 238, 240, 242, 244, 246, 248
federated learning 1, 2, 3, 4, 5, 6, 7, 8, 9, 11, 13, 14, 15, 35, 36, 37, 38, 41, 48, 49, 51, 52, 53, 54, 56, 57, 58, 78, 79, 80, 81, 82, 83, 84, 85, 86, 87, 88, 101, 102, 103, 105, 106, 107, 108, 110, 111, 112, 113, 114, 115, 116, 117, 118, 120, 121, 122, 128, 129, 130, 131, 132, 133, 137, 141, 142, 144, 145, 150, 151, 157, 158, 159, 170, 171, 172, 173, 174, 175, 176, 177, 179, 181, 182, 183, 184, 185, 186, 187, 188, 189, 190, 191, 193, 194, 195, 197, 198, 208, 210, 211, 212, 214, 215, 216, 217, 219, 220, 221, 222, 224, 231, 232, 239
federated transfer techniques 224

251

framework 4, 6, 7, 8, 14, 21, 35, 37, 38, 39, 40, 42, 43, 45, 48, 50, 51, 52, 53, 55, 56, 57, 62, 69, 79, 103, 106, 110, 111, 114, 115, 116, 118, 119, 120, 121, 128, 129, 130, 131, 132, 133, 135, 140, 141, 145, 146, 150, 151, 152, 155, 156, 157, 158, 162, 177, 178, 179, 180, 181, 182, 183, 184, 189, 197, 214, 215, 216, 217, 218, 220, 221, 222, 225, 226, 228, 229, 230, 231, 232, 239, 241

healthcare applications 4, 11, 12, 13, 47, 81, 101, 105, 115, 136, 137, 154, 156, 157, 180, 182, 187
healthcare challenges 27, 78, 79, 81, 82, 83, 85, 87, 106
healthcare informatics 74, 88, 129, 158, 190, 207, 208, 209, 210, 211, 212, 213, 215, 216, 217, 218, 219, 220, 221, 223
healthcare management 222
healthcare systems 23, 73, 78, 107, 133, 134, 138, 140, 142, 143, 144, 158, 176, 177, 182, 189, 201, 202, 219, 222
homomorphic encryption 4, 6, 16, 35, 36, 43, 116, 140, 152, 156, 179, 187, 188, 189, 190, 218, 226, 227, 232

Internet of Things 13, 52, 79, 88, 109, 128, 131, 142, 143, 145, 147, 149, 151, 153, 155, 157, 158, 159, 161, 169, 173, 187, 189, 192, 205, 221

machine learning 1, 8, 13, 14, 15, 19, 23, 25, 28, 30, 32, 48, 49, 51, 57, 59, 60, 61, 63, 65, 67, 69, 71, 73, 74, 75, 76, 77, 79, 80, 81, 82, 83, 84, 86, 88, 89, 91, 93, 95, 97, 99, 101, 103, 108, 109, 117, 127, 129, 131, 141, 143, 151, 152, 153, 154, 155, 156, 161, 169, 170, 184, 187, 192, 197, 198, 204, 205, 210, 211, 213, 215, 216, 217, 218, 219, 221, 222, 223, 224, 226, 227, 228, 231, 232, 233, 247, 248, 249

medical applications 3, 49, 50, 55, 134, 142, 156
model distillation 52

personalized healthcare 85, 102, 145, 199, 200, 201, 202, 203, 204, 205, 219, 221
predictive models 14, 120, 234
regulatory compliance 24, 86, 106, 107, 213, 214, 218

resource efficiency 82, 137

smart healthcare 4, 13, 14, 57, 107, 141, 157, 177, 181, 182, 187, 207, 208, 209, 216, 217, 218, 219, 220, 222
stroke prediction 234, 235, 236, 237, 247, 248
systematic analysis 109

tailoring medicine 199, 200, 201, 202, 203, 204, 205
transfer learning 4, 6, 14, 40, 49, 56, 79, 81, 82, 86, 135, 137, 145, 150, 151, 157, 158, 192, 220, 221, 224, 225, 226, 227, 228, 230, 232

wearable healthcare 4, 6, 14, 145, 157, 207, 208, 209, 210, 211, 213, 214, 215, 216, 217, 218, 219, 220, 225, 232